DATE DUE

			PRINTED IN U.S.A.

SOMETHING ABOUT THE AUTHOR

ISSN 0276-816X

something ABOUT the Author

Facts and Pictures about Authors
and Illustrators of Books for Young People

EDITED BY
ANNE COMMIRE

VOLUME 39

GALE RESEARCH COMPANY
BOOK TOWER
DETROIT, MICHIGAN
48226

Editor: Anne Commire

Associate Editors: Agnes Garrett, Helga P. McCue

Senior Assistant Editor: Joyce Nakamura

Assistant Editors: Dianne H. Anderson, Lori J. Bell, Linda Shedd, Cynthia J. Walker

Sketchwriters: Rachel Koenig, Eunice L. Petrini

Researcher: Kathleen Betsko

Editorial Assistants: Lisa Bryon, Carolyn Kline, Marilyn O'Connell,
Susan Pfanner, Catherine Ruello, Elisa Ann Sawchuk, Libby York

Production Director: Carol Blanchard

External Senior Production Associate: Mary Beth Trimper

External Production Associate: Dorothy Kalleberg

Internal Senior Production Assistant: Louise Gagné

Internal Production Assistant: Sandy Rock

Layout Artist: Vivian Tannenbaum

Art Director: Arthur Chartow

Special acknowledgment is due to the members of the *Contemporary Authors* staff
who assisted in the preparation of this volume.

Publisher: Frederick G. Ruffner

Executive Vice-President/Editorial: James M. Ethridge

Editorial Director: Dedria Bryfonski

Director, Literature Division: Christine Nasso

Senior Editor, Something about the Author: Adele Sarkissian

Library of Congress Catalog Card Number 72-27107

ISBN 0-8103-0074-5
ISSN 0276-816X
Computerized photocomposition by
Typographics, Incorporated
Kansas City, Missouri
Printed in the United States

Contents

Introduction

As the only ongoing reference series that deals with the lives and works of authors and illustrators of children's books, *Something about the Author (SATA)* is a unique source of information. The *SATA* series includes not only well-known authors and illustrators whose books are most widely read, but also those less prominent people whose works are just coming to be recognized. *SATA* is often the only readily available information source for less well-known writers or artists. You'll find *SATA* informative and entertaining whether you are:

—a student in junior high school (or perhaps one to two grades higher or lower) who needs information for a book report or some other assignment for an English class;

—a children's librarian who is searching for the answer to yet another question from a young reader or collecting background material to use for a story hour;

—an English teacher who is drawing up an assignment for your students or gathering information for a book talk;

—a student in a college of education or library science who is studying children's literature and reference sources in the field;

—a parent who is looking for a new way to interest your child in reading something more than the school curriculum prescribes;

—an adult who enjoys children's literature for its own sake, knowing that a good children's book has no age limits.

Scope

In *SATA* you will find detailed information about authors and illustrators who span the full time range of children's literature, from early figures like John Newbery and L. Frank Baum to contemporary figures like Judy Blume and Richard Peck. Authors in the series represent primarily English-speaking countries, particularly the United States, Canada, and the United Kingdom. Also included, however, are authors from around the world whose works are available in English translation, for example: from France, Jean and Laurent De Brunhoff; from Italy, Emanuele Luzzati; from the Netherlands, Jaap ter Haar; from Germany, James Krüss; from Norway, Babbis Friis-Baastad; from Japan, Toshiko Kanzawa; from the Soviet Union, Kornei Chukovsky; from Switzerland, Alois Carigiet, to name only a few. Also appearing in *SATA* are Newbery medalists from Hendrik Van Loon (1922) to Robin McKinley (1985). The writings represented in *SATA* include those created intentionally for children and young adults as well as those written for a general audience and known to interest younger readers. These writings cover the spectrum from picture books, humor, folk and fairy tales, animal stories, mystery and adventure, science fiction and fantasy, historical fiction, poetry and nonsense verse, to drama, biography, and nonfiction.

Information Features

In *SATA* you will find full-length entries that are being presented in the series for the first time. This volume, for example, marks the first full-length appearance of Benjamin Appel, Ted De Grazia, Fred D'Ignazio, Paul Fleischman, Gyo Fujikawa, Jane Gardam, Bettina Hürlimann, Katherine Anne Porter, and Shigeo Watanabe, among others. Since Volume 25, each *SATA* volume also includes newly revised and updated biographies for a selection of early *SATA* listees who remain of interest to today's readers and who have been active enough to require extensive revision of their earlier entries. The entry for a given biographee may be revised as often as there is substantial new information to provide. In Volume 39 you'll find a revised entry for Robert McCloskey.

Brief Entries, first introduced in Volume 27, are another regular feature of *SATA*. Brief Entries present essentially the same types of information found in a full entry but do so in a capsule form and without illustration. These entries are intended to give you useful and timely information while the more time-consuming process of compiling a full-length biography is in progress. In this volume you'll find Brief Entries for Poul Anderson, Barbara Dillon, Penelope Farmer, René Goscinny, Bruce and Carole Hart, Patrick Moore, Roger Zelazny, and Kaethe Zemach, among others.

Obituaries have been included in *SATA* since Volume 20. An Obituary is intended not only as a death notice but also as a concise view of a person's life and work. Obituaries may appear for persons who have entries in earlier *SATA* volumes, as well as for people who have not yet appeared in the series. In this volume Obituaries mark the recent deaths of Helen Boylston, Nora Kramer, Bill Libby, Virgil Partch, Philip Van Doren Stern, Clara Winston, and others.

Each *SATA* volume provides a cumulative index in two parts: first, the Illustrations Index, arranged by the name of the illustrator, gives the number of the volume and page where the illustrator's work appears in the current volume as well as all preceding volumes in the series; second, the Author Index gives the number of the volume in which a person's biographical sketch, Brief Entry, or Obituary appears in the current volume as well as all preceding volumes in the series. These indexes also include references to authors and illustrators who appear in *Yesterday's Authors of Books for Children*. Beginning with Volume 36, the *SATA* Author Index provides cross-references to authors who are included in *Children's Literature Review*.

Illustrations

While the textual information in *SATA* is its primary reason for existing, photographs and illustrations not only enliven the text but are an integral part of the information that *SATA* provides. Illustrations and text are wedded in such a special way in children's literature that artists and their works naturally occupy a prominent place among *SATA*'s listees. The illustrators that you'll find in the series include such past masters of children's book illustration as Randolph Caldecott, Kate Greenaway, Walter Crane, Arthur Rackham, and Ernest L. Shepard, as well as such noted contemporary artists as Maurice Sendak, Edward Gorey, Tomie de Paola, and Margot Zemach. There are Caldecott medalists from Dorothy Lathrop (the first recipient in 1938) to Trina Schart Hyman (the latest winner in 1985); cartoonists like Charles Schulz, ("Peanuts"), Walt Kelly ("Pogo"), Hank Ketcham ("Dennis the Menace"), and Georges Remi ("Tintin"); photographers like Jill Krementz, Tana Hoban, Bruce McMillan, and Bruce Curtis; and filmmakers like Walt Disney, Alfred Hitchcock, and Steven Spielberg.

In more than a dozen years of recording the metamorphosis of children's literature from the printed page to other media, *SATA* has become something of a repository of photographs that are unique in themselves and exist nowhere else as a group, particularly many of the classics of motion picture and stage history and photographs that have been specially loaned to us from private collections.

What a *SATA* Entry Provides

Whether you're already familiar with the *SATA* series or just getting acquainted, you will want to be aware of the kind of information that an entry provides. In every *SATA* entry the editors attempt to give as complete a picture of the person's life and work as possible. In some cases that full range of information may simply be unavailable, or a biographee may choose not to reveal complete personal details. The information that the editors attempt to provide in every entry is arranged in the following categories:

1. The "head" of the entry gives

       —the most complete form of the name,
       —any part of the name not commonly used, included in parentheses,
       —birth and death dates, if known; a (?) indicates a discrepancy in published sources,
       —pseudonyms or name variants under which the person has had books published or is publicly
         known, in parentheses in the second line.

2. "Personal" section gives

 —date and place of birth and death,
 —parents' names and occupations,
 —name of spouse, date of marriage, and names of children,
 —educational institutions attended, degrees received, and dates,
 —religious and political affiliations,
 —agent's name and address,
 —home and/or office address.

3. "Career" section gives

 —name of employer, position, and dates for each career post,
 —military service,
 —memberships,
 —awards and honors.

4. "Writings" section gives

 —title, first publisher and date of publication, and illustration information for each book written; revised editions and other significant editions for books with particularly long publishing histories; genre, when known.

5. "Adaptations" section gives

 —title, major performers, producer, and date of all known reworkings of an author's material in another medium, like movies, filmstrips, television, recordings, plays, etc.

6. "Sidelights" section gives

 —commentary on the life or work of the biographee either directly from the person (and often written specifically for the *SATA* entry), or gathered from biographies, diaries, letters, interviews, or other published sources.

7. "For More Information See" section gives

 —books, feature articles, films, plays, and reviews in which the biographee's life or work has been treated.

How a *SATA* Entry Is Compiled

A *SATA* entry progresses through a series of steps. If the biographee is living, the *SATA* editors try to secure information directly from him or her through a questionnaire. From the information that the biographee supplies, the editors prepare an entry, filling in any essential missing details with research. The author or illustrator is then sent a copy of the entry to check for accuracy and completeness.

If the biographee is deceased or cannot be reached by questionnaire, the *SATA* editors examine a wide variety of published sources to gather information for an entry. Biographical sources are searched with the aid of Gale's *Biography and Genealogy Master Index*. Bibliographic sources like the *National Union Catalog*, the *Cumulative Book Index*, *American Book Publishing Record*, and the *British Museum Catalogue* are consulted, as are book reviews, feature articles, published interviews, and material sometimes obtained from the biographee's family, publishers, agent, or other associates.

For each entry presented in *SATA*, the editors also attempt to locate a photograph of the biographee as well as representative illustrations from his or her books. After surveying the available books which the biographee has written and/or illustrated, and then making a selection of appropriate photographs and illustrations, the editors request permission of the current copyright holders to reprint the material. In the case of older books for which the copyright may have passed through several hands, even locating the current copyright holder is often a long and involved process.

We invite you to examine the entire *SATA* series, starting with this volume. Described below are some of the people in Volume 39 that you may find particularly interesting.

Highlights of This Volume

MAGINEL WRIGHT BARNEY......who enhanced the world of children's book illustration with quaint drawings known for their simple elegance and charming color. Barney's childhood was happily spent in the lush Wisconsin valley during the 1880s, years she shared with her older brother, Frank Lloyd Wright. Her nostalgic illustrative style appeared in classics like *Hans Brinker; or, The Silver Skates* and *Heidi*, as well as books like Caroline Snedeker's *Downright Dencey* and Ethel Calvert Phillips's *Calico*. Barney was a great influence on the writing career of her daughter, Newbery medalist Elizabeth Enright, who observed: "My mother was largely responsible for the revolutionizing of textbook illustration .... What [she] did was to bring grace, liveliness and, above all, imagination to the pages of these books."

BETTINA HÜRLIMANN......German author, illustrator, editor, and publisher of children's books who issued the works of artists and writers like Joseph Domjan, Chiyoko Nakatani, and Paul Nussbaumer. The daughter of publishers, Hürlimann was quite naturally drawn into the book publishing field and later married the founder of the German publishing house Atlantis Verlag, Martin Hürlimann. Also an avid collector of rare editions of children's books, she remembered the time when her husband presented her with a first edition of Grimm's *Tales*. "This was a high point in my life as a collector," she recalled. "I was completely taken by surprise and burst into tears as I held the volumes in my hands...." Hürlimann's love for children's literature resulted in studies like *Three Centuries of Children's Books in Europe* and *Picture-Book World*.

ELLEN MacGREGOR......creator of the popular "Miss Pickerell" science-fiction series. Miss Lavinia Pickerell made her debut in 1951 with the publication of *Miss Pickerell Goes to Mars* and appeared in three subsequent books before MacGregor's death in 1954. MacGregor, who once revealed a penchant for "delightful absurdity and utter logic," was among the first science-fiction writers for young readers to combine scientific accuracy with humorous fantasy. Also featured in this volume is DORA PANTELL who, ten years after MacGregor's death, accepted the challenge of continuing the adventures of the dauntless Miss Pickerell with her trademark umbrella and companion cow. Pantell has since written twelve books in the series, making some minor changes in the original concept. "Miss Pickerell had only a cow when I inherited her," she relates. "She has since accumulated a cat, a dog, a lamb, a deaf old plow horse, even a home for retired and disabled animals...."

ROBERT McCLOSKEY......Caldecott Award-winning author who began writing and illustrating books for children simply because he wanted his pictures to be looked at and enjoyed. "I don't know anything about children's literature ....," he confesses. "I fill in between pictures with words." In spite of this indirect approach, through the years McCloskey has produced children's favorites like *Make Way for Ducklings* and *Time of Wonder*, both Caldecott Award winners, *Blueberries for Sal* and *One Morning in Maine*, and the now-classic *Homer Price*. McCloskey remains, however, an artist first and illustrator second. "Yes, I'm working on children's illustration...," he admits. "But I'm still for hire—to paint, sculpt, whittle, or blast . . . whether it be in a bank, post office, or chicken coop."

JON STONE......one of the four original producers of the highly acclaimed children's television program "Sesame Street." It was Stone who called in puppeteer Jim Henson when the format for "Sesame Street" was first being developed twenty years ago. The two collaborated on a cavalcade of characters who have since delighted countless preschoolers: Oscar the Grouch, Bert and Ernie, Cookie Monster, Big Bird, and others. A nine-time Emmy award winner for "Sesame Street"-related work, Stone initially used his own children as a built-in test audience for the show. "They used to shoot down all my best stuff," he says, "and tell me how they like Mister Rogers better. . . ." Although he relinquished his position as executive producer of "Sesame Street" in 1978, Stone continues to entertain children through television specials and books like *The Monster at the End of This Book* and *Would You Like to Play Hide and Seek in This Book with Loveable, Furry Old Grover?*

These are only a few of the authors and illustrators that you'll find in this volume. We hope you find all the entries in *SATA* both interesting and useful. Please write and tell us if we can make *SATA* even more helpful for you.

Forthcoming Authors

A Partial List of Authors and Illustrators Who Will Appear in Forthcoming Volumes of *Something about the Author*

Abels, Harriette S.
Allard, Harry
Allen, Agnes B. 1898-1959
Allen, Jeffrey 1948-
Anders, Rebecca
Anderson, Leone C. 1923-
Andrist, Ralph K. 1914-
Ardley, Neil (Richard) 1937-
Austin, R. G.
Axeman, Lois
Ayme, Marcel 1902-1967
Bains, Rae
Baker, Olaf
Balderson, Margaret 1935-
Barkin, Carol
Bartlett, Margaret F. 1896-
Batey, Tom 1946-
Bauer, Caroline Feller 1935-
Bauer, John Albert 1882-1918
Beckman, Delores
Beim, Jerrold 1910-1957
Beim, Lorraine 1909-1951
Bernheim, Evelyne 1935-
Bernheim, Marc 1924-
Birnbaum, Abe 1899-
Boegehold, Betty 1913-
Boning, Richard A.
Bonners, Susan
Bourke, Linda
Bowen, Gary
Bracken, Carolyn
Brewton, Sara W.
Bridgman, Elizabeth P. 1921-
Bromley, Dudley 1948-
Bronin, Andrew 1947-
Bronson, Wilfrid 1894-
Brooks, Ron(ald George) 1948-
Brown, Roy Frederick 1921-
Brownmiller, Susan 1935-
Buchanan, William 1930-
Buchenholz, Bruce
Budney, Blossom 1921-
Burchard, Marshall
Burke, David 1927-
Burstein, Chaya M.
Butler, Dorothy 1925-
Butler, Hal 1913-
Calvert, Patricia
Camps, Luis 1928-
Carley, Wayne
Carlson, Nancy L.
Carrie, Christopher
Carris, Joan D. 1938-
Carroll, Ruth R. 1899-

Cauley, Lorinda B. 1951-
Chang, Florence C.
Charles, Carole
Charles, Donald 1929-
Chartier, Normand
Chase, Catherine
Chessare, Michele
Cline, Linda 1941-
Cohen, Joel H.
Cole, Brock
Cooper, Elizabeth Keyser 1910-
Cooper, Paulette 1944-
Cosgrove, Margaret 1926-
Coutant, Helen
Dabcovich, Lydia
D'Aulnoy, Marie-Catherine
    1650(?)-1705
David, Jay 1929-
Davies, Peter 1937-
Davis, Maggie S. 1942-
Dawson, Diane
Dean, Leigh
Degens, T.
Deguine, Jean-Claude 1943-
Demarest, Chris L. 1951-
Deweese, Gene 1934-
Ditmars, Raymond 1876-1942
Drescher, Henrik
Duggan, Maurice (Noel) 1922-1975
Dumas, Philippe 1940-
East, Ben
Edelson, Edward 1932-
Edens, Cooper
Edwards, Linda S.
Eisenberg, Lisa
Elder, Lauren
Elwood, Roger 1943-
Endres, Helen
Eriksson, Eva
Erwin, Betty K.
Etter, Les 1904-
Everett-Green, Evelyn 1856-1932
Falkner, John Meade 1858-1932
Fender, Kay
Filson, Brent
Fischer, Hans Erich 1909-1958
Flanagan, Geraldine Lux
Flint, Russ
Folch-Ribas, Jacques 1928-
Foley, Louise M. 1933-
Fox, Thomas C.
Freschet, Berniece 1927-
Frevert, Patricia D(endtler) 1943-
Funai, Mamoru R. 1932-

Gans, Roma 1894-
Garcia Sanchez, J(ose) L(uis)
Gardner, John Champlin, Jr. 1933-1982
Garrison, Christian 1942-
Gathje, Curtis
Gelman, Rita G. 1937-
Gemme, Leila Boyle 1942-
Gerber, Dan 1940-
Goldstein, Nathan 1927-
Goode, Stephen 1943-
Gordon, Shirley
Gould, Chester 1900-
Graeber, Charlotte Towner
Gregory, Diana 1933-
Gutman, Bill
Harris, Marilyn 1931-
Hayman, LeRoy 1916-
Healey, Larry 1927-
Heine, Helme 1941-
Heller, Linda 1944-
Henty, George Alfred 1832-1902
Herzig, Alison Cragin
Hicks, Clifford B. 1920-
Higashi, Sandra
Hockerman, Dennis
Hollander, Zander 1923-
Hood, Thomas 1779-1845
Howell, Troy
Hull, Jessie Redding
Hunt, Clara Whitehill 1871-1958
Hunt, Robert
Inderieden, Nancy
Irvine, Georgeanne
Iwamura, Kazuo 1939-
Jackson, Anita
Jackson, Kathryn 1907-
Jackson, Robert 1941-
Jacobs, Francine 1935-
Jameson, Cynthia
Janssen, Pierre
Jaspersohn, William
Jewell, Nancy 1940-
Johnson, Harper
Johnson, Maud
Johnson, Sylvia A.
Jukes, Mavis
Kahn, Joan 1914-
Kalan, Robert
Kantrowitz, Mildred
Kasuya, Masahiro 1937-
Keith, Eros 1942-
Kirn, Ann (Minette) 1910-
Koenig, Marion
Kohl, Herbert 1937-

Kohl, Judith
Kramer, Anthony
Kredenser, Gail   1936-
Krensky, Stephen   1953-
Kurland, Michael   1938-
Laure, Jason   1940-
Lawson, Annetta
Leach, Christopher   1925-
Lebrun, Claude
Leckie, Robert   1920-
Leder, Dora
Le-Tan, Pierre   1950-
Lewis, Naomi
Lindgren, Barbro
Lindman, Maj (Jan)
Lines, Kathleen
Livermore, Elaine
Lye, Keith
MacKinstry, Elizabeth   (?)-1956
Mali, Jane Lawrence
Manes, Stephen   1949-
Marryat, Frederick   1792-1848
Marsh, Carole
Marxhausen, Joanne G.   1935-
May, Dorothy
Mayakovsky, Vladimir   1894-1930
McCannon, Dindga
McKim, Audrey Margaret   1909-
McLenighan, Valjean   1947-
McLoughlin, John C.   1949-
McReynolds, Ginny
Melcher, Frederic G.   1879-1963
Michel, Anna   1943-
Miller, J(ohn) P.   1919-
Mills, Claudia   1954-
Molesworth, Mary L.   1839(?)-1921
Molly, Anne S.   1907-
Moore, Lilian
Moskowitz, Stewart
Muntean, Michaela
Murdocca, Sal
Newsom, Carol
Nickl, Peter
Nicoll, Helen
Obligado, Lillian Isabel   1931-
Odor, Ruth S.   1926-
Oppenheim, Shulamith (Levey)   1930-
Orr, Frank   1936-

Orton, Helen Fuller   1872-1955
Overbeck, Cynthia
Owens, Gail   1939-
Packard, Edward   1931-
Parenteau, Shirley L.   1935-
Parker, Robert Andrew   1927-
Paterson, A(ndrew) B(arton)   1864-1941
Patterson, Sarah   1959-
Pavey, Peter
Pelgrom, Els
Peretz, Isaac Loeb   1851-1915
Perkins, Lucy Fitch   1865-1937
Peterson, Jeanne Whitehouse   1939-
Phillips, Betty Lou
Plowden, David   1932-
Plume, Ilse
Poignant, Axel
Pollock, Bruce   1945-
Pollock, Penny   1935-
Polushkin, Maria
Porter, Eleanor Hodgman   1868-1920
Poulsson, Emilie   1853-1939
Powers, Richard M.   1921-
Prager, Arthur
Prather, Ray
Preston, Edna Mitchell
Pursell, Margaret S.
Pursell, Thomas F.
Pyle, Katharine   1863-1938
Rabinowitz, Solomon   1859-1916
Rappoport, Ken   1935-
Reese, Bob
Reich, Hanns
Reid, Alistair   1926-
Reidel, Marlene
Reiff, Tana
Reiss, Elayne
Reynolds, Marjorie   1903-
Rohmer, Harriet
Rosier, Lydia
Ross, Pat
Roy, Cal
Rudstrom, Lennart
Sargent, Sarah   1937-
Saunders, Susan   1945-
Schneider, Leo   1916-
Sealy, Adrienne V.
Seidler, Rosalie

Shea, George   1940-
Shreve, Susan   1939-
Silbert, Linda P.
Slepian, Jan(ice B.)
Smith, Alison
Smith, Catriona (Mary)   1948-
Smith, Ray(mond Kenneth)   1949-
Smollin, Michael J.
Steiner, Charlotte
Stevens, Leonard A.   1920-
Stine, R. Conrad   1937-
Stubbs, Joanna   1940-
Sullivan, Mary Beth
Suteev, Vladimir Grigor'evich
Sutherland, Robert D.   1937-
Sweet, Ozzie
Thaler, Mike
Thomas, Ianthe
Timmermans, Gommaar   1930-
Todd, Ruthven   1914-
Tourneur, Dina K.   1934-
Treadgold, Mary   1910-
Velthuijs, Max   1923-
Villiard, Paul   1910-1974
Waber, Bernard   1924-
Wagner, Jenny
Walker, Charles W.
Walsh, Anne Batterberry
Watts, Franklin   1904-1978
Wayne, Bennett
Werner, Herma   1926-
Weston, Martha
Whelen, Gloria   1923-
White, Wallace   1930-
Wild, Jocelyn
Wild, Robin
Winter, Paula   1929-
Winterfeld, Henry   1901-
Wolde, Gunilla   1939-
Wong, Herbert H.
Woolfolk, Dorothy
Wormser, Richard   1908-
Wright, Betty R.
Yagawa, Sumiko
Youldon, Gillian
Zaslow, David
Zistel, Era
Zwerger, Lisbeth

In the interest of making *Something about the Author* as responsive as possible to the needs of its readers, the editor welcomes your suggestions for additional authors and illustrators to be included in the series.

Acknowledgments

Grateful acknowledgment is made to the following publishers, authors, and artists
for their kind permission to reproduce copyrighted material.

ATHENEUM PUBLISHERS, INC. Illustration by Jochen Bartsch from *My Great-Grandfather, the Heroes and I* by James Krüss. Translated from the German by Edelgard von Heyde Kampf Bruhl. Copyright © 1967 by Verlag Friedrich Oetinger. English translation copyright © 1973 by Atheneum Publishers, Inc./ Photograph by J. Morton Cone and Ferne Geller Cone from *Crazy Crocheting* by Ferne Geller Cone. Copyright © 1981 by Ferne Geller Cone. Both reprinted by permission of Atheneum Publishers, Inc.

BANTAM BOOKS, INC. Illustration by Paul Granger from *Your Very Own Robot* by R. A. Montgomery. Text copyright © 1982 by R. A. Montgomery. Illustrations copyright © 1982 by Bantam Books, Inc. Reprinted by permission of Bantam Books, Inc.

BEHRMAN HOUSE, INC. Photograph courtesy of Israel Government Tourist Office from *The Jews of Israel* by Nora Benjamin Kubie. Copyright © 1968, 1975 by Franklin Watts, Inc. Copyright © 1975 by Behrman House, Inc. Reprinted by permission of Behrman House, Inc.

THE BODLEY HEAD LTD. Sidelight excerpts from *Seven Houses: My Life with Books* by Bettina Hürlimann. Copyright © 1977 by T. Y. Crowell, Inc./ Illustration by Yasuo Ohtomo from *Ready, Steady, Go!* by Shigeo Watanabe. Text copyright © 1980 by Shigeo Watanabe. Illustrations copyright © 1980 by Yasuo Ohtomo. English text copyright © 1980 by The Bodley Head Ltd. Both reprinted by permission of The Bodley Head Ltd.

CHILDREN'S PRESS. Illustration by P. K. Hallinan from *Where's Michael?* by P. K. Hallinan. Copyright © 1978 by Regensteiner Publishing Enterprises, Inc. Reprinted by permission of Children's Press.

CROSSWAY BOOKS. Illustration by Marilyn Churchill Theurer from *The Kingdom of Wundle* by Robert Siegel. Copyright © 1982 by Robert Siegel. Jacket and interior illustrations copyright © 1982 by Marilyn Churchill Theurer. Reprinted by permission of Crossway Books.

T. Y. CROWELL, INC. Illustration by Joe Lasker from *The Cobweb Christmas* by Shirley Climo. Text copyright © 1982 by Shirley Climo. Illustrations copyright © 1982 by Joe Lasker./ Photograph by Ron and Nancy Goor from *In the Driver's Seat* by Ron and Nancy Goor. Copyright © 1982 by Ron and Nancy Goor./ Jacket photographs by Ron Goor from *Shadows: Here, There, and Everywhere* by Ron and Nancy Goor. Copyright © 1981 by Ron and Nancy Goor./ Sidelight excerpts from *Seven Houses: My Life with Books* by Bettina Hürlimann. Copyright © 1977 by T. Y. Crowell, Inc./ Illustration by Denise Saldutti from *My Brother Ange* by Mary McCaffrey. Text copyright © 1982 by Mary McCaffrey. Illustrations copyright © 1982 by Denise Saldutti. All reprinted by permission of T. Y. Crowell, Inc.

DILLON PRESS, INC. Illustration by Reg Sandland from *Jacques Cousteau: Free Flight Undersea* by Paul Westman. Copyright © 1980 by Dillon Press, Inc. Reprinted by permission of Dillon Press, Inc.

DOBSON BOOKS LTD. Jacket design by Beryl Sanders from *Shadows on the Sand* by Terry Roche. Copyright © 1979 by Peggy Poole. Reprinted by permission of Dobson Books Ltd.

DOUBLEDAY & CO., INC. Illustrations by Maginel Wright Barney from *Downright Dencey* by Caroline Dale Snedeker. Copyright 1927 by Double, Page & Co./ Photograph from *The Missilemen* by Mel Hunter. Copyright © 1960 by Mel Hunter./ Illustration by Diane Paterson from *Monnie Hates Lydia* by Susan Pearson. Text copyright © 1975 by Susan Pearson. Illustrations copyright © 1975 by Diane Paterson. All reprinted by permission of Doubleday & Co., Inc.

E. P. DUTTON, INC. Sidelight excerpts and photographs from *The Valley of the God-Almighty Joneses* by Maginel Wright Barney, with Tom Burke. Copyright © 1965 by Maginel Wright Barney./ Illustration by Emily Arnold McCully from *Fifth Grade Magic* by Beatrice Gormley. Text copyright © 1982 by Beatrice Gormley. Illustrations copyright © 1982 by Emily Arnold McCully./ Painting by Robert Andrew Parker from *Izzie* by Susan Pearson. Text copyright © 1975 by Susan Pearson. Paintings copyright © 1975 by Robert Andrew Parker./ Illustration by Trinka Hakes Noble from *Karin's Christmas Walk* by Susan Pearson. Text copyright © 1980 by Susan Pearson. Illustrations copyright © 1980 by Trinka Hakes Noble./

Illustration by Ben Shahn from *A Christmas Story* by Katherine Anne Porter. Text copyright 1946, © 1967 by Katherine Anne Porter. Illustrations copyright © 1967 by Ben Shahn./ Jacket illustration by Ann Kobayashi from *Reina the Galgo* by Nicole de Messières. All reprinted by permission of E. P. Dutton, Inc.

EMC CORPORATION. Illustration by Art Scott from *My Mom and Dad Are Getting a Divorce* by Florence Bienenfield. Copyright © 1980 by EMC Corporation. Reprinted by permission of EMC Corporation.

FABER & FABER LTD. Jacket illustration by Renate Belina from *Isabel's Double* by Kenneth Lillington. Copyright © 1984 by Kenneth Lillington. Reprinted by permission of Faber & Faber Ltd.

FLAMMARION. Illustration by Janusz Grabiański from "Toomai et les Eléphants" by Rudyard Kipling in *Histoires d'animaux sauvages.* Copyright © 1964 by Flammarion./ Illustration by Janusz Grabiański from "Jeux Aquatiques" by Henry Williamson in *Histoires d'animaux sauvages.* Copyright © 1964 by Flammarion. Both reprinted by permission of Flammarion.

FUKUINKAN SHOTEN PUBLISHERS. Illustration by Yasuo Ohtomo from *Ready, Steady, Go!* by Shigeo Watanabe. Text copyright © 1980 by Shigeo Watanabe. Illustrations copyright © 1980 by Yasuo Ohtomo. English text copyright © 1981 by The Bodley Head. Reprinted by permission of Fukuinkan Shoten Publishers.

FUNK & WAGNALLS, INC. Sidelight excerpts from an article "Preface to the Original Edition," by Maria Leach in *The Standard Dictionary of Folklore, Mythology, and Legend,* edited by Maria Leach. Reprinted by permission of Funk & Wagnalls, Inc.

LES EDITIONS GAUTIER-LANGUEREAU. Illustration by Carmen Batet from *Si tu vas...à Paris* by Michèle Lochak. Copyright © 1983 by Les Editions Gautier-Languereau. Reprinted by permission of Les Editions Gautier-Languereau.

GREENWILLOW BOOKS. Illustration by Donald Carrick from *Alex Remembers* by Helen V. Griffith. Text copyright © 1983 by Helen V. Griffith. Illustrations copyright © 1983 by Donald Carrick./ Illustration by Frank Modell from *Toby in the Country, Toby in the City* by Maxine Zohn Bozzo. Text copyright © 1982 by Maxine Zohn Bozzo. Illustrations copyright © 1982 by Frank Modell./ Illustration by Nancy Tafuri from *Across the Stream* by Mirra Ginsburg. Text copyright © 1982 by Mirra Ginsburg. Illustrations copyright © 1982 by Nancy Tafuri. All reprinted by permission of Greenwillow Books.

HARCOURT BRACE JOVANOVICH, INC. Illustration from *Barry: The Story of a Brave St. Bernard* by Bettina Hürlimann. Translated and adapted from the German by Elizabeth D. Crawford. Copyright © 1967 by Atlantis Verlag AG./ Illustration by Paul Nussbaumer from *William Tell and His Son* by Bettina Hürlimann. Copyright © 1965 by Atlantis Verlag AG./ Illustration by Lady McCrady from *Tulla's Summer* by Rose Lagercrantz. Copyright © 1973 by Rose Lagercrantz. Illustrations and English translation copyright © 1977 by Harcourt Brace Jovanovich, Inc. All reprinted by permission of Harcourt Brace Jovanovich, Inc.

HARPER & ROW, PUBLISHERS, INC. Illustration by Marcia Sewall from *The Birthday Tree* by Paul Fleischman. Text copyright © 1979 by Paul Fleischman. Illustrations copyright © 1979 by Marcia Sewall./ Illustration by Jacqueline Bardner Smith from *Davey Come Home* by Margaret Teibl. Text copyright © 1979 by Margaret E. Teibl. Illustrations copyright © 1979 by Jacqueline Bardner Smith. Both reprinted by permission of Harper & Row, Publishers, Inc.

HERALD PRESS. Illustration by Seho Park from *Loaves and Fishes* by Linda Hunt, Marianne Frase, and Doris Liebert. Copyright © 1980 by Herald Press. Reprinted by permission of Herald Press.

HOLIDAY HOUSE, INC. Illustration by Tomie de Paola from *Ghost Poems,* edited by Daisy Wallace. Text copyright © 1979 by Holiday House, Inc. Illustrations copyright © 1979 by Tomie de Paola. Reprinted by permission of Holiday House, Inc.

HOLT, RINEHART & WINSTON GENERAL BOOK. Illustration by Victor Kalin from *Groundhog's Horse* by Joyce Rockwood. Text copyright © 1978 by Joyce Rockwood Hudson. Illustrations copyright © 1978 by Victor Kalin. Reprinted by permission of Holt, Rinehart & Winston General Book.

THE HORN BOOK, INC. Sidelight excerpts from an article "On Writing for Children: Some Wasps in the Marmalade, Part I," by Jane Gardam, October, 1978 in *The Horn Book./* Sidelight excerpts from an article "On Writing for Children: Some Wasps in the Marmalade, Part II," by Jane Gardam, December, 1978 in *The Horn Book./* Sidelight excerpts from

Illustrators of Children's Books: 1957-1966 by Lee Kingman and others, compilers. Copyright © 1968 by The Horn Book, Inc./ Sidelight excerpts from an article by Robert McCloskey, "Caldecott Medal Acceptance, 1958," in *Newbery and Caldecott Medal Books: 1956-1965,* edited by Lee Kingman. Copyright © 1965 by The Horn Book, Inc./ Sidelight excerpts from an article by Robert McCloskey, "Caldecott Medal Acceptance, 1942," in *Caldecott Medal Books: 1938-1957,* edited by Bertha Mahoney Miller and Elinor Whitney Field. Copyright © 1957 by The Horn Book, Inc. All reprinted by permission of The Horn Book, Inc.

HOUGHTON MIFFLIN CO. Illustration by Merle Peek from *Roll Over! A Counting Song,* lyrics from "Sally Go Round the Sun" by Edith Fowke. Copyright © 1969 by McClelland & Stewart Ltd. Illustrations copyright © 1981 by Merle Peek. Reprinted by permission of Houghton Mifflin Co.

ALFRED A. KNOPF, INC. Frontispiece illustration by Kenneth Dewey from *Lawyers for the People* by Elizabeth Levy. Text copyright © 1974 by Elizabeth Levy. Illustrations copyright © 1974 by Alfred A. Knopf, Inc./ Illustration by Charles McVicker from *Addie and the King of Hearts* by Gail Rock. Text copyright © 1976 by Gail Rock. Illustrations copyright © 1976 by Alfred A. Knopf, Inc. Both reprinted by permission of Alfred A. Knopf, Inc.

LERNER PUBLICATIONS CO. Photograph by Gary Garnett from *Custom Cars* by Kirk L. Ready. Copyright © 1982 by Lerner Publications Co. Reprinted by permission of Lerner Publications Co.

J. B. LIPPINCOTT CO. Illustration by Susan Jeschke from *Saturday I Ran Away* by Susan Pearson. Text copyright © 1981 by Susan Pearson. Illustrations copyright © 1981 by Susan Jeschke. Reprinted by permission of J. B. Lippincott Co.

LITTLE, BROWN & CO. Jacket illustration by Wendell Minor from *Far from Home* by Ouida Sebestyen. Text copyright ©1980 by Ouida Sebestyen. Jacket illustration copyright © 1980 by Wendell Minor. Reprinted by permission of Little, Brown & Co.

MACMILLAN PUBLISHING CO. Illustration by Peggy Fortnum from *A Few Fair Days* by Jane Gardam. Copyright © 1971 by Jane Gardam. Illustrations copyright © 1971 by Peggy Fortnum./ Illustration by Robert Shore from *Moby Dick* by Herman Melville. Both reprinted by permission of Macmillan Publishing Co.

McGRAW-HILL BOOK CO. Illustrations by Charles Geer from *Miss Pickerell and the Supertanker* by Ellen MacGregor and Dora Pantell. Copyright © 1978 by McGraw-Hill, Inc./ Illustration by Jessica Ann Levy from *She Was Nice to Mice* by Alexandra Elizabeth Sheedy. Text copyright © 1975 by Alexandra Elizabeth Sheedy. Illustrations copyright © 1975 by Jessica Ann Levy./ Illustration by Paul Galdone from *Miss Pickerell Goes Undersea* by Ellen MacGregor. Copyright 1953 by Robert Noble MacGregor and John MacGregor./ Illustration by Charles Geer from *Miss Pickerell on the Trail* by Ellen MacGregor and Dora Pantell. Copyright © 1982 by McGraw-Hill, Inc. All reprinted by permission of McGraw-Hill Book Co.

DAVID McKAY CO. Illustration by Kathleen Elgin from *Twenty-Eight Days* by Kathleen Elgin and John F. Osterritter. Copyright © 1973 by Kathleen Elgin and John F. Osterritter./ Jacket illustration by Maginel Wright Enright from *Hans Brinker; or, The Silver Skates* by Mary Mapes Dodge. Both reprinted by permission of David McKay Co.

WILLIAM MORROW & CO., INC. Illustration by Imero Gobbato from *The Practical Man* by George Mendoza. Text copyright © 1968 by George Mendoza. Illustrations copyright © 1968 by Imero Gobbato./ Illustration by Imero Gobbato from *A Bucketful of Moon* by Toby Talbot. Text copyright © 1976 by Toby Talbot. Illustrations copyright © 1976 by Imero Gobbato. Both reprinted by permission of William Morrow & Co., Inc.

THE PUTNAM PUBLISHING GROUP. Jacket illustration by Gyo Fujikawa from *That's Not Fair* by Gyo Fujikawa./ Illustration by Gyo Fujikawa from *Oh, What a Busy Day!* by Gyo Fujikawa. Copyright © 1976 by Gyo Fujikawa./ Illustration by Jeanne Titherington from "Queen Pig," in *A Taste for Quiet: And Other Disquieting Tales* by Judith Gorog. Text copyright © 1982 by Judith Gorog. Illustrations copyright © 1982 by Jeanne Titherington./ Illustration by Tony King from *The Moving Alphabet Book* by Tony King. Copyright © 1982 by Tony King./ Illustration by Kurt Werth from *Noodles, Nitwits and Numskulls* by Maria Leach. Copyright © 1961 by Maria Leach./ Illustration by Colin McNaughton from *A Book of Opposites at Home* by Colin McNaughton./ Illustration by Yasuo Ohtomo from *Where's My Daddy?,* adapted from a story by Shigeo Watanabe. Text copyright © 1979 by Shigeo Watanabe. Illustrations copyright © 1979 by Yasuo Ohtomo. American text copyright © 1982 by Philomel Books. All reprinted by permission of The Putnam Publishing Group.

RAINTREE PUBLISHERS, INC. Illustration by Dennis Hockerman from *Beginning to*

Learn about Summer by Richard L. Allington and Kathleen Krull. Copyright © 1981 by Raintree Publishers, Inc. Reprinted by permission of Raintree Publishers, Inc.

RAND McNALLY & CO. Illustrations by Maginel Wright Enright from *Heidi* by Johanna Spyri. Copyright 1921 by Rand McNally & Co./ Sidelight excerpts from *Conversations* by Roy Newquist. Copyright © 1967 by Rand McNally & Co. All reprinted by permission of Rand McNally & Co.

RANDOM HOUSE, INC. Illustration by J. K. Lambert from *Heart of Ice* by Comte De Caylus. Adapted by Benjamin Appel. Text copyright © 1977 by Benjamin Appel. Illustrations copyright © 1977 by Random House, Inc./ Illustration by Robert Shore from "The Pram" by A. W. Bennett in *Alfred Hitchcock's Supernatural Tales of Terror and Suspense.* Copyright © 1973 by Random House, Inc. Both reprinted by permission of Random House, Inc.

CHARLES SCRIBNER'S SONS. Sidelight excerpts from *Writers and Writing* by Robert van Gelder./ Illustration by Carole M. Byard from *Under Christopher's Hat* by Dorothy M. Callahan. Text copyright © 1972 by Dorothy M. Callahan. Illustrations copyright © 1972 by Carole M. Byard. Both reprinted by permission of Charles Scribner's Sons.

SIMON & SCHUSTER, INC. Illustration by Charles Geer from *Miss Pickerell on the Moon* by Ellen MacGregor and Dora Pantell. Copyright © 1965 by McGraw-Hill, Inc./ Illustration by Charles Geer from *Miss Pickerell Takes the Bull by the Horns* by Ellen MacGregor and Dora Pantell. Copyright © 1976 by McGraw-Hill, Inc./ Illustration by Paul Galdone from *Miss Pickerell Goes to the Arctic* by Ellen MacGregor. Copyright 1954 by McGraw-Hill, Inc. All reprinted by permission of Simon & Schuster, Inc.

THE VIKING PRESS. Illustration by Robert McCloskey from *Junket* by Anne H. White. Copyright 1955 by Anne H. White and Robert McCloskey./ Illustrations by Robert McCloskey from *Homer Price* by Robert McCloskey. Copyright 1943, renewed © 1971 by Robert McCloskey./ Illustration by Robert McCloskey from *One Morning in Maine* by Robert McCloskey. Copyright 1952, renewed © 1980 by Robert McCloskey./ Frontispiece illustration by Robert McCloskey from *Blueberries for Sal* by Robert McCloskey. Copyright 1948, renewed © 1976 by Robert McCloskey./ Illustration by Robert McCloskey from *Journey Cake, Ho!* by Ruth Sawyer. Copyright 1953, renewed © 1981 by Ruth Sawyer and Robert McCloskey./ Illustration by Robert McCloskey from *Lentil* by Robert McCloskey. Copyright 1940, renewed © 1968 by Robert McCloskey./ Illustration by Robert McCloskey from *Make Way for Ducklings* by Robert McCloskey. Copyright 1941, renewed © 1969 by Robert McCloskey./ Sidelight excerpts from an article "Katherine Anne Porter," in *Writers at Work: The Paris Review Interviews,* second series, edited by George Plimpton. Copyright © 1963 by The Paris Review, Inc. All reprinted by permission of The Viking Press.

FRANKLIN WATTS, INC. Photograph from *An Album of the Sixties* by Carol A. Emmens. Copyright © 1981 by Carol A. Emmens./ Illustration by Janusz Grabiański from *Grabiański's Cats* by Janusz Grabiański. Copyright © 1966 by Carl Ueberreuter Druck und Verlag./ Illustration by Janusz Grabiański from *Grabiański's Horses* by Janusz Grabiański. Copyright © 1966 by Carl Ueberreuter Druck und Verlag./ Photograph from *They Triumphed over Their Handicaps* by Joan Harries. Copyright © 1981 by Joan Harries Katsarakis. All reprinted by permission of Franklin Watts, Inc.

WAYLAND PUBLISHERS LTD. Photograph from *The Danube* by C.A.R. Hills. Copyright © 1979 by Wayland Publishers Ltd. Reprinted by permission of Wayland Publishers Ltd.

Sidelight excerpts from an article "May Hill Arbuthnot Honor Lecture: One of the Dozens," by Shigeo Watanabe, Spring, 1977 in *Top of the News.* Copyright © 1977 by American Library Association. Reprinted by permission of American Library Association./ Sidelight excerpts from *Why the Russians Are the Way They Are* by Benjamin Appel. Reprinted by permission of Willa Appel./ Illustration by De Grazia from *Caves and Canyons* by Sister M. Angela. Copyright © 1979 by Benedictine Sisters of Perpetual Adoration. Reprinted by permission of Benedictine Sisters of Perpetual Adoration./ Illustration by De Grazia from *God and a Mouse* by Sister M. Angela. Copyright © 1979 by Benedictine Sisters of Perpetual Adoration. Reprinted by permission of Benedictine Sisters of Perpetual Adoration./ Sidelight excerpts from *Books Are by People* by Lee Bennett Hopkins. Copyright © 1969 by Scholastic Magazine, Inc. Reprinted by permission of Curtis Brown Ltd./ Sidelight excerpts from an article "Long Point for Decorative Accessories," by Elizabeth Enright, Nov.-Dec., 1954 in *Craft Horizons.* Reprinted by permission of *Craft Horizons.*/ Sidelight excerpts from an article "The Computer Playground," by Fred D'Ignazio, July, 1982 in *Compute!* magazine. Copyright © 1982 by Small System Services, Inc. Reprinted by permission of *Compute!* magazine.

Illustration by Linda Strauss Edwards from *The Turtle Street Trading Co.* by Jill Ross Klevin.

Text copyright © 1982 by Jill Ross Klevin. Illustrations copyright © 1982 by Linda Strauss Edwards. Reprinted by permission of Linda Strauss Edwards./ Illustration by Stan Gilliam from *Katie and the Computer* by Fred D'Ignazio. Text copyright © 1979 by Fred D'Ignazio. Illustrations copyright © 1979 by Stan Gilliam. Reprinted by permission of Stan Gilliam./ Photograph by Blaise Levai from *Young Hungary: Children of Hungary at Work and at Play* by Marianna Norris. Copyright © 1970 by Marianna Norris. Reprinted by permission of Marianna Norris./ Photograph from *The Baseball Book*, edited by Zander Hollander. Copyright © 1982 by Associated Features, Inc. Reprinted by permission of United Press International./ Sidelight excerpts from "Kids, Parents and Software," by Fred D'Ignazio, October 2, 1983 in *Washington Post* "Book World." Copyright © 1983 by *Washington Post*. Reprinted by permission of *Washington Post*./ Sidelight excerpts taken from the film "Robert McCloskey." Produced by Weston Woods, 1964. Reprinted by permission of Weston Woods./ Sidelight excerpts from an article "When I Illustrate a Story I Play All the Parts," by Robert Shore, February 26, 1968 in *Publishers Weekly*. Copyright © 1968 by Xerox Corporation. Reprinted by permission of Xerox Education Publications./ Sidelight excerpts from an article "Robert McCloskey, Master of Humorous Realism," by Miriam Horrman and Eva Samuels in *Authors and Illustrators of Children's Books*. Reprinted by permission of Xerox Education Publications.

PHOTOGRAPH CREDITS

Benjamin Appel: Sol Libsohn; Peter Briggs: Larry Lauve; Shirley Climo: *Los Alamos Town Crier;* Ferne Geller Cone: Lyn Gardner; Margaret Stuyvesant Cuyler: Jan Perkins; Ted De Grazia: Bernard Coyle; De Grazia's "Gallery in the Sun": Col. Sherman Chuck; Nicole de Messières: Philippe Vaughan; Peter Desbarats: Ron Nelson Photography; Nancy Goor: Ron Goor; Jill Ross Klevin: copyright © 1982 by Sloane Mallory Klevin; Nora Benjamin Kubie: Bernice B. Perry; Colin McNaughton: Michael Ann Mullen; R. A. Montgomery: Ethan Hubbard; Katherine Anne Porter: (at eighteen months) Estate of Katherine Anne Porter, (in 1933) George Platt Lynes, (on her eighty-fifth birthday) Paul Porter, ("The Jilting of Granny Weatherall") courtesy of Learning in Focus; Robert Shore: Walter Hortens.

SOMETHING ABOUT THE AUTHOR

ALLINGTON, Richard L(loyd)   1947-

PERSONAL: Born May 13, 1947, in Grand Rapids, Mich.; son of George C. (a farmer) and Eldona (an advertising copywriter; maiden name, Weller) Allington; married Susan Gordon, April 6, 1968 (divorced May 5, 1978); married Anne McGill Franzen (a legislative assistant), January 11, 1980; children: Heidi, Tinker, Margaret, Bo, Michael. *Education:* Western Michigan University, B.A., 1968, M.A., 1969; Michigan State University, Ph.D., 1973. *Home:* 246 Van Wie Point Rd., Glenmont, N.Y. 12077. *Office:* Department of Reading, State University of New York at Albany, Albany, N.Y. 12222.

CAREER: Belding (Mich.) Area Schools, reading director, 1969-71; State University of New York at Albany, Albany, N.Y., assistant professor, 1973-78, associate professor of reading, 1978—, chairman of department, 1982—. Co-editor of *Journal of Reading Behavior,* 1977-82. Soccer Coach, Bethlehem Soccer Club. *Member:* International Reading Association, American Educational Research Association, National Conference of Researchers in English, National Reading Conference. *Awards, honors:* Grants from State University of New York Research Foundation, 1976, 1979, National Institute of Education, 1977-78, National Institutes of Health, 1977-79, and International Reading Association, 1983-84.

WRITINGS: The Reading Fact, Macdonald-Raintree, 1978; (with Michael Strange) *Learning through Reading in the Content Areas,* Heath, 1980; (with others) *Focus: Reading for Success,* Scott, Foresman, 1985.

"Beginning to Learn About" series; all for children; all published by Raintree: *Beginning to Learn about Colors* (illustrated by Noel Spangler), 1979; . . . *Numbers* (illustrated by Tom Garcia), 1979; . . . *Opposites* (illustrated by Eulala Conner), 1979; . . . *Shapes* (illustrated by Lois Ehlert), 1979; . . . *Letters* (illustrated by T. Garcia), 1983.

"Beginning to Learn About" series; all with Kathleen Cowles (pseudonym of Kathleen Krull); all published by Raintree, 1980: *Beginning to Learn about Feelings* (illustrated by Brian Cody); . . . *Hearing* (illustrated by Wayne Dober); . . . *Looking* (illustrated by Bill Bober); . . . *Smelling* (illustrated by Rick Thrun); . . . *Tasting* (illustrated by N. Spangler); . . . *Touching* (illustrated by Yoshi Miyake).

"Beginning to Learn About" series; all with Kathleen Krull; all published by Raintree: *Beginning to Learn about Reading* (illustrated by Joel Naprstek), 1980; . . . *Talking* (illustrated by R. Thrun), 1980; . . . *Thinking* (illustrated by T. Garcia), 1980; . . . *Writing* (illustrated by Y. Miyake), 1980; . . . *Autumn* (illustrated by Bruce Bond), 1981; . . . *Spring* (illustrated

(From *Beginning to Learn about Summer* by Richard L. Allington and Kathleen Krull. Illustrated by Dennis Hockerman.)

RICHARD L. ALLINGTON

by Dee Rahn), 1981; . . . *Summer* (illustrated by Dennis Hockerman), 1981; . . . *Winter* (illustrated by John Wallner), 1981; . . . *Measuring* (illustrated by N. Spangler), 1983; . . . *Science* (illustrated by James Teason), 1983; . . . *Stories* (illustrated by Helen Cogancherry), 1983; . . . *Time* (illustrated by Y. Miyake), 1983; . . . *Words* (illustrated by Ray Cruz), 1983.

WORK IN PROGRESS: Descriptive study of compensatory education instruction.

SIDELIGHTS: "I was born in Cedar Springs, Michigan, the eldest of six children. I was raised on a dairy farm and attended a one room country school. Now I work as a university professor and live in an old Victorian summer home on the Hudson River south of Albany, N.Y. I have five children, all of whom think it is quite nice to be able to go to the library and check out a book written by their father."

ANDERSON, Poul (William) 1926-
(A. A. Craig, Michael Karageorge, Winston P. Sanders)

BRIEF ENTRY: Born November 25, 1926, in Bristol, Pa. Novelist, short story writer, and translator. Best known in the realm

of science fiction, Anderson is an extremely prolific writer who has produced over fifty novels and two hundred shorter works. In his creation of alien worlds and their inhabitants, critics have especially noted his blend of scientific accuracy, historical perspective, and powerful grasp of Nordic mythmaking elements. Unlike other science fiction writers, Anderson has never restricted himself to one literary genre. His works encompass a wide range—not only science fiction, but songs, poems, parodies, essays, historicals, mysteries, and horror stories. He has written broad farce, adventure, comedy, sociopolitical drama, and romantic and heroic fantasy; he is also an adept translator of Danish folktales.

Anderson's first published story, "Tomorrow's Children," appeared in the March, 1947 issue of *Astounding Science Fiction.* The following year he graduated from the University of Minnesota with a degree in physics. Although he immediately became a free-lance writer and never pursued a career in science, his background in the study has always been evident in his writings through his expert handling of scientific phenomena and premises. In 1952 his first science fiction novel, *Vault of the Ages,* was published. It marked the beginning of his "Technic Civilization" series that has since grown to include eleven novels and over twenty-nine shorter works, spanning a publication period of twenty-eight years and more than five millennia of galactic history. Anderson's short stories are contained in volumes like *The Book of Poul Anderson* (DAW Books, 1975), *The Worlds of Poul Anderson* (Ace Books, 1974), and *The Earth Book of Stormgate* (Putnam, 1978). More works are represented in numerous anthologies such as *Masters of Science Fiction* (Belmont Books, 1964) and *The Future at War* (Ace Books, 1979). In 1961 he received the first of six Hugo awards in the best short fiction catagory for "The Longest Voyage"; about ten years later, "The Queen of Air and Darkness" and "Goat Story" received both the Hugo and Nebula awards. In addition, he is the recipient of the first annual Cock Robin Mystery Award and the Tolkien Memorial Award. *Home:* 3 Las Palomas, Orinda, Calif. 94563. *For More Information See: Contemporary Literary Criticism,* Volume 15, Gale, 1980; *Contemporary Authors, New Revision Series,* Volume 2, Gale, 1981; *Dictionary of Literary Biography,* Volume 8, Part 1, Gale, 1981; *Science Fiction Writers,* Scribner, 1982.

APPEL, Benjamin 1907-1977

PERSONAL: Born September 13, 1907, in New York, N.Y.; died April 3, 1977, in Princeton, N.J.; son of Louis and Bessie (Mikofsky) Appel; married Sophie Marshak, October 31, 1936; children: Carla, Willa, Marianna Consideration. *Education:* Attended University of Pennsylvania, 1925-26, and New York University, 1926-27; Lafayette College, B.S., 1929. *Politics:* "Utopian." *Residence:* Roosevelt, N.J.

CAREER: Writer, 1929-77, with some short stints during depression years as bank clerk, farmer, lumberjack, tenement house inspector, and other positions. During World War II worked as aviation mechanic; served with various government agencies, including U.S. Office of Civilian Defense, and War Manpower Commission, 1943-45; special assistant to U.S. Commissioner for the Philippines, 1945-46, with simulated rank of colonel in Manila. Visiting author at University of Pennsylvania, spring, 1974. *Member:* Authors Guild, P.E.N. *Awards, honors:* Louis Rabinowitz Foundation Grants, 1965-66; New Jersey Authors Award from New Jersey Institute of Technology, 1966, for *Why the Russians Are the Way They*

His Majesty was lying on a rich Persian carpet surrounded by several spaniels who, like dutiful pages, were engaged in chasing away flies hovering over their monarch. ■ (From *Heart of Ice* by Comte De Caylus. Adapted by Benjamin Appel. Illustrated by J. K. Lambert.)

Are, 1967, for *Man and Magic,* and 1968 and 1975, for *Why the Chinese Are the Way They Are.*

WRITINGS: Mixed Vintage (poems), Richard G. Badger, 1929; *Brain Guy* (novel), Knopf, 1934; *Four Roads to Death* (novel), Knopf, 1935; *Runaround* (novel), Dutton, 1937; *The Power House* (novel), Dutton, 1939.

The People Talk (nonfiction), Dutton, 1940; *The Dark Stain,* Dial, 1943; *But Not Yet Slain,* Wyn, 1947; *Fortress in Rice,* Bobbs-Merrill, 1951, revised edition, Pocket Books, 1960; *Plunder,* Gold Medal, 1952, *Hell's Kitchen* (short stories; young adult), Lion Books, 1952, published as *Hell's Kitchen: A Novel,* Pantheon, 1977; *Dock Walloper* (short stories), Lion Books, 1953; *Sweet Money Girl,* Fawcett, 1954; *Life and Death of a Tough Guy,* Avon, 1955; *We Were There in the Klondike Gold Rush* (juvenile; illustrated by Irv Docktor), Grosset, 1956; *We Were There at the Battle for Bataan* (juvenile; illustrated by I. Docktor), Grosset, 1957; *The Raw Edge,* Random House, 1958; *We Were There with Cortes and Montezuma* (juvenile; illustrated by Reynold C. Pollak), Grosset, 1959; *The Funhouse* (science fiction), Ballantine, 1959, another edition published as *The Death Master,* Popular Library, 1959.

The Illustrated Book about South America, including Mexico and Central America (juvenile; illustrated by Tran Mawicke), Grosset, 1960; *A Big Man, a Fast Man,* Morrow, 1961; *Shepherd of the Sun* (juvenile; illustrated by Bernarda Bryson), Obolensky, 1961; *With Many Voices: Europe Talks about America,* Morrow, 1963; *A Time of Fortune,* Morrow, 1963; *Hitler: From Power to Ruin,* Grosset, 1964; *Ben-Gurion's Israel* (juvenile), Grosset, 1965; *Man and Magic* (young adult; illustrated by Jacob Landau), Pantheon, 1966; *Why the Russians Are the Way They Are* (juvenile; illustrated by Samuel Bryant), Little, Brown, 1966; *The Age of Dictators* (juvenile), Crown, 1968; *Why the Chinese Are the Way They Are* (juvenile; illustrated by S. Bryant), Little, Brown, 1968, revised edition, 1973; *The Fantastic Mirror: Science Fiction across the Ages* (juvenile), Pantheon, 1969; *Why the Japanese Are the Way They Are* (juvenile), Little, Brown, 1973; *The Devil and W. Kaspar,* Popular Library, 1977; (adapter) Comte de Caylus, *Heart of Ice* (fairy tale; illustrated by J. K. Lambert), Pantheon, 1977.

Short stories anthologized in *O. Henry Memorial Award Prize Stories* and O'Brien's *Best Short Stories,* 1934, 1935, and in *Best Short Stories, 1915-39.* Contributor of essays on writers of the 1930s and short stories to magazines, such as *Carleton Miscellany, Literary Review,* and *New Letters.*

ADAPTATIONS: "Cry of Battle" (motion picture, starring Van Heflin and Rita Moreno; based on novel, *Fortress in the Rice*), Petramonte Productions, 1963.

SIDELIGHTS: Appel was born in New York City on September 13, 1907. Because his parents had come from wealthy families in Poland, they attempted to shield their children from the day-to-day poverty and crime in their neighborhood. Nevertheless, life in New York's midtown West Side, known as "Hell's Kitchen," made a profound impression on Appel. The world of "Hell's Kitchen" later formed the background for several of his novels. "Of course, I never found any glamour in crime. It is just part of the life that I knew, and you can't call the life of Hell's Kitchen glamorous. There are quite a number of people up the river in Sing Sing who were just neighbors. For instance, for a while my father did very well as a real estate operator. He had an office at Fortieth Street and Eighth Avenue, and a lot of other people who were doing well in politics or

BENJAMIN APPEL

one thing and another would come to his office and sit in a very big poker game that ran there.

"I was about sixteen years old, but very naive for that age, when we had a chauffeur, Red. I hung out a lot with Red and on many afternoons he'd take me downtown with him on visits to the Tombs [prison]. He'd bring presents to men in the Tombs, and once I said something about it being kind of funny that he should have so many friends who were in jail. Red said that lots of people were in jail and that their friends on the outside should help them. I asked what his friends were in jail for and he told me they were all in for speeding.

"Red was good to me but I guess the money he saw kicking around my father's office made him restless. One day when the poker game was big, some stick-up men came in and knocked it off. A couple of months later there was another stick-up in the office. And this time there was proof that Red was the finger man—that he had tipped off the stick-up crowd that there was a lot of cash available. But as I say, Red was just someone I knocked around with." [Robert van Gelder, *Writers and Writing,* Scribner, 1946.[1]]

Social rules in the ghetto-world of "Hell's Kitchen" were uncompromising and structured. "The Irish Catholics were the top dogs and they considered that they outrated Americans, Germans and Jews in that order. After that came the Italians, the Greeks and the Negroes. Every block had a gang, and when you went off your own block and a gang caught you there was considerable chance that you'd be beaten up. But, of course, there was also some chance that you'd be beaten up on your own block. When I went to the University of Pennsylvania I talked from the side of my mouth the way they do in prison pictures and I pronounced words in what is the Hell's Kitchen accepted style."[1]

(From *Shepherd of the Sun* by Benjamin Appel. Illustrated by Bernarda Bryson.)

After a year at the University of Pennsylvania, Appel transferred to New York University, and then to Lafayette College, from which he graduated in 1929. That same year his first book—a book of poetry entitled *Mixed Vintage*—was published. Appel held a variety of odd jobs while he continued to write.

In 1934 his first novel, *Brain Guy* was published. It formed the first book of a trilogy that focused on the relationship of vice and society. *Brain Guy* traced the relationship of poverty to crime. The second novel in the trilogy, *The Powerhouse*, traced the development of petty crime to organized mob violence and lawlessness. In the third novel, *The Dark Stain*, crime moved into racial relations.

Appel's first nonfiction book, *The People Talk,* was published in 1940. For this book the author traveled cross-country to gather material about how people talked and what they were talking about. "I went out in Wisconsin, for example, and pitched hay with a crew. Whenever any one made a comment that I thought I could use I'd stop and make a note—right there in the field. Just as well I did. I wasn't used to heaving hay around and the notes gave me a breathing spell." [Robert van Gelder, "Mr. Ben Appel of Hell's Kitchen," *New York Times*, June 16, 1940.[2]]

Soon after World War II Appel was sent to the Philippines as a special assistant to the United States commissioner. His 1951 book, *Fortress in Rice*, grew out of his experiences there.

For children Appel wrote many nonfiction books about special historical events that formed a series entitled "We Were There." Appel also wrote several nonfiction books about people from other cultures for children, including *Why the Russians Are the Way They Are*. "Before writing the book I thought it would be a good idea to find out what American kids knew about Russia or the Soviet Union, and *also* what they would like to know.

"What I did was speak or write to school principals and teachers in different parts of the United States. I needed their co-operation.

"I also got in touch with friends of mine and asked them to help me by speaking to the school authorities in their communities. The *Library Journal* was good enough to print a few paragraphs about my plans, and what I wanted.

"Since I am not a Gallup Poll, but a writer living in a small town in the middle of New Jersey, I didn't expect to get replies from all over the United States. But there were enough replies to make up what could be called a sample.

"When I read through everything, a pattern began to emerge. I'm reasonably sure it would hold up even if I had been a Gallup Poll and could have covered, say, fifty cities, towns, and rural townships in each of the fifty states in the Union.

"What did the pattern show? Some kids knew nothing or next to nothing, and said so. One Pittsburgh kid wrote: 'I don't know anything.'

"Some kids put down all sorts of fantastic notions. For example: 'I imagine that the Russians are huge men with hard blue eyes and very strong.' 'The religion is Jewish or Protestant.'

"These two replies came from some big town kids who lived in New York. But across the country in Concord, California, there were replies just as fantastic: 'Russia had a very bad background. She killed off all the Christians.' 'The boys are put in military schools. Their heads are shaved. They drill all day and sleep all night.'

"A few kids, not many, very few in fact, knew quite a bit: 'We believe in democracy and the Russians believe in Communism. The Russians once had tsars and nobility but the blue-blooded people took all the riches and land themselves. They profited from the poor peasants and poverty-stricken people. After many years of torture the poor people could stand it no longer; they revolted. The land and the money was divided between all of them and that was the start of Communism.'

"Well, I read all the replies and thought it all over. It seemed to me that the best way to answer, not only the questions, but the worries and fears and anger behind the questions—as well as to satisfy the widespread curiosity—all depended on finding an answer to one key question. It could be put in these words: *Why are the Russians the way they are?*

"I found that I had to write about the 1917 Revolution and the long cruel years of Stalin's dictatorship. But I also had to go back to the times of such tsars as Ivan the Terrible and Peter the Great.

"This book, however, is not a question-and-answer book. The plan is my own. For example, I begin with the Second World War, in which twenty-five million Soviet citizens, men, women and children, were killed by the Nazis. Today the fear of a new war, a nuclear war, haunts the minds of the Soviet people, just as it haunts our minds. I felt that if we really wished to understand why the Russians (or more correctly all the varied Soviet nationalities) are the way they are, we would have to begin with the terrible bloodletting of 1941-45.

"This great democracy of ours has always been a land interested in knowing the truth about other nations. Of course, there are many definitions of what the truth is. This book is a try at understanding *why* the Russians are the way they are." [Benjamin Appel, *Why the Russians Are the Way They Are*, Little, Brown, 1966.³]

Shortly before his death in 1977, Appel adapted an eighteenth-century French fairy tale for children entitled *Heart of Ice.*

HOBBIES AND OTHER INTERESTS: Fishing. "I have fished since I was ten, spending most of my summers, as far as I can remember, on lakes and in the woods."

FOR MORE INFORMATION SEE: New York Times, June 16, 1940; Robert van Gelder, *Writers and Writing,* Scribner, 1946; *Oxford Companion to American Literature,* 4th edition, Oxford University Press, 1965. *Obituaries: New York Times,* April 4, 1977; *Publishers Weekly,* April 25, 1977; *AB Bookman's Weekly,* June 27, 1977.

ARAGONÉS, Sergio   1937-

BRIEF ENTRY: Born September 6, 1937, in Castellon, Spain; came to the United States in 1962. Cartoonist and illustrator. Aragonés is one of *Mad* magazine's most popular cartoonists, noted especially for his large mural-cartoons. As a child growing up in Mexico City, Aragonés was a constant doodler. By the time he was sixteen his work was appearing in various Mexican magazines. Later, he studied mime under French pantomimist Marcel Marceau and worked for a while as a clown.

Aragonés credits this training for his cartoon style which consists mainly of wordless gags. His affiliation with *Mad* began in 1962, shortly after his arrival in America. He soon began contributing to other magazines (including work for DC Comics), illustrating books, and designing storyboards for cartoon specials. Aragonés has made numerous television appearances and has executed drawings for television productions featuring celebrities like Cher, Jim Stafford, and Shirley MacLaine. He has also supplied drawings for shows such as "Laugh-In," "Speak Up America," and "Real Kids." Over ten of his books feature trademark *Mad* cartoons, including *Viva Mad* (New American Library, 1968), *Mad-ly Yours* (Warner, 1972), *Mad as a Hatter* (Warner, 1981), and *Mad Menagerie* (Warner, 1983). He is also the illustrator of over twenty books for both children and adults. *Office:* Mad Magazine, 485 Madison Ave., New York, N.Y. 10022. *For More Information See:* Nick Meglin, *The Art of Humorous Illustration,* Watson-Guptill, 1973; *The World Encyclopedia of Comics,* Volume 1, Chelsea House, 1976.

ARNDT, Ursula (Martha H.)

BRIEF ENTRY: Born in Düsseldorf, Germany. An illustrator of books for children, Arndt attended the Academy of Arts in Düsseldorf from 1942 to 1947. She eventually immigrated to the United States and settled in New York where, beginning in 1963, she worked as a Christmas card designer for H. G. Caspari, Inc. A free-lance illustrator, she also contributed illustrations to numerous magazines. Her first illustrated book, Alfred Slote's *The Princess Who Wouldn't Talk,* was published in 1964. Through the years she has illustrated over a dozen books, including Mike Thaler's *The Prince and the Seven Moons* (Macmillan, 1966), Elizabeth Coatsworth's *Troll Weather* (Macmillan, 1967), and Phyllis Purscell's *Old Boy's Tree House and Other Deep Forest Tales* (Weybright, 1968). In 1970 Arndt illustrated *Lilies, Rabbits, and Painted Eggs: The Story of the Easter Symbols,* the first in a series of six books written by Edna Barth. All published by Seabury, the books explore the origin and symbolic meaning of different holidays, including Christmas (*Holly, Reindeer, and Colored Lights,* 1971), Halloween (*Witches, Pumpkins, and Grinning Ghosts,* 1972), Valentine's Day (*Hearts, Cupids, and Red Roses,* 1974), and St. Patrick's Day (*Shamrocks, Harps, and Shillelaghs,* 1977). Arndt has most recently provided the illustrations for James C. Giblin's *Fireworks, Picnics, and Flags* (Clarion Books, 1983). She is also the illustrator of several books published in German.

ASHLEY, Bernard   1935-

BRIEF ENTRY: Born April 2, 1935, in London, England. British author and educator. A teacher in England for nearly thirty years, Ashley's young adult novels reveal a deep understanding and empathy for how youths think and feel; his focus is on the "troubled" child whose attitude and behavior in the classroom is often a symptom of pressures being exerted by an undesirable home life situation. In books like *The Trouble with Donovan Croft, All My Men, Break in the Sun,* and *High Pavement Blues,* critics have praised his realistic fiction whereby the life of the pre-adolescent is accurately depicted as possibly lonely, painful, confusing, and, at times, even threatening. Although his stories are set specifically in the urban working-class environment of inner London, the truths he reveals are universal. The problems range from racial prejudice to dealing with the class bully to neglectful parents who can be accused of alcoholism and battering.

In *A Kind of Wild Justice* (S. G. Phillips, 1979), young Ronnie Webster must deal with life in London's East End—a criminal father, a deserting mother, and a desperate struggle against the recognized family of power in the slums. *Horn Book* observed: ". . . Tension is created through skillful use of details. . . . The narrative utilizes street argot, thus enabling the reader to perceive events through the haunted eyes of the hunted and intensifying the sense of urgency and terror." As in his other novels, Ashley not only creates a thrilling adventure story but provides the reader with insight into existing social problems, in this case, life in a poor, multi-ethnic neighborhood. In 1976 he was the recipient of the Children's Rights Workshop Other Award for *The Trouble with Donovan Croft;* three years later he was commended for the Carnegie Medal for *A Kind of Wild Justice.* In addition to his young adult novels, Ashley has written several novels for younger readers. All published by Julia MacRae, they are part of a series designed to accomodate the "in-between" reader who has out-grown picture books but is not quite ready for the full-length novel. His titles include: *Dinner Ladies Don't Count* (1981) and *Linda's Lie* (1982), both illustrated by Janet Duchesne, and *Your Guess Is as Good as Mine* (1983), illustrated by Steven Cain. *Home:* 128 Heathwood Gardens, London SE7 8ER, England. *For More Information See: Contemporary Authors,* Volumes 93-96, Gale, 1980; *Children's Literature Review,* Volume 4, Gale, 1982; *Twentieth-Century Children's Writers,* 2nd edition, St. Martin's, 1983.

BAIRD, Thomas (P.)   1923-

BRIEF ENTRY: Born April 22, 1923, in Omaha, Neb. Novelist and educator. Baird graduated from Princeton University and received his M.F.A. from the same university in 1950. He also taught there for three years before becoming a lecturer in art history at the Frick Collection in New York City. After working as a member of the curatorial staff at the National Gallery of Art and as associate director at Dumbarton Oaks in Washington, D.C., he went to Trinity College where, since 1970, he has been a professor of art history, Primarily an adult novelist, Baird has written two novels for young adults. In *Finding Fever* (Harper, 1982), fifteen-year-old Benny O'Bryan sets out to find his little sister's dog which has disappeared. With the help of a schoolmate he begins to unravel the existence of a dognapping ring. *Booklist* observed: "Baird's novel functions well as both a mystery and a portrait of friendship between two boys whose . . . distinctly different backgrounds make for an odd pairing. The interplay between Benny and Strill is as taut as the developing mystery. . . ." *Horn Book* called the characterization "outstanding, even of the minor figures, " adding that "the many narrative strands are admirably interwoven."

In his second young adult novel, *Walk Out a Brother* (Harper, 1983), Baird again combines mystery with the development of interpersonal relationships. Following the death of his father, sixteen-year-old Don Rennie sets out on a backpacking trip through the mountains of Wyoming—where a murderer is at large. *Booklist* again had praise for this "first-person coming-of-age narrative within an exciting adventure story that imparts a vivid sense and appreciation of nature and wilderness. . . ." Among Baird's adult novels, all published by Harper, are: *Triumphal Entry* (1962), *Sheba's Landing* (1964), *People Who Pull You Down* (1970), *The Way to the Old Sailors Home*

(1977), and *Poor Millie* (1978). His latest work is *Villa Aphrodite* (St. Martin's, 1984). *Home:* 70 Lorraine St., Hartford, Conn. 06105. *For More Information See: Contemporary Authors, New Revision Series,* Volume 4, Gale, 1981.

BAKER, Gayle C(unningham)   1950-

PERSONAL: Born April 23, 1950, in Elmhurst, Ill.; daughter of David John (a commercial illustrator; also in sales) and Gladys (in merchandising; maiden name, Morrison) Cunningham; married Clifford D. Baker (a professor of special education), August 17, 1974; children: Brian Cunningham, Scott Morrison. *Education:* Drake University, B.S.E., 1972; University of Northern Colorado, M.S., 1973, graduate study, 1974—. *Home:* 2330 21st Ave., Greeley, Colo. 80631.

CAREER: Teacher of handicapped children at elementary school in Englewood, Colo., 1973-74; Weld Board of Cooperative Educational Services, LaSalle, Colo., designer of remedial reading and mathematics program for middle school in Milliken, Colo., 1974-76, writer for career education project, 1975-77, designer of pre-primary and primary program for severely handicapped and multi-handicapped students, 1979-80; designer of program for mentally handicapped students at elementary school in Kersey, Colo., 1976-78; Platte Valley Elementary School, Kersey, designer of pre-first grade program, 1980—. Guest lecturer at University of Northern Colorado, 1977—, and Metropolitan State College, Denver, Colo., 1979. Colorado Department of Education, member of career education resource team, 1977, grant reader and evaluator, 1979. Presenter at Colorado Federation Council for Exceptional Children, 1977, and at mainstreaming seminar in Thailand, 1981.

MEMBER: International Reading Association, National Association for Retarded Citizens, National Education Association, Association for the Severely and Profoundly Handicapped, Council for Exceptional Children, Polk County Association for Retarded Citizens (citizen advocate, 1971—), Women's Panhellenic Association of Greeley, Cesarean Support Group of Greeley (charter board member), Platte Valley School District Education Association (member of executive board, 1981-82), University of Northern Colorado Faculty Dames, Alpha Phi, Gamma Gamma, Kappa Delta, Pi Lambda Theta. *Awards, honors:* Named Outstanding Young Woman of America, 1981, by U.S. Jaycees.

WRITINGS: (With Vivian M. Montey) *Special Delivery: A Book for Kids about Cesarean and Vaginal Birth* (edited by Linda D. Meyer; illustrated by Debbie Hillyer), Charles Franklin Press, 1981. Developed book on language for Glenwood State School (Iowa), 1971. Author with husband, Cliff Baker, of article published in *Special Education in Canada, Council for Exceptional Children Journal,* 1983.

SIDELIGHTS: "I believe that in today's society it is extremely difficult for a woman to blend her family and career together without feeling outside pressure from people and dealing with her own guilt resulting from decisions she's made. Personally I have had to do a great amount of reading and attending classes to educate myself about child rearing, family structure, and women. I also spent a good part of my everyday conversations with people in surveying each about their beliefs, concerns, and feelings pertaining to motherhood and outside-the-home careers. I would strongly recommend every mother-to-be to do

GAYLE C. BAKER

the same to assist her in fitting all the pieces of her life together. It's still a struggle, but I'm beginning to feel better about my life because of my ongoing research.

"After having worked outside the home for five years in an established teaching career, I had my first baby. During my year-and-a-half maternity leave I felt it was important to keep myself stimulated so that I wouldn't fall into the trap of a 'stereotyped' housewife and mother. This led to writing *Special Delivery*.

"It's extremely important to me that my sons and any future children, and *all* the children of the world, understand their own special delivery. *Special Delivery* is the first complete book on the market to explain to preschool through preteen children about conception, development, nature's way of intending a baby to be born, reasons for a Cesarean, the actual Cesarean birth, and the recovery of the mother after delivery. I believe that my own Cesarean birth experience was a blessing in disguise to trigger the initial idea for this book.

"Now that I have returned to my outside-the-home career I want to comment on my philosophy of education. I have been formally trained and have had a wide variety of teaching experiences, working with numerous handicapping conditions. I believe in assisting every child to reach his/her highest potential during the very short time I know him/her. A teacher should find as many different ways as possible of teaching the same concept to motivate the student. Teaching is similar to the field of entertainment; a good teacher needs to turn the student on to life so that he/she isn't conscious of his/her actual learning. To be able to accomplish this in teaching, a good teacher needs

to be re-evaluating his/her life as a person. A teacher needs to experience as much as possible through travel, hobbies, reading and people so he/she, too, is turned on to life."

BARKER, Cicely Mary 1895-1973

BRIEF ENTRY: Born June 28, 1895, in Croydon, Surrey, England; died February 16, 1973. Painter, and author and illustrator of children's books. Barker briefly attended Croydon School of Art, but as an artist was largely self-educated. Her work—done in oil, watercolor, and pastel—was exhibited at the Royal Institute of Painters in Watercolours and the Society of Woman Artists, among others. Also a designer and painter of screens and stained glass, she did work for St. Georges, Waddon, and other churches in Surrey, England. She is best remembered for her children's books featuring the "flower fairies" which she began producing in the 1920s. Among these are the volumes of poetry *Flower Fairies of the Spring, Flower Fairies of the Summer,* and *Flower Fairies of the Autumn, with the Nuts and Berries They Bring.* She also wrote and illustrated fictional works such as *The Lord of the Rushie River* and *Groundsel and Necklaces,* reissued as *The Fairy's Gift.* In reviewing reprinted editions of her work, *Books and Bookmen* found *The Lord of the Rushie River* "delightfully illustrated" with a "timeless charm," while *Publishers Weekly* called *The Fairy's Gift* "fresh and new . . . a welcome change from the many 'problem' books." *For More Information See: Twentieth-Century Children's Writers,* 2nd edition, St. Martin's, 1983. *Obituaries: Times* (London), February 21, 1973.

BARNEY, Maginel Wright 1881-1966 (Maginel Wright Enright)

PERSONAL: Born June 19, 1881, in Weymouth, Mass.; died April 18, 1966, in East Hampton, N.Y.; daughter of William Cary (a minister) and Anna (a schoolteacher; maiden name, Lloyd-Jones) Wright; married Walter J. Enright (an illustrator and political cartoonist; divorced); married Hiram Barney (a lawyer; died, 1925); children: Elizabeth Enright Gillham. *Education:* Studied under brother, Frank Lloyd Wright; attended Chicago Art Institute. *Residence:* East Hampton, N.Y.

CAREER: Illustrator of children's books, artist, and craftsperson. Following art school, worked for an engraving company; painted covers for *Woman's Home Companion* and other magazines; during the Depression, created "long point" pictures using colored wools; in the early 1940s, designed high-fashion jeweled and sequinned shoes. Work has been exhibited at Marie Sterner Gallery, 1940, French & Company Galleries, 1945; and Sagittarius Gallery, New York City, 1962. *Awards, honors:* Illustrator of Caroline D. Snedeker's *Downright Dencey* which was selected as a Newbery honor book, 1928.

WRITINGS: The Baby's Record through the First Year in Song and Story (self-illustrated), Harper, 1928; (compiler) *Weather Signs and Rhymes* (juvenile; self-illustrated), Knopf, 1931; *The Valley of the God-Almighty Joneses* (autobiography), Appleton-Century, 1965.

Illustrator; all for children: (Under name Maginel Wright Enright) Clara Whitehill Hunt, *About Harriet,* Houghton, 1916; (under name M. W. Enright) Mary Mapes Dodge, *Hans Brinker; or, The Silver Skates,* McKay, 1918; (under name M. W.

Maginel Wright Barney, as a young woman.

Enright) *Songs from Mother Goose, for Voice and Piano,* Macmillan, 1920; (under name M. W. Enright) Johanna Spyri, *Heidi: A Story for Children and Those Who Love Children,* translated by Philip S. Allen, Rand McNally, 1921; Ruth Sawyer, *This Way to Christmas,* Harper, 1924, revised edition, 1967; Caroline D. Snedeker, *Downright Dencey,* Doubleday, 1927; Sophie de Ségur, *Sophie: The Story of a Bad Little Girl,* translated from the French by Marguerite Fellows Melcher, Knopf, 1929; Philip Broughton, *Pandy,* P. F. Volland, 1930; Ethel Calvert Phillips, *Calico,* Houghton, 1937.

Under name Maginel Wright Enright; all written by Laura Bancroft (pseudonym of L. Frank Baum); all published by Reilly & Britton, except as indicated: *Bandit Jim Crow,* 1906; *Mr. Woodchuck,* 1906; *Prairie-Dog Town,* 1906; *Sugar-Loaf Mountain,* 1906; *Prince Mud-Turtle,* 1906; *Twinkle's Enchantment,* 1906; *Policeman Bluejay,* 1907, facsimile reprint, Scholars' Facsimilies & Reprints, 1981, also published as *Babes in Birdland,* 1911; *Twinkle and Chubbins: Their Astonishing Adventures in Nature-Fairyland,* 1911.

Also contributor of illustrations to various periodicals, including *Everybody's, Woman's Home Companion, Ladies' Home Journal, McClure's* and *Woman's World.*

SIDELIGHTS: **June 19, 1881.** Born in Weymouth, Massachusetts. Barney was the third child born to William Cary and Anna Lloyd-Jones Wright. "". . . I like to imagine my mother,

bareheaded, curly haired, sitting straight in the saddle, her beautiful intelligent eyes appreciating all they saw, and a strand of traveler's joy, pulled from a hedgerow, wreathed around the pommel. Nature and knowledge: those were her early and abiding passions.

"If neighbors, seeing her intensity and pride, thought her eccentric she would not have cared. She was emancipated before the emancipated woman became the vogue; perhaps she was a little formidable, though, in her adherence to principle. She did not marry till she was twenty-nine.

"At that time William Russell Cary Wright came to Lone Rock, a town not far from the Valley. At this stage of his life he was a circuit rider, a musician who went about the countryside to teach singing. He had already tried law, then medicine, then preaching, to which he would return, but music remained his first love.

"It was inevitable, I suppose, that my mother should be attracted to this man from the East. He was highly educated, a member of the singular New England family that produced James Russell and Amy Lowell, and in another connection he was related to the two lady-poets, Phoebe and Alice Cary. He was strikingly different from the young men who had courted my mother till then: she found him attractive, puzzling, and romantic. He was seventeen years older than she, a widower with three children, but my mother, like her mother before her, made up her mind, and nothing, not even Grandfather, could stand in her way. If she had foreseen the clash of their two positive natures, I think she would have gone ahead and married him anyway to prove to the Lloyd-Joneses that she knew her mind.

"At first his restlessness charmed her and she encouraged it. She thought it noble that he had abandoned a professional life in order to teach music. She thought it noble that he was able to give up teaching music in order to be a clergyman again. But as time went by it became apparent that he cared nothing for money, had no financial sense whatever. Sometimes there was no food to cook for supper. It was not so easy to be patient then.

"Their first child was a son. She had wished for a son, and even before he was born she had wished that this son would grow up to be an architect.

"A few years after Frank was born, my father's father, in Massachusetts, took his candle and went up to bed. He was ninety-nine years old and in full possession of his faculties. He sat down and wrote a farewell letter to each of his three sons. Then he went to bed and never woke up again.

"My father's letter came; and reading it he felt a great longing to return to his native New England. When he was called, soon afterward, to a pastorate in Weymouth, near Boston, he welcomed the offer as a gift from God. He took his family, left the Lloyd-Joneses [her mother's family] and their lush valley [in rural Wisconsin], and set out for the East.

"In Weymouth he was given the narrow gray parish house next to the church; it was not poorer than the other houses in the town but it was a far cry from the warm homesteads of my mother's girlhood. The people, New Englanders, offered a restrained cordiality: they gave the family a sort of reception, each bringing a comestible for the new pastor's cupboard. When they had gone my mother found she was wealthier by twenty-three pumpkin pies and very little else.

"In Weymouth, as it would have been anywhere, the most absorbing, rewarding fact in her life was her son, Frank.

"From the start, her devotion to Frank was overwhelming, and as it grew, the gulf between her and father widened. He retired more and more into his interior world, he walked backward, closing the few doors he had opened to her, until he was locked in a place inaccessible to everyone else; a kingdom he could rule in peace and silence. Frank could not enter it, he was relinquished once and for all to his mother." [Maginel Wright Barney, *The Valley of the God Almighty Joneses,* Appleton-Century, 1965.[1]]

1883. Following the separation of the parents, the family of three children and their mother moved to Madison, Wisconsin. " . . . Weymouth had grown hostile to my father, as he continued to preach the Baptist creed in a place that more and more embraced Unitarianism. And my mother was homesick for the Valley, for the air of Wisconsin. She wanted Frank to know the Uncles, to work for and with them in the Valley. She felt that he was becoming too sensitive and introspective. So, in the end, we moved to Madison.

"And it was not very long after that—not many years—that her marriage ended, too. I don't know what went wrong between my father and mother. I remember that he was often away for long stretches—teaching or preaching?—I don't even know. One scene has remained vivid in my memory all my life.

"It was a gray November day with a chill wind blowing. Wet falling leaves flew past the window. I was clinging to my mother's skirts as usual. Father faced us on the doorstep.

"'I will stay if you ask me to,' he said.

"'I do not ask you to,' my mother said.

"He turned and went down the steps without a word. My mother closed the door and took me into the living room where a coal stove was crackling: flames winked cheerfully from its isinglass window. She lifted me to her lap, reached into her pocket and drew out the old wine-colored wallet she always called her *portemonnaie* (I thought it sounded like 'pork money'). She opened it and took out a big fifty-cent piece.

"'This is all the money I have in the world,' she said.

"I leaned my head against her comfortably. I thought the coin looked very wealthy. But I knew something was wrong. Perhaps I sensed my mother's sadness; her deep knowledge of failure. And while I never had been very close to my father, something in the way he had turned and left us made me want to cry. But Mother's eyes were dry and bright, and so I didn't.

"I saw my father only one more time. It was a spring day and I was walking home from kindergarten. Suddenly, there he was, standing in my path. I stopped short; for a second I didn't recognize him. He puzzled me, and I felt a vague dread, looking up at him. Clearly he knew me, expected something of me. He smiled, and called me by name, and I felt terribly foolish: it was Father, only Father. I smiled uncertainly at him.

"Picking me up, he lifted me to his shoulder in one easy swing, kissed my cheek, and asked me the usual questions: Had I been good? Did I like kindergarten? I made the stock replies, hoping he would not kiss me again. I knew that I was supposed to feel something, but I did not. It was disturbing.

(Copy of the original 1918 jacket illustration by Maginel Wright Enright from *Hans Brinker; or, The Silver Skates* by Mary Mapes Dodge.)

"But he had put me down, and was examining my plain dress and scuffed, worn slippers. He considered critically; then off he strode, leading me by the hand to the town's best clothing store. I was not consulted. Father glanced over the display of children's shoes and made his decision: little cowhide shoes with copper toes that both interested and annoyed me. Before I knew it, they were on my feet. I regarded my blinking toes, and my father regarded me, smiling, waiting for a response.

"When I had shyly said my thanks, he put his hand out, stroked my hair, and asked the saleslady to show him some hats for little girls. Again he made the selection: blue and white straw it was, with a polka-dotted cotton ribbon. It was a cheap hat and I hated it on sight; Mother never bought anything shoddy. I thanked him, though.

"He walked with me a little way along the street, in the fitful sunlight, then he stopped and surveyed the improvements he had made in my appearance. He opened his mouth to speak, but changed his mind and did not. I often wonder what he wanted to say.

"He lifted me and kissed me once more, put me down, and smiled.

"'Go straight home, now,' he said. Then he turned and went his way along the muddy street.

(From *Downright Dencey* by Caroline Dale Snedeker. Illustrated by Maginel Wright Barney.)

"Mother waited on the step. Usually I did come straight home from kindergarten and as she knew of no reason why I should be late, she was anxious. When I was close enough for her to see my new hat and shoes, her look of relief gave way to one of profound bewilderment.

"I told her how I had come by my new things. She looked up and away from me, down the road toward town; then, taking my hand, she led me gently through the hall into the big warm kitchen, to the old wood range. Carefully she removed the hat, then sat me down and took off my fancy shoes. Without hesitation, she lifted the stove lid and committed the new accessories to the fire. She stared into the stove, watching the clothes burn. There was a short bright flash as the flames snatched the straw; then the odor of charred leather filled the room.

"I did not regret my loss, nor did Mother's action surprise or shock me. In some vague way I understood. She had destroyed Father's presents not so much because they came from him, but because he had done the one thing she could not abide: he had compromised, and bought cheap, gauche, eye-catching things, rather than plain, solid goods of quality, tastefully turned out. Mother believed that you bought a good dress, if you bought only one a year. Though it might become faded with age and countless washings, it was fine material—therefore you wore it with pride until it was beyond mending. That afternoon she took me uptown and bought me the finest pair of little French kid shoes she could find."[1]

Barney's childhood was spent with many aunts and uncles in the Wisconsin valley. "The thing I remember first about the Valley, aside from the Valley itself, is the Uncles.

"There were five of them: Uncle Thomas, Uncle John, Uncle Jenkin, Uncle James, and Uncle Enos.

"They were all farmers except Uncle Jenkin. They were tall, vigorous, strong men, able to do any heavy task. They were all bearded and had great shocks of dark curly hair.

"When I became aware of my Uncles in the Valley, they were middle-aged. To me they seemed gigantic beings who would toss me up for a kiss and I would shrink as my face was embedded in beard. Sometimes it would be damp with rain or fog, and then it was rather like kissing a swamp. The Uncles, as I've said, had a Biblical, apostolic look and once when four of them were driving through Madison in an open carriage someone yelled from the sidewalk: 'Hey, where's the other eight?'

"If there were troubles in those summers, we, the children, didn't know it. If there were illnesses, worries, or disappoint-ments, we didn't remember them. Looking back, all of it seems one long sunny day; and every hour was interesting.

"There was the excitement of threshing time, when my aunts served enormous midday meals out of doors, and I sat with the others at a big table in the fields, the chaff of wheat clinging to the neck of my dress, . . . stunned with the sight of food: meats, breads, vegetables, pies, cakes, cookies, fresh butter, fresh milk. Watermelons broken open: hot-colored, ice-cold, winking with jetty seeds, and cucumbers that we peeled and ate the way one eats bananas.

"There were the picnics, usually instigated by Uncle Thomas, in the chapel yard: all the Clan and all the children settled down companionably among the graves, eating again. (How we ate in those summers!) . . .

"I remember the peaceful satisfaction at the end of the day when one had played hard, and laughed a lot. Laughed enough to know the best sort of tiredness and, going to bed, to fall into sleep as a stone falls into a well.

"And so it went, summer after glorious summer. The Valley is a landscape in my memory forever, various, changing with weather and seasons, magnificently peopled with the grownups of our family: the Lloyd-Joneses. Tall, wise, protective, they seemed almost as immortal and invincible as gods. They were knowledge and authority and strength. They would be there always, and no harm could come to them—would dare to come to them. Or that is how it seemed to us."[1]

Barney was educated at home by her mother and brother, and later at her aunt's school, the Hillside Home School, which was designed by her brother, Frank Lloyd Wright. ". . . When I took my graduation year at Hillside I had a room there, too. I loved it; it had a balcony from which I could see the houses of all the Uncles, and the Valley fanning out beyond.

"It was a wonderful year. I think, during the course of it, I learned more than in all the other years of my schooling put together. At commencement I was to give the valedictory address, and for the occasion I designed a piece of oratory that was notable for its didactic splendor and thundering clichés. It was a little too much for Aunt Jennie; I remember how tactfully she tried not to smile, when I showed it to her, and how gently she pointed out the fact that I could say things, perhaps, a little more simply. So I did it all over, and delivered it in the chapel before everybody: teachers, classmates, Aunts, Uncles, and visitors. The relatives were admiring, and all the bearded Uncles cried. Very gratifying. But I'm afraid Aunt Jennie failed to deal with all my youthful sententiousness even then. Not too many years ago my daughter found the valedic-

(Maginel Wright Barney's illustration for the Christmas issue of *Woman's Home Companion*, December, 1928. This drawing was used as a greeting card for UNICEF.)

(From *Downright Dencey* by Caroline Dale Snedeker. Illustrated by Maginel Wright Barney.)

tory address and read it aloud with irreverent enjoyment. 'The fruitage of duty is ever joy and peace,' she read with delight. She has never been gracious enough to let me forget the phrase. Oh, Lord! I cringe with embarrassment for that fool adolescent even now. But the Uncles seemed to like it.''[1]

Barney and her mother moved to Chicago to be near brother Frank who was starting his career as an architect in that city. "We took a while to settle—at least Mother did. She found, after looking it over, that she disliked the North Shore by the lake because the wind was cruel there; and the South Side, adjacent to her powerful brother, didn't please her either. At last she decided on Oak Park, a village suburb half an hour by train from Chicago. Its pleasant homes were buried in shrubs, and surrounded by oak trees, and the schools were good, and it was time I went to school.

"Our first home was a big, ugly, red brick house on Forest Avenue, where we took up residence with the Reverend Augusta Chapin, a Universalist minister. . . .

"I started school that year. I was twelve years old, terrified of the idea, of the teacher, and the children. I didn't understand the rules or routine, so different from those at Hillside, and I was shy and miserable. I didn't know how to belong. I had lived a pretty solitary life except for my beautiful summers in the Valley. Finally, the most popular girl in the school, Florence Talbot, began to notice me and single me out. She did a blessed and generous thing; she made me feel that I was pretty, that I was liked, and could 'belong.' She was very pretty herself, the type all the boys preferred, with blond curls and blue, blue eyes. It was she who established after-school parties where we met in different houses, usually at hers, and someone played the piano and we danced and had hot chocolate and cookies. She did more for my morale than anyone ever has. She gave me courage and confidence in myself and I began to know how to deal with boys.

"We finally left Mrs. Chapin's and Mother and Frank together bought a large piece of property on the corner of Forest and Chicago Avenues. We lived in the house on the lot. . . .''[1]

When brother Frank married he built another house on the property for his family, which eventually grew to six children.

Barney began her career as an illustrator by working as a commercial artist in an engraving house. ''. . . I had one year at the Art Institute; it was all we could afford. I wanted desperately to be an illustrator, and would in time become one, but in the meanwhile I had to earn a living and took a job in the Chicago engraving house of Barnes, Crosby Co., with three or four other Institute girls.

"I earned fifty dollars a week in the engraving house, which was a very good salary for a girl in those days. With the other girls, I worked on catalogues. In the hottest months of the years, samples of next winter's furs and wool coats would pour into the office from Sears Roebuck, and Butler Brothers. Great cardboard sheets, the page layouts for the catalogues, would be hurried in from the drafting room. It was our job to draw the figures on which the clothes would be shown; elegant and formal ladies, posed statuesquely on tiny feet, done up in buttoned boots. For the faces we used pictures of stage and opera stars, cut from magazines, as models. Anyone turning the pages of the Sears Roebuck catalogue might see Maxine Elliott, glamorous in Hudson seal, or Julia Marlow, jaunty in raccoon.

"When we had finished our drawings one of us would take the cardboard sheets out to the layout men, pleasantly aware of the stares of the young draftsman and clerks.

"The hours were nine to five. At noon, when we were feeling poor, we bought bananas and salted peanuts from an Italian peddler for our lunch; and when we were not, we ordered cottage cheese and baked potatoes in the somber splendor of Marshall Field's. Sometimes I took my mother there, too, and I remember how she would always look at the prices first and choose the least expensive thing, no matter what it was.

"After working at Barnes, Crosby for three years I had saved up enough money to take a trip to Europe; enough to take Mother, too. I left my job for good, planning to be married on my return to a young illustrator, Walter J. Enright.

"I was wild to see Paris. Mother was anxious to return to Llandyssil where she had been born. Uncle John had kept contact with a distant Welsh cousin named John Thomas who, learning of our prospective visit, sent us an invitation to stay with him. I must say I wasn't too pleased at the prospect but I couldn't disappoint Mother.

"We took a cattle boat to Liverpool. We went to London, then to Paris, then to Venice. Wherever we went I sketched and made water colors: the umbrella pines of Italy, the pollarded trees of France, and everywhere, in every country, the enchanting children in the parks. I was wildly happy, sensitized to every impression; but I could feel that Mother was anxious to be off: to go to Wales. And so we went.

"That little country in the north was tourist-ridden, though lovely. But as we journeyed south in our small train, the land beyond the windows seemed suddenly familiar: the wooded hills, the streams and waterfalls and fields. I could understand very well why my grandfather had settled in the Valley.''[1]

Upon return to the States, Barney married Walter Enright, an illustrator and cartoonist, whose nickname was "Pat." "Pat and I lived on in Oak Park for a few years until our baby, Elizabeth, was born. Soon after that we went to New York to pursue our careers as artists.

"We lived far, far uptown on the top floor of a building that overlooked the Hudson. Pat had a studio in the Flatiron Building, and I had one at home. Though we were in the most modest circumstances, we could, in that day and in that neighborhood, afford a flat of seven spacious rooms as well as a 'cook general,' and someone to look after the baby. We soon had all the work we could do, and dozens of new friends: Gelett Burgess, William Glackens, Maud Tousey Fangel, Wallace Morgan, and many others. I bought a Steinway piano that it took me three years to pay for, and whenever Frank came

(From *Heidi* by Johanna Spyri. Illustrated by Maginel Wright Enright.)

to see us in New York he went straight to it before he took his hat off, and began to play.

"Our life was happy and busy; the views from our windows were beautiful; we loved our work. We loved meeting our friends in the evenings, too, dining at Mouquin's, or Delmonico's, or the Cafe Martin. When we could afford it we went to the theater and saw Yvette Guilbert, Maxine Elliott, William Gillette . . . New York seemed a glamorous, exciting place to live; not both dangerous and monotonous to look at, as it is now."[1]

Barney's first marriage ended in divorce. She subsequently married a lawyer named Hiram Barney who died in 1925. Her daughter Elizabeth became a popular author and illustrator.

Barney's own life as a New York illustrator was a successful one. Her nostalgic pictures made her very popular. In addition to her work for children's books, she painted covers for *Woman's Home Companion* and other magazines.

During the Depression, she created pictures with colored wools, which she called "long point" because of the long, vigorous stitches that distinguished it from ordinary tapestry.

1939. Daughter Elizabeth Enright (Gillham) won the Newbery Medal for *Thimble Summer,* a children's book about a girl on a Wisconsin farm. Barney's career as an artist was an important influence on her daughter's development as a writer. About her mother's work, daughter Elizabeth recalled: "Almost my earliest memory of my mother is the sight of her at work. Sometimes she would interrupt it for a moment, rubbing the tired muscles at the back of her neck, to gaze at the splendid view of the Hudson river and its Palisades beyond the window. I remember seeing her do this often, for when I was not at kindergarten or in the Park, I in the same way would sometimes interrupt my play to come and stare at her.

"I watched her through the glass doors of the little room she used as a studio, my nose snubbed resentfully against the pane, for I was forbidden to enter while she was at work. I can see her now as I saw her then, her drawing board tilted against the worktable before her. In her dark curly hair two or three pencils were stabbed like geisha ornaments, and a water color brush was often gripped between her teeth. Another, the one she was using at the moment, was in her fingers. Almost always there would be an aboriginal stripe of paint or ink across her cheek, and her whole attitude as she applied the brush—then leaned away from the picture and bent her head from side to side, narrowing her eyes at it, then leaned forward again—was the attitude of an artist at work; alone, concentrated, for the moment wholly self-sufficient. To a child this attitude is sometimes disconcerting, and I did my share of whining and snuffling at the door, trying to force her attention to myself. Sometimes, though not often, I was allowed to come in and watch for a while. I liked to see the picture growing on the board; I liked the little round porcelain dishes in which fat worms of color had been squeezed: crimson lake and cobalt blue and

(From *Heidi* by Johanna Spyri. Illustrated by Maginel Wright Enright.)

Maginel Wright Barney with her brother, Frank Lloyd Wright.

emerald green. I liked the lions on the Winsor & Newton paint tubes, and the tiny chime of the brush as it knocked against the rim of the glass when she dipped it in the water.

"The only times I didn't enjoy going into her studio were the times when she wanted me to pose. I hated staying still as much as any child, and didn't hesitate to say so.

"I took my mother's work for granted. It was just something that some parents did; not till much later did I realize the importance of it in my own life. For she took the responsibility of my upbringing nearly single-handed; and in her case the phrase is particularly apt, because she did this by means of her skillful right hand guided by her imagination

"As for the importance of her work in the lives of others, it is certainly true that her illustrations enhanced the book in many a nursery and that they enlivened the pages of thousands of school readers, for my mother was largely responsible for the revolutionizing of textbook illustration. Up to that time most primers had been adorned with stolid, utilitarian illustrations, nearly as deadly as the text: 'Ned has gone to the shed, Tom has a red sled. . . .' What my mother did was to bring grace, liveliness and, above all, imagination to the pages of these books. The unpretentious beauty and gaiety of her drawings must have quickened many young perceptions. In addition, she did magazine illustrations and magazine covers, all distinguished by their charm and informality and lovely color." [Elizabeth Enright, "'Long Point' for Decorative Accessories," *Craft Horizons*, November-December, 1954.²]

1940s. Distinguished herself as a shoe designer. Barney created high-fashioned jeweled and sequinned shoes, which were made by Capezio, with American House as an outlet.

1965. Published her autobiography, *The Valley of the God-Almighty Joneses*, which focused on her mother's family, the Lloyd-Joneses, who had settled in rural Wisconsin. The book also focused on her relationship with her famous brother, Frank Lloyd Wright.

April 18, 1966. Died at the Huntting Lane Rest Home in East Hampton, Long Island, at the age of eighty-four.

FOR MORE INFORMATION SEE: Bertha E. Mahony and others, compilers, *Illustrators of Children's Books: 1744-1945*, Horn Book, 1947; *Craft Horizons*, February, 1948, November-December, 1954; Maginel Wright Barney, *The Valley of the God-Almighty Joneses* (autobiography), Appleton-Century, 1965; Walt Reed, editor, *The Illustrator in America: 1900-1960's*, Reinhold, 1966. Obituaries: *New York Times*, April 19, 1966; *Publishers Weekly*, May 9, 1966.

BARTSCH, Jochen 1906-

PERSONAL: Born December 30, 1906, in Striegau, Silesia, Germany; married wife in 1953; children: one son. *Education:* Attended School for Applied Art, Breslau, Germany, Academy for Applied Art, Munich, and Reimannschule, Berlin.

CAREER: Artist, illustrator, author. Has also worked in the manufacturing of china and as a press-illustrator. *Military service*: German Army, 1940; French prisoner of war, 1945. *Awards, honors:* Jugendbuchpreis of Germany, 1959, for *Mein Urgrossvater und Ich; Der Nette König Mandolin* was on the honor list of Austrian prizes, 1965.

WRITINGS: (With Max Kruse) *Windkinder* (title means "Children of the Wind"), Ensslin, 1968; (with Barbara Teutsch) *Die fliegende Strassenbahn* (title means "The Flying Trolley-car"), Betz, 1973.

Illustrator: James Krüss, *Mein Urgrossvater und Ich*, Oetinger, 1961, translation by Edelgard von Heyderkampf Bruhl published as *My Great-Grandfather and I* (juvenile, *Horn Book* honor list), Atheneum, 1964; Josef Hausen, compiler, *Was nicht in den Annalen steht* (title means "That Which Is Not Recorded in the Annals"), 4th edition, Verlag Chemie, 1964, 6th edition, revised, 1969; Marielis Hoberg, *Heiner und Elsie fahren nach Afrika*, translated by R. J. Hollingdale published as *The Voyage to Africa* (juvenile), Abelard, 1964; *Mixtura mirabilis*, Verlag Chemie, 1965; Gunhild Paehr, *Das Wirtshaus zum schwarzen Kater*, translated by Marion Koenig published as *The Lonely Witch* (juvenile), A. Whitman, 1965; J. Krüss, *Pauline and the Prince in the Wind* (juvenile), translated from the German by E. H. Bruhl, Atheneum, 1966; J. Krüss, *Mein Urgrossvater, die Helden, und Ich*, Oetinger, 1967, translation by E. H. Bruhl published as *My Great-Grandfather, the Heroes, and I* (juvenile), Atheneum, 1973; J. Krüss, *In Tante Julies Haus* (title means "In Aunt Julie's House"), Oetinger, 1969; Siegfried von Vegesack, *Schnüllermann sieht das Leben heiter an* (title means "Schnüllermann Looks Cheerfully at Life"), A. Langen-G. Muller, 1969; Erich F. Karrer, compiler, *Alle Jahre wieder: Eine Sammlung von weihnachtl* (title means "All Through the Years: A Collection from Christmas"), Lingen, 1970; J. Krüss, *Die Abenteuer der Berta Besenbinder*

Each night he stepped into his bath fully dressed. If an insect had found its way during the day into the folds of the king's clothing, it would rise to the top of the water. . . . ■ (From *My Great-Grandfather, the Heroes and I* by James Krüss. Illustrated by Jochen Bartsch.)

(juvenile picture book; title means "The Adventure of Berta Broom-binder"), Englebert, 1972; Sigrid Munro, *Plitsch und Platsch,* Gundert, 1973; J. Krüss, *Geschichten aus allen Winden; oder, Sturm um Tante Julies Haus* (title means "Stories from the Winds; or, Storm around Aunt Julie's House"), Oetinger, 1973.

Also author of *Der Nette König Mandolin* (title means "Nice King Mandolin"), c. 1965.

BECKER, Joyce   1936-

PERSONAL: Born August 27, 1936, in Brooklyn, N.Y.; daughter of Martin (a salesman) and Lillian (Feinberg) Levitan; married Elliott R. Becker (a treasurer), October 12, 1958; children: Caryn, David, Leslie, Nicole. *Education:* Attended Pratt Institute, 1955, Brooklyn College, 1960, Middlesex College, 1964—. *Religion:* Hebrew. *Home:* 78 Calvert Ave. E., Edison, N.J. 08820.

CAREER: Author and illustrator of craft books for children. Freelance short story writer and illustrator. Also lecturer and teacher of craft classes, co-owner and general manager of Nourishing Nibbles (a health food snack pack company), co-owner of own book distribution company. Member of planning board, Body, Emotion And Mind (BEAM; a self-help research group).

WRITINGS—For children; all self-illustrated: *Jewish Holiday Crafts,* Hebrew Publishing, 1977; *Hanukkah Crafts,* Hebrew Publishing, 1978; *Bible Crafts,* Volume 1, Holiday House, 1982. Also writer and illustrator of greeting cards.

WORK IN PROGRESS: Bible Crafts, Volume 2, based on the New Testament; adult romance novel.

SIDELIGHTS: "I come from a religious household. Under our roof lived several generations of our family. We worked, played, and prepared for festive occasions together. This is the kind of family life that is so sorely missed today.

"From these memories came the desire to teach the love of family life and heritage. I do this via creative craft classes, workshops and the writing and illustrating of books. Even slow learners respond. When it is difficult to communicate in words, communication runs through the fingers in crafts. Along with the items crafted, pride in oneself is created as well.

"I have a headstart with my own family in developing craft ideas. I have four children who range in age from fourteen to twenty-three and a mother in her 80s. They comprise my at-home laboratory. Our tabletops are buried beneath experimental projects—our house looks like a museum.

"From where do I gather inspiration? Sometimes this is a puzzle to me, too; but once I get started, it is hard to stop the flow of ideas.

"There is much that can be done that is innovative. Ideas infiltrate my head from different sources and eventually come out in different forms. This transmutation is the innovation. Every project reflects the uniqueness of its creator.

"Once I touch the life of a single person, either through a class, workshop, or a book, there is no way of knowing how many others will be influenced.

JOYCE BECKER

"In addition to being an author and illustrator, I am co-owner of Nourishing Nibbles, a healthfood snack pack company. We primarily mail order to customers such as college students (care packages), schools (fund raising), professionals (thank-you for referrals and holiday gift giving), and to individuals throughout the United States and abroad.

"I designed the name and logo of BEAM (Body, Emotion And Mind), a self-help group sponsored by the American Association of University Women. I am on the planning board to develop this newly formed group. We offer to individuals of all ages lectures, workshops, and study groups so that they can be made aware of their own well-being, physically, emotionally, and mentally.

"My teaching experience for the past twelve years includes craft classes for the mentally retarded as well as for individuals on all age levels.

"I co-own, with my husband, a book distribution company. We are now the sole distributors of *Jewish Holiday Crafts* and *Hanukkah Crafts.*"

FOR MORE INFORMATION SEE: Judaica Book News, fall/winter, 1977; *Home News,* April, 1977, December, 1979; *The Jewish Voice,* January, 1978.

George I. Bernard with a Thysania Agrippina butterfly.

BERNARD, George I.   1949-

PERSONAL: Born September 13, 1949, in Paris, France; married Joanna Blinkhorn (an artistic consultant), January 29, 1983. *Education:* Attended Bryanston School, Dorset, England, 1963-68; University of Aston, England, honours degree in biological sciences, 1972; University of Keele, U.K., post-graduate certificate of education, 1973. *Home and office:* 23 Prospect Road, Banbury, Oxfordshire, England.

CAREER: Biologist and photographer. Oxford Scientific Films, England, stills photographer, 1977-83; Bernard Photo Productions, Oxfordshire, England, free-lance stills photographer, 1983—. *Awards, honors:* National Science Teacher Association Award, Outstanding Science Books for Children, 1979, for *Common Frog* and *The Chicken and the Egg,* 1980, for *Dragonfly* and *Common Rabbit,* both 1981, for *Harvestmouse,* 1982, for *Mosquito* and *Grey Squirrel;* Times Junior Book Award, 1979, for *The Common Frog;* Royal Photographic Society Progress Medal, 1980; *Natural History* magazine, merit award, 1981; Society of Publication Design XVII, merit award, 1982.

ILLUSTRATOR—All illustrated with photographs; all by Oxford Scientific Films Ltd.: *Squirrel on My Shoulder,* BBC Publications, 1979; *The Secret Life of the Harvest Mouse,* Hamlyn, 1979; *The Wild Rabbit,* Putnam, 1980; *Snowy and Co,* Collins, 1981; *Focus on Nature,* Faber, 1981; *The Grand Design,* Dent, 1982; *Pond,* Collins, 1984.

"Nature in Action" series; all illustrated with photographs; all by Oxford Scientific Films Ltd.; all published by Purnell Books, 1979: *Living Together; The Quest for Food; How Creatures Multiply; Growing Up.*

"Nature's Way" series; all illustrated with photographs; all by Oxford Scientific Films Ltd., except as noted: *The Common Frog,* Putnam, 1979; *The Chicken and the Egg* (illustrated with Peter Parks), Putnam, 1979; *Dragonfly,* Whizzard/Deutsch, 1980; *Common Rabbit,* Whizzard/Deutsch, 1980; *Harvestmouse* (illustrated with others), Whizzard/Deutsch, 1981, Putnam, 1982; Jennifer Coldrey, *Mosquito* (illustrated with John Cooke), Putnam, 1982; J. Coldrey, *Grey Squirrel* (illustrated with John Paling), Putnam, 1982; *The Silkworm Story,* Deutsch, 1983.

WORK IN PROGRESS: Field Guide to Ponds, Junior Field Guide to Ponds and Gems, Ponds All in the Pipeline, all for Collins; natural history and commercial photography.

SIDELIGHTS: "My curiosity of the natural world started when I was very young. My prep school, set in 100 acres of private land, dotted with lakes and ponds and woodlands, could not help but sow the seed of interest. The germination continued through my school years and became obvious, to me, that the natural sciences—zoology, botany, geography and geology, was to be at the very least a hobby and at best a career. Between 1971 and 1977, five two-man exhibitions into the Venezuelan and Colombian cordilleras sponsored by the Royal Society, the

Royal Geographical Society, the British Museum of Natural History, the Explorers' Club of New York, Mount Everest Foundation and the Universities of Aston and Cambridge, resulted in the discovery and naming of six new genera and twenty-three new species to science, in the butterfly world. As an aide memoire, I took along on these expeditions a camera and a few rolls of film.

"At twenty-seven years old, and still determined to stay in the world of natural history, though now with the advantage of a developing eye for photography, I joined the filmmaking company—Oxford Scientific Films, as their still photographer. With a free rein and with much experimenting, I developed my skills—and I was still in natural history. Greatly encouraged by the response to my work and the ever increasing experimental nature of my photography, I became a free-lance natural history photographer in 1983."

FOR MORE INFORMATION SEE: Focus on Nature, Faber, 1981.

BIENENFELD, Florence L(ucille) 1929-

PERSONAL: Born December 29, 1929, in Los Angeles, Calif.; daughter of Jack (a sign painter) and Gertrude (Lewis) Gottlieb; married Milton Bienenfeld (a business executive), September 7, 1952; children: Ruth Bienenfeld Barrett, Joel, Daniel. *Education:* California State University, B.A., 1950; University of California, Los Angeles, M.A., 1968; doctoral study at University of Southern California, 1972-73; Columbia Pacific University, Ph.D., 1981. *Politics:* Democrat. *Religion:* Jewish. *Residence:* Marina del Rey, Calif. *Office:* Conciliation Court of Los Angeles County, 1725 Main St., Room 225, Santa Monica, Calif. 90401.

CAREER: Montebello Unified School District, Montebello, Calif., elementary school teacher, 1948-49; educational therapist and private practitioner in marriage and family counseling, 1968-74; Conciliation Court of Los Angeles County, Santa Monica, Calif., senior family mediator/counselor, 1974-76, 1977—; Superior Court of Los Angeles County, Los Angeles,

(From *My Mom and Dad Are Getting a Divorce* by Florence Bienenfeld. Illustrated by Art Scott.)

FLORENCE L. BIENENFELD

Calif., child custody investigator, 1977. Workshop leader; lecturer; guest on radio and television programs. *Member:* American Association for Marriage and Family Therapy (clinical member), Association of Family Conciliation Courts. *Awards, honors:* Award of merit from Association of Family Conciliation Courts, 1980, for outstanding service to children of divorce, their parents and to A.F.C.C.

WRITINGS: My Mom and Dad Are Getting a Divorce (juvenile; illustrated by Art Scott), EMC Corp., 1980; (contributor) H. Norman Wright, editor, *Marital Counseling: A Biblically Based Cognitive Approach*, Christian Marriage Enrichment, 1981; *Child Custody Mediation* (adult), Science and Behavior Books, 1983; *Making a Magnificent Marriage* (adult), Pine Mountain Press, 1985. Author of columns, "For Better or Worse," 1977-81. Contributor to counseling journals.

WORK IN PROGRESS: Helping Your Child Succeed after Divorce, for adults.

SIDELIGHTS: "Hundreds of thousands of children are involved in divorce courts each year when their parents battle over child custody. These children are victims of a legal system which promotes competition between parents rather than cooperation. Warring parents go into court trying to 'win' their children. During the battle children are often pressured by their parents to take sides. Some are actually asked to choose where they want to live, with mom or with dad. This puts children in a no-win situation. If they pick dad, they feel guilty about not picking mom.

"I want to ease tension and pain for children involved in marital or postmarital conflicts. Most children take divorce very hard and they take custody battles even harder. Children can recover from the divorce when their parents allow them to heal. Regrettably, some parents continue to argue and fight after the separation and divorce. The children become the focal point for their arguments and bitterness. Parental hostility often escalates and never ends. For some children there is no relief from parental conflict throughout their entire childhood. When these children grow up many of them carry unhappy memories of this experience into adulthood, and this can ruin their lives.

"In an age of much violence and harshness throughout the world, there are small inroads being made toward humanizing life for children. In some birth centers and hospitals newborns are being placed in a warm bath to soothe their entrance to the world. There is much talk and action being taken to protect children from physical and sexual abuse. One very important inroad is divorce counseling and mediation for parents as a measure for protecting children from the ravages during and after the divorce."

BOYLSTON, Helen (Dore)   1895-1984

OBITUARY NOTICE—See sketch in *SATA* Volume 23: Born April 4, 1895, in Portsmouth, N.H.; died September 30, 1984, in Trumbull, Conn. Nurse and author best known as the creator of the "Sue Barton" nurse series. Boylston served with British forces as a nurse during World War I and later used her experiences in her stories. In addition to the "Sue Barton" series, Boylston produced the "Carol Page" series, a biography of a Civil War heroine entitled *Clara Barton: Founder of the American Red Cross*, and an autobiography of her war experiences, *Sister: The War Diary of a Nurse. For More Information See: Authors of Books for Young People*, 2nd edition, Scarecrow, 1971; *Contemporary Authors*, Volumes 73-76, Gale, 1978; *Twentieth-Century Children's Writers*, 2nd edition, St. Martin's, 1983; *The Writers Directory: 1984-1986*, St. James Press, 1983. *Obituaries: New York Times*, October 5, 1984; *School Library Journal*, November, 1984.

BRENT, Hope   1935(?)-1984

OBITUARY NOTICE: Born about 1935; died of cancer August 17, 1984. Expert on children's literature. The wife of bookstore owner Stuart Brent and the mother of eight children, Brent was responsible for the children's floor at Chicago's Stuart Brent Book Store. She also created the Children's Book Club, which now possesses a membership of over 300 children who receive a personally selected book each month. *Obituaries: Publishers Weekly*, September 21, 1984.

What are you able to build with your blocks?
Castles and palaces, temples and docks.
Rain may keep raining, and others go roam,
But I can be happy and building at home.

Let the sofa be mountains, the carpet be sea,
There I'll establish a city for me:
A kirk and a mill and a palace beside,
And a harbor as well where my vessels may ride.
                —Robert Louis Stevenson

PETER BRIGGS

BRIGGS, Peter 1921-1975

PERSONAL: Born April 15, 1921, in St. Paul, Minn.; died of cancer, July 18, 1975, in New York, N.Y.; son of Allan and Winifred (Douglas) Briggs; divorced; children: Andy. *Education:* University of Chicago, B.A., 1942. *Residence:* New York, N.Y. *Agent:* McIntosh & Otis, Inc., 475 Fifth Ave., New York, N.Y. 10017.

CAREER: Worked in book advertising department at A. S. Barnes, and as promotion manager at Columbia University Press, Henry Holt, G. P. Putnam's Sons, John Day & Co., and Coward McCann, 1946-51; *Ladies' Home Journal,* New York City, non-fiction editor, 1951-63; free-lance writer, 1963-75. *Military service:* U.S. Naval Reserve, 1942-45; became ensign. *Member:* American Association for the Advancement of Science, Antarctic Press Club (McMurdo Sound, Antarctica).

WRITINGS—All for young people: *Water: The Vital Essence,* Harper, 1967; *Men in the Sea,* Simon & Schuster, 1968; *The Great Global Rift,* Weybright, 1969; *Science Ship: A Voyage Aboard the Discoverer,* Simon & Schuster, 1969; *Rivers in the Sea,* Weybright, 1969; *Mysteries of the Sea,* McKay, 1969; *Mysteries of Our World: Unanswered Questions about the Continents, the Seas, the Atmosphere, the Origins of Life,* McKay, 1969; *Buccaneer Harbor: The Fabulous History of Port Royal, Jamaica,* Simon & Schuster, 1970; *Laboratory at the Bottom of the World,* McKay, 1970; *200,000,000 Years beneath the Sea,* Holt, 1971; *Will California Fall into the Sea?,* McKay, 1972; *What Is the Grand Design?: The Story of Evolving Life and the Changing Planet on Which It Is Lived,* McKay, 1973; *Rampage: The Story of Disastrous Floods, Broken Dams, and Human Fallibility,* McKay, 1973; *Population Policy: The Social Dilemma,* British Book Center, 1974. Also contributor of articles to magazines.

SIDELIGHTS: Briggs's books are concerned with oceanography and the forces of nature. He traveled to Antarctica to conduct personal research for his book, *Laboratory at the Bottom of the World.* In 1968 he voyaged on the *Giomar Challenger* which explored the geology of the ocean. This expedition resulted in his book, *200,000,000 Years beneath the Sea.*

FOR MORE INFORMATION SEE: Contemporary Authors, Permanent Series, Volume 2, Gale, 1978. *Obituaries: New York Times,* July 19, 1975; *AB Bookmen's Weekly,* August 4, 1975.

BROWN, Roy (Frederick) 1921-1982

OBITUARY NOTICE: Born December 10, 1921, in Vancouver, British Columbia, Canada; died September 14, 1982. Educator, radio and television writer, and author of books for children. Employed by British schools for nearly thirty years, Brown began as a primary school teacher and later served as deputy headmaster at the Helen Allison School for autistic children in Gravesend, Kent, England. The author of more than thirty books for young people, he wrote the first of his numerous mystery and suspense novels, *A Saturday in Pudney,* prior to 1966. His book about the disappearance of a mentally disturbed teenager, *Find Debbie,* was named by *School Library Journal* as one of the best books of 1976. He also wrote *The Day of the Pigeons, Flight of Sparrows, The Battle of Saint Street, Chubb on the Trail, The Cage, The Wing of the Gate,* and *Octopus,* among others. His detective series featuring Chips Regan includes the books *Undercover Boy, Chips and the Crossword Gang,* and *Chips and the Black Moth.* In addition, Brown was a writer for the popular British television program "Jackanory," as well as the author of a series of radio plays. Two of his books, *A Saturday in Pudney* and *The Day of the Pigeons,* were adapted into motion pictures and *The Viaduct* was twice aired on British television. *For More Information See: Contemporary Authors,* Volumes 65-68, Gale, 1977; *Fourth Book of Junior Authors,* H. W. Wilson, 1978; *Twentieth-Century Children's Writers,* 2nd edition, St. Martin's, 1983; *The Writers Directory, 1984-86,* St. James Press, 1983.

BRYAN, Dorothy (Marie) 1896(?)-1984

OBITUARY NOTICE: Born about 1896; died September 12, 1984, in Glen Cove, N.Y. Publishing executive, editor, and author. Founder of the children's book division at Dodd, Mead & Co. in 1934, Bryan also became that company's first woman vice-president in 1958. Prior to that, she had worked in the junior books department at Doubleday-Doran. Books she brought to Dodd, Mead & Co. include Maureen Daly's *Seventeenth Summer,* Walter D. Edmonds's Newbery Award-winning *The Matchlock Gun,* Phil Stong's *Honk the Moose,* and over sixty career books written by successful professionals about their respective careers. With her sister, Marguerite Bryan, she wrote the children's books *Johnny Penguin, Michael Who Missed His Train, There Was Tammie, Bobby Wanted a Pony,* and *Frisky Finding a Home,* among others. *For More Information See: Catholic Authors,* Volume 2, St. Mary's Abbey, 1952; *Foremost Women in Communications,* Foremost Americans Publishing Corp., in association with Bowker, 1970. *Obituaries: Publishers Weekly,* October 12, 1984.

BULL, Peter (Cecil)   1912-1984

OBITUARY NOTICE: Born March 21, 1912, in London, England; died of a heart attack, May 21, 1984, in London, England. Actor and author. Bull's acting career spanned more than fifty years and included roles on the London stage and in such motion pictures as ''The African Queen,'' ''Tom Jones,'' and ''Doctor Strangelove,'' in which he played the Russian ambassador. Considered one of the world's leading authorities on teddy bears, he was the author of *The Teddy Bear Book* and the ''Bully Bear'' series of children's books. Included in the series are *Bully Bear Goes to a Wedding, . . . Punk, . . . to Hollywood, . . . to Harrods.* Bull also wrote a number of reminiscences, including *To Sea in a Sieve, I know the Face But—, Not on Your Telly!,* and *I Say, Look Here! For More Information See: The Writers Directory: 1984-1986,* St. James Press, 1983; *Contemporary Authors, New Revision Series,* Volume II, Gale, 1984. *Obituaries: New York Times,* May 22, 1984; *Times* (London), May 22, 1984; *Time,* June 4, 1984; *Facts on File,* June 8, 1984; *Publishers Weekly,* June 8, 1984.

CALLAHAN, Dorothy M.   1934-

PERSONAL: Born December 24, 1934, in Bronx, N.Y.; daughter of Eugene T. (a bookkeeper) and Irene (a bookkeeper; maiden name, Schmidt) Monahan; married Robert L. Callahan (a director of Office on Aging), May 3, 1958; children: Christopher, Kathleen. *Education:* College Misericordia, B.A., 1956; William Paterson College, M.A., 1972, certificate of learning disabilities, 1974. *Home:* 45 Summit Rd., Hamburg, N.J. 07419. *Office:* Lafayette School, Augusta, N.J. 07822.

"I've been wounded," he said, slumping into a chair. ■ (From *Under Christopher's Hat* by Dorothy M. Callahan. Illustrated by Carole M. Byard.)

DOROTHY M. CALLAHAN

CAREER: Woman's Home Companion, New York, N.Y., assistant copy editor, 1956; free-lance writer, 1956—; Shell Oil Co., Flushing, N.Y., copy editor, 1957-59; Lafayette School, Lafayette, N.J., teacher of remedial reading, 1970—. Chairperson, Hamburg Democratic Municipal. *Member:* New Jersey Education Association. *Awards, honors:* New Jersey Institute of Technology Authors Award, 1972, for *Under Christopher's Hat,* and 1980, for *Jimmy: The Story of the Young Jimmy Carter.*

WRITINGS—All for children; all nonfiction, except as indicated: *Under Christopher's Hat* (fiction; illustrated by Carole M. Byard), Scribner, 1972; *Jimmy: The Story of the Young Jimmy Carter,* Doubleday, 1979; *Ruffian,* Crestwood House, 1983; *Thoroughbreds,* Crestwood House, 1983. Also contributor of articles and short stories to periodicals and newspapers, including *Coed, Ranger Rick's Nature Magazine, Career World, Modern Maturity, Backstretch, American Turf Monthly, Thoroughbred Record, Scholastic Scope, Youth, Seventeen, Lady's Circle, Women's News Service, New York Times, New York News, Associated Press,* and others.

WORK IN PROGRESS: Additional books about famous racehorses such as Secretariat; *Amish Is Always,* a fictional work about an Amish girl faced with ''The Outsiders.''

SIDELIGHTS: ''I took education courses in college because my friends were planning to teach. I didn't want to be the only one not doing my practice semester. But I *knew* I would *never* enter such a dull profession. I wanted to travel and write and work for a big newspaper or magazine! But Life has a way of twisting plans into even greater opportunities.

"After a short time in publishing, I married and moved to the country where there were more cows than people and only one weekly newspaper.

"When my children were both in school, I was offered the challenging position of remedial reading teacher. Seventeen years later, I still feel that the classroom is a great place for me to expend 'creative juices.'

"Young people have always been my best resource in writing. My son Christopher lived the title role in *Under Christopher's Hat* before I wrote it. My daughter Kathy's detailed knowledge of thoroughbred horseracing provided me with information as well as inspiration for *Ruffian*.

"The world of horseracing has infected me with its drama and I want to write more stories about its heroes and heroines, both human and equine.

"Being able to go through life with your eyes and ears and all your senses wide open to experience and curiosity is the blessing and curse of a writer. We ask a million questions and get emotionally involved, and so we can empathize and then write from experience.

"My visit to an Amish one-room schoolhouse in Lancaster County, Pennsylvania, was a good example of this. It set my senses reeling back a century and helped me understand how the main character in my book-in-progress, *Amish Is Always*, will think."

CAREY, Mary (Virginia) 1925-
(M. V. Carey)

BRIEF ENTRY: Born May 19, 1925, in New Brighton, England; came to the United States in 1925; became naturalized citizen, 1955. Author of books for young readers. Carey graduated in 1946 from the College of Mount St. Vincent and went to work as an editorial associate for *Coronet* magazine in New York City. In 1955 she began a fourteen-year association with Walt Disney Productions in Burbank, Calif., where she was employed as assistant editor of publications. During her stay there she adapted into book form seven Disney films, including *Babes in Toyland* (Golden Press, 1961), *The Sword in the Stone* (Whitman Publishing, 1963), *The Misadventures of Merlin Jones* (Whitman Publishing, 1964), and *Donald Duck and the Lost Mesa Ranch* (Whitman Publishing, 1966).

A free-lance writer since 1969, she has written (as M. V. Carey) over ten books in the popular "Alfred Hitchcock and the Three Investigators" series which is based on characters created by the late Robert Arthur. Published by Random House and aimed at reluctant readers, her titles include: *The Mystery of the Flaming Footprints* (1971), *The Secret of the Haunted Mirror* (1974), *The Mystery of the Sinister Scarecrow* (1979), *The Mystery of the Scar-Faced Beggar* (1981), and *The Mystery of the Trail of Terror* (1984). The series is described by *Booklist* as "better than the Hardy Boys and others; this has humor, real suspense, and a satisfying resolution. All in all, it's good formula fiction that makes for pleasant, escapist reading." In addition to the mystery series, Carey has written several books for younger children published by Golden Press, among them *Raggedy Ann and the Glad and Sad Day* (1972), *The Owl Who Loved Sunshine* (1977), and *Mrs. Brisby's Important Package* (1982), adapted from the animated film "The Secret of Nimh."

Home: 645 Hampshire Rd., Apt. 137, Westlake Village, Calif. 91361. *For More Information See: Contemporary Authors,* Volumes 81-84, Gale, 1979; *Who's Who of American Women: 1983-1984,* 13th edition, Marquis, 1983.

CELESTINO, Martha Laing 1951-
(Martha Laing)

PERSONAL: Born July 9, 1951, in Delhi, N.Y.; daughter of John Mathias (a farmer) and Viola (a nurse; maiden name, Mathis) Laing; married William J. Celestino (a Latin teacher), May 25, 1974; children: Alexandra, Adriana, Gregory. *Education:* Boston University, B.S., 1973. *Home:* 479 Merrimac St., Newburyport, Mass. 01950.

CAREER: Raytheon Service Co., Cambridge, Mass., technical writer and editor, 1973-82; Digital Equipment Corp., Lawrence, Mass., technical editor, 1984—.

WRITINGS: (Under name Martha Laing) *Grandma Moses: The Grand Old Lady of American Art* (young adult), edited by Steve D. Rahmas, SamHar Press, 1972. Contributor of articles to newspapers, including *The Newburyport Daily News.*

CHAMBERS, Bradford 1922-1984

OBITUARY NOTICE: Born February 4, 1922, in New York, N.Y.; died of a cerebral hemorrhage, September 22, 1984. Organization director and editor. Chambers is best remembered as director of the Council on Interracial Books for Children, an organization dedicated to promoting bias-free textbooks and children's storybooks. During his eighteen-year leadership, the council established guidelines for determining if books were racist or sexist, published the *Interracial Books for Children Bulletin,* and established a Racism and Sexism Resource Center, for which it received the National Education Association's Human and Civil Rights Award in 1982. Before joining the council, Chambers had worked with the New York County District Attorney's office and as children's book editor at *Parents Magazine.* He compiled and wrote the commentary for the young adult book, *Chronicles of Negro Protest* and wrote and edited other books. *For More Information See: Authors of Books for Young People,* 2nd edition supplement, Scarecrow, 1979. *Obituaries: New York Times,* September 24, 1984; *Publishers Weekly,* October 5, 1984; *School Library Journal,* November, 1984.

CHANDLER, Linda S(mith) 1929-

PERSONAL: Born February 4, 1929, in Wadesboro, N.C.; daughter of Clinton Ashe and Emma (Sikes) Smith; married Gordon Yearby Chandler (a pressman), October 17, 1948; children: Gordon Lee, Judi Chandler Crouse, Linda Ann. *Education:* Attended Croft Secretarial School, 1947-48, and Duke University. *Politics:* Democrat. *Religion:* Southern Baptist. *Home:* 106 Stallings Rd., Durham, N.C. 27703. *Office:* Chapel, Duke University, Durham, N.C. 27706

CAREER: Held part-time secretarial positions in Durham, N.C., 1957-75; Duke University, Durham, hostess at university chapel, 1975—. Taught at Ridgecrest and Glorieta conference centers.

LINDA S. CHANDLER

Member of Durham County Board of Health, 1972-83, Durham County Board of Education, 1976—, North Carolina Interagency Council on Community Schools, 1979-84, board of trustees of North Carolina Baptist Homes, 1981-83, member of board of directors of North Carolina School Boards Association, 1983—, advisory committee of Child Abuse and Prevention of Parental Stress (CAPPS), Durham Citizens' Safety Council, Durham Democratic Women, and advisory board of Parents Involved in Preschool Education (PIPE). *Member:* Society of Children's Book Writer, National Writers Club, North Carolina Poetry Society, North Carolina Community Education Association, Durham County Association for Childhood Education, Delta Kappa Gamma.

WRITINGS—For children: *My Family Loves Me,* Convention Press, 1978; *Hello, My Church,* Broadman, 1980; *Uncle Ike,* Broadman, 1981; *David Asks, "Why?",* Broadman, 1981; *When I Talk to God,* Broadman, 1984; *Dr. Harms, the Helper,* WMU Press, 1984.

Curriculum writer for Southern Baptist Convention Sunday School Board. Author of series "Parents, Enjoy Your Children," in *Living with Preschoolers,* 1984—. Contributor to magazines, including *Christian Advocate, Child Life, Biblical Recorder, Look and Listen, Living with Teenagers,* and *Church Administration.*

WORK IN PROGRESS: A book for young children dealing with the importance of nonsexist lifestyle; "Just-for-Fun" stories for children; a book on prayer for adults.

SIDELIGHTS: "Writing for children has been an important part of my life. I have made two child-study trips abroad,

visiting schools in Italy, Israel, Switzerland, and England. I am also involved in conducting book fairs in different parts of the country and enjoy going into classrooms to talk to children about writing, books, and the importance of self-expression. I believe we should do everything we can to help children learn to love books and think of them as friends."

FOR MORE INFORMATION SEE: Durham Herald, April 20, 1980, October 11, 1981; *Raleigh News and Observer,* January 31, 1982.

CLIMO, Shirley   1928-

PERSONAL: Born November 25, 1928, in Cleveland, Ohio; daughter of Morton J. (a paving contractor) and Aldarilla (a writer; maiden name, Shipley) Beistle; married George F. Climo III (a corporate historian), June 17, 1950; children: Robert, Susan, Lisa. *Education:* Attended DePauw University, 1946-49. *Politics:* "Variable." *Religion:* Protestant. *Home:* 24821 Prospect Ave., Los Altos, Calif. 94022. *Agent:* Ruth Cantor, 156 Fifth Ave., New York, N.Y. 10010.

CAREER: WGAR-Radio, Cleveland, Ohio, scriptwriter for weekly juvenile series, "Fairytale Theatre," 1949-53; freelance writer, 1976—. President, Los Altos Morning Forum, 1971-73. *Member:* California Writers, Society of Children's Book Writers.

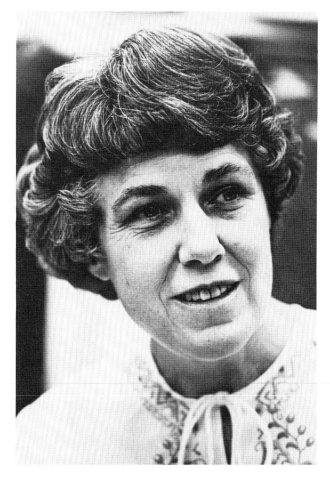

SHIRLEY CLIMO

Christkindel touched the spokes of each web with his finger. The twisted strands turned shiny gold; the dangling threads sparkled like silver. ■ (From *The Cobweb Christmas* by Shirley Climo. Illustrated by Joe Lasker.)

WRITINGS: (Reteller) *Piskies, Spriggans, and Other Magical Beings: Tales from the Droll-Teller* (juvenile; illustrated by Joyce Audy dos Santos), Crowell, 1981; *The Cobweb Christmas* (juvenile; illustrated by Joe Lasker), Crowell, 1982; (contributor) Sylvia K. Burack, *Writing and Selling Fillers, Light Verse, and Short Humor,* Writer, Inc., 1982; *Gopher, Tanker, and the Admiral* (juvenile; illustrated by Eileen McKeating), Crowell, 1984; *Someone Saw a Spider,* Harper, 1985. Contributor to magazines, including *Family Weekly, The Writer, Cricket, Ranger Rick,* and *Seventeen,* and to newspapers.

WORK IN PROGRESS—Three children's books: *Betty Stoggs and the Small People,* edited by Nina Ignatowicz, for Harper; and *The Tortoise-Shell Talisman; King of the Birds,* a fable.

SIDELIGHTS: "Between 1953 and 1976, I raised children. Now, once again, I write for them and plug in the typewriter instead of the vacuum cleaner. From 1976 until 1980, I fulfilled a typical writer-reentry apprenticeship doing a series of newspaper articles and selling a number of travel and humor pieces to adult magazines. I learned a great deal, but all along my target was not bigger but smaller. I kept my eye on other people's kids. A trip to Cornwall and a stay in a four-hundred-year-old cottage provided the necessary information and inspiration for my first juvenile book, a collection of Cornish folklore called *Piskies, Spriggans, and Other Magical Beings.*

My second book, *The Cobweb Christmas,* is also a folktale, from Germany. Writing it turned a fear of spiders into a fascination, and now I'm thoroughly enmeshed in spider lore and legend and have just completed a collection of spidery tales called *Someone Saw a Spider.* My book, *Gopher, Tanker and the Admiral* is strictly a contemporary humor/adventure story for youngsters and the *Tortoise-Shell Talisman* is a historical novel for pre-teens that borders on being a ghost story. With the picture book version of *Betty Stoggs and the Small People* (one of the Cornish tales) and *King of the Birds,* I'm back in the realm of folklore.

Except for a yearly travel article, I do very little magazine work of late. But the urge to write has become a persistent itch, relieved only by a thick soft pencil and a yellow ruled legal pad. It proves the quotation from Somerset Maugham that's pasted on my desk lamp: 'Until you're fifty, writing is hard work. Then it becomes just another bad habit.'''

FOR MORE INFORMATION SEE: The Writer, June, 1978, December, 1979; *Booklist,* November, 1980; *Horn Book,* December, 1980, December, 1982; *Publishers Weekly,* March 20, 1981, August 6, 1982; *Kirkus Reviews,* April 1, 1981; *New York Times Book Review,* July 5, 1981.

CONE, Ferne Geller 1921-

PERSONAL: Born October 9, 1921, in Portland, Ore.; daughter of Borus H. (a salesman) and Sadie (a volunteer worker) Geller; married J. Morton Cone (in printing), March, 1948; children: Carol Ann Cone Gulan, Wendy Lee Cone Dore. *Education:* Attended University of Washington, Seattle, 1960. *Home:* 6401 Sand Point Way N.E., Seattle, Wash. 98115.

CAREER: War Relief Agency, San Francisco, Calif., assistant to director, 1943-46; knit designer, 1946-63; Yarn Boutique, Seattle, Wash., owner, 1963-67; knit designer, 1967-80; University of Washington, Seattle, community development specialist in Office of Community Development, 1980. Member of board of directors of Pacific Northwest Writers Conference, 1979—, and KUOW-Radio, and advisory board of Washington

Ferne Geller Cone leaning on her knitted and crocheted "Bagel, Lox and Cream Cheese."

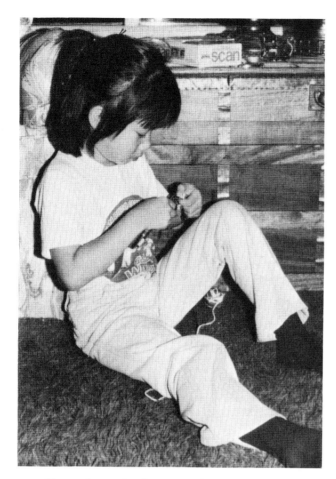

(From *Crazy Crocheting* by Ferne Geller Cone. Photographs by J. Morton Cone and Ferne Geller Cone.)

Volunteer Lawyers for the Arts; past member of board of directors of Group Homes of Washington and steering committee of Friends of the Crafts. Seminar organizer; conducts workshops; public speaker; craft work exhibited throughout the West Coast, Hawaii, and British Columbia.

MEMBER: Fashion Group International (member of Seattle board of directors and education chairperson, 1973-75), World Crafts Council, International Guild of Craft Authors, Photographers, and Journalists, Women in Communications, American Crafts Council, Washington Athletic Club, Seattle Freelances (president, 1983), Pacific Northwest Writers Conference. *Awards, honors:* Awards from Society of Technical Writers, 1980, for *Knutty Knitting for Kids*, 1981, for *Knit with Style*, and 1982, for *Crazy Crocheting*.

WRITINGS: Knit Art, Van Nostrand, 1975; *Knutty Knitting for Kids* (juvenile), Follett, 1977; *Knit with Style* (illustrated with photographs by F. Cone and her husband, J. Morton Cone), Madrona, 1979; *Crazy Crocheting* (juvenile; illustrated with line drawings by Rachel Osterlof and with photographs by F. Cone and J. M. Cone), Atheneum, 1981; *Classy Knitting*, Atheneum, 1984. Author of "Craft Talk," a weekly column in *University Herald*, 1972, 1973. Contributor to magazines and newspapers, including *Trumpet, Cast On* and *Flying Needle*.

WORK IN PROGRESS: Signature Knits: Knits for All Sizes.

SIDELIGHTS: "I never dreamed my knitting needles would take me on so many exotic excursions. And I never imagined that I would be writing books!

"All my life I seemed to have been able to mix business with pleasure, which added dashes of enthusiasm, imagination, and creativity to my several careers.

"I have owned and managed my own knit shop, where I organized seminars, directed workshops, arranged fiber displays, designed the shop itself, and learned many tough lessons about being the proprietor of a small business. Those experiences taught me some of the most valuable lessons I've ever learned about interpersonal communication and how to speak with authority. They were also an effective foundation that helped make my skill, knit art, into a recognized art form.

"Although more than thirty years of technical background were important, I was also fortunate enough to be involved with people of vision and I became wiser in my judgment of what will succeed, stylistically, economically, artistically, and was willing to take risks in order to achieve my goals. From my work with professionals in my field, I established a network of communication between practitioners of various crafts.

"My world travels have added breadth to my knowledge of my craft, and whatever writing skills I have acquired along the way. While at Ulpan Akiva, an international study center located in Netanya in Israel, I wrote six newspaper articles on my experiences there. I have lectured in Hawaii, Canada, Israel, and Japan, and have traveled to England, France, Denmark, Sweden, Indonesia, Austria, Italy, Greece, Puerto Rico, and Mexico. In the fall of 1978, I visited the People's Republic of China, with a specially selected group of craft artists, writers, and museum directors.

"I came to writing as a senior citizen. At age fifty-four, my first book was published. My message was 'Don't just learn by rote, let yourself enjoy your creativity.' *Knutty Knitting for Kids* came out of my work with hearing impaired youngsters and youngsters with emotional problems at local elementary schools. 'I like knitting because it is fun,' wrote a ten-year-old child, 'and you can make mistakes if you want. It is much more fun than plane (sic) knitting.' I knew, somehow instinctively, that children could excel at this traditionally utilitarian craft and that it would add much to their self-esteem. Their enthusiasm was exhilarating! Photographs of the children and their creations appear throughout the book.

"In *Knit with Style*, I also urged creativity, and encouraged the reader to experiment with design and texture independently. My husband and I took most of the photographs for that book. *Crazy Crocheting* is another book for children, although adults are using it, too. My husband and I also took the photos for that book.

"My latest book, *Classy Knitting* is a book for both teens and adults. In order to understand their response to my way of teaching some fashion tricks, and the knitting techniques, several Campfire Girls agreed to be my guinea pigs. They were delightful to work with, and they enjoyed the results.

"From time to time I have been invited to present mini-workshops at libraries in San Francisco, Seattle, Honolulu and New York City, mainly for elementary school children. That special moment of 'light' is truly a joy to behold.

"In order to write any book for children, for me it is necessary to work directly with them to record their responses. I watch their reactions, listen to their comments, and praise their efforts. I consider abstract knitting a viable art form which has no particular structure—somewhat like freehand drawing. Children are more apt to accept this concept with open minds, and are willing to experiment.

"In each of my books is included a cartoon drawn especially for me, which tips off the reader that having fun is what it's all about.

"What I call my abstract knitting of clothing, wall hangings, soft jewelry, and sculptures, has progressed into workshops, exhibits, and finally into books. I love knitting (and crocheting) because it is practical, therapeutic, and portable, and so many things inspire me—colors and shapes in nature, junk yards, or a building. I believe that knitting, and life, should be fun. Dropped stitches, like some mistakes, can be chuckled over and used to enhance the overall 'appearance' of the work and life.''

FOR MORE INFORMATION SEE: Baltimore Jewish Times, January 15, 1970; *University Herald,* February 4, 1970; *Seattle Times,* July 14, 1972, May 22, 1975, November 7, 1976, April 10, 1979, August 26, 1979, October 3, 1982; *Oregon Journal,* June 12, 1975; *St. Louis Globe Democrat,* October 29, 1975; *San Francisco Chronicle,* November 11, 1978; *Artnews,* May 8, 1976; *Fiber Arts,* May/June, 1978; *Seattle Post-Intelligencer,* December 10, 1979; *Oakland Tribune,* February 10, 1980; *Seattle Times,* October, 1982; *Honolulu Advertiser,* November, 1982; *New York Times,* May 27, 1983; *Lynwood Enterprise,* July, 1983.

MARIBELLE B. CORMACK

CORLETT, William   1938-

BRIEF ENTRY: Born October 8, 1938, in Darlington, Durham, England. Playwright, actor, and author of books for young people. Corlett received his diploma from the Royal Academy of Dramatic Art and has performed in the theater and on television. A stage and television playwright for both children and adults, he is the recipient of a 1978 Pye television award for children's drama and, in 1980, a New York film and television international award for the children's series "Barriers." His other plays for children are "Orlando the Marmalade Cat Buys a Cottage" and "Orlando's Camping Holiday," both adapted from stories by Kathleen Hale. For young adults, Corlett has written a trilogy of novels that includes *The Gate of Eden, The Land Beyond,* and *Return to the Gate.* Featuring an unnamed protagonist, the books follow the character's life from his teen years to an elderly age. Corlett later adapted *The Gate of Eden* into a television play. Among his other juvenile works are *The Dark Side of the Moon* and *Barriers* (both Hamish Hamilton, 1981), and a book of poetry entitled *The I Deal Tale* (Compton Russell, 1975). He is also the author of "Questions" (Hamish Hamilton, 1978-79), a nonfiction series written with John Moore that presents answers to questions of human existence from major world religions. Corlett is currently working on an adaptation of his novel, *Return to the Gate. Home:* Cottesbrook, Great Bardfield, Essex, England. *For More Information See: Contemporary Authors,* Volume 103, Gale, 1982; *Twentieth-Century Children's Writers,* 2nd edition, St. Martin's, 1983; *The Writers Directory: 1984-1986,* St. James Press, 1983.

When I am dead, I hope it may be said:
'His sins were scarlet, but his books were read.'
                                        —Hilaire Belloc

CORMACK, Maribelle B.   1902-1984

PERSONAL: Born January 11, 1902, in Buffalo, N.Y.; died in 1984; daughter of Adam Horne and Hollis (Marshall) Cormack. *Education:* Cornell University, A.B., 1923; graduate study at University of Vienna, 1924-25, and University of Geneva, 1925; Brown University, A.M., 1928; graduate study at University of Connecticut, 1955. *Religion:* Congregationalist. *Residence:* Providence, R.I.

CAREER: Buffalo Museum of Science, Buffalo, N.Y., lecturer, 1923-26; Park Museum, Providence, R.I., head of education department, assistant director, 1926-47, director of museum, beginning 1947, director of planetarium, beginning 1953. Member of Brown University Skyscrapers eclipse expeditions to Mt. Katahdin, Maine, 1932, Roblin, Manitoba, Canada, 1945, and Araxa, Brazil, 1947; lecturer on birds, wild flowers, popular astronomy, and writing. *Member:* American Association of Museums, Middle Atlantic Planetarium Society, Rhode Island Astronomical Society (former president), Natural Science for Youth Foundation, Bishop Museum Association (Honolulu), Daughters of the American Revolution, Business and Professional Women's Association, Alpha Xi Delta. *Awards, honors:* Recipient of an award from Daughters of the American Revolution, 1950; Award of merit from American Legion of Rhode Island, 1965.

WRITINGS—All for young readers, except as indicated: (With William P. Alexander) *The Museum Comes to Life* (illustrated by Henry J. Meloy), American Book Co., 1931; (with W. P. Alexander) *Horns of Gur* (illustrated by Gordon L'Allemand), American Book Co., 1935; *Runner of the Trail: A Mystery of the Hudson Bay Country* (illustrated by Robert K. Stephens), Appleton-Century, 1934; *Wind of the Vikings: A Tale of the*

Orkney Isles (illustrated by Robert Lawson), Appleton-Century, 1937; (with W. P. Alexander) *Jacques, the Goatherd: A Story of the High Alps* (illustrated by Pierre Brissaud), Appleton-Century, 1938; (with W. P. Alexander) *Land for My Sons: A Frontier Tale of the American Revolution* (illustrated by Lyle Justis), Appleton-Century, 1939.

(With W. P. Alexander) *Last Clash of Claymores: A Story of Scotland in the Time of Prince Charles* (illustrated by Norman Price), Appleton-Century, 1940; (with W. P. Alexander) *The Luck of the Comstocks: A Story of Block Island* (illustrated by Hilda Frommholtz), Appleton-Century, 1941; *A Recruit for Abe Lincoln* (illustrated by Hamilton Greene), Appleton-Century, 1942; *Road to Down Under* (illustrated by Edward Shenton), Appleton-Century, 1944; (with Pavel Bytovetzski) *Underground Retreat* (illustrated by Margaret Ayer), Reynal & Hitchcock, 1946; (with P. Bytovetzski) *Swamp Boy: A Story of the Okefinokee Swamp in Georgia* (illustrated by Winfield Hoskins), McKay, 1948; *The First Book of Stones* (illustrated by M. K. Scott), F. Watts, 1950; *The First Book of Trees* (illustrated by Helene Carter), F. Watts, 1951; *Timber Jack*, F. Watts, 1952; *The Lady Was a Skipper: The Story of Eleanor Wilson, Missionary Extraordinary to the Marshall and Caroline Islands*, Hill & Wang, 1956; *The Star-Crossed Woman* (adult fiction), Harrap, 1961, Crown, 1962; *Imhotep, Builder in Stone*, F. Watts, 1965.

HOBBIES AND OTHER INTERESTS: Travel, languages (both living and dead).

FOR MORE INFORMATION SEE: Times Literary Supplement, June 12, 1937, June 24, 1939; *New York Herald Tribune Books*, May 7, 1939, November 10, 1940, November 15, 1942, October 28, 1956; *New York Times*, May 7, 1939; *Christian Science Monitor*, November 3, 1942; Stanley J. Kunitz and Howard Haycraft, editors, *Junior Book of Authors*, 2nd edition, revised, H. W. Wilson, 1951; Martha E. Ward and D. A. Marquardt, *Authors of Books for Young People*, Scarecrow Press, 1964.

CUYLER, Margery Stuyvesant   1948-
(Daisy Wallace)

PERSONAL: Born December 31, 1948, in Princeton, N.J.; daughter of Lewis Baker (a retired banker) and Margery Pepperell (Merrill) Cuyler; married John Newman Hewson Perkins (a psychoanalyst), August 23, 1979. *Education:* Sarah Lawrence College, B.A., 1970. *Politics:* Democrat. *Home:* 261 Fillow St., West Norwalk, Conn. 06850. *Agent:* McIntosh & Otis, Inc., 475 Fifth Ave., New York, N.Y. 10017. *Office:* Holiday House, 18 East 53rd St., New York, N.Y. 10022.

CAREER: Atlantic Monthly Press, Boston, Mass., assistant to editor of children's books, 1970-71; Walker & Co., New York, N.Y., editor of children's books, 1972-74; Holiday House, New York City, vice president and editor-in-chief of children's books, 1974—. Lecturer on children's book editing, Rutgers University, 1974, New School for Social Research, 1975, Vassar College, 1984. Board member, Women's National Book Association Children's Book Council, 1980-82. Library trustee and member of alumnae board, Sarah Lawrence College.

WRITINGS—All for children: *Jewish Holidays* (illustrated by Lisa C. Wesson), Holt, 1978; *The All-Around Pumpkin Book* (illustrated by Corbett Jones), Holt, 1980; *The All-Around*

MARGERY STUYVESANT CUYLER

Christmas Book (illustrated by C. Jones), Holt, 1982; *The Trouble with Soap*, Dutton, 1982; *Sir William and the Pumpkin Monster* (illustrated by Marcia Winborn), Holt, 1984.

Editor; under pseudonym Daisy Wallace; all for children; all published by Holiday House: *Monster Poems* (illustrated by Kay Chorao), 1976; *Witch Poems* (illustrated by Trina Schart Hyman), 1976; *Giant Poems* (illustrated by Margot Tomes), 1978; *Ghost Poems* (illustrated by Tomie De Paola), 1979; *Fairy Poems* (illustrated by T. S. Hyman), 1980.

WORK IN PROGRESS: Rufus and Max: A Valentine Story.

SIDELIGHTS: "I grew up in a large family, with four siblings and four cousins who lived with us after their mother died, and learned early how to fend for myself. I'm a great supporter of the type of small institution that allows the creative spirit to flourish. For example, both Sarah Lawrence and Holiday House value independent thinking, and provide the kind of nourishing environment where new ideas can take seed and ripen naturally.

"My passion has been editing children's books, but I also enjoy writing, since it exercises my imagination in a more personal and introspective fashion."

HOBBIES AND OTHER INTERESTS: Jungian psychology and mythology.

TEENY TINY GHOST

A teeny tiny ghost
no bigger than a mouse,
at most,
lived in a great big house.

It's hard to haunt
a great big house
when you're a teeny tiny ghost
no bigger than a mouse,
at most.

He did what he could do.

So every dark and stormy night—
the kind that shakes a house with fright—
if you stood still and listened right,
you'd hear a
teeny
tiny
BOO!

LILIAN MOORE

ECHO

Hello!
    hello!
Are you near?
    near, near.
Or far from here?
    far, far from here.
Are you there?
    there, there
Or coming this way,
Haunting my words
Whatever I say?

Halloo!
    halloooo
Listen, you.
Who are you, anyway?
    who, who, whoooo?
      SARA ASHERON

(From *Ghost Poems,* edited by Daisy Wallace. Illustrated by Tomie de Paola.)

DALE, Margaret J(essy) Miller 1911-
(Margaret J. Miller)

PERSONAL: Born August 27, 1911, in Edinburgh, Scotland; daughter of James (a professor of pathology) and Margaret (Clare) Miller; married C. R. Dale, September 3, 1938 (divorced); children: Anna Clare, Richard, Diana. *Education:* Lady Margaret Hall, Oxford, B.A. (second class honours), 1933. *Home:* 26 Greys Hill, Henley-on-Thames, Oxon RG9 1SJ, England. *Agent:* John Johnson, Clerkenwell House, 45-47 Clerkenwell Green, London EC1R 0HT, England.

CAREER: Associated Screen News, Montreal, Quebec, Canada, scenario writer, 1935-36; Asiatic Petroleum Co., London, England, assistant editor of *Shell* magazine, 1937-39; writer. *Member:* International P.E.N.

WRITINGS—Under name Margaret J. Miller; children's books: *Seven Men of Wit,* Hutchinson, 1960; *Gunpowder Treason,* Macdonald & Co., 1968; *Plot for the Queen,* Macdonald & Co., 1969; *Emily: The Story of Emily Bronte,* Lutterworth, 1969; *King Robert the Bruce,* Macdonald & Co., 1970; *The Fearsome Road,* Abelard, 1974; *The Fearsome Island,* Abelard, 1975; *The Fearsome Tide* (illustrated by Carol Tarrant), Abelard, 1976; *The Far Castles,* Blackie & Son, 1978; *The Big Brown Teapot* (illustrated by Janina Ede), Hodder & Stoughton, 1979; *Roald Amundsen,* Hodder & Stoughton, 1981; *The Mad Muddle,* Hodder & Stoughton, 1982; *A Pocketful of Mice,* Hodder & Stoughton, 1984.

Published by Brockhampton Press, except as indicated: *The Queen's Music,* 1961; *The Powers of the Sapphire,* 1962; *Dr. Boomer,* 1964; (contributor) Margery Fisher, editor, *Open the Door* (anthology), 1965; *Mouse Tails,* 1967; *Willow and Albert,* 1968; (editor) *Knights, Beasts and Wonders: Tales and Legends from Mediaeval Britain* (illustrated by Charles Keeping), 1968, David White, 1969; *Willow and Albert Are Stowaways,* 1970.

Also author of about 200 scripts for Schools Broadcasting and of several scripts for Schools Television. Contributor to *London Times* and *Times Educational Supplement.*

SIDELIGHTS: "When I was twelve or thirteen I started a magazine called the 'Felix Magazine' to which my sisters and friends contributed. We had a love story, always written by one of my sisters, a serial detective story, written by me, fashion notes, humorous articles and poetry."

Dale gathers the material for her children's fantasies from her travels to remote parts of Scotland. She has traveled to Rhodesia, South Africa, and Portuguese East Africa and has written about these countries in an historical and educational manner.

HOBBIES AND OTHER INTERESTS: Music especially choral singing, boating and fishing, travel, especially in the western islands of Scotland; historical and literary research, and folklore.

De GRAZIA, Ted 1909-1982
(De Grazia; Ettore De Grazia)

PERSONAL: Born June 14, 1909, in Morenci, Ariz.; died September 17, 1982, in Tucson, Ariz.; son of Domenico (a miner) and Lucia (Gagliarei) De Grazia; married second wife, Marion Sheret, 1948; children: three. *Education:* University

TED De GRAZIA

of Arizona, B.A., 1944, B.F.A., 1945, M.A., 1945. *Residence:* Tucson, Ariz. 85705.

CAREER: Artist. Owner and director of Gallery in the Sun and De Grazia Studio Shops in Tucson, Ariz. and of Superstition Mountain Gallery in Apache Junction, Ariz. *Member:* Sinfonia. *Awards, honors:* Achievement award from University of Arizona, 1968.

WRITINGS—All self-illustrated: *Impressions of Papago and Yaqui Indians,* De Grazia Studios, 1950; *Mission in the Santa Catalinas: A Tale of Apache Indians, Mexicans, and a Mission in Arizona South,* De Grazia Studios, 1951; *The Flute Player: A Fantasy with Dances Inspired by Pottery of Ancient Indians Called Hohokam . . . ,* De Grazia Studios, 1952; *Padre Nuestro: A Strange Story of Now and Long Ago,* De Grazia Studios, 1953; *The Blue Lady: A Desert Fantasy of Papago Land,* De Grazia Studios, 1957; *Padre Kino: A Portfolio Depicting Memorable Events in the Life and Times of the Heroic and Immortal Priest-Colonizer* (portfolio of twenty prints), Arizona South, 1962; *The Way of the Cross* (fifteen painting reproductions), De Grazia Associates, 1964; *Ah Ha Toro,* Northland Press, 1967; *The Rose and the Robe: The Travels of Fray Junipero Serra in California,* Best-West Publications, 1968: *De Grazia Paints the Yaqui Easter: Forty Days of Lent in Forty Paintings,* University of Arizona Press, 1968.

(With William Neil Smith) *The Seri Indians: A Primitive People of Tibouron Island in the Gulf of California,* Northland Press, 1970; *De Grazia Paints the Signs of the Zodiac* (limited proof edition), Gallery in the Sun, 1971; *De Grazia and His Mountain, The Superstition,* Gallery in the Sun, 1972; *De Grazia Paints Cabeza De Vaca: The First Non-Indian in Texas,*

New Mexico, and Arizona, Gallery in the Sun, 1973; *De Grazia Moods in Gold, Silver, Precious Gems, and Cookies,* Gallery in the Sun, 1974; *De Grazia Paints the Papago Indian Legends,* Gallery in the Sun, 1975; *De Grazia Paints the Apache Indians and Myths of the Chiricahua Apaches,* Gallery in the Sun, 1976; *Christmas Fantasies,* Gallery in the Sun, 1977; *De Grazia Paints the Signs of the Zodiac,* Gallery in the Sun, 1978; *De Grazia and Padre Kino,* Gallery in the Sun, 1980; *De Grazia in Graphics, 1949-1979, 30 Years,* Gallery in the Sun, 1980. Contributor of articles to *Arizona Highways, Desert,* and *Mountain States Architecture.*

Illustrator: Patricia Benton, *The Young Corn Rises,* Vantage Press, 1953; Patricia Paylore, *Kino, A Commemoration,* Arizona Pioneers' Historical Society, 1961; Alvin Gordon, *Inherit the Earth: Stories from Mexican Ranch Life,* University of Arizona Press, 1963; A. Gordon, *Brooms of Mexico,* Best-West Publications, 1965; LaVerne Clark, *They Sang for Horses: The Impact of the Horse on Navajo and Apache Folklore,* University of Arizona, 1966; A. Gordon, *Journeys with Saint Francis of Assisi,* Best-West Publications, 1966; Ray Brandes, editor, *Troopers West: Military and Indian Affairs in the American Frontier,* Frontier Heritage Press, 1970; Mildred Feague, *The Little Indian and the Angel,* Children's Press, 1970; A. Gordon, *Of Vines and Missions,* Northland Press, 1971; Marion S. De Grazia, *M Collection,* Gallery in the Sun, 1971; Dick Frontain, *San Xavier del Bac: Poem of the Desert,* Los Amigos, 1972; Sister M. Angela, *God and a Mouse: A Festival of Reflective Jubilation,* Benedictine Sisters, 1972; Rita Daven-

port, *De Grazia and Mexican Cookery,* Arizona Highways, 1976; Sister M. Angela, *Caves and Canyons: A Refreshing Journey of the Spirit to Inner Realities,* Benedictine Sisters, 1979; Sister M. Angela, *God and a Mouse,* Benedictine Sisters, 1980.

SIDELIGHTS: **June 14, 1909.** Born in the desert mountains of Morenci, Arizona, the third of seven children. "From childhood, I have been interested in color. To some people, Morenci looks harsh and barren. To me, it has always been a world of beauty and color. Often I would go on long hikes with my father, and we would fill our pockets with colored minerals. These rocks I crushed with a hammer for color. Color fascinated me. It made a deep impression which has persisted to this day. I treasure a head of Christ I modeled in native red clay, baked hard in my mother's oven." [William Reed, *De Grazia: The Irreverent Angel,* Frontier Heritage Press, 1971.[1]]

1920. With his Italian family, returned to Italy for an extended, five-year visit. "While there I got a good education in Church art. I watched the Church decorators and artists and soon began to work with clay. Then I got some paints and tried to paint pictures, always with the religious theme. I still consider the church art of Italy to be some of the finest ever painted by man."[1]

1925. Returned to Morenci. De Grazia had to relearn English and start over in school, entering the first grade when he was

De Grazia's "Gallery in the Sun," which opened in 1965.

(From *Caves and Canyons* by Sister M. Angela.
Illustrated by De Grazia.)

sixteen years old. Seven years later, he graduated from high
school at the age of twenty-three.

1932. Entered the University of Arizona. Relying on work in
the mines of Morenci and money he earned from playing his
trumpet, De Grazia attended the University for four years. A
few months before he was to receive his bachelor's degree in
music, however, he dropped out of school.

1930s. Attempted to establish himself as an artist, but acceptance came slowly. "... I did sell a few [paintings], but
damned few. Those were pretty dark days, and more than once
I considered throwing in the towel and going back into business. It was a constant struggle between the call of the artist
and the demands of economics."[1]

1942. Moved to Mexico City, where he worked with noted
Mexican artists José Clemente Orozco and Diego Rivera. "In
college, the professor usually looks down upon you as a dumb
bastard. It was not like that with Rivera and Orozco; they
treated me as an equal. They made me feel—for the first time
in my life—that maybe I was somebody after all.

"I worked on murals with both men; on the second-floor of
the National Palace with Rivera, and with Orozco at the Hospital of Jesus in Mexico City. It was a good experience—and
those were good days!"[1]

In November of that year De Grazia had his first one-man show
in Palacio de Bellas.

1943. Returned to the University of Arizona. Received two
bachelor's degrees, one in art and one in music, and a master's
degree in art in 1945. His master's thesis developed the relationship between art and music. In later years he earned a
reputation as a master in the field of color. "I was very surprised to discover during research for my thesis that my ideas
concerning music and art were certainly not original. Sometime
before 322 B.C. Aristotle commented that, '... we find colors
may mutually relate like musical concords for their pleasantest
arrangements like those concords mutually proportion.'

"It is true that as we look at a painting that is a masterpiece
of art which has survived through the ages, we find that what
makes it great is not whether it is realistic or not, or because
of its subject matter ... its merit depends upon the play of
light and color and the relationship of one form to another,
making a composition expressive and alive. ... In our own
age especially, when the camera has surfeited us with realism
and the true-to-life possibilities of painting have been ade-
quately developed, we must turn to abstract painting in order
to have more freedom in expressing in a creative way what we
feel rather than what we see ... a kind of painting that can
suggest motion, speed, action.

"Basically, music and painting are the same, the common root
being emotion ... probably *feeling* is a better word to use
than emotion, since feeling means more. ... One thinks of
feeling as referring to the whole of man."[1]

De Grazia built his first gallery in Tucson, Arizona. "It took
years to complete. Sometimes I would just say 'The hell with
it!' and go off prospecting for gold in the Superstition Mountains. I've always been obsessed with the idea of finding gold,
but on the other hand, I've always been afraid I might find it.
Somehow, the hunt has always meant more to me than the kill.

"In those days, we couldn't make a penny no matter how we
tried. I once got a call from a fellow who wanted one of my
paintings, and he said he would drop by to see a few. I rushed
outside and put some lobster and crab shells around my hammock—so he would be impressed with the fact that I was eating
high-class food—then stretched out in the hammock and tried
to look bored.

"He wasn't impressed. Turned out he was a grocer, and I
wound up trading a 4x8 foot canvas for $18.00 worth of gro-
ceries. Funny thing though ... the grocer got a divorce a few
years later, and he cut that painting in half as part of the
settlement. He hung his unsigned half of the painting in the
front window of a junk shop, and advertised it for $50.00.
Some guy who recognized my work drove by one day and saw
it, so he slammed on his brakes, went in and bought it.

"This same guy sold that one-half of a painting for $1000.00!
No one knows what happened to the other half."[1]

1947-1951. Painted numerous works, and also visited New
York, where he explained the possibilities of reproducing paintings on cards and prints. "I wanted in the worst way to see
some of my work reproduced in prints, so I worked up my
courage and approached an engraver in Southern California. I
showed him a few paintings.

"I said, 'You know, if you print these, I think I can sell them.'

"I didn't know the first damned thing about color separations, or procedure, or cost. I just knew I wanted to see some of my things reproduced.

"He said, 'Where you from?'

"I told him, and he said, 'How many can you buy?'

"'That depends upon how much they cost.'

"He said, 'Oh, about a dollar each.'

"He was, of course, thinking in terms of doing quantities of a few thousand. I said, 'Well, in that case I think I can afford about fifteen!'

"The printer thought that was very funny, but he went out on a limb and carried me. Sure enough, I began to sell prints quite successfully. Today, of course, we sell prints by the millions.''[1]

Built Gallery in the Sun, which is listed among the architectural wonders of Arizona. "People in the art business always want to know, 'How did you make it?' There is no formula for success in an art career. I got in through the back door. I've always spoken my mind. I tell people to go to hell if I don't agree with them. I'm not saying that this is the way to make it, but I will say that if you do make it this way, you will sure as hell enjoy it more!

"And, it isn't getting money that counts anyway. Having no money conditions you. You never really change, even when you finally get it. I remember I used to sleep in the car on the side of the road because I didn't have three dollars for a motel room. I ate crackers and sardines instead of a meal in a restaurant. I still have an inclination to turn off the lights in a motel, and take the extra bars of soap for future use.

"You always come back to your basic principles. You may stray away while experimenting with superficial 'kicks,' but you always come back. I used to get a kick out of spending money simply because it was a new experience. I had always dreamed of owning a convertible car. Finally I got one; a bright, new red one. After that, there were many. Now I just want something to take me where I'm going . . . I no longer care about impressing anybody.''[1]

1958. Hallmark cards put his art work on Christmas cards, which brought him national recognition.

1960. Painting, "los Ninos," sold over five million boxes of greeting cards. "I'm not impressed with the fact that I'm supposed to be famous. All that really means—once you start to believe it—is that people have some kind of an unnatural 'hold' on your life. I don't want anybody, or any situation, to dictate how I live my life.

"As an example, my insurance man called me some time back and insisted that I carry the same insurance as one of our more famous loud mouth politicos from Arizona.

"'Why?' I asked him.

"'Well,' he said, 'you're a famous person. You have more in assets now. At least, you should let us insure your hands.'

"'I'll tell you what,' I replied, 'I'll save you a lot of worry. You just cancel everything. Cancel all my insurance. You guys

(From *God and a Mouse* by Sister M. Angela. Illustrated by De Grazia.)

have me at the point now that I'm afraid to live and afraid to die!'

"'You're joking!' he said.

"'Like hell I am! I figure I've paid enough taxes to cover the cost of my burial. If I can't afford to pay for my own funeral, then let the county do it.''[1]

1982. Died in Tucson, Arizona. During the height of his popularity as an artist, De Grazia reflected on his success. "Sure I get tired. After a week of traveling, meeting thousands of people and signing hundreds of books, cards, and prints, anyone would be tired, but that's part of the price you have to pay. They are my public . . . they put me on top. I love them and they love me. Still, the more you are exposed, the less time you have to call your own. That's what I mean when I say I'm fighting overexposure. I need time alone—'brooding' time.

"If I were a 'technician' instead of a creative artist, then there would be no problem. I can't do it that way. I can't really create something unless I have time to live with it for awhile, alone. You can't be an artist unless you know what 'aloneness' means. You don't become an artist by going to school, where they 'sugar coat' you. To become an artist, you start inside and work out. You must be dedicated, and you'll sweat it out every minute of every day. It's difficult, and there's no guarantee of anything, and you will pay dearly and nobody will know and nobody will care.

"I was once asked on a television show to give advice to young art students. I said, '. . . first you must be able to grow a beard, and then you must wait until it turns white!'"[1]

FOR MORE INFORMATION SEE: New Mexico Magazine, January, 1965; *San Diego Magazine,* December, 1968; William Reed, *De Grazia: The Irreverent Angel,* Frontier Heritage Press, 1971; Frontain, *De Grazia in Fotos,* Los Amigos, 1977; Harry Redl and Buck Saunders, *World of De Grazia: An Artist of the American Southwest,* Chrysalis, 1981; (obituary) *New York Times,* September 9, 1982.

de MESSIÈRES, Nicole   1930-

PERSONAL: Born January 26, 1930, in Alès, France; came to the United States in 1938, naturalized citizen, 1956; daughter of René E. (a professor) and Marguerite (a painter; maiden name, Delfau) de Messières; married Alan Benjamin Spurney (in international trade); children: Philippe, Chantal. *Education:* Wellesley College, B.A., 1950; attended Parsons School of Design, 1950-52; University of Geneva, Certificat Propédeutique, 1965: *Religion:* Roman Catholic. *Residence:* Kensington, Md. *Office:* c/o Virginia Buckley, Lodestar Books, Dutton, 2 Park Ave., New York, N.Y. 10016.

CAREER: Muller-Barringer (interior design studio), New York City, assistant designer, 1952-53; Brunschwig & Fils (textile firm), New York City, designer and colorist, 1953-56; Editions Nagel (publisher), Geneva, Switzerland, editor and translator, 1965; Pictures Publishing Co., New York City, Swiss correspondent, 1966-68; *Weekly Tribune,* Geneva, art critic, 1967-68; volunteer worker in the slums of Lima, Peru, 1969-72; Montgomery Ward, interior decorating instructor in Springfield, Va., 1973, manager of consumer education program and lecturer to schools and women's organizations in Wheaton, Md., 1974-79; writer, 1980—. *Member:* Washington Wellesley Club, Women's Community Club of Kensington. *Awards, honors: Reina the Galgo* was chosen as one of twenty best novels for children by the New York Public Library, 1981, chosen a children's book of the year by Child Study Association, 1982, and selected by the Library of Congress for production on tapes and/or braille for their National Library Service for the Blind and Physically Handicapped.

WRITINGS: (Editor and translator) *Who's Who in Switzerland,* Editions Nagel, 1965; *Reina the Galgo* (juvenile), Elsevier/Nelson, 1981. Swiss correspondent for *Pictures on Exhibit,* 1966-68. Author of a weekly column in *Geneva Tribune,* 1967-68. Contributor of articles and a story to magazines and newspapers, including *Americas.*

WORK IN PROGRESS: Shake Hands with the Wind, a juvenile novel about a young mill worker's dream to become a pilot; a novel for juveniles; *Dreamers of the Day,* a novel for adults, set in Peru.

SIDELIGHTS: "My two brothers and I were born in France but were raised and educated in the United States. Growing up, I felt torn between two languages, two cultures. Because World War II was in progress, returning to what I still considered 'home' was impossible. Communication with relatives

across the Atlantic was difficult and infrequent. We were constantly anxious over their fates and over the future of occupied France. During those years I developed an acute nostalgia for what I dimly remembered as a lost paradise. I yearned for a promised land that beckoned, inaccessible—perhaps for ever.

"It took years of maturing to lay this feeling to rest. Later on, I went through the process all over again with my own children. Born in the States, their growing up was spread halfway around the globe; they speak three languages fluently. In their late teens, the usual adolescent crisis over identity was magnified by a feeling of rootlessness. Eventually they came to realize—as I had done—that a multinational background could be an asset rather than a handicap.

"Following my husband in foreign posts gave me an opportunity to know people of many lands, cultures, and religions. Residence in Bangladesh, Pakistan, Switzerland, and Peru (with visits to other countries) showed me that similarities far outweigh differences in the family of man.

"Yet people, especially young people, suffer everywhere from a sense of alienation when they must cope with a different environment. They tend to believe that their problem is unique, that no one understands. They need reassurance that, out of their painful readjustments, they can become better human beings with a more tolerant, compassionate view of the world.

"It is no coincidence, then, that in my writing I return to an underlying common theme: conflict arising from a clash of different cultures.

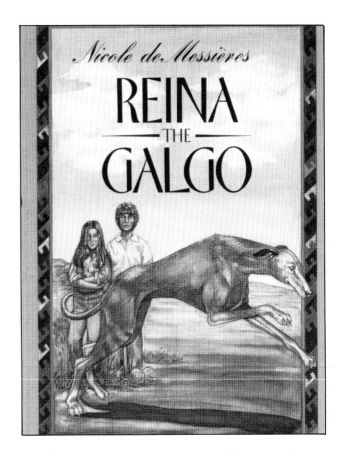

(Jacket illustration by Ann Kobayashi from *Reina the Galgo* by Nicole de Messières.)

NICOLE de MESSIÈRES

'In *Reina the Galgo,* Colette and Mark must first adjust to Peru, then to the States. Their memories of growing up in Peru, focused on the beloved greyhound Reina, is in the light of a 'lost paradise.' In *Shake Hands with the Wind,* Natalie and her elder brother and sister are in conflict with the French Canadian traditions which their father attempts to preserve in a small Massachusetts mill town. Natalie's dream of flying is a wish to escape to a 'promised land,' far from family and factory conflicts. In *Dreamers of the Day,* a Catholic priest encounters a family fleeing from their Andean village to Lima, an unknown world full of promise. But they find there only more civil strife, injustice, and poverty as the priest faces a growing sense of alienation from his church.

"I grew up in a house full of books. My father, a professor of French literature, stressed a sound knowledge of the classics. My brothers and I read everything in sight. Dick Tracy, Jules Verne, Mark Twain, Louisa May Alcott, Dickens, Victor Hugo, James Fenimore Cooper and so on, were welcome reliefs from Homer and Racine. I think most children of ten or twelve need no simplified juvenile style or specialized vocabulary. (I have not written for the very young.) Nevertheless, while children today seem more precocious and sophisticated than ever, we should not be fooled into treating them like little adults. Childhood is a time for dreams, for heroes and heroines, for 'promised lands.' Reading can provide them.

"Too many juvenile books are featuring the negative side of life. While we adults strive to correct the ills of the world, we have no business inflicting this burden on our children. Even—perhaps especially—those very children who have had to face real life tragedies need books which are entertaining, uplifting, and which offer hope—hope that our world is a pretty good place after all.

"My view is based on speaking to many hundreds of school children, usually in small informal groups. It is they, the children themselves, who have told me what they like to read. To say that we must compete with television, that children's books won't sell unless they deal with sordid subjects, is a cop-out. If we choose to write for children, we have a sacred responsibility.

"Another strong influence in my life was my mother, a talented painter. Among the books which filled our house were many art books. I can remember rainy afternoons spent copying drawings of Degas or Michelangelo. At Wellesley College, I majored in art history. After graduation, I accepted a scholarship to Parsons School of Design. This led to jobs, first with an interior design studio, then with Brunschwig & Fils, a firm manufacturing decorator fabrics. Later it led to a position with Montgomery Ward, where I directed a district-wide program of interior decorating classes, and then to the publication of articles on interior decorating. In the meanwhile, during our stay in Switzerland, I had written a newspaper column reviewing exhibits in art galleries; I was also Swiss correspondent for a New York based magazine addressed to art collectors.

"All my life, visiting museums and art galleries has been a joy. To a very modest degree, I inherited some of my mother's talent. I have spent many happy hours working on a sketch or a watercolor. But I often think I turned to writing because I knew that I could never be a really good artist. So I try to paint with words.

"I think for a long time about a book before starting to write. I do a rough draft in pencil on a yellow pad then, as each chapter is completed, I type another draft on newsprint. It's a long, painstaking process calling for much rewriting.

"Every writer is often asked: where do you get your ideas? *Reina the Galgo* is taken from personal experience. When we buried Reina, our beautiful greyhound and a cherished member of the family, I remember thinking: someday I will write her story. But when children want to know if this or that actually happened, I have to pause and define in my own mind that blurred line between 'real' and 'made up.' Then I explain that life has no convenient beginnings, middles, and ends; that a story needs to be structured. Writers have a chance to correct, improve on what happens in life, whether or not the story is based directly on personal experience.

"The seed of *Shake Hands with the Wind* [awaiting publication] was planted years ago when a friend told me of her childhood dream to become a pilot. She never made it. My story turned out vastly different from my friend's brief tale, but I gave my heroine the same dream and I had her succeed.

"*Dreamers of the Day* [in progress] really began (although I didn't know it then) when I worked in slums near Lima, Peru. I met there priests who were grappling with a spiritual crisis: poverty and social injustice vs. the Kingdom of God. (The 'updating' of Vatican II resulted in a deepening split in the Catholic Church on this, and other, issues.) I set out to solve, or, at least, understand their dilemma by writing a novel.

"My husband is a specialist on international trade. We collect art; our walls are covered with paintings, etchings, and posters of exhibits. On weekends, my husband and I like to walk our two greyhounds in the woods near our house. Occasionally, we take short trips to Chesapeake Bay or other rural spots. Our favorite vacation retreat is on the Outer Banks of North Carolina. On a recent trip to the Virgin Islands, we discovered scuba diving. Perhaps a story will emerge from it. Who knows?"

FOR MORE INFORMATION SEE: Children's Books of the Year, Child Study Association, 1982.

DESBARATS, Peter   1933-

PERSONAL: Surname is pronounced *Deb*-ah-rah; born July 2, 1933, in Montreal, Quebec, Canada; son of Hullett John (a printer) and Margaret (Rettie) Desbarats. *Education:* Attended Loyola College, Montreal, Quebec, Canada. *Home:* 524 Princess Ave., London, Ontario N6B 2B7, Canada. *Agent:* Curtis Brown Ltd., 575 Madison Ave., New York, N.Y. 10022. *Office:* Graduate School of Journalism, University of Western Ontario, London, Ontario N6A 5B7, Canada.

CAREER: Canadian Press, copy boy and writer, 1952; *Montreal Gazette,* Montreal, Quebec, writer, 1952-55; Reuters,

London, England, writer, 1955; *Winnipeg Tribune,* Winnipeg, Manitoba, writer, 1956, legislative reporter, 1957-60; *Montreal Star,* Montreal, staff writer, 1960-65; *Parallel* (magazine), Montreal, editor, 1965; CBC-TV, Montreal, host of nightly news and public affairs show "Hourglass," 1966-70; *Toronto Star,* editor in Ottawa, Ontario, 1970-72; Global TV, bureau chief in Ottawa, 1973-80; Royal Commission on Newspapers, Ottawa, senior consultant, 1980-81; University of Western Ontario, Graduate School of Journalism, London, Ontario, dean, 1981—. Canadian correspondent, *National Observer,* Washington, D.C., 1962-65. *Awards, honors:* National award as "best news broadcaster," 1977, Ottawa award as "best television interviewer," 1980, both from Association of Canadian Television and Radio Artists.

WRITINGS: Halibut York (verse for children), privately printed, 1964; *The State of Quebec: A Journalist's View of the Quiet Revolution,* McClelland & Stewart, 1965; *Halibut York and More* (verse for children), privately printed, 1965, revised edition published as *The Night the City Sang* (illustrated by Frank Newfeld), McClelland & Stewart, 1977; "The Great White Computer" (three-act play), first produced at Centaur Theatre, Montreal, c.1966; *Gabrielle and Selena* (juvenile; illustrated by Nancy Grossman), Longmans, 1968; (editor and author of introduction) *What They Used to Tell About: Indian Legends from Labrador,* McClelland & Stewart, 1969.

The Canadian Illustrated News, McClelland & Stewart, 1970; *René: A Canadian in Search of a Country,* McClelland & Stewart, 1976; (with Terry Mosher) *The Hecklers,* McClelland & Stewart, 1979.

Canada Lost/Canada Found: The Search for a New Nation, McClelland & Stewart, 1981; *Newspapers and Computers: An*

PETER DESBARATS

(From the film "Gabrielle and Selena," based on the story by Peter Desbarats. Produced by Stephen Bosustow. Released by BFA/Phoenix Films, 1972.)

Industry in Transition, Royal Commission on Newspapers, Minister of Supply and Services, 1981; *Collins and the Computer,* McClelland & Stewart, 1985; "Nurses" (two-act play), first produced at CentreStage, 1985. Also author of the official publication of the Canadian Pavilion at the World's Fair in Osaka, Japan, 1970. Author of scripts for National Film Board of Canada, British Broadcasting Corp., and other organizations. Contributor to *Weekend, Maclean's Magazine, The Western Producer, Saturday Night, The Times, Canadian Forum,* and *Canadian Commentator.*

ADAPTATIONS: "Gabrielle and Selena" (film), Stephen Bosustow Production, c.1970.

WORK IN PROGRESS: Studies in development of Canadian television news and the future of videotex news services.

SIDELIGHTS: "I've been interested in writing for as long as I can remember . . . starting with poems and stories in elementary school. My first published work was a poem printed in *The Montreal Star* when I was sixteen years of age. No byline since then has seemed as exciting.

"In more than three decades, I have written and spoken millions of words of journalism but the words that seem destined to outlive me, if anything does, are the hundreds in my few verses and stories for children, particularly *Halibut York* and the other Christmas verses for children. Every year at Christmas, they are read over radio stations and networks in different parts of Canada. The story, *Gabrielle and Selena,* about two little girls, one black and the other white, has gone through far more editions than anything else I have written. It seems to endure while all the political journalism disappears into the archives to be read in future years by a few scholars, if at all.

"I don't know what the moral in all this is, or whether this is of any use to anyone else. You don't choose to be a writer in the first place; constant work makes one more efficient as a writer but not necessarily any better; the ideas that are the germ of creative writing come at odd moments and for no apparent reason. Today we can transmit and produce the work of writers far more effectively than ever before, through print, radio, TV and various computer systems, but we have made little progress in understanding creativity, in supporting it and in discovering how to identify and to esteem the few creative works that do appear from time to time. The marketing of mass culture seems to work against this."

HOBBIES AND OTHER INTERESTS: Theatre, music, sports (cross-country skiing and swimming).

DEWEY, Ken(neth Francis) 1940-

PERSONAL: Born October 5, 1940, in New York, N.Y.; son of Frank and Katherine (Heatherington) Dewey; children: one son, Killian Cooper-Dewey. *Education:* Attended School of Visual Arts, New York, N.Y., 1958-60. Studied with B. Hogarth and Philip Hayes. *Residence:* New York, N.Y. *Office:* 220 Fifth Ave., New York, N.Y. 10001. *Agent:* Daniele Deverin, 226 E. 53rd St., New York, N.Y. 10022. *Dealer:* Yares Gallery, P.O. Box 1662, Scottsdale, Ariz. 85252.

CAREER: Painter and book illustrator. Exhibited work in one-man shows at Dal Bohrer's Design Gallery, Scottsdale, Ariz., 1969, and Yares Gallery, Scottsdale, Ariz., 1972. Also exhibited work at Firebird Festival of Fine Arts, 1970, Strathmore Paper International, 1970, and Southwest Graphics International, 1972. *Awards, honors:* Modern Publicity International Award, 1970; Strathmore Paper Award, 1970; bronze medal, two awards from Communigraphics, 1971.

WRITINGS: Onyamarks: A Collection of Thoughts and Drawings (self-illustrated), Arizona State University, 1972.

Illustrator: *Rip Van Winkle*, Simon & Schuster, 1970; Elliott Arnold, *The Spirit of Cochise*, Scribner, 1972; Elizabeth Levy, *Lawyers for the People: A New Breed of Defenders and Their Work*, Knopf, 1974; Ruth Maxwell, *Look with May Ling*, Ginn, 1974; Peter R. Limburg, *Termites*, Hawthorn, 1974; S. E. Ambrose, *Crazy Horse and Custer*, Doubleday, 1975; William Styron, *The Confessions of Nat Turner*, Franklin Library, 1976; Millicent E. Selsam, *Up, Down, and Around: The Force of*

(From *Lawyers for the People* by Elizabeth Levy. Illustrated by Kenneth Dewey.)

Gravity, Doubleday, 1977; William Stegner, *Angle of Repose*, Franklin Library, 1978; Sean O'Casey, *Six Plays*, Franklin Library, 1980; James Joyce, *Ulysses*, Franklin Library, 1980; William Faulkner, *The Sound and the Fury*, Franklin Library, 1980; Truman Capote, *Breakfast at Tiffany's*, Franklin Library, 1983.

WORK IN PROGRESS: A series of watercolors on New York City; a series of prints of the Statue of Liberty; a series of prints on the history of military small arms; a revival of the posters called "Catch All the Trains You Missed," for the New York Transit Authority.

"I am now forming a company, Penthouse Studios, dedicated to creating prints and posters, where the artist has more control and financial involvement."

SIDELIGHTS: "My motivation and artistic aesthetics are open to change, depending upon the assignment and seasonal variation. In my work I use pen and ink and watercolors.

"I can only learn on a technical level. . . . I am not concerned so much with learning from other artists, because the devel-

KEN DEWEY

opment of one artist does not necessitate his understanding of another.

". . . I create from peoples' conditions that have paralleled with mine at one time or another. . . . There are elements in society that encompass a whole spectrum of feeling and they need to be expressed, to be told. I am a medium, a transistor, and via my work these people, their positions, can be amplified, can be explained, so they can be viewed with a little more understanding. . . . You cannot remove, isolate or exile yourself from the origins of your culture. . . . I can only express that which I have intuitive knowledge of, that which I have lived with.

". . . The artist should be less impressed with himself and the categorical isms, and get down to a basic stick of communicating with another human being. . . .

"From 1972 to 1983 I have received fifteen awards of excellence from the Society of Illustrators and several New York Art Directors Awards. I have worked on several projects for *Time* magazine, including 'Man of the Year, Jimmy Carter.' The original drawings are in the President's permanent collection."

DeWIT, Dorothy (May Knowles)   1916-1980

PERSONAL: Born May 24, 1916, in Youngstown, Ohio; died June 19, 1980; married Adriaan DeWit (a doctor), April, 1951; children: Erica, Rick, Brian, Carolyn. *Education:* Shauffler College, B.S., 1940; Cleveland State University, B.A., 1941; Case Western Reserve University, M.S.L.S., 1965; post-master's courses in library work at Case Western Reserve University; further graduate work at University of Chicago. *Residence:* Garfield Heights, Ohio.

CAREER: Maple Heights Regional Library, Cuyahoga County Public Library, Maple Heights, Ohio, assistant children's librarian, 1960-65, children's librarian, 1965-66, head of children's services, 1966-80. Director of religious education, Union Church, 1947-51. Member, Notable Books Re-evaluation Committee, Association for Library Services to Children, 1971-75, and 1978-80; member, Children's Work Committee, Ohio Library Association, 1976-77; member, Newbery-Caldecott-Wilder Awards Committee, 1981. Book reviewer for *School Library Journal, Top of the News,* and *Previews. Member:* American Library Association, Ohio Library Association, Netherlands America Club (northeast chapter). *Awards, honors: The Talking Stone: An Anthology of Native American Tales and Legends* was selected as a notable children's book by the American Library Association, 1979.

WRITINGS: Children's Faces Looking Up: Program Building for the Storyteller, American Library Association, 1979; (editor) *The Talking Stone: Native American Tales and Legends* (juvenile; illustrated by Donald Crews; ALA Notable Book), Greenwillow, 1979.

SIDELIGHTS: "Before and during my college years, I worked in a marionette troupe, in the younger girls' department of the YWCA, for a public library and the college library, and among Appalachian and Spanish-speaking agricultural migrants, as a children's worker.

"After graduation I served as a co-director of a rural community program. I worked for five years on the midwest mi-

grant staff for the National Council of Churches, in the editorial office of a national magazine, and finally, for four years was director of religious education for the Union Church of Balboa, Canal Zone. Since 1961 I have been on the staff of the Cuyahoga County Public Library, Ohio in bookmobile, in the children's department, and since 1966, as Regional Children's Librarian at the Maple Heights Regional Branch. I was also a school librarian for the Garfield Heights and the Maple Heights systems."

For recreation DeWit and her family enjoyed camping. "The family has camped all over the United States, and Canada, in a little Apache tent trailer, in Padre Island National Seashore, Acadia, Olympic National Park, Southern California and in Europe. We have read scores of books aloud on these expeditions!"

DeWit died on June 19, 1980.

HOBBIES AND OTHER INTERESTS: Camping, music and puppets and marionettes. "For eight months I was part of a marionette troupe, and have taken courses in this, as well as making and using them in library work."

FOR MORE INFORMATION SEE—Obituaries: *School Library Journal,* August, 1980; *Horn Book,* October, 1980.

D'IGNAZIO, Fred   1949-

PERSONAL: Surname is pronounced Dig-*nay*-zee-oh; born January 6, 1949, in Bryn Mawr, Pa.; son of Silvio Frederick (a restaurateur) and Elizabeth (McComas) D'Ignazio; married Janet Letts (a manager in urban transit), September 5, 1969; children: Catie, Eric. *Education:* Brown University, B.A. (honors), 1970; Tufts University, M.A., 1971; graduate study at Harvard University, American University, and University of North Carolina. *Home and office:* 2117 Carter Rd. S.W., Roanoke, Va. 24015. *Agent:* Steve Axelrod, 126 Fifth Ave., New York, N.Y. 10011.

CAREER: The Futurist magazine, Washington, D.C., assistant editor, 1971-72; The Institute, Dickerson, Md., co-founder and president, 1971-76; Computer Sciences Corp., Chapel Hill, Washington, D.C., computer analyst and programmer, 1974-76; University of North Carolina, Chapel Hill, manager and consultant on computer systems, 1976-79; full-time editor, writer, television and radio commentator, and lecturer, 1979—. Regular commentator on ABC-TV's "Good Morning America," PBS's "The New Tech Times," and National Public Radio's "All Things Considered." Computers and robots' consultant for children's programming, ABC-Entertainment; consultant to schools, computer software and hardware companies, toy companies, publishers, robotics companies, and communications companies. Researcher, Harvard University, 1969-70; member of board of educational advisors, Terrapin, Inc., 1981—, and Tar Heel Computer Camps, 1982. *Member:* Brazilian International Relations Institute (fellow), National Association for the Preservation and Perpetuation of Storytelling (NAPPS). *Awards, honors:* Fellow, Gulbenkian Foundation; recipient of grant, National Science Foundation, 1974.

WRITINGS—Of interest to young readers, except as indicated; all nonfiction, except as indicated: *Katie and the Computer* (fiction; illustrated by Stan Gilliam), Creative Computing, 1979; *The Creative Kid's Guide to Home Computers: Super Games and Projects to Do with Your Home Computers* (illustrated by

S. Gilliam), Doubleday, 1981; *Small Computers: Exploring Their Technology and Future*, F. Watts, 1981; *The First Book of Electronic Games*, F. Watts, 1982; *The New Astronomy: Probing the Secrets of Space*, F. Watts, 1982; *Working Robots*, Lodestar, 1982; *Chip Mitchell: The Case of the Stolen Computer Brains* (fiction; illustrated by Larry Pearson), Lodestar, 1982; *The Star Wars Question and Answer Book about Computers* (illustrated by Ken Barr), Random House, 1983; *The Computer Parade* (fiction; sequel to *Katie and the Computer*; illustrated by S. Gilliam), Creative Computing, 1983; *Invent Your Own Computer Games*, F. Watts, 1983; *Atari Wonderland: 43 Learning Games for Your Atari Computer*, Hayden, 1983; *Messner's Introduction to the Computer*, Messner, 1983; *How to Get Intimate with Your Computer: Ten Easy Steps to Conquer Your Computer Anxiety* (adult; illustrated by S. Gilliam), McGraw, 1984; (with Allen L. Wold) *The Science of Artificial Intelligence*, F. Watts, 1984; *Chip Mitchell: The Case of the Robot Warriors* (fiction; illustrated by L. Pearson), Lodestar, 1984. Author of an early-learning series of "Wonderland" and "Playground" books for all popular computers (including Atari, Commodore 64, and Apple), Hayden, 1984.

Also associate editor and author of monthly columns for *Compute!*, *Compute!'s PC & PC jr.*, and *Compute!'s Gazette;* contributing editor and columnist for *Enter* (a children's magazine published by the Children's Television Workshop) and *Video Movies;* and contributor of articles to periodicals, including *Highlights for Children, The Washington Post, Better Homes and Gardens, Publishers Weekly,* and *USA Today.*

WORK IN PROGRESS: Various books on robots and computers, both fiction and nonfiction, including "Sandbox" and "Building Blocks" for all major computers (continuation of the Hayden early learning series); two new titles for the "Chip Mitchell Micro-Mystery" series.

SIDELIGHTS: D'Ignazio studied computer programming in college, and, after several years of working with computers, entered graduate school in the field of computer science. At the same time he began to write books about robots and computers. "Back in 1974, I was a programmer working on a mammoth Honeywell 6000 computer in the basement of the Pentagon, coding and decoding top-secret military systems. I guess it's safe now to admit what I was doing. My job was to program the computer to send soldiers' socks and underwear to Army bases all over the world.

"Programming soldiers' underwear and socks is a more demanding job than you might imagine. One day I decided to call it quits, and I picked up a briefcase-size computer terminal and smuggled it out of the Pentagon. I took a city bus over the Potomac River and ended up in a mid-town elementary school. I hooked up the terminal, via a telephone, to a giant computer in Chicago. I spent the entire day, with the teacher's permission, teaching 5-, 6-, and 7-years-olds how to program and play computer games. It was one of the most exhilarating experiences of my life. After Snurkle and Hunt the Wumpus, it was hard to go back to socks and underwear.

"The following year (1975), the first personal computer appeared—the Altair computer from the MITS Corporation in Albuquerque, New Mexico. And my daughter was born. I became fascinated with the idea of a personal-computer book for a little kid (a very little kid—Catie was only a month old

He took off, charging through the deep snow. Katie chased after him. ■ (From *Katie and the Computer* by Fred D'Ignazio. Illustrated by Stan Gilliam.)

Fred D'Ignazio, his daughter Catie, and "Ged" the home computer.

at the time). My wife suggested that the book would be most successful if it were a picturebook adventure story like *Alice in Wonderland.*

"I began the project immediately. But writing a book and getting it published was a much harder task than I imagined. The book, *Katie and the Computer* didn't appear until Catie's fourth birthday in 1979. . . .

"Between 1979 and 1982, only a few new children's computer books appeared. Then, suddenly, the home computer market exploded. By 1982, home computers could be bought for less than $200 apiece, than for less than $100 apiece. . . ." [Fred D'Ignazio, "Kids, Parents and Software," *Washington Post* "Book World," October 2, 1983.[1]]

About his own writing, D'Ignazio commented: "I like to pretend that I am a genie and that I can take my readers on a magic carpet ride into the past, the future, and into worlds invisible to human eyes. 'What if?' I ask my readers. 'What if you could shrink so small that one of your hairs was as big as the Empire State Building?' I encourage my readers to invent, create, imagine, and speculate along with me. My writing is playful, informative, enthusiastic, and, often, silly."

D'Ignazio has been a guest on numerous national and local television and radio programs. Since 1979 he has been a full-time writer and house-husband to his two children, Catie and Eric. While attempting to explain the functions of a computer to his daughter, D'Ignazio received the inspiration for his first computer storybook for children. "I love the mixture of fantasy

and reality; I love to teach, especially children. They have such lovely minds. My wife calls my writing 'fiction/non-fiction.'

"My writing has really taken off. My interest in computers coincided with society's interest. If I'd picked something less hot, it would have made it much harder to sell." [Lynn Jaluvka, "Author Took a Trip into Wonderland—and Stayed," *Durham Sun,* March 12, 1982.[2]]

D'Ignazio has written more than twenty juvenile books exploring the various facets of computers and robotics. His writing emanates from his home, which is crammed with books, magazines, robots and, at last count, twenty-three computers. It has become the neighborhood arcade. "I have several computers and mountains of software, and I have turned my study into a videogame arcade and a computer programming workshop for neighborhood kids.

"The kids can use all the computers in the room except one, my writing computer. That computer is 'supposed' to be off limits.

"One day, while the kids were banging away at the other computers, I got up from my computer to stretch and make a snack in the kitchen. On my way back into the room, five minutes later, I happened to glance at my computer screen. Before I left, the screen had been filled with words—a section of a new book chapter I was writing. Now the screen was empty.

"I panicked. I ran into the room yelling at the kids. 'Who messed with my computer?' I hollered. 'My chapter's gone. I've lost hours of work.'

"Then I checked the computer. I was sure it had been turned off, but it was still on. I did some more checking. Finally, I noted the screen brightness switch. I turned it. Magically, my words reappeared. My chapter was untouched. Nothing was lost.

"Just then, a very contrite five-year-old boy came up to me with his head drooping. 'I did it, Mr. D'Ignazio,' he said. 'I didn't mean to kill your computer.'

"Another time, I was in the kitchen eating dinner with my family. Several children were still playing computer games in the study. All of a sudden, from the study came shouts and scuffling noises.

"'It's my turn to blast them!' one child cried.

"'You just blasted them!' cried another child. 'Now it's my turn!'

"I ran into the study and found a six-year-old and a nine-year-old (brother and sister) doing their best to rip two joysticks out of a computer.

"'What are you two doing?' I shouted.

"The kids turned toward me. Frightened, they dropped their joysticks. One broke open on the study's hardwood floor.

"'Out! Out!' I yelled.

"They dashed past me and ran out the front door of the house.

"Given these tales of abused and violated computers, what is the best strategy for mixing young people and computers?

"You could put a lock on the computer room door until the kids all turn sixteen. Or until they leave home.

"You could keep the computer in the car trunk and only bring it in the house after the kids are asleep.

"You could even fortify the computer, beef it up, and make it indestructible, the way the military does with computers on tanks, guided missiles, and submarines.

"You could do these things, but I would advise against it. In their place, I would advise a brief discussion of computer 'manners,' followed by frequent 'refresher' courses. I would also recommend a few simple precautions. And trust—lots of trust.

"If you make your kids' computer time synonymous with drudgery, with work, with tension, or with pressure, they won't grow up liking computers." [Fred D'Ignazio, "The Computer Playground," *Compute!*, July, 1982. Amended by the author.[3]]

HOBBIES AND OTHER INTERESTS: "Storytelling, tree climbing, science fiction, collecting dragons and dinosaurs, travelling with my children, aerobic dancing, roller skating, science and technology."

FOR MORE INFORMATION SEE: Delaware County Daily Times, January 15, 1980; *Chapel Hill Newspaper*, March 8, 1981; *(Raleigh, N.C.) News and Observer People*, March 9, 1982; *Durham Sun*, March 12, 1982; *Compute!*, July, 1982; *U.S.A. Today*, August 1, 1983; *Washington Post* "Book World," October 2, 1983; *Roanoke Times and World News*, October 11, 1983, February 14, 1984, February 21, 1984; *Newsweek*, June, 1984; *Roanoke* magazine, July, 1984.

DILLON, Barbara   1927-

BRIEF ENTRY: Born September 2, 1927, in Montclair, N.J. Dillon graduated from Brown University in 1949; for the following eight years she worked as an editorial assistant for the *New Yorker* in New York City. She married in 1952 and, after her three daughters had grown, decided to enter the field of children's writing. It was a world, she recalls, "in which I had dwelt so happily with my children for so many years. My own childhood memories are, for some reason, most vivid at the third and fourth grade level, so it was to this age group that I naturally gravitated." Her first book, *The Good-Guy Cake* (Morrow, 1980), was described by *Publishers Weekly* as "a warm and decidedly original comedy" about an obnoxious little boy who becomes unbearably angelic after eating some magic cake. *Booklist* called it "a neat little fantasy," adding, "Dillon not only knows the formula for amusing children, . . . her matter-of-fact style converts everyday oddities of life into something worth reading about."

In her second book, *The Beast in the Bed* (Morrow, 1981), she creates a playful, pea-green Beast who befriends a little girl. *Bulletin of the Center for Children's Books* observed: "There are so many stories about children's imaginary companions, it's nice to have one told from the viewpoint of the companion, and told with a gentle, cheerful tone. . . ." Dillon followed with *Who Needs a Bear?* (Morrow, 1981) and *What's Happened to Harry?* (Morrow, 1982). In a review of her latest book, *The Teddy Bear Tree* (Morrow, 1982), *Publishers Weekly* called her "an expert at weaving tales children believe in willingly." This one was described as "a far out fantasy" in which young Bertine buries the remains of a tattered teddy bear and

soon finds herself with an entire tree full of "magic cuddlers." Currently, Dillon is working on two more books for children, *The Disappearance of Danny Dinkel* and *The Kingswood Key Caper*, both from Morrow. *Home:* 29 Harbor Rd., Darien, Conn. 06820. *For More Information See: Contemporary Authors*, Volume 110, Gale, 1983.

DORMAN, N. B.   1927-

PERSONAL: Born in 1927, in Iowa; daughter of a mail carrier and a dietitian; divorced, 1973; children: two sons. *Education:* California State University, Chico, B.A., 1963. *Residence:* Chico, Calif. *Office address:* Box 775, Chico, Calif. 95927.

CAREER: Worked in clerical and sales positions; assistant county librarian; free-lance typesetter and copy editor; writer, 1972—. Volunteer in alcohol recovery programs.

WRITINGS: Laughter in the Background (juvenile fiction), Elsevier/North Holland, 1980. Contributor of stories to magazines.

WORK IN PROGRESS: Daddy's Sick and *What Daddy Can Do*, primers on parental alcoholism; *Petey and Miss Magic*, a book on family rejection; *The Mystery of the Red Hen*, a juvenile mystery dealing with child abuse; *The Secret Summer*, a juvenile adventure; *The Day of the Great Apple Sale*, a juvenile set during the Depression and dealing with a death in the family; *The Smallest Farm*, a juvenile on urban homesteading; *Sister to Sheauna*, a juvenile on mental retardation; *What's Wrong?*, a book on parental alcoholism; *Mad Olga* and *The Beekeeper's Tale*, both collections of essays on urban homesteading; children's mysteries; stories for children involving three themes: normal kids with normal life situations, hardship stories, and animal stories; three fantasies, *After the Iridescent Mushroom*, *The Buzzings of Bees*, and *Cross Country Carnival*.

SIDELIGHTS: "Why did I begin to write? I had been told—and believed—I was utterly, completely incompetent . . . but my mother had never thought to forbid me to write stories. By the time she might have, I was earning money at it. I started because (1) What can you do if you can't do anything but you do have a typewriter? and (2) I had a need to make some sense, some happy ending, put some emotional control into my life. Sanity and compassion had been in short supply around me, but I could fantasize. That is an avenue which most easily leads into real mental illness. By some miracle, I quite sanely put my dreams on paper, more sanely spent the time and effort reworking them—and then editors began buying them. It was unbelievable.

"With my emotional background I gave myself several wretched years because I did not know how to live comfortably with myself, with life, or with people. That is a skill which must be learned, and if you do not have the chance to while young, it is like not having had the opportunity to learn Chinese. You simply grow up without it. However, I have had a good deal of help from some very wonderful people, and make progress despite my shortcomings. And as my own pain has ebbed, I realize I have not been the only hopelessly miserable child.

"That's perhaps why I now write mainly for children. I repeat the same things, subtly or obviously; about personal responsibility; about situations never lasting forever; about awareness of child abuse and doing something about it; about finding solutions, solving problems, going on, no matter how hard or hopeless or frightening it seems. As I work things out for myself, my work gets brighter and more delightful, which says more about my own sanity and peace of mind than any writing skill. Two I've worked on, for instance, have identical themes—of knuckling down to problems, of finding solutions—and yet within a fantasy framework. I guess I basically try to talk about awareness, about a sure knowledge that we can begin to do things which will increasingly solve problems and change situations, no matter how bad life seems now. If I stop being my own first enemy, I can make real improvements in my life.

"Life is struggle, uncertainty, confusion, unceasing confrontation with my own ignorances and inadequacies, but it is also increasingly rich and rewarding as I deal with these realities. Often that simply means accepting this is the way it is and most probably will be, and how do I get comfortable with such a state of affairs?

"I refuse to be defeated. I am a writer—selling or not. My joy ultimately lies in doing what I want and must do. That is its own reward, my well done effort. Even if it goes no farther, my work is enough.

"*How* do I write? Each piece probably begins with a question such as 'What if—?' What if, say, you found yourself seven and one half inches tall in this world? Why would this have happened? What size would other family members be? How would you get about—say climbing stairs—and feed or dress yourself? How might you handle winter? What would happen if others saw you? There is, you see, a great deal of logical thought following the simplest 'What if—?' A friend to whom I described this cried, 'That's how I've felt all my life—too small and weak for what people expect from me!' so perhaps I have struck a universal theme. It is not new—look at Gulliver, or Alice down the rabbit hole, or the Borrowers. Maybe we are all too small sometimes. That is an emotional reality. What do we do about it? That is the greater reality.

"The actual process of writing? I stare at the typewriter, my fingernails, leaves outside, or the wall. A few words dribble out. A few more. I go outside to check for fresh eggs or see how noticeably the asparagus has grown since breakfast. I moan through another sentence as painfully as if I give birth to a giraffe, all unwieldy limbs that sprawl too far in a great many directions I wish they didn't. I rewrite it. No better. I make a pot of tea. Write one line. Go measure the asparagus against the height of my nose and talk to a duck. She talks back! I return to the typewriter. Another four words—only one phrase. The tea is cold. I reheat it. The rest of that dangling sentence. . . . I lie down and stare at the ceiling, exhausted.

"Then there are days when my fingers race far faster than I can type. My characters fly rapidly as wind driven clouds across the pages while I try frantically to capture them . . . after, I know how God felt, creating a world in which everything works well. . . .

"I would be nothing else on earth than what I am.

"I was made copy editor and typesetter for a small publishing company located three blocks from my home. I can bring much of the work home. How delighted I am in smoothing out rumpled sentences or setting the spelling straight."

DRUCKER, Malka　1945-

PERSONAL: Born March 14, 1945, in Tucson, Ariz.; daughter of William (a clothing manufacturer) Treiber and Francine (a

MALKA DRUCKER

writer; maiden name, Epstein) Chermak; married Steven Drucker (a certified public accountant), August 20, 1966; children: Ivan, Max. *Education:* University of California, Los Angeles, B.A., 1967; University of Southern California, teaching credential, 1968. *Home:* 863 Manning Ave., Los Angeles, Calif. 90024.

CAREER: Writer, 1975—. *Member:* Society of Children's Book Writers, Association of Jewish Librarians, California Council on Literature for Children and Young People, PEN. *Awards, honors:* Jewish Book Award nomination, 1982, for *Passover: A Season of Freedom,* 1984, for *Shabbat: A Peaceful Island;* Southern California Council on Literature for Children and Young People Award for Excellence in a series, 1982, for the Jewish holiday series.

WRITINGS—Juveniles; all published by Holiday House, except as noted: (With Tom Seaver) *Tom Seaver: Portrait of a Pitcher,* 1978; (with George Foster) *The George Foster Story,* 1979, revised edition, 1980; *Hanukkah: Eight Nights, Eight Lights* (illustrated by Brom Hoban), 1980; *Passover: A Season of Freedom* (illustrated by B. Hoban), 1981; *Rosh Hashanah and Yom Kippur: Sweet Beginnings* (illustrated by B. Hoban), 1981; *Sukkot: A Time to Rejoice* (illustrated by B. Hoban), 1982; *Shabbat: A Peaceful Island* (illustrated by B. Hoban), 1983; (with Elizabeth James) *Series TV: How a Television Show Is Made,* Clarion, 1983; *Celebrating Life: Jewish Rites of Passages,* 1984.

WORK IN PROGRESS: Eliezer Ben-Yehuda: The Reviver of Hebrew, for Dutton.

EDENS, (Bishop) David   1926-

PERSONAL: Born February 11, 1926, in Sumter, S.C.; married wife, Virginia, 1950; children: two. *Education:* Wake Forest College (now Wake Forest University), B.A., 1950; Southern Baptist Theological Seminary, B.D., 1953, Th.M., 1954; Columbia University, Ed.D., 1957. *Office:* Stephens College, Columbia, Mo. 65201.

CAREER: Riverside Hospital, New York, N.Y., chaplain, 1955-57; San Antonio College, San Antonio, Tex., instructor in psychology, marriage, and family life, 1958-67; Stephens College, Columbia, Mo., director of marriage and family program, 1967—. Director of counseling and family life, Trinity Baptist Church, 1957—. *Military service:* U.S. Navy, 1944-46. *Member:* American Psychological Association, American Sociological Association, American Association of Marriage and Family Counselors. *Awards, honors:* Fellow, Merrill-Palmer Institute, 1954-55; fellow, Columbia University, 1956.

WRITINGS: Sexual Understanding among Young Married Adults, Family Life Publications, 1955; (with wife, Virginia Edens) *Why God Gave Children Parents,* Broadman, 1966; (with V. Edens) *Making the Most of Family Worship,* Broadman, 1968; *Teen Sense: A Guide to the Turbulent Teens* (for young adults), Warner Press, 1971; *The Changing Me* (juvenile; illustrated by Bill McPheeters), Broadman, 1973; *Marriage: How to Have It the Way You Want It,* Prentice-Hall, 1981.

ELGIN, Kathleen   1923-

PERSONAL: Born January 13, 1923, in Trenton, N.J.; daughter of Charles P. (an engineer) and Mary (Poore) Elgin. *Education:* Attended Dayton Art Institute, Dayton, Ohio, 1940-43, and Columbia University, 1948-52. *Home:* 1002 Fleming St., Key West, Fla. 33040. *Agent:* Evelyn Singer Agency, Inc., Box 163, Briarcliff Manor, N.Y. 10510.

CAREER: Artist, and author and illustrator of children's books. Began career as an artist working in a glass studio on a window depicting the history of medicine for Mayo Clinic; illustrated technical manuals for U.S. Army Air Forces during World War II; began free-lance illustrating for magazines in New York, N.Y., 1945, and started illustrating books a few years later. *Awards, honors:* Graphic Prize for Children's Books from Bologna Children's Book Fair, 1969, for *The Heart.*

WRITINGS—All self-illustrated: *First Book of Mythology,* F. Watts, 1955; *First Book of Norse Legends,* F. Watts, 1956; *Nun: A Gallery of Sisters,* Random House, 1964; (with John F. Osterritter) *The Ups and Downs of Drugs,* Knopf, 1972; (with J. F. Osterritter) *Twenty-Eight Days,* McKay, 1973; *The Fall Down, Break a Bone, Skin Your Knee, Book,* Walker, 1975.

"Human Body" series; all published by F. Watts: *The Eye,* 1967; *The Ear,* 1967; *The Brain,* 1967; *The Hand,* 1968; *The Heart,* 1968; *The Female Reproductive System,* 1969; *The Male Reproductive System,* 1969; *The Respiratory System,* 1970; *The Skin,* 1970; *The Skeleton,* 1971; *The Glands,* 1971; *The Digestive System,* 1973; *The Muscles,* 1973.

"Freedom to Worship" series; all self-illustrated; all published by McKay: *The Quakers: The Religious Society of Friends,* 1968; *The Mormons: The Church of Jesus Christ of Latter-Day Saints,* 1969; *The Episcopalians: The Protestant Episcopal Church,* 1970; *The Unitarians,* 1971.

Illustrator: Ethel S. Berkley (pseudonym of Ethel S. Berkowitz), *The Size of It: A First Book about Sizes,* W. R. Scott, 1950; E. S. Berkley, *Ups and Downs: A First Book about Space,* W. R. Scott, 1951; May Garelick, *Let's Start Cooking,* W. R. Scott, 1952; Jay Sherman (pseudonym of Jane Sherman), *Real Book about Bugs, Insects and Such,* Garden City Books, 1952; Helen Mears, *First Book of Japan,* F. Watts, 1953; Isabel J. Peterson, compiler, *The First Book of Poetry,* F. Watts, 1953; August W. Derleth, *Land of Grey Gold,* Alad-

DAVID EDENS

din, 1953; Edith E. Sproul, *Science Book of the Human Body*, F. Watts, 1955; Leone Adelson, *All Ready for Winter* (Junior Literary Guild selection), McKay, 1955; L. Adelson, *All Ready for Summer* (Junior Literary Guild selection), McKay, 1956; L. Adelson, *All Ready for School* (Junior Literary Guild selection), McKay, 1957; Millicent E. Selsam, *Plants That Heal*, Morrow, 1959.

KATHLEEN ELGIN

M. E. Selsam, *How to Grow House Plants*, Morrow, 1960; Keith W. Jennison, *From This to That* (Junior Literary Guild selection), McKay, 1961; M. E. Selsam, *Underwater Zoos*, Morrow, 1961; Barnett D. Laschever, *Getting to Know India*, Coward, 1961; Charles R. Joy, *Getting to Know Israel*, Coward, 1961; M. E. Selsam, *Language of Animals*, Morrow, 1962; *Passage to Texas*, Aladdin, 1962; Peter Farb, *The Story of Life: Plants and Animals through the Ages*, Harvey House, 1962; Jane Yolen, *See This Little Line?*, McKay, 1963; M. E. Selsam, *How Animals Live Together*, Morrow, 1963; R. Holland, *Bad Day*, Morrow, 1964; James P. Wood, *Golden Swan*, Seabury, 1965; Stuart D. Currie, *Beginnings of the Church*, John Knox, 1967; John Pallister and John Ripley Forbes, *In the Steps of the Great Entomologist, Frank Eugene Lutz*, M. Evans, 1967; J. R. Forbes, *In the Steps of the Great American Zoologist, William Temple Hornaday*, M. Evans, 1967; Robert Froman, *Billions of Years of You*, World Publishing, 1967; R. Froman, *Great Reaching Out: How Living Beings Communicate*, World Publishing, 1968; James Tasker, *African Treehouse*, Harvey House, 1973.

SIDELIGHTS: At sixteen Elgin attended Dayton Art Institute where she developed an interest in stained glass. She later worked in a glass studio for two years on the execution of a "History of Medicine" window for the Mayo Clinic.

During World War II Elgin illustrated manuals for the Air Force. After the war, her career branched into free-lance illustration work, first for advertising agencies and later for books. Besides illustrating children's books written by others, Elgin has written and illustrated her own books. She has also exhibited her work at one-man shows, including: a 1962 New York show of her brush drawings, a 1981 one-man exhibition in New York City, and a 1983 show in Key West, Florida.

Outside of art, one of Elgin's interests is American history. She feels that "it is vital to relate the history of past truths and mistakes to today." Many of her self-illustrated books reflect her interest in the past. She was responsible for the text and

(From *Twenty-Eight Days* by Kathleen Elgin and John F. Osterritter. Illustrated by Kathleen Elgin.)

illustration of the books for children in the "Freedom to Worship" series, published by McKay. Concentrating on events in nineteenth century America, the books showed how people of faith, living in times as perilous as ours, tried to solve the issues of their day. Each book acted as an introduction to the religion discussed, presented an outstanding individual of the sect, and emphasized the effect of the individual's life and work on American history.

FOR MORE INFORMATION SEE: Bertha Mahony Miller, and others, compilers, *Illustrators of Children's Books: 1946-1956*, Horn Book, 1958; Lee Kingman and others, compilers, *Illustrators of Children's Books: 1957-1966*, Horn Book, 1968.

ELLIS, Mel(vin Richard) 1912-1984

OBITUARY NOTICE—See sketch in *SATA* Volume 7: Born February 21, 1912, in Beaver Dam, Wis.; died September 1, 1984, in Waukesha, Wis. Journalist and author. Ellis had been a columnist and contributor to the *Milwaukee Journal* for more than thirty-five years and had served as an associate editor of

Field and Stream for twelve years. A winner of five awards from the Wisconsin Council of Writers, he received an honorable mention in the juvenile category for *Sidewalk Indian* in 1975 and was named runner up for another juvenile book, *The Wild Horse Killers*, in 1977. Two of his other books, *Wild Goose, Brother Goose* and *Flight of the White Wolf*, were made into Walt Disney movies. He also wrote *Run, Rainey, Run, Sad Song of the Coyote, Ghost Dog of Killicut, When Lightning Strikes*, and *Caribou Crossing. For More Information See: Contemporary Authors*, Volumes 13-16, revised, Gale, 1975. *Obituaries: Chicago Tribune*, September 4, 1984.

EMMENS, Carol Ann 1944-

PERSONAL: Born October 12, 1944, in Newark, N.J.; daughter of Carmine John and Antoinette (Rosano) Rossi; married Christopher Emmens, June 26, 1966; children: Scott Christopher. *Education:* Fairleigh Dickinson University, B.S., 1966; Rutgers University, M.L.S., 1971. *Religion:* Society of Friends (Quakers). *Home:* 213 Highfield Lane, Nutley, N.J. 07110.

... **The top performers of the decade sang at the three-day music festival in Woodstock, New York, in 1969. Over 400,000 fans showed up, and traffic was blocked for miles.** ■ (From *An Album of the Sixties* by Carol A. Emmens. Photograph courtesy of United Press International.)

CAREER: Rutherford Junior High School, Rutherford, N.J., English teacher, 1966-69; New York Public Library, Donnell Library Center, New York, N.Y., young adult librarian, 1966-70; Belleville Public Library, Belleville, N.J., librarian, 1970-71, part-time reference librarian, 1971-73; Educational Film Library Association, New York, N.Y., film reference librarian, 1974-77; free-lance writer, 1977—. Assistant editor of *Sightlines,* 1971-77; television editor of *Children's World;* video editor for *School Library Journal.* Writer, host, and producer of "TV Tips and Thoughts," a television program for United Artists and Columbia cable television, 1981. *Member:* Society of Children's Book Writers, National Organization of Women.

WRITINGS: Famous People on Film, Scarecrow, 1977; *An Audio-Visual Guide to American Holidays,* Scarecrow, 1978; *Short Stories on Film,* Libraries Unlimited, 1978; *An Album of Television* (juvenile), F. Watts, 1979; *An Album of the Sixties* (juvenile), F. Watts, 1981; *Stunts and Stunt People* (juvenile), F. Watts, 1982. Contributor of articles and reviews to magazines, including *Scholastic Scope, Class, Right On!* and *Ms.*

Filmstrips: "Persian Tales" (four-part series), ACI Media, 1979; "Make-It-Yourself Games" (four-part series), ACI Media, 1979; "The Middle East" (eight-part series), Denoyer-Geppert, 1980.

WORK IN PROGRESS: A biography of John Lennon, publication by F. Watts; a book on suffrage, publication by F. Watts.

SIDELIGHTS: "It is important for parents and educators to discuss television with children and to note its effects on them. But let's not lose sight of the fact that in homes where love, honesty, and humanistic values are in evidence every day, TV will not harm our children. Let's work on creating an atmosphere of caring and sharing so we will not have to worry so much about television."

HOBBIES AND OTHER INTERESTS: Flying, travel, silk, antique jewelry, indoor plants, watching television.

EMMONS, Della (Florence) Gould   1890-1983

OBITUARY NOTICE: Born August 12, 1890, in Glencoe, Minn.; died November 6, 1983, in Tacoma, Wash. Author. Best known for her stories about pioneer days, Emmons wrote her first book, *Sacajawea of the Shoshones,* while traveling West with her husband. A recreation of the Lewis and Clark expedition ordered by President Thomas Jefferson in 1804, the juvenile book was made into the Paramount motion picture, "The Far Horizon." Among Emmons's other books are *Leschi of the Nisquallies, Jay Gould's Million Dollar Gems,* and *Northwest History in Action,* a collection of plays and stories that has been used as a text in junior and senior high schools. Some of her juvenile plays include "The Charm of the Seventh Orphan," "A Territory Is Born," "Medicine Creek Treaty," and "Out to Win." *For More Information See: Minnesota Writers,* T. S. Dennison & Co., 1961; *Who's Who Among Pacific Northwest Authors,* 2nd edition, Pacific Northwest Library Association, 1969; *Who's Who of American Women,* 9th edition, Marquis, 1975; *International Authors and Writers Who's Who,* 8th edition, Melrose, 1977. *Obituaries: New York Times,* November 10, 1983; *Washington Post,* November 11, 1983.

ERNST, (Lyman) John   1940-
(Dorothy A. Chernoff, David Allen Clark)

PERSONAL: Born September 1, 1940, in New York, N.Y.; son of Richard Charles (an investor) and Susan (Bloomingdale) Ernst; married Bronwyn Jones, June 24, 1962; married Kathryn Fitzgerald (an editor and writer), December 11, 1971; married Margot Paul, December 31, 1980; children: Alexandra, Matthew Lyman, Jessica Paul. *Education:* Harvard University, B.A., 1962; University College, Oxford, graduate study, 1962-63. *Home and office address:* R.D. 2, Box 344, Red Hook, N.Y. 12571.

CAREER: Doubleday & Co., Inc., New York, N.Y., 1963-71, began as editorial assistant, became associate editor, then assistant manager, editorial director of books for young readers, 1968-71; Manuscript Evaluation Service, Inc., Red Hook, N.Y., president, 1974-76; Lyman Realty Corp., president, 1980—. Member of board of directors of Children's Book Council, 1970-71.

*WRITINGS—*For young people: (Editor) *Favorite Sleuths: Ellery Queen [and others],* Doubleday, 1965; (editor) Rudyard Kipling, *Phantoms and Fantasies,* Doubleday, 1965; (editor, under pseudonym Dorothy A. Chernoff) *Call Us Americans,* Doubleday, 1968; (editor, under pseudonym David Allen Clark) *Jokes, Puns, and Riddles,* Doubleday, 1968; *Escape King: The Story of Harry Houdini* (illustrated by S. Martin and others), Prentice-Hall, 1975; *Jesse James* (illustrated by Ted Miller), Prentice-Hall, 1976.

WORK IN PROGRESS: Book about American Indians.

HOBBIES AND OTHER INTERESTS: Poetry, classic Navajo blankets, skiing, travel in England, France, Spain, Italy, Germany, Peru and Japan.

FOR MORE INFORMATION SEE: New York Times Book Review, June 16, 1968.

FARMER, Penelope (Jane)   1939-

BRIEF ENTRY: Born June 14, 1939, in Westerham, Kent, England. Full-time writer. Farmer received a B.A. with second-class honors from St. Anne's College and later was awarded a diploma in social studies from Bedford College. From about 1961 to 1963, Farmer taught school in London for the London County Council Education Department. Since that time she has written several books of fiction for children. She is best known for her fantasy works which include *The Summer Birds* (an ALA Notable Book), *Emma in Winter,* and *Charlotte Sometimes,* all featuring the characters Charlotte and Emma Makepeace. Reviewers have praised Farmer's originality in blending fantasy with realism. *Times Literary Supplement* commented that Farmer can "slip easily from the world of everyday reality to that of enchantment without ruffling a hair." In *A Castle of Bone* (McElderry Book, 1972), a magical cupboard leads four children into surrealistic adventure. *New York Times Book Review* found it "an exhilarating, troubling book, unlike any other, and unforgettable," while *Library Journal* noted the "believable characters, and . . . spellbinding descriptions." The same qualities are evident in *William and Mary: A Story* (McElderry Book, 1974), described by *Bulletin of the Center for Children's Books* as having "strongly defined characters . . . a sustaining theme . . . and a strong evocation of place."

Other books by Farmer include the retelling *Daedalus and Icarus* (Harcourt, 1971), the young adult novel *Year King* (McElderry Book, 1977), and the collection of myths *Beginnings: Creation Myths of the World* (McElderry Book, 1979). *Home:* 39 Mount Ararat Rd., Richmond, Surrey, England. *For More Information See:* "Penelope Farmer: The Popular British Novelist Talks about the Craft of Writing" (sound recording), Center for Cassette Studies, 1975; *Fourth Book of Junior Authors,* H. W. Wilson, 1978; *Contemporary Science Fiction Authors II,* Gale, 1979; *Contemporary Authors, New Revision Series,* Volume 9, Gale, 1983: *Twentieth-Century Children's Writers,* 2nd edition, St. Martin's, 1983.

FLEISCHMAN, Paul   1952-

PERSONAL: Born September 5, 1952, in Monterey, Calif.; son of Albert Sidney (an author of books for children) and Beth (a brailer; maiden name, Taylor) Fleischman; married Becky Mojica (a nurse), December 15, 1978. *Education:* Attended University of California, Berkeley, 1970-72; University of New Mexico, 1975-77. *Home:* 1101 Vassar Dr. N.E., Albuquerque, N.M. 87106.

CAREER: Author. Has been employed as a bagel baker, bookstore clerk, and proofreader. *Member:* Society of Children's Book Writers. *Awards, honors: The Half-a-Moon Inn* received the juvenile award from the Commonwealth Club of California, and was selected as a Golden Kite Honor Book by the Society of Children's Book Writers, both 1980; *Graven Images: Three Stories* was selected as a Newbery Honor Book, 1983; *Path*

of the Pale Horse* was selected as a Golden Kite Honor Book by the Society of Children's Book Writers, 1983.

WRITINGS—All juvenile: *The Birthday Tree* (illustrated by Marcia Sewall), Harper, 1979; *The Half-a-Moon Inn* (illustrated by Kathy Jacobi), Harper, 1980; *Graven Images: Three Stories* (illustrated by Andrew Glass), Harper, 1982; *The Animal Hedge* (illustrated by Lydia Dabcovich), Dutton, 1983; *Path of the Pale Horse,* Harper, 1983; *Phoebe Danger, Detective, in the Case of the Two-Minute Cough* (illustrated by Margot Apple), Houghton, 1983; *Finzel the Farsighted* (illustrated by M. Sewall), Dutton, 1983.

WORK IN PROGRESS: Four stories entitled *Coming-and-Going Men,* for Harper; a book of poems entitled *Birdsongs,* for Harper; a picture book, *Shadow Play; Prelude and Fugue,* a novella based on the musical form of the same name.

SIDELIGHTS: "My father, as it happens, writes children's books—books he read aloud to us chapter by chapter as he wrote them. So, writing for children always seemed as honorable and possible profession.

"Despite which, I was never much of a reader as a child and have always been more attracted to music than to books. Had I the talent to write music, I'd be doing that instead. I don't have the talent, but I've found it possible to bring many musical elements into my writing: my sentences all scan (or are supposed to), as if set to music; I spend half my time attending to sound as opposed to sense (alliteration, internal rhyme). I enjoy writing long, multi-clause sentences, working out their shapes as if they were musical phrases. *Birdsong,* a forthcom-

PAUL FLEISCHMAN

One night a sharp wind sprang up and rain spattered the earth. ■ (From *The Birthday Tree* by Paul Fleischman. Illustrated by Marcia Sewall.)

ing book, is a set of poems, for two voices to be read simultaneously, just as in a musical duet. My current work is modeled on the form of a prelude and fugue. The story, I should add, I regard as the foremost element. But playing with sounds and rhythms and shapes—the writing out of the story—is the most satisfying part of the process for me.''

FOX, Mary Virginia   1919-

BRIEF ENTRY: Born November 17, 1919, in Richmond, Va. An author of biographies for children, Fox began her career as a short story writer. A visit to New York and the Statue of Liberty inspired her first book, *Apprentice to Liberty* (Abingdon, 1960). Since then she has written several biographies of historical and prominent figures whose personal achievements have influenced the political and governmental character of the United States. In 1976 *Lady for the Defense: A Biography of Belva Lockwood* (Harcourt, 1975) was runner-up for the Council of Wisconsin Book Award. Described by *Horn Book* as ''meaty and inspirational,'' the book is considered a credible depiction of the first woman to run for the presidency of the United States. In *Mr. President: The Story of Ronald Reagan*

(Enslow, 1982), Fox focuses on Reagan's personal life and experiences en route to the presidency. As *School Library Journal* observed, she makes the book highly readable through the ''little-known personal glimpses [that] provide insight into Reagan's personal philosophy.'' Fox is also the author of radio scripts and travel articles. Her other juvenile biographies include *Ethel Barrymore: A Portrait* (Reilly & Lee, 1971), *Pacifists: Adventures in Courage* (Reilly & Lee, 1971), *Barbara Walters: The News Her Way* (Dillon, 1980), *Jane Fonda: Something to Fight For* (Dillon, 1980), *Jane Goodall: Living Chimp Style* (Dillon, 1981), and *Justice Sandra Day O'Connor* (Enslow, 1983). *For More Information See: Contemporary Authors,* Volumes 29-32, revised, Gale, 1978.

'Reeling and Writhing, of course, to begin with,' the Mock Turtle replied; 'and then the different branches of Arithmetic—Ambition, Distraction, Uglification, and Derision.'

—Lewis Carroll
(pseudonym of Charles L. Dodgson)
(From *Alice's Adventures in Wonderland*)

"I'll be Fourth-of-July Bunny!" he said to himself. And he started re-painting his eggs red, white and blue. ■ (From *The Easter Bunny That Overslept* by Priscilla and Otto Friedrich. Illustrated by Adrienne Adams.)

FRIEDRICH, Priscilla 1927-

PERSONAL: Born August 13, 1927, in Peru, South America; daughter of Charles and Hilde Boughton; married Otto Friedrich (a writer), April 13, 1950; children: Liesel, Molly (Mrs. Mark Carson), Nicholas, Amelia, Charles Anthony. *Education:* Attended Bryn Mawr College, 1945-47. *Religion:* Episcopalian. *Address:* Box 549, Locust Valley, N.Y. 11560.

CAREER: Author of books for children.

WRITINGS—All for children; all with husband, Otto Friedrich; all published by Lothrop, except as indicated: *The Easter Bunny That Overslept* (illustrated by Adrienne Adams), 1957, new edition, 1983; *Clean Clarence* (illustrated by Louis Slobodkin), 1959; *Sir Alva and the Wicked Wizard* (illustrated by Talivaldis Stubis), 1960; *The Marshmallow Ghosts* (illustrated by L. Slobodkin), 1960; *The Wishing Well in the Woods* (illustrated by Roger Duvoisin), 1961; *Noah Shark's Ark* (illustrated by Peter Fellin), A. S. Barnes, 1962; *The Christmas Star* (illustrated

by Burton Groedel), A. S. Barnes, 1962; *The April Umbrella* (illustrated by R. Duvoisin), 1963; *The League of Unusual Animals* (illustrated by Carol Rogers), Steck, 1965.

FUJIKAWA, Gyo 1908-

PERSONAL: Born November 3, 1908, in Berkeley, Calif.; daughter of Hikozo (an interpreter) and Yu (a journalist and poet) Fujikawa. *Education:* Attended Chouinard Art Institute. *Residence:* New York, N.Y.

CAREER: Illustrator and author of books for children. Walt Disney Studios, Burbank, Calif., designer in the promotion department, 1939-41; Fox Film Co., New York, N.Y., worked in advertising and promotion, 1941-43; William Douglas McAdams (pharmaceutical advertising agency), New York, N.Y., art director, 1943-51. Work includes three U.S. commemorative postage stamps including Lady Bird Johnson's

(Jacket illustration by Gyo Fujikawa from *That's Not Fair* by Gyo Fujikawa.)

I'm up! I'm up! ■ (From *Oh, What a Busy Day!* by Gyo Fujikawa. Illustrated by the author.)

beautification program; Eskimo Pies advertisements; Beech-Nut Baby Foods advertisements; cover illustrations for the *Saturday Evening Post*. Instructor of color and design, Chouinard Art Institute, 1933-39. *Awards, honors: Oh, What a Busy Day* was chosen for inclusion in the American Institute of Graphic Arts Book Show, 1976.

WRITINGS—All for children; all self-illustrated; all published by Grosset: *Babies*, 1963; *Baby Animals*, 1963; *A to Z Picture Book*, 1974; *Let's Eat*, 1975; *Let's Play*, 1975; *Puppies, Pussycats, and Other Friends*, 1975; *Sleepy Time*, 1975; *Gyo Fujikawa's Oh, What a Busy Day!*, 1976; *Babes of the Wild*, 1977; *Betty Bear's Birthday*, 1977; *Can You Count?*, 1977; *Our Best Friends*, 1977; *Millie's Secret*, 1978; *Let's Grow a Garden*, 1978; *My Favorite Thing*, 1978; *Surprise! Surprise!*, 1978; *Come Follow Me . . . to the Secret World of Elves and Fairies and Gnomes and Trolls*, 1979; *Jenny Learns a Lesson*, 1980; *Welcome Is a Wonderful Word*, 1980; *Come Out and Play*, 1981; *Dreamland*, 1981; *Fairyland*, 1981; *Faraway Friends*, 1981; *The Flyaway Kite*, 1981; *Good Morning!*, 1981; *Here I Am*, 1981; *Jenny and Jupie*, 1981; *The Magic Show*, 1981; *Make-Believe*, 1981; *My Animal Friends*, 1981; *One, Two, Three, A Counting Book*, 1981; *Shags Has a Dream*, 1981; *Mother Goose*, 1981; *A Tiny Word Book*, 1981; *Year In, Year Out*, 1981; *Jenny and Jupie to the Rescue*, 1982; *Fraidy Cat*, 1982; *Me Too!*, 1982; *Sam's All-Wrong Day*, 1982; *Shags Finds a Kitten*, 1983; *That's Not Fair*, 1983.

Illustrator: Robert L. Stevenson, *A Child's Garden of Verses*, Grosset, 1957; Clement C. Moore, *The Night Before Christmas*, Grosset, 1961; *Mother Goose*, Grosset, 1968; *A Child's Book of Poems*, Grosset, 1969; Eve Morel, editor, *Fairy Tales and Fables*, Grosset, 1970, revised edition published as *Fairy Tales*, Platt, 1980; *Poems for Children*, Platt, 1980.

SIDELIGHTS: Fujikawa's first name, Gyo, comes from an ancient Chinese emperor whom her father admired. Even though "Gyo" is a masculine Japanese name similar to "Charles" in America, the name stuck.

Born in Berkeley, California in 1908, Fujikawa and her brother grew up in an Asian household. Their father was a Japanese translator for Van Kamp Seafoods Company and their mother was a Japanese journalist, poet, and an early suffragette. The Japanese children received a traditional American schooling.

Showing an early propensity toward art, Fujikawa studied at the Chouinard Art Institute in Los Angeles on a scholarship. "I have no degrees from Chouinard. In my day (pre-World War II) degrees were not given. I attended Chouinard from 1926 on, through several years. Somewhere from about 1930 I was a free-lance artist in Los Angeles. I was teaching color and design also, but I continued to take classes in drawing and painting from time to time. After I joined the Disney Studios I took night classes at Chouinard in painting until I left Los Angeles to go to New York. You could call me a perennial student.

"1932 and 1933 saw me living in Tokyo, absorbing my cultural background. I then returned to Los Angeles and resumed free-lancing. In 1937 I took a trip to New York, fell in love with the city, and vowed to return someday.

"1939-41 were happy years in the employ of the Walt Disney Studios in Burbank, California. I was put in charge of art-directing and designing promotional material for 'Fantasia.' The major work was the designing of the Simon & Schuster book, *Fantasia*, written by Deems Taylor.

"In early spring, 1941, at the end of my stint with 'Fantasia,' I was sent to New York to work in Disney merchandising, of which the books were an important part. As a Disney employee for a short time, I designed Disney books in an office at Western Printing and Publishing. (They printed and published Disney books.) Although I did not work with them, I was fortunate to meet Georges Duplaix, Dick Small and Lucille Ogle there. They were responsible for the forward thrust that children's books were making creatively at that time. It was heady and exciting to watch these talented people launching a new era in well-designed and imaginative children's books.

"As enthusiastic as I was to be involved with books, to continue in this field was not to be. I was in it only a few short months when I was offered a job as a designer with the Hal Horne Organization in motion picture advertising and promotion. It was while I was working here that Pearl Harbor occurred.

"In 1942 the Horne Organization was absorbed into the 20th Century-Fox advertising department in New York. I designed movie ads there. My time with 20th Century-Fox was very short. I was grateful for the job. There was a war on and as a Japanese-American I would have had a hard time had I not had a job.

"Sometime during 1943 I was offered a position of art director with William Douglas McAdams, an advertising agency specializing in medical and pharmaceutical accounts. I accepted. I stayed with McAdams eight years and left to become a free-lance artist in 1951. While pursuing this endeavor, in 1955 or 1956 I was approached by Doris Duenewald, juvenile editor of Grossett & Dunlap to illustrate *A Child's Garden of Verses*. I took it on the proviso that I work on it between my commercial assignments. It was a dream of a book for me to do and I wanted to very much. There was also a challenge of whether or not there would be an acceptance by the buying public to my particular style."

As a free-lance commercial artist Fujikawa's baby drawings were chosen for baby food campaigns, and her illustrations of children, animals, and food appeared in leading magazines such as *Family Circle, Ladies' Home Journal, McCalls*, and *The Saturday Evening Post*. She has also designed United States postage stamps. In 1960 she designed the centennial stamp honoring the first treaty between the United States and Japan.

Since the 1963 publication of *Babies*, Fujikawa's books have been translated into seventeen languages and are read in more than twenty-two countries. At the suggestion of Grosset & Dunlap editor Doris Duenewald, Fujikawa illustrated *A Child's Garden of Verses*, which initiated her study of the world of children. "For a long time I thought I would like to draw pictures for children about children. With the Stevenson verses I had a chance to see if there was a market for my ideas. Besides, it was fun to illustrate a good book."

In the late sixties, after illustrating *Mother Goose, A Child's Book of Poems*, and *Fairy Tales and Fables*, Fujikawa decided to develop her own stories and concentrate on the two-to-six age group. "To complete one little book takes months of engrossing work; sometimes I don't go out of my apartment studio for days on end. But it is so rewarding to think that I can reach out and touch small children through words and pictures and make friends with them." Her most popular books include: *A to Z Picture Book, Oh, What a Busy Day!, Come Follow Me*, two series of board books, and her "Checkerboard Books."

Beginning in 1974, Fujikawa has devoted herself exclusively to children's books. The year 1983 marked the publication of

GYO FUJIKAWA

her thirty-second juvenile book. ''In illustrating for children, what I relish the most is trying to satisfy the constant questions in the back of my mind—will this picture capture a child's imagination? What can I do to enhance it further? Does it help to tell a story?

''I am *far* from being successful (whatever that means) but I am ever so grateful to small readers who find something in any book of mine.

''Sometimes I wonder if I have any convictions about what I do. I think I do, but in the daily pressures of working on a book I have to bring myself back constantly to what my purpose is—to entertain children from the printed page.''

FOR MORE INFORMATION SEE: American Artist, May, 1954; Diana Klemin, *The Art of Art for Children's Books,* Clarkson Potter, 1966; *Illustrators of Children's Books: 1957-1966,* Horn Book, 1968; *Publishers Weekly,* January 4, 1971; Selma C. Lanes, *Down the Rabbit Hole,* Atheneum, 1971; *Illustrators of Books for Young People,* 2nd edition, Scarecrow, 1975; *Fourth Book of Junior Authors and Illustrators,* Wilson, 1978.

GARDAM, Jane 1928-

PERSONAL: Born July 11, 1928, in Coatham, Yorkshire, England; daughter of William (a schoolmaster) and Kathleen (Helm) Pearson; married David Gardam (a Queen's counsel), April 20, 1952; children: Timothy, Mary, Thomas. *Education:* Bedford College, London, B.A. (honors), 1949, graduate study, 1949-52. *Politics:* Liberal. *Religion:* Anglo-Catholic. *Home:*

53 Ridgeway Pl., London SW19 4SP, England; and Fell House, Hartley Kirk by Stephen, Westmorland, England.

CAREER: Weldons Ladies Journal, London, England, sub-editor, 1952-53; *Time and Tide,* London, assistant literary editor, 1953-55, author, 1971—. Organizer of hospital libraries for Red Cross, 1950. *Member:* Royal Society of Literature (fellow). *Awards, honors: A Long Way from Verona* received special mention from the Guardian Award for children's fiction, and was selected an honor book by *Book World's* Spring Book Festival award, both 1972; David Higham Prize for fiction, 1975, for *Black Faces, White Faces; Boston Globe-Horn Book* honor book for text, 1974, for *The Summer after the Funeral;* Winifred Holtby Memorial Prize, 1976, for *Black Faces, White Faces;* Whitbread Literary Award, 1981, for *The Hollow Land;* Carnegie Medal ''highly recommended'' award, for *The Hollow Land* and ''commended'' award, for *Bridget and William,* both 1983.

WRITINGS: A Few Fair Days (short stories; illustrated by Peggy Fortnum), Macmillan, 1971; *A Long Way from Verona*

"The Princess of Cleves," said Lucy, looking down her nose, **"has wigs of her own. . . ."** She picked up an eiderdown of cress and arranged it on her head. ∎ (From *A Few Fair Days* by Jane Gardam. Illustrated by Peggy Fortnum.)

(novel; ALA Notable Book), Macmillan, 1971; *The Summer after the Funeral* (novel), Macmillan, 1973; *Black Faces, White Faces* (short stories), Hamish Hamilton, 1975, published as *The Pineapple Bay Hotel,* Morrow, 1976; *Bilgewater* (novel), Hamish Hamilton, 1976, Greenwillow, 1977; *God on the Rocks* (novel), Morrow, 1978; *The Sidmouth Letters,* Hamish Hamilton, 1980; *Bridget and William* (illustrated by Janet Rawlings), MacRae, 1981, F. Watts, 1983; *The Hollow Land* (illustrated by J. Rawlings; ALA Notable Book), MacRae, 1981, Greenwillow, 1982; *Horse,* F. Watts, 1982; *The Pangs of Love,* Hamish Hamilton, 1982; *Kit,* MacRae, 1983. Contributor of short stories to magazines.

WORK IN PROGRESS: Another short story collection; *Through the Doll's House Door,* a book for children; a novel.

SIDELIGHTS: Gardam read few books as a child. ". . . It seems extraordinary that our house was a schoolmaster's house, but there were only three bookshelves. My father taught mathematics and physics, and I don't think had ever read a novel. My mother was an Anglo-Catholic, and all her books seemed to be by Dean Inge. There was no book shop in the town, no public library, no library at my kindergarten or at the junior part of the high school to which I went when I was eleven. In the senior school there was the county library cupboard, locked with a padlock, which contained forty books, changed at monthly intervals and unlocked for an hour on alternate Wednesdays. I went back to my old school three years ago to present the prizes there—I had written a book about it, a book which I had thought modestly (like Dickens) might cause the establishment to be closed. But no. I was invited back and shown a library of such splendor that I was humbled and ashamed and decided that the bi-Wednesday cupboard must have been a myth. And it certainly seems a myth that through this cupboard . . . I achieved a place to read English literature at a university and, several happy years afterward, in the reading room of the British Museum." [Jane Gardam, "On Writing for Children: Some Wasps in the Marmalade, Part II," *Horn Book,* December, 1978.¹]

A children's writer, Gardam commented on the development of her career. ". . . Each book I have written I have desperately wanted to write. Whether or not they had anything to do with children has never occurred to me. . . . I have not the faintest idea where I am going, whom I am writing for, or why I am compelled to write fiction at all. . . .

"Once upon a time I did try to write a children's book—a book children would really love. I wrote it in the early sixties in the public library at Wimbledon after dropping my eldest children at their nursery school. I wrote painlessly for two hours a day with a smile upon my face.

". . . My book was called 'The Astonishing Vicarage' and I wrote away among all the other Wimbledon mothers writing books with roughly the same titles. . . . When I had finished—it was a book about boarding-school children, tunnels, butterfly collections, and clergymen—I confidently sent if off to a distinguished publishing house where I had a friend, and expected to hear from her immediately.

"But time passed and grew heavy, and it was several weeks before an embarrassed voice on the telephone asked if she could talk to me about 'The Astonishing Vicarage.' . . . 'The book is funny,' she said, 'but it is very strange.'

"So I burnt it up, thank goodness, for it was quite hideously bad, not analyzing at that moment the line—if there is one—

JANE GARDAM

between the novel and the tale for the young, which has always, anyway, been a very wavering one.

". . . If writing a book for children was beyond me, considering a void was harder still. I returned . . . to an almost bookless life—shepherd's pie by day and sewing name tapes by night and only the old comforters to read to the children of an evening, like *Biggles* and *Tin-Tin* and Beatrix Potter and Laura Ingalls Wilder and Richmal Crompton's *William.* It was a harrowing time, ending after some years when it occurred to me to write a book which sprang from a single image of a child very young, under five, alone on a long beach, and to try to recreate the mystery of this time, the temporary freedom from fear and anxiety and the need for people which occurs now and then in very early childhood.

". . . Both characters in fiction and children often need to be left alone to grow. Children ought not to be in need of consolation all the time, of fantasy, of myth, of being stroked like queen bees. In fact, I think it's bad for them.

"So I tried to describe childhood in very bare words and clear colors, and whether I thought I was writing poetry or painting, I don't know. The exercise was impossible: trying to recreate moments of absolute peace that one is lucky if one remembers at all as soon as one is out of the pram—moments which appear afterward to be on the edge of dream. I didn't bring the experiment off at all, but I liked trying. It felt like real work, and when the book was published as a children's book, the critics said that I had entered the field of children's literature."

[Jane Gardam, "On Writing for Children: Some Wasps in the Marmalade, Part I," *Horn Book,* October, 1978.[2]]

". . . In the first book there was a sort of seed of a second. I wanted to examine somebody growing up in the landscape I had described which was then partly removed from her by a war, and I had touched on this in the last page or two of my first book.

"I wrote a few new chapters of this new book. They were no good, so I did them again. Then what I was doing got hold of me, and I could think of nothing else. The girl in the new book possessed me. When I'd finished with her—and what a small step on I'd got! How little I knew of her and what she would become and when; or if there is any when, or becoming—or real understanding!—; when I'd finished with her, I felt quite lost." [Jane Gardam, "Mrs. Hookaneye and I," in *The Thorny Paradise: Writers on Writing for Children,* edited by Edward Blishen, Kestrel, 1975.[3]]

"And when I wrote [*A Long Way from Verona*] about an older child and found that I was now called a children's writer, I was very pleased. The field was interesting, and I certainly didn't make for the gate. Once . . . I stepped outside to write a book about Jamaica which would not interest any child unless he were very peculiar—it wouldn't, as Robert Louis Stevenson said, 'fetch the kids.' But even though, perhaps because, the critics said that they were pleased that I had moved to something serious, I found myself back in the field again writing another book about a child. . . ."[2]

". . . I write only to entertain. . . . I can only write very tame tales, mostly about the tragicomedy of being young. I sometimes even sing of vicars' daughters. If people read my books, and particularly if they sometimes laugh at them, I could not ask for any more."[1]

FOR MORE INFORMATION SEE: Jane Gardam, "Mrs. Hookaneye and I," *The Thorny Paradise: Writers on Writing for Children,* edited by Edward Blishen, Kestrel, 1975; J. Gardam, "On Writing for Children: Some Wasps in the Marmalade," Part I, *Horn Book,* October, 1978, Part II, December, 1978; D. L. Kirkpatrick, *Twentieth-Century Children's Writers,* St. Martin's, 1978.

GARRET, Maxwell R. 1917-

PERSONAL: Born April 18, 1917, in New York, N.Y.; son of Harry and Esther (Lieber) Goldstein; married Diana Rosen, April 3, 1943; children: Roger, Roberta, Esther, Bruce. *Education:* City College of New York (now of the City University of New York), B.Ed., 1939; University of Illinois, M.S., 1942; further study at Washington and Lee University, 1943 and 1945; accredited fencing master by the National Fencing Coaches Association of America (now United States Fencing Coaches Association). *Home:* 633 Easterly Pkwy., State College, Pa. 16801. *Office:* Pennsylvania State University, 301 Recreation Building, University Park, Pa. 16802.

CAREER: Teacher of health education at public schools in New York, N.Y., 1939-41 and 1946; University of Illinois, Urbana, fencing coach, 1940-42 and 1946-72, instructor, 1947-53, assistant professor, 1953-58, associate professor of recreation, 1958-72; Pennsylvania State University, University Park, associate professor of recreation and parks, 1972-82, varsity fencing coach, 1972-82. Director, Camp Illini, 1954-68, and Israel

MAXWELL R. GARRET

Academy for Fencing Teachers, 1969-70. U.S. fencing coach, World University Games, Torino, Italy, 1970, World Fencing Championships, Ankara, Turkey, 1970, Junior World Championships, South Bend, Ind., 1971, and Maccabiah Games, 1981, United States Fencing Team manager, National Sports Festival, Colorado Springs, Colo., 1983. *Military service:* U.S. Army Air Forces, 1942-46.

MEMBER: National Recreation and Park Association, National Education Association, National Fencing Coaches Association of America (now United States Fencing Coaches Association; president, 1982-84), U.S. Fencing Association (member of board of directors, 1982-84), Olympic Fencing Committee, 1982, U.S. Academy of Arms, American Society of Testing and Materials, American Camping Association, American Youth Hostels, Pennsylvania Recreation and Park Association, National Collegiate Athletic Association, B'nai B'rith, Alpha Epsilon Pi, Chi Gamma Iota, Phi Delta Kappa, Phi Epsilon Kappa. *Awards, honors:* Certificate of merit from the Amateur Fencers League of America, 1952; Fred K. Moskowitz Award from Central Illinois Council of B'nai B'rith, 1958; named B'nai B'rith man of the year, 1959; elected to Helm's Hall of Fame for Fencing, 1960; named fencing coach of the year, 1962 and 1965; named National Fencing Coach of Israel, 1969-70; inducted into City College of New York Athletic Hall of Fame, 1975.

WRITINGS: (Consultant) *How to Improve Your Fencing,* Athletic Institute, 1960; (with Mary F. Heinecke) *Fencing,* Sterling, 1961, revised edition, Allyn & Bacon, 1971; *Science-Hobby Book of Boating* (juvenile), Pastimes (Morton Grove, Ill.), 1967, revised edition, Lerner, 1968; (with Mary Heinecke

Poulson) *Foil Fencing: Skills, Safety, Operations, and Responsibilities,* Pennsylvania State University, 1981.

Contributor of articles to journals, including *Parks and Recreation, Physical Educator, Illinois Parks, Pennsylvania Recreation and Parks.* Contributing editor, *American Fencing,* 1950-52; member of editorial board, *Physical Educator,* 1958-61, and *Mentor,* 1958-68; editor, *The Swordmaster Journal,* 1982—.

SIDELIGHTS: ''Fencing, camping, and all forms of physical and cultural recreational activities should be considered lifelong pursuits. They can provide enjoyment, improved health, and well-being for all participants. I have always had a keen interest in helping young people to develop their utmost potential through such activities.''

HOBBIES AND OTHER INTERESTS: Athletics, carpentry, camping, dancing, reading, writing, music.

GILLIAM, Stan 1946-

PERSONAL: Born April 16, 1946, in Kannapolis, N.C.; son of Lawrence F. (in newspaper advertising) and Idelle (a secretary; maiden name, Collins) Gilliam. *Education:* University of North Carolina, Chapel Hill, B.A., 1968, M.Ed., 1982, Greensboro, M.F.A., 1972. *Home:* 122 Hazel Dr., Dalton, Ga. 30720.

CAREER: Livingstone College, Salisbury, N.C., art instructor, 1972-74; free-lance artist, 1975—. *Wartime service:* Civilian Public Service, 1969-71. *Member:* American Association of Museums, Georgia Association for Instructional Technology.

ILLUSTRATOR—Juvenile, except as noted: Fred D'Ignazio, *Katie and the Computer,* Creative Computing, 1979; F. D'Ignazio, *The Creative Kids Guide to Home Computers: Super Games and Projects To Do with Your Home Computers,* Doubleday, 1981; F. D'Ignazio, *The Computer Parade* (fiction; sequel to *Katie and the Computer*), Creative Computing, 1983; F. D'Ignazio, *How to Get Intimate with Your Computer: Ten Easy Steps to Conquer Your Computer Anxiety* (adult), McGraw, 1984; N. Healy and B. Kurshan, *Computer FUNdamentals,* Reston, 1984. Also contributing illustrator to various publications, including *Creative Computing, Softside Magazine,* and *Chapel Hill Sun.*

WORK IN PROGRESS: The Crazy Robot by F. D'Ignazio, for Creative Computing; calligraphy for ''The Highwayman'' by Alfred Noyes.

The Colonel dived the plane between the Bug's legs, but the Bug lassoed them with his sticky bubble gum rope, and began reeling them in like frightened flounder. The Colonel jammed the gas pedal to the floor, and in a loop they spun, like a merry-go-round gone crazy. The Bug pulled them closer and closer to his hungry jaws.

(From *Katie and the Computer* by Fred D'Ignazio. Illustrated by Stan Gilliam.)

STAN GILLIAM

SIDELIGHTS: "It's fascinating to be able to create an imaginary world. I work almost entirely from my memory and imagination. My favorite artists are Van Gogh, Disney, Cliff Sterrett, George Herriman, and R. Crumb.

"I play and sing country bluegrass and old time music with the good ol' boys and girls of North Georgia. I sharpen my wits by drawing companions and contrasts between 'fine arts' and 'popular arts.'

"I also enjoy visiting elementary school classes and giving 'chalk talks' about my books and about art."

GOBBATO, Imero   1923-

PERSONAL: Born December 28, 1923, in Milan, Italy; naturalized U.S. citizen. *Education:* Attended Liceo Artistico, Milan, Italy, Institute of Fine Arts, Venice, Italy, and Academy of Fine Arts, Milan and Venice. *Residence:* Camden, Me.

CAREER: Artist and illustrator of books for children. Began career illustrating books and magazines in Italy; has worked as a professional naval architect, set designer for films, Los Angeles, Calif., and art restorer, New York, N.Y.; spent twelve years in extensive travels throughout Europe, Latin America, and the United States.

ILLUSTRATOR—All for children: Carol Kendall, *The Whisper of Glocken* (*Horn Book* honor list), Harcourt, 1965; Eve Merriam, *Catch a Little Rhyme,* Atheneum, 1966; Gunnel Linde, *The White Stone* (*Horn Book* honor list), translated by Richard Winston and Clara Winston, Harcourt, 1966; Jane L. Curry, *Beneath the Hill,* Harcourt, 1967; Anita Hewett, *The Bull beneath the Walnut Tree, and Other Stories,* McGraw, 1967 (Gobbato was not associated with original British edition); Padraic Colum, *The Girl Who Sat by the Ashes,* new edition (Gobbato was not associated with earlier editions), Macmillan, 1968; Marguerita Rudolph, adapter, *I Am Your Misfortune: A Lithuanian Folk Tale,* Seabury, 1968; Jay Williams, *The King with Six Friends,* Parents Magazine Press, 1968; Solveig P. Russell, *The Mushmen,* Dodd, 1968; George Mendoza, *The Practical Man,* Lothrop, 1968; Howard Fast, *Tony and the Wonderful Door,* Knopf, 1968; Abraham Rothberg, *The Boy and the Dolphin,* Norton, 1969; J. Williams, *The Good-for-Nothing Prince,* Norton, 1969; Jean Van Leeuwen, *The Great Cheese Conspiracy,* Random House, 1969; Christopher B. Wilson, *Oliver at Sea,* Norton, 1969.

Aileen Olsen, *Big Fish,* Lothrop, 1970; M. Rudolph, adapter, *The Brave Soldier and a Dozen Devils: A Latvian Tale,* Seabury, 1970; Aleksandr N. Afanas'ev, *Foma the Terrible: A Russian Folktale,* translated by Guy Daniels, Delacorte, 1970; Bryan MacMahon, *Patsy-O and His Wonderful Pets,* Dutton, 1970; Lesley Conger (pseudonym of Shirley Shuttles), adapter, *Tops and Bottoms* (folk tale), Four Winds, 1970; Carolyn Lane, *Uncle Max and the Sea Lion,* Bobbs-Merrill, 1970; Carol Panter, *Beany and His New Recorder,* Four Winds, 1972; Anne

(From *A Bucketful of Moon* by Toby Talbot. Illustrated by Imero Gobbato.)

. . . Hirple kicked the trunk. ■ (From *The Practical Man* by George Mendoza. Illustrated by Imero Gobbato.)

E. Bunting, *Barney the Beard,* Parents Magazine Press, 1975; Toby Talbot, *A Bucketful of Moon,* Lothrop, 1976.

SIDELIGHTS: "I inherited my inclination for drawing and painting from my maternal grandfather. He died the year I was born but very early in life I became acquainted with his studies in pen and ink and water color. I was also given some of his materials to play with when still a small child. Pen and ink became soon my favorite medium and, in many ways, still is. My father chose for me a classical education, but when I reached sixteen, he became convinced of the strength of my vocation and consented to send me to an art school." [Lee Kingman and others, compilers, *Illustrators of Children's Books: 1957-1966,* Horn Book, 1968.[1]]

In addition to his work as an illustrator, Gobbato has worked as an architect, designer and art restorer. "For years I worked as a professional naval architect. I also built boats myself and for two years lived with my wife aboard a houseboat which I designed and built at the edge of the Everglades in Florida. I have worked as a set designer for the movie industry in Los Angeles and as an art restorer in New York. And I travelled rather extensively for twelve and more years across Europe, Latin America and the United States. I am now living in Maine, alternating between a house on the mainland and a small fisherman's cottage on one of the outer islands. Maine and its people are still vastly uncontaminated by the soul-destroying cult of the superfluous that almost everywhere else undermines man's sense of value."[1]

Gobbato comments on his work as an illustrator: "I am a narrative artist, a teller of stories by means of images. I illustrate children's books because I love illustrated books. Of the new media, the colored acetate sheets by Bourges seem to be the most valuable. They allow perfectly controlled color separations giving a final effect half-way between color woodcuts and multi-layered graffitos. I have not found yet a new medium which surpasses the old pen and ink in capacity for detail, chiaroscural richness or affinity for photographic reproduction.''[1]

Gobbato's works are included in the Kerlan Collection at the University of Minnesota.

FOR MORE INFORMATION SEE: Lee Kingman and others, compilers, *Illustrators of Children's Books: 1957-1966,* Horn Book, 1968; L. Kingman and others, compilers, *Illustrators of Children's Books: 1967-1976,* Horn Book, 1978.

GOOR, Nancy (Ruth Miller)   1944-

PERSONAL: Born March 27, 1944, in Washington, D.C.; daughter of Martin H. (a government worker) and Helen (a teacher; maiden name, Zarkower) Miller; married Ronald S. Goor (a health administrator, writer, and photographer), March 12, 1967; children: Alexander, Daniel. *Education:* University of Pennsylvania, B.S., 1965; Boston University, M.F.A., 1966. *Address:* c/o Harper & Row Publishers, Inc., 10 East 53rd St., New York, N.Y. 10022.

CAREER: Teacher of art at public high school in Bethesda, Md., 1966-70; Smithsonian Institution, Natural History Museum, Washington, D.C., director of Insect Zoo, summer, 1971, scientific illustrator, 1975-78; author of children's books, 1981—. *Member:* Children's Book Guild, Guild of Natural Science Illustrators (corresponding secretary), Phi Beta Kappa. *Awards, honors: Shadows: Here, There, and Everywhere* was chosen as outstanding children's science book by the National Science Teacher's Association/Children's Book Council Joint Committee, and as one of the Library of Congress's best books of the year, both 1981; *In the Driver's Seat* was chosen as one of the best children's books of the year by the *New York Times* and *School Library Journal,* both 1982.

WRITINGS—Nonfiction for children; all illustrated with photographs by husband, Ron Goor: (With R. Goor) *Shadows: Here, There, and Everywhere* (ALA Notable Book), Crowell, 1981; *In the Driver's Seat* (Junior Literary Guild selection), Crowell, 1982; *Signs,* Crowell, 1983; *All Kinds of Feet,* Crowell, 1984.

WORK IN PROGRESS: (With Ronald Goor) a book about Pompeii, for children, a photographic essay which reveals the life of a small Roman city, specifically Pompeii in 79 A.D., the story of the burial of Pompeii by the volcano, Vesuvius, and the rediscovery of the ancient city.

SIDELIGHTS: ''I have always considered myself an artist. I majored in art in college, taught art in a public high school, did scientific illustration, and enjoy silkscreening, painting, and drawing. Although I have written and illustrated stories since childhood, it was not until the publication in several newspapers of my article on 'Traveling to Italy with Children' that I seriously considered writing as a vocation. My career as an author of children's books began with *Shadows: Here, There, and Everywhere,* the first of many books on which I have worked with my husband, Ron.

''Ron and I work well together. When he was special assistant to the director of the Smithsonian's National Museum of Nat-

NANCY GOOR

ural History, he thought of having a live insect zoo in the museum. He asked me to create and direct the insect zoo. I eagerly agreed. That summer (1971) opened my eyes to the fascinating world of insect behavior.

''We're often asked where we get the ideas for our books. Our ideas arise from our everyday experiences. For example, when my son was in first grade he told me, 'Mommy, I like to read signs.' 'Aha,' said I. Then, Ron and I set to work. Ron took hundreds of pictures of signs. I organized, reorganized, and reorganized them again, wrote several texts, and *Signs* was published.

''Neither Ron nor I remember which one of us thought of the idea for *In the Driver's Seat.* However, we both were convinced that driving a tank, supersonic jet, or front-end loader would be something any kid—or even old kids like us—would love to do. While researching the book I got to ride in an army tank, an electric engine, and an eighteen-wheel truck, on a combine, and to sit in the driver's seat of the Concorde, a front-end loader, and a race car!

''Each book brings new adventures. I rode in the cab of an old-time steam engine and pulled the horn! To get a picture of a beach umbrella making a shadow for *Shadows,* we went to the beach for the day. We buried our eleven-year-old son up to his neck in the sand. Children kept running over his sand-covered body thinking he was only a head. We took pictures of killer guard dogs—a frightening but fascinating experience—to illustrate the 'Beware of Dog' sign for *Signs*.

"Writing nonfiction for young children is a challenge. You have to write simply about subjects that are often difficult or complicated. How does a blimp work? What is a shadow? The text must be clear, and, as in all writing, the words must have rhythm and sound right when placed together.

"The aim of our books is to expand a child's awareness and interest in the common, everyday things around him. The advantage of using photography is that photographs capture the real thing—what a child actually finds in his environment.

"We have two sons who have been extremely helpful in doing all our books, from collecting insects, to posing, to reading manuscripts for clarity.

"[Recently] we took our fifth trip to Europe with our sons. We began traveling abroad when Danny was two and Alex was five-and-a-half. Although we have no Italian background, we are enchanted with Italy. We learned Italian well enough to converse. My French was adequate to help us communicate in France. Traveling with two young boys in a rented car with no reservations and a vague itinerary made every trip an adventure."

GOOR, Ron(ald Stephen) 1940-

PERSONAL: Born May 31, 1940, in Washington, D.C.; son of Charles G. (a statistician) and Jeanette (a statistician; maiden name, Mindel) Goor; married Nancy Ruth Miller (an author and illustrator), March 12, 1967; children: Alexander, Daniel. *Education:* Swarthmore College, B.A. (magna cum laude), 1962; graduate study, University of Chicago, 1962-63; Harvard University, Ph.D., 1967, Master of Public Health, 1977. *Address:* c/o Harper & Row Publishers, Inc., 10 East 53rd St., New York, N.Y. 10022. *Office:* National Heart, Lung and Blood Institute, National Institutes of Health, Bethesda, Md. 20205.

CAREER: Worked for the National Institutes of Health, Bethesda, Md., 1967-70; Smithsonian Institution, Natural History Museum, Washington, D.C., special assistant to director, 1970-72; National Science Foundation, Washington, D.C., program manager, 1972-76; Has worked at National Institutes of Health, National Heart, Lung and Blood Institute, Bethesda, since 1976. *Member:* American Chemical Society, American Association for the Advancement of Science, Children's Book Guild. *Awards, honor: Shadows: Here, There, and Everywhere* was chosen as outstanding children's science book by the National Science Teacher's Association/Children's Book Council Joint Committee, and as one of the Library of Congress's best books of the year, both 1981; *In the Driver's Seat* was chosen as one of the best children's books of the year by the *New York Times* and *School Library Journal,* both 1982; Phi Beta Kappa.

Shadows are everywhere. ■ (Jacket photographs by Ron Goor from *Shadows: Here, There, and Everywhere* by Ron and Nancy Goor.)

Like a gigantic metal monster, the front-end loader takes a bite out of the side of a wrecked building. ■ (From *In the Driver's Seat* by Ron and Nancy Goor. Photographs by Ron and Nancy Goor.)

WRITINGS—Nonfiction for children; all self-illustrated with photographs: (With Millicent Selsam) *Backyard Insects*, Scholastic Book Services, 1981; (with wife, Nancy Goor) *Shadows: Here, There, and Everywhere* (ALA Notable Book), Crowell, 1981; (with N. Goor) *In the Driver's Seat* (Junior Literary Guild selection), Crowell, 1982; (with N. Goor), *Signs*, Crowell, 1983; (with N. Goor), *All Kinds of Feet*, Crowell, 1984.

WORK IN PROGRESS: (With Nancy Goor) a book about Pompeii, for children—a photographic essay which reveals the life of a small Roman city, specifically Pompeii in 79 A.D., the story of the burial of Pompeii by the volcano, Vesuvius, and the rediscovery of the ancient city.

SIDELIGHTS: "I was born and raised in Washington, D.C. Ever since I can remember I have been interested in biology, but it was not until I had a Ph.D. in biochemistry and was doing laboratory research that I found I wanted both to express myself and to teach. While at the Smithsonian Institution developing biological exhibits for the lay public, I began to take photographs and discovered that photography opened up new avenues of self-expression as well as exploring and documenting the world.

"Writing books for children has been a natural outgrowth of my interest in photography. Good photography helps us see the world through fresh eyes. In my books I share with the reader a heightened awareness and appreciation of the beautiful and intricate natural world and new ways to see the complex man-made world.

"*Backyard Insects*, my first book, explores the many ways shapes and colors of insects protect them from their enemies. Ever since my wife Nancy and I started the nation's first live Insect Zoo at the Smithsonian's Natural History Museum in 1971, I became aware of the natural interest most children have in insects. These tiny ubiquitous creatures illustrate many of the most important biological principles and are so easily found, observed and raised that they make ideal teaching tools for understanding biology.

"The enlarged photographs of the insects in the book help the reader see the insects in more detail than is possible with the naked eye. The text, written together with Millicent Selsam, explains the variety of ways color and shape protects the insects. The lessons learned in the book provide a basis for seeing the animal world with fresh eyes. The use of domestic insects, easily found in both city and countryside, as examples in the book encourages readers to go outside to observe first-hand the phenomena described. Armed with this knowledge, the reader can go beyond the examples to understand and appreciate new observations in the field.

"In *Shadows: Here, There, and Everywhere*, my wife, Nancy, and I explore the world of shadows using carefully conceived black-and-white photographs. Set-ups consisting of a child's blocks and hand-held flashlight accompany each environmental scene and show how shadows are formed. Shadows are all around us—on the floor, the ground, the walls. They are long, short, bent, folded. They are beautiful, useful, scary. Yet, how often do we notice them? The book is designed not only to heighten awareness of shadows but to increase understanding of the interactions of light, objects and surfaces in the making of shadows.

"With *In the Driver's Seat*, we explore what it is like to drive a variety of vehicles—a blimp, a tank, an engine, the Concorde supersonic jet, a race car, a combine, a wrecking crane, a

RON GOOR

front-end loader, and an eighteen-wheel truck. Fisheye pictures put the reader in the driver's seat of these nine different vehicles. The text explains how to drive each vehicle and what it is like to operate. Additional pictures show the vehicle in action."

The Goors live in Bethesda, Maryland, a suburb of Washington, D.C. with their two sons, Alex and Danny. "Both boys help with the books by posing for pictures (Alex is on the cover of *Shadows*), finding insects, reading and critiquing text and suggesting topics for new books. When he was learning to read, Danny observed that he liked to read signs. We questioned a number of children and discovered that all either learned to read or practiced their reading on signs. From this we developed *Signs* for reading-ready children and children who are just learning to read."

The husband-and-wife team have developed a compatible working method when producing their books. "Nancy and I are often asked how we work together on a book. Generally, I begin by exploring the topic photographically. At the same time, Nancy and I begin to develop conceptual approaches to the subject matter. As Nancy develops the text, she suggests specific pictures which I have not yet taken during the early photographic exploration. Likewise, the photographs sometimes suggest changes in the text. Obviously, it is most helpful to have the writer and photographer working so closely together. Also, it is more fun that way!"

FOR MORE INFORMATION SEE: Popular Photography, February, 1982.

"Just hold it up at arm's length in a stable manner"—she held up her own baggy-sleeved arm—"and relax while I chant." ■ (From *Fifth Grade Magic* by Beatrice Gormley. Illustrated by Emily Arnold McCully.)

GORMLEY, Beatrice 1942-

PERSONAL: Born October 15, 1942, in Glendale, Calif.; daughter of Louis Kirk (an office supervisor for the California State Department of Employment) and Elizabeth (Fisher) LeCount; married Robert J. Gormley (college textbook publisher), September 4, 1966; children: Catherine, Jennifer. *Education:* Pomona College, B.A. (magna cum laude), 1964. *Home:* 37 Western Way, Box 1407, Duxbury, Mass. 02331.

CAREER: Addison-Wesley Publishing Co., Menlo Park, Calif., assistant English editor, 1966-67; free-lance editor, 1968-77; full-time writer. *Member:* Society of Children's Book Writers.

WRITINGS—Juvenile: Mail-Order Wings (illustrated by Emily Arnold McCully), Dutton, 1981; *Fifth Grade Magic* (illustrated by E. A. McCully), Dutton, 1982; *Best Friend Insurance* (illustrated by E. A. McCully), Dutton, 1983; *The Ghastly Glasses* (illustrated by E. A. McCully), Dutton, 1985. Also contributor of articles and essays to various newspapers, including the *Boston Globe.*

WORK IN PROGRESS: Paul's Volcano, a juvenile novel "in a realistic contemporary setting, with a fantasy element."

SIDELIGHTS: "When I was eight, I wanted to become a cowgirl when I grew up. By the time I was ten I had changed my mind, deciding to become a writer instead. That has been my heart's desire ever since.

"All through school I was encouraged in my ambition. Teachers were enthusiastic about my writing; I even won awards. I was confident that I would know, when the time came, *how* to become a writer. But I graduated from college with my final prize for student fiction and still no idea of how to go about earning my living as a professional writer. Instead, I went into textbook publishing, and edited and rewrote other people's prose. This was interesting work, but not exactly what I had in mind when I was ten. I wrote short stories now and then, dreary aimless stories that I would never want to read myself, and sent them to the *New Yorker.* They were always sent back with printed rejection slips.

"About eight years ago, it began to dawn on me that perhaps I hadn't worked hard enough at becoming a writer. Maybe I had to give it more time and effort—maybe I had to risk failing. So I worked up my courage, stopped accepting free-lance editing jobs (I was lucky to have this option, because my husband could support us on his salary) and spent that time on my own writing. At first I concentrated on articles and essays, and I was delighted to see my work in print in newspaper and magazines. But I couldn't stop trying to write fiction, even though I was still totally unsuccessful in getting it published. Then, in the year that my two daughters were eight and ten, I began to write stories for children. They were the kind of stories *I* liked to read at that age—adventure stories, especially with some magic or science fiction.

"I enjoyed writing these stories so much, I couldn't understand why I'd never tried them before. In June of 1979 I took my latest attempt, *Mail-Order Wings,* to a writer's conference. To my great good fortune, Jane Langton was teaching the writing for children section. She encouraged me, helped me revise *Mail-Order Wings,* and advised me to send it to Ann Durell at Dutton. I felt that my fairy godmother had appeared!

"Ann Durell thought my manuscript was promising, but outlined major revisions, and I saw right away that the story could

BEATRICE GORMLEY

be ten times better if I did what she said. Working and sweating to make these revisions, I had my first revelation about how hard one has to work to write a good story.

"After writing *Mail-Order Wings* in a haphazard way, and with a great deal of advice, I knew that I would have to find a more organized method of working if I was going to make a career out of this. I did some painful and unsuccessful trial-and-error work, and then a friend told me about Phyllis Whitney's *Writing Juvenile Stories and Novels.* I began to keep a notebook, as Whitney advises, with sections for outline, theme, characters, etc. Her method has been invaluable to me.

"A word about fantasy: I have always enjoyed reading fantasy (C. S. Lewis's Narnia books, the Tolkien trilogy, Ursula LeGuin's Earthsea trilogy), but it wasn't until I started to write it myself that I learned that this most fanciful fiction must be based on the most solid psychological truth. I was amazed that I had to be so honest with myself in order to write a good story. The writing of each novel has evoked surprisingly strong feelings, strong enough to distort the story if I don't face up to them. So the core of each book is something important to me as an adult. Of course it is equally important to entertain my readers; I think a dull or dreary novel is worthless.

"I believe I was attracted to writing for the middle grades, ages eight to eleven, partly because those were happy years for me. In my spare time, when I wasn't reading, I was playing in the sagebrush-covered hills behind my family's house in

Burbank, California. Sometimes I explored the canyons and ridges and their absorbing variety of wildflowers and shrubs and trees. Sometimes I played fantasy games in which I was shipwrecked or captured by Indians. Sometimes I just sat under a bush and smelled the pungent sage and felt peaceful and happy.

"At that time I took my environment for granted. But years later, when my children were babies and we were living in a cramped housing development on the San Francisco Peninsula, with not even sidewalks, let alone hills to walk in, I missed my open space terribly. And when we moved to Massachusetts in 1971, to a town south of Boston with woods and fields and overgrown cranberry bogs, I rediscovered the joy I felt in nature when I was ten. This pleasure in the New England countryside comes out clearly, I think, in my first book, *Mail-Order Wings*."

GOROG, Judith (Allen) 1938-

PERSONAL: Born December 16, 1938, in Madison, Wis.; daughter of Henry (a pilot and an electrical engineer) and Harriett (a secretary; maiden name, Teckemeyer) Allen; married István Gorog (a research scientist), November 13, 1965; children: Antonia, Nicole, Christopher. *Education:* Attended San Jose State College, 1957-59; University of California, Berkeley, B.A., 1961; Mills College, M.A., 1963. *Residence:* Princeton, N.J.

CAREER: Writer. Mobil Research Corp., Princeton, N.J., editor and writer, 1964-67; R.C.A.-Astro Corp., Princeton, production editor and writer, 1969-71; free-lance technical writer, 1971-73. *Member:* Society of Children's Book Writers.

WRITINGS—Juvenile: *A Taste for Quiet: And Other Disquieting Tales* (illustrated by Jeanne Titherington), Philomel Books, 1982; *Caught in the Turtle* (illustrated by Ruth Sanderson), Philomel Books, 1983.

WORK IN PROGRESS: *Summerpits,* a novel about a family during a dreadful summer; *Bavek,* a scary novel for young readers, ages seven to ten; a novel about a family that lives in a country during a political terror; a novel about a family in which parents are abducted.

SIDELIGHTS: Gorog recollected her life. "Somewhere back there is a little girl. She's tall and skinny, with knees full of scabs. Her fine blond hair is in braids so tight they pull at her eyes. The braids, four of them, are done because 'braiding makes the hair strong and keeps it out of your eyes.' It doesn't work.

(From "Queen Pig" in *A Taste for Quiet: And Other Disquieting Tales* by Judith Gorog. Illustrated by Jeanne Titherington.)

JUDITH GOROG

"Her dresses are short, with ties that tear out every day when she plays on the school ground at recess. She is the new girl in five grammar schools. To her that's all the time. She does not make friends easily. I now suspect that she is moody and stubborn. She reads, makes up stories and plays, daydreams, rewrites the Greek myths with herself taming Pegasus. In real life everything she does is wrong, and she does not fit in anywhere. She is said, in the family, to be her grandmother's favorite, a love she returns completely.

"In high school she meets other girls who feel that they somehow don't fit the picture of an American teenage girl. They call themselves the 'clank' to distinguish themselves from the 'clique,' pronounced in California in those days as 'click,'

"Then comes another move, to Europe, where she learns about living in a town rather than in a vast, desolate suburb. The town has opera, ballet, cafes, a good library, and a stable.

"Back home again, the girl begins college, where her mind and her looks are somehow magically transformed. Everybody praises them. She meets and comes to know her other grandmother; again it is an incredibly rich relationship.

"From college she goes to university, then graduate school. Along with academic success comes the awful realization that she is not as good a writer as Dostoevsky. She gives up writing fiction, but wants to stay at the university. Her friend says, 'Writers write. Don't hide in academia!,' a phrase he repeats, with variations, even after twenty years of marriage.

"The whole story sounds like a bad movie from 1930 or so.

"Then the young woman works as an editor and technical writer, marries, and has three children. As any woman with one child can tell you, there is no time to write. Ergo, exit writer's block, and begin work, which then continues. At this moment there are four books more or less in progress, and a pie in the oven.

"Pamela McCorduck, a dear friend who is a well-known science writer, says that when graduate students come to talk with her about me, they will ask discreetly about my weight problem, for food is always in my books and in my life. I love to cook, eat, read about food, grow food, feed people, teach cooking to children, and share recipes with anyone willing or too courteous to refuse.

"I look with a mixture of fear and delight at my own children, who are decidely not late bloomers and wonder what they will do with their many talents.

"My eldest, who is twelve, reports that her life is miserable."

HOBBIES AND OTHER INTERESTS: "I enjoy telling stories, reading to and cooking with children in the schools."

GOSCINNY, René   1926-1977

BRIEF ENTRY: Born in 1926, in Paris, France; died of a heart attack, November 5, 1977, in Paris, France. Comic strip writer and creator of the internationally known strip "Astérix." Goscinny spent his childhood in Argentina and, in 1945, came to the United States harboring a secret ambition to work as a cartoonist for Walt Disney. Although his dream never materialized, he did hold a variety of positions in New York, including that of cartoonist for *Mad* magazine. In 1954 he returned to his place of birth where he began contributing scripts for comic features in publications such as *Spirou* and *Jours de France*. In 1959 he founded his own comic weekly, *Pilote*. It was in the first issue of this publication that Goscinny's most famous comic strip made its appearance. Accompanied with illustrations by Albert Uderzo, the strip featured Astérix the Gaul, a feisty little warrior with a droopy moustache and winged helmet, his companion Obélix, and dog Idéfix (known in translation as Dogmatix)—all of whom waged perpetual battle against the Roman forces occupying their land. Originally published in French, "Astérix" was eventually translated into dozens of languages. It was also published in book form and sold millions of copies worldwide. In 1970 three of the books were made available in the United States by Morrow: *Astérix the Gaul*, *Astérix and Cleopatra*, and *Astérix the Legionary*. Recently, Dargaud issued 1984 paperback editions of *Astérix and the Great Crossing* and *Astérix at the Olympic Games*.

Publishers Weekly compared the popularity of "Astérix" in Europe to that of "Superman" and "Charlie Brown" in the United States, noting that the strip contained "free play of incidental humor and broad satire, . . . sufficiently universal to appeal to American readers." Although "Astérix" was by far Goscinny's most popular creation, he also produced the strip "Les Dingodossiers" and assisted creator Maurice de Bevére on the "Lucky Luke" western cowboy series. All three strips were eventually adapted to animated film. Among Goscinny's lesser-known series were "Le Petit Nicolas," "Haroun El Poussah," and "La Fée Aveline." He was the recipient of numerous awards and honors throughout his career, including the title of Chevalier of Arts and Letters. *For More Information See: The World Encyclopedia of Comics*, Volumes 1 and 2, Chelsea House, 1976. *Obituaries: New York Times*, November 7, 1977; *Contemporary Authors*, Volume 113, Gale, 1984.

To read without reflecting is like eating without digesting.

—Edmund Burke

GRABIAŃSKI, Janusz 1929-1976

PERSONAL: Born July 24, 1929, in Szamotuly, Poland; died October 20, 1976, in Warsaw, Poland; married wife, Joanna; children: two daughters, Kascha and Ditta. *Education:* Attended Academy of Fine Arts, Cracow, Poland. *Religion:* Catholic. *Residence:* Warsaw, Poland.

CAREER: Artist, author and illustrator of books for children. *Awards, honors:* Received awards in Poland, Austria, England, and Switzerland; prize for outstanding achievement in the field of illustration from the Polish government, 1958, for collected illustrations; Milan Triennale Gold Medal, 1960; *The Big Book of Animal Stories* was named among the ten best illustrated books of the year by the *New York Times*, 1961; honorable mention, from Polish Association of Publishers, for *Bajki* (title means "Fairy Tales"), and for *Wiersze dla Kaji* (title means "Poems for Kaja"), both 1971; prize for the best typographically designed children's book, Fair Association of Bologna, 1978, for *Grabiański's Stadtmusikanten* (title means "Grabiański's Town Musicians").

WRITINGS—Self-illustrated juvenile books: *Chodzi, chodzi baj po scianie*, Nasza Ksiegarnia, 1960; *Grabiański's Wild Animals*, F. Watts, 1969 (published in England as *Grabiański's Animals*, Dent, 1969); *Grabiański's Stadtmusikanten* (title means "Grabiański's Town Musicians"), Ueberreuter, 1977.

Illustrator: Jadwiga Wernerowa, *Rudzia*, Nasza Ksiegarnia, 1958; Lucyna Krzemieniecka, *Slomkowy lancuszek*, Czytelnik, 1960; *Big Book to Grow On*, F. Watts, 1960; *Frohes Singen, frohes Klingen* (title means "Happy Singing, Happy Ringing"), Ueberreuter, 1960; *Kauneimmat elaeinsadut*, Soederstrom, 1961; Margaret Green, editor, *The Big Book of Animal Stories*, F. Watts, 1961; Jakob Grimm and Wilhelm Grimm, *Fairy Tales*, Duell, Sloan & Pearce, 1962; Hans Christian Andersen, *Fairy Tales*, Duell, Sloan & Pearce, 1963; *Tales from the Arabian Nights*, selected by Hedwig Smola, English translation and adaptation by Charlotte Dixon, Duell, Sloan & Pearce, 1964; *Histoires d'animaux sauvages*, Flammarion, 1964; M. Green, editor, *The Big Book of Wild Animals*, F. Watts, 1964; *Ueberreuter-Kinderkalender*, Ueberreuter, 1964; *Das grosse Fabelbuch* (title means "The Big Book of Animal Fables"), Ueberreuter, 1965; M. Green, editor, *The Big Book of Animal Fables*, F. Watts, 1965; H. C. Andersen, *Eventyr*, Aschehoug, [Oslo], 1965.

Bertl Hayde, *Das grosse Buch fuer unsere Kleinen* (title means "The Big Book for Little People"), Ueberreuter, 1966; *Das grosse Buch der kleinen Freunde* (title means "The Big Book

(From "Toomai et les Eléphants" by Rudyard Kipling in *Histoires d'animaux sauvages*. Illustrated by Janusz Grabiański.)

(From "Jeux Aquatiques" by Henry Williamson in *Histoires d'animaux sauvages.* Illustrated by Janusz Grabiański.)

of Little Friends''), Ueberreuter, 1966; Mira Lobe, *Meine kleine Welt* (title means ''My Small World''), Ueberreuter, 1966; *Le grande livre des enfants et des betes,* Flammarion, 1966; Valentin P. Kataev, *Das Erdbeermaennchen* (title means ''The Little Strawberry Man''), Ueberreuter, 1966; Irena Jurgielewiczowa, *Wie ein Maler einen gluecklichen Schmetterling malen wollte* (title means ''How an Artist Wanted To Paint a Happy Butterfly''), Kinderbuchverlag, 1966; Theo Riegler, *Die bunte Maerchenwiese* (title means ''The Colorful Fairy Meadow''), Suedwest Verlag, 1966; M. Green, editor, *The Big Book of Pets,* F. Watts, 1966; Charles Perrault, *Classic French Fairy Tales,* Meredith, 1967; Bruno Horst Bull, *Katzen,* Ueberreuter, 1967, translation published as *Cats,* F. Watts, 1967; B. H. Bull, *Pferde,* Ueberreuter, 1967, translation published as *Horses,* F. Watts, 1967; Josef Guggenmos, *Hunde,* Ueberreuter, 1968, translation published as *Dogs,* F. Watts, 1968; J. Guggenmos, *Voegel,* Ueberreuter, 1968, translation published as *Birds,* F. Watts, 1968; Charles Lamb and Mary Lamb, *Ten Tales from Shakespeare,* F. Watts, 1969; Christiane de Haas, *Contes des quatre saisons,* Editions des Deux coqs d'or, 1969.

Wilhelm Hauff, *The Big Book of Stories,* F. Watts, 1970; *Androcles and the Lion,* F. Watts, 1970; Joanna Kulmowa, *Wiersze dla Kaji* (title means ''Poems for Kaja''), Krajowa Agencja Wydawnicza, 1970; C. Perrault, *Bajki* (title means ''Fairy Tales''), adapted by Hanna Januszewska, Nasza Ksiegarnia, 1971; Louis Enault, *The Captain's Dog,* F. Watts, 1971; Gertrud Fussenegger, *Bibel-Geschichten* (title means ''Bible Stories''), Ueberreuter, 1972; Maria Dabrowska, *Marcin Kozera,* Nasza Ksiegarnia, 1972; Norman Vincent Peale, *Bible Stories,* F. Watts, 1973; Enid Blyton, *Before I Go to Sleep,* Brockhampton Press, 1975; Silvia Sherry, *Mat, the Little Monkey,* Scribner, 1977.

Also illustrator of M. Konopnicka's *Franek,* 1956; S. Jachowicz' *Chory kotek,* 1959; K. Illakowiczówna's *Zwierzaki i ziola,* 1960; C. Lewandowska's *Bogatki z jabloniowej dziupli,* 1960; V. Kataev's *Dudoczka i kuwszyncik,* 1963; E. Leitgeb's *Das Buch vom Osterhasen* (title means ''The Easter Bunny Book''), 1965; K. Wölfflin's *Tiere der Wildnis* (title means ''Animals of the Wilderness''), 1969. Also illustrated *Strupp geht an Bord* (title means ''Strupp Goes on Board''), *Flughafen* (title means ''Airport''), and *Tom Sawyer.*

SIDELIGHTS: Born in Szamotuly, Poland, Grabiański ''drew from early childhood,'' even though playing with airplanes occupied more of his boyhood hours. The two interests came

(From *Grabiański's Horses,* illustrated by Janusz Grabiański.)

It is wonderful the cool way a cat takes possession of any spot he likes. He may be sitting on the very book you are just wanting to read, but you haven't the heart to chase him away.

(From *Grabiański's Cats,* illustrated by Janusz Grabiański.)

together during the dark days of World War II when Poland was occupied by the Nazis. According to Grabiański, he discovered a booklet, printed by the underground movement, which told the story of the fighting done by the Polish Fighter Division in the Battle of Britain. Finding the book fascinating, he created illustrations for it, making it the first story that he had ever illustrated.

After World War II, Grabiański was a glider pilot for several years. When a defect in young Grabiański's eyes was detected, his career as a glider pilot ended and he turned to art. Studying at the Academy of Fine Arts in Cracow, Poland for six years, he began his career in book illustration.

Grabiański's work was first noticed by Helen Hoke Watts, of the American publishing company, Franklin Watts, when she attended the 1958 International Book Fair in Frankfurt, Germany. Shortly thereafter, one of his German publications was translated into English and published in Watts's "Big Book" series. Grabiański's talent for painting animals was internationally known.

Before his early death in 1976, the artist lived near Warsaw, Poland in a house that he designed with his wife and two talented daughters, Kascha and Ditta. Kascha's picture of a butterfly was included by her father in one of his books.

Grabiański preferred to work in watercolor, tempera, and also in chalks. He once said that "a sense of unfulfillment and looking for better ways has always been with me." On yet another occasion when a reporter questioned what he wanted most for himself, he replied: "To paint what I want to paint!"

HOBBIES AND OTHER INTERESTS: Travel, meeting people, children, flowers, animals, birds, and fast cars.

FOR MORE INFORMATION SEE: Lee Kingman and others, *Illustrators of Children's Books: 1957-1966,* Horn Book, 1968; Doris de Montreville and Donna Hill, editors, *Third Book of Junior Authors,* H. W. Wilson, 1972; *Children's Book Illustration,* Graphis Press, 1975; *Bookbird,* Volume 4, 1976. *Obituaries: Publishers Weekly,* November 22, 1976; *Graphis,* Volume 34, May/June, 1979.

JANUSZ GRABIAŃSKI

GREENBANK, Anthony Hunt 1933-
(Nigel Hunt)

PERSONAL: Born December 21, 1933, in Settle, Yorkshire, England; son of Anthony and Marjorie Greenbank; divorced; children: Heather, Mark, Hannah. *Education:* Giggleswick School, Yorkshire, England, 1944-50, and Newcastle School of Librarianship, 1956. *Home:* Crag Cottage, The Green, Ambleside, Cumbria, England.

CAREER: Writer. Worked briefly as a librarian. Outward Bound instructor in Cumberland, England, 1959-60, and Marble, Colo., summer, 1964. *Military service:* Royal Air Force, 1952-54. *Member:* London Press Club, Fell and Rock Climbing Club of the English Lake District.

WRITINGS: Instructions in Rock-Climbing, Museum Press, 1963; (with Donald Robinson) *Caving and Potholing,* Constable, 1964; *Climbing, Canoeing, Ski-ing and Caving,* Elliot Right Way Books, 1964; (under pseudonym Nigel Hunt) *Adventures in Canoeing,* Pelham, 1964; *Instructions in Mountaineering,* Museum Press, 1967; *The Book of Survival: How to Save Your Skin When Disaster Strikes without Warning,* Wolfe, 1967, revised edition, Bell & Hyman, 1985, published in the U.S. as *The Book of Survival: Everyman's Guide to Staying Alive and Handling Emergencies in the City, the Suburbs, and the Wild Lands Beyond,* Harper, 1968; *Mr. Tough: The Powerkit of Fitness and Strength for All Men,* Wolfe, 1969, published as *Mr. Tough,* Harper, 1970, published as *Build a New Body,* New English Library, 1973; (under pseudonym Nigel Hunt) *Camping,* Brockhampton Press, 1969; *Survival in the City,* Wolfe, 1974, Harper, 1975; *Survival for Young People,* Harrap, 1975, published as *A Handbook for Emergencies: Coming Out Alive,* Doubleday, 1976; *Enjoy Your Rock-Climbing,* Pelham, 1976; *Climbing for Young People,* Harrap, 1977; *Walking, Hiking and Backpacking,* Constable, 1977; *Camping for Young People,* Harrap, 1979; *Getting About in the Great*

ANTHONY HUNT GREENBANK

Outdoors, Kestrel Books, 1984.

HOBBIES AND OTHER INTERESTS: Rock climbing, mountaineering, and checkers.

FOR MORE INFORMATION SEE: Library Journal, February 15, 1968; *Book World*, March 3, 1968.

GRIFFITH, Helen V(irginia)   1934-

PERSONAL: Born October 31, 1934, in Wilmington, Del.; daughter of John (a railroad machinist) and Helen (a wholesale building materials company president; maiden name, Williams) Griffith. *Education:* Attended high school in Woodcrest, Del. *Home:* 2200 West 18th St., Wilmington, Del. 19806. *Office:* S. G. Williams & Bros. Co., 301 Tatnall St., Wilmington, Del. 19801.

CAREER: Secretary and clerk at various companies, 1953-76; S. G. Williams & Bros. Co. (building products distributors), Wilmington, Del., secretary-treasurer, 1976—. *Member:* Authors Guild, Society of Children's Book Writers, Delmarva Ornithological Society. *Awards, honors:* International Reading Association/Children's Book Council "Children's Choice," 1981, for *Mine Will, Said John; Alex and the Cat* was chosen one of *School Library Journal*'s "Best Books 1982."

WRITINGS—For children: *Mine Will, Said John* (illustrated by Muriel Batherman), Greenwillow, 1980; *Alex and the Cat* (illustrated by Joseph Low; Junior Literary Guild selection), Greenwillow, 1982; *Alex Remembers* (illustrated by Donald Carrick; Junior Literary Guild selection), Greenwillow, 1983; *More Alex and the Cat* (illustrated by D. Carrick; Junior Literary Guild selection), Greenwillow, 1983; *Foxy*, Greenwillow, 1984.

SIDELIGHTS: "I have been writing and drawing since I could handle a pencil, but I never took it seriously. When I was very young I wrote poetry, usually about animals. Later I began several novels which I illustrated profusely, but never finished. In high school I wrote funny sketches which still make me laugh—interviews with my dog, Wooly, about current events and little skits about school life that were very unflattering (and unfair) to our teachers.

"My tenth grade English teacher liked my writing (she never saw the skits) and encouraged me to send a poem to a magazine for teenagers. They published it and paid me, and if I'd had any sense that would have been the beginning of my writing career. Instead, I never submitted another thing anywhere until I was forty years old.

"I started out writing non-fiction articles for magazines. Then I had an idea for a story about some boys and a tape recorder. I wrote it and found that I preferred writing fiction and that's what I've done ever since.

"I have always liked animals and so far a dog has had a featured role in every book I've written. I don't begin by thinking, 'I'm going to write a book about a dog,' but that's what happens.

"I love nature, too, with birdwatching my only hobby. I don't count reading as a hobby—it's more of a vice. I wish I would spend less time reading and more time writing."

"Look at the moon," Robbie said. "I've never seen it so big and orange." ■ (From *Alex Remembers* by Helen V. Griffith. Illustrated by Donald Carrick.)

HELEN V. GRIFFITH

HALLINAN, P(atrick) K(enneth) 1944-

PERSONAL: Born November 1, 1944, in Los Angeles, Calif.; son of Kenneth Frank (a salesman) and Marguerite (Rommel) Hallinan; children: Kenneth P., Michael T. *Education:* Attended University of California, Berkeley, 1962, Foothill College, 1963-65, and California State University, Northridge, 1969. *Home:* 1101 Valencia Dr., Escondido, Calif. 92025.

CAREER: J. C. Penney & Co., Saratoga, Calif., sporting goods manager, 1967-69; Lockheed Aircraft Corp., Burbank, Calif., project scheduler, 1969-72; Attal, Champion & Associates Advertising, San Diego, Calif., copy writer, 1973-74; Rohr Industries (aerospace manufacturing), Chula Vista, Calif., expediter, 1974-76; Topaz, Inc., San Diego, Calif., marketing communications manager, 1976—.

WRITINGS—All self-illustrated children's books; all published by Children's Press, except as indicated: *How Really Great to Walk This Way*, 1972; *The Looking Book*, 1973; *We're Very Good Friends, My Brother and I*, 1973; *Just Being Alone*, 1976; *That's What a Friend Is*, 1977; *I'm Glad to Be Me*, 1977; *Where's Michael?*, 1978; *I'm Thankful Each Day*, Ideals Publishing, 1979; *Just Open a Book*, 1980.

WORK IN PROGESS: Self-illustrated books for Children's Press: *When I Grow Up, Imagine Me, My Silent Day, All by Myself,* and *Nothing To Do; Famous People I Almost Met*, for adults.

SIDELIGHTS: "From the very first time I attempted to write and illustrate for children, I was fascinated with how animated kids are. There are simply no shades of grey. Kids are either wildly ecstatic or totally crushed. I love that about them, and I strive hard to capture it in my illustrations. I also feel strongly that a children's book should be completely honest; that the value presented not be masked behind impossible, imaginary

(From *Where's Michael?* by P. K. Hallinan. Illustrated by the author.)

P. K. HALLINAN

creatures! For this reason, I never write about talking animals or dancing refrigerators. I state the truth as well as I can and then try to capture the spirit of it with my cartoons. And then, if my kids laugh at my manuscript, I figure I'm doing okay.''

HAMLEY, Dennis   1935-

PERSONAL: Born October 14, 1935, in Crockham Hill, Kent, England; son of Charles Richard (a post office engineer) and Doris May (Payne) Hamley; married Agnes Moylan (a nurse), August 6, 1965; children: Peter Richard John, Mary Elizabeth Carmel. *Education:* Jesus College, Cambridge, M.A., 1959; University of Bristol, P.G.C.E., 1960; University of Manchester, diploma in advanced studies in education, 1965; University of Leicester, Ph.D., 1980. *Politics:* ''Generally leftward inclined. But hating Communism, despairing of Labour Party and not impressed with Social Democratic Party, wondering how one can take the political process seriously anymore.'' *Religion:* ''Lapsed Anglican, but still with Christian belief.'' *Home:* ''Hillside,'' 2 King's Rd., Hertfordshire SG13 7EY, England. *Office:* Education Department, Country Hall, Hertfordshire SG13 8DF, England.

CAREER: English master at grammar and secondary modern schools in England, 1960-67; Milton Keynes College of Ed-

ucation, Bletchley, Milton Keynes, England, lecturer, 1967-69, senior lecturer in English, 1969-78; Hertfordshire Local Education Authority, Hertfordshire, England, County Adviser for English and drama, 1978—. Counselor and tutor for Open University, 1971-78. *Military service:* Royal Air Force, 1954-56. *Member:* Society of Authors (chairman, educational writers group, 1981-1983), National Association of Educational Inspectors and Advisers, Eastern Arts Association (member of literature panel, 1983—).

WRITINGS: Three Towneley Plays (adapted into modern English), Heinemann, 1963; *Pageants of Despair* (juvenile novel), S. G. Phillips, 1974; (with Colin Field) *Fiction in the Middle School,* Batsford, 1975; *Very Far from Here* (juvenile novel), Deutsch, 1976; *Landings* (juvenile novel), Deutsch, 1979; (contributor) Jean Russell, editor, *The Methuen Book of Sinister Stories,* Methuen, 1982; *The Shirt Off a Hanged Man's Back,* Deutsch, 1984; *The Fourth Plane at the Flypast* (juvenile novel), Deutsch, 1985.

Adapter into English; all written by Gian Paolo Ceserani; all published by Kestrel: *The Travels of Columbus,* 1979; *The Travels of Livingstone,* 1979; *The Travels of Marco Polo,* 1980; *The Travels of Captain Cook,* 1980.

Contributor to anthology: Bryan Newton, editor, *Aliens,* Collins, 1985.

Author of two radio plays, ''Pageants of Despair'' (based on his novel of the same title), and ''Court Jester,'' both for BBC-Radio, both 1979. Also author of ''Julius Caesar, Study Guide and Cassette,'' Argo Records, 1980. Reviewer for *School Librarian.*

WORK IN PROGRESS: Juvenile novel, tentatively titled *Haunted United,* the story of a once great football club which is being haunted.

SIDELIGHTS: ''I was born into what will probably be regarded as one of the most fortunate generations in history—just old enough after World War II to benefit from the 1944 Butler Education Act which enabled me to go to Cambridge University. I don't claim great gifts here—I was carried on a tide of history into areas absolutely uncharted by any members of my family before. I had a quiet and happy childhood, despite the war, spent in various parts of the south and middle of England—with one marvellous interlude in the Lake District, bits of which I can still recall. When the war ended we found ourselves in the little Buckinghamshire market town of Winslow which proved a lasting influence on my life and writing.

''I suppose, if there is any theme in my books, it is this idea of the young person—older than child, younger than youth—realising there are big changes afoot and trying to come to terms with them. It's always disguised—but it's always there because my mind seems naturally drawn to this eleven- to fourteen-year-old period in my life which was so important to me.

''I have always loved the art of narrative—but for many years as a listener, not a teller until I started to write for myself—when I discovered that the end of a story is implicit in its beginning, If you begin it, you will end it. You don't always see the destination at the start of the journey, but you'll get there all right. This to me is now a simple fact which only writing as a sort of act of faith taught me. Not realising it delayed my start as a writer of stories for many years because, try as I would—and I thought one had to—I could never work out a story before I started writing it.

DENNIS HAMLEY

"I am not a full-time writer. All my working life has been concerned with teaching, schools, and education. I don't find the two careers at odds; they complement each other. In my work as County English Adviser, visiting schools in Hertfordshire for all age groups, I find I keep in touch in a way being a full-time writer would not so easily allow. Contact with children is vital. Which is why I share in and promote authors' visits to schools, our local Eastern Arts Association's Visiting Writers Scheme and any other means of de-mystifying the writing process so that children will know it for what it is—not some sort of esoteric trick but a process shared by all and at the very centre of all human volition.

"I've mentioned 'themes' in perhaps a pretentious way. There's another way of looking at the way I write—that is, finding some*thing* I'm deeply interested in and some*one* I'm deeply interested in, putting them together and seeing what happens. So twelve-year-old Peter in *Pageants of Despair* finds himself in the middle of the Wakefield Mystery Cycle of Plays. Fourteen-year-old Philip in *Landings* learns to fly sailplanes, takes a secret train journey across England, and sees his grandfather's ghost from World War I. All the raw material of things I was fascinated by long before I thought of writing children's books is becoming a part of my writing. I long ago stopped playing soccer (I was never any good anyway) and have never believed in ghosts. But always the two have intrigued me. Football can be a way of expressing character and conflict; ghosts are messengers from the past—which must be why they are used by so many writers who presumably, like me, don't believe in them. But both football and ghosts are turning up more and

more in my stories. In fact, in my new book there is actually a story about a ghost playing football. It's called 'The Substitute,' story in *The Shirt Off a Hanged Man's Back*. I've read it aloud to a lot of children and they seem to like it.

"My own children, Peter and Mary, have always been helpful and assiduous critics. They've given advice I ignore at my peril, suggestions I always use, on occasions have changed the course of stories for me—always correctly. They—and a marvellous editor at Andre Deutsch—have been very good for me."

HOBBIES AND OTHER INTERESTS: Music, railways, watching football, drama, camping, motoring.

HANSEN, Caryl (Hall)   1929-
(Caryl Hall)

PERSONAL: Born November 3, 1929, in Berkeley, Calif.; daughter of Edward Harrison (a shipping executive) and Winifred (a writer: maiden name, MacNally Johnson) Harms; married Jordan D. Hall, April 24, 1955 (divorced, June, 1967); married Robert F. Hansen (a social worker), March 15, 1975; children: (first marriage) Jennifer Ann, Rebecca Jean. *Education:* Stanford University, A.B., 1951. *Religion:* Christian Scientist. *Residence:* Palo Alto, Calif. *Agent:* Ruth Cohen, Inc., P.O. Box 7626, Menlo Park, Calif. 94025.

CARYL HANSEN

(From the television special "I Think I'm Having a Baby," broadcast on the "CBS Afternoon Playhouse," March 3, 1981. Hansen novelized the teleplay by Blossom Elfman who won an Emmy for Best Writer in Children's Programming.)

CAREER: Piedmonter (newspaper), Oakland, Calif., managing editor, 1954-62; Oakland Public Library, Oakland, educational assistant, 1962-64; United Way of the Bay Area, San Francisco, Calif., press director, 1964-67; Children's Home Society of California, Golden Gate District, Oakland, public relations director, 1967-76. Consultant in public relations and fundraising, 1976—. President, California Crafts Museum, 1982—. _Military service:_ U.S. Marine Corps, active duty, 1951-54; became captain. _Member:_ Women Marines Association, Glass Art Society, California Writers Club (president, 1970-72), Marine Corps Combat Correspondents Association.

WRITINGS: (Under name Caryl Hall) _Gold on Her Shoulder_ (juvenile), Funk, 1964; (under name Caryl Hall) _The Prettiest Politician_ (juvenile), Funk, 1968; _Your Choice: A Young Woman's Guide to Making Decisions about Unmarried Pregnancy_ (young adult), Avon Flare Books, 1980; _I Think I'm Having a Baby_ (young adult; adapted from the teleplay by Blossom Elfman), Avon Flare Books, 1982; _One for the Road_ (young adult), Silhouette First Love, 1984. Past contributing editor of _Home;_ past associate editor of _Glass Art Society Journal._

WORK IN PROGRESS: Rich Man's Bluff, a romantic suspense novel; a young adult novel; research for an historical novel set in California.

SIDELIGHTS: "My first book began as a picture book about a cat and finished as a young adult novel about a woman Marine (_Gold on Her Shoulder_). This unlikely metamorphosis took place when (1) I discovered that being the mother of a toddler did not necessarily make me a writer for young children and (2) a writing teacher at the University of California-Berkeley learned that I had served in the Marine Corps and exclaimed, 'What a great setting for a career romance!' (as such teenage novels were then known). Writing a novel proved to be much easier for me than the picture book, despite the latter's deceptively short and simple format. I was learning how important it is for a writer to find the kind of writing most natural to his or her style.

"My only nonficion work to date (_Your Choice_) was the culmination of nine years on the staff of a nonprofit private agency which counsels unmarried pregnant women. I knew that for every young woman who had the opportunity to talk with a counselor, like those at Chidren's Home Society, many others went through the pregnancy and made life-changing decisions with no one to talk to and very few facts to go on. My book has, I hope, reached out to some of these young women and provided them with information about the choices open to them.

"_I Think I'm Having a Baby_ began as a television drama, written by Blossom Elfman and shown on the CBS Afternoon

Playhouse. When the broadcast won an Emmy award, I was asked to turn the teleplay into a book. I worked from the script and from a videocassette of the program and tried to remain faithful to the original story while adding the detail necessary to expand the TV show into a book. Writing this way was both easier and harder than writing 'my own' novels. Easier because plotting is always a tussle for me, and the story line was already there. Harder because I had to get inside someone else's characters and make them real to me before I could make them real to the reader.

"Obviously my own career experiences and interests provide much of the inspiration and background for my writing. Recently I have become very much interested in fine contemporary crafts, particularly the work of today's glass artists. Because of my affiliation with the Glass Art Society, I have had the opportunity to watch many of the very best of these artists in their studios and at the furnaces where they turn hot molten glass into extraordinary and beautiful objects. I find both the process and the results tremendously exciting—so perhaps there is a book in there someplace, someday!"

HANSEN, Joyce   1942-

BRIEF ENTRY: Born October 18, 1942, in New York, N.Y. A teacher and author of books for young people, Hansen received her B.A. from Pace University and her M.A. from New York University. Since 1973 she has been an English and reading teacher for the New York City Board of Education. A member of the Harlem Writers Guild, she has written two books for young people, *The Gift-Giver* (Clarion Books, 1980) and *Home Boy* (Clarion Books, 1982), a young adult novel. Both of her books are set in New York City's Bronx and have black youths as characters. Critics agree on Hansen's ability to effectively portray this setting in her books. In *The Gift-Giver*, she introduces Amir, a foster child new to his fifth grade class who affects the lives of many of his classmates through his thoughtfulness and kind deeds. *Bulletin of the Center for Children's Books* cited *The Gift-Giver's* "strong characters," and *Publishers Weekly* mentioned that the book's "dialogue . . . was vivid," adding that it "jumps with humor." *Home Boy* tells the turbulent story of Marcus who, after moving to New York with his parents from the Caribbean, becomes involved in drug dealing and the stabbing of a fellow student. *Voice of Youth Advocates* called it "a memorable story, . . . a . . . very credible tale," while *Publishers Weekly* stated that "the author compels earnest attention to, and sympathy with, everyone involved [in the story]." *Home:* 19 Dongan Pl., New York, N.Y. 10040. *For More Information See: Contemporary Authors,* Volume 105, Gale, 1982.

HARRIES, Joan   1922-
(Joan Harries Katsarakis)

PERSONAL: Born October 23, 1922, in Pembroke, South Wales; came to the United States in 1928, naturalized citizen, 1935; daughter of John (a minister) and Margaret (Jones) Harries; married George Katsarakis (works in the field of electronics), April 17, 1963; children: Louise. *Education:* Elizabethtown College, B.S., 1943; Northwestern University, M.S., 1969. *Politics:* Independent. *Religion:* Unitarian-Universalist. *Home:* 10 Briar Lane, Essex Junction, Vt. 05452.

CAREER: Teacher at public elementary schools in Middletown, Pa., 1943-51, and in Illinois, 1962-80; Lancaster Newspapers, Inc., Lancaster, Pa., special features editor, 1951-59; children's editor for publishing house in Illinois, 1959-61; Chicago Board of Education, Doolittle Pre-Vocational Center (federally-funded poverty program), Chicago, Ill., teacher of vocational skills to young adults, 1965, teacher of basic reading and mathematical skills to adults, 1965-66, teacher of English to foreign-speaking adults, 1965-68. Writer. *Member:* Society of Children's Book Writers, League of Vermont Writers.

WRITINGS: They Triumphed over Their Handicaps (juvenile), F. Watts, 1981.

Adapter of "Gateway Fact Books"; published by Warwick Press, 1982: David Lambert, *Birds;* D. Lambert, *Animal Life;* D. Lambert, *Dinosaur World;* Anne Millard, *Early People;* Christopher Maynard and David Jefferis, *Weapons and Warfare;* John Paton, editor, *Astronomy;* Stewart Cowley, *Space Flight;* C. Maynard and J. Paton, *The History of Aircraft.*

Contributor to magazines and journals, including *Pennsylvania School Journal.*

WORK IN PROGRESS: Is Your Classmate Disabled?; Anemone, a romantic mystery novel for young adults.

SIDELIGHTS: "Peter Pan didn't want to grow up. I think that, to some extent, most young people feel the same way. As a child I hated to think that in a few years I'd no longer be able to become Tarzan by swinging on the branches of my neighbor's willow trees, or a test pilot by zooming through the air in my backyard swing. No longer would I be able to change into a princess simply by dressing up in my mother's gowns. Even playing with dolls would be a joy of the past.

JOAN HARRIES

. . . Kitty O'Neil, substituting for Lynda Carter in an episode of the TV show "Wonder Woman."
. . . Kitty O'Neil is 5 feet 3 inches (1.58 m.) tall. She weighs 95 pounds (43 kg.). And she is deaf. ■
(From *They Triumphed over Their Handicaps* by Joan Harries. Photograph courtesy of Wide World.)

"My grandmother must have understood how I felt because one day she told me that, though people get older and taller and take on adult responsibilities, they don't really have to grow up. Of course, she said, most adults don't feel free to walk down the sidewalk on their hands or play kick-the-can as children do. But, no matter how old a person is, she can be a queen, king, famous actor, cop, robber, or anyone else she wishes. According to Grandma, the secret is to keep your imagination in good working order.

"As the years go by, I find more and more examples that show Grandma was right. Most adults won't say what they're dreaming, but a friend told me that every time the electric-eye door opens for her in the supermarket she becomes a movie star making a grand entrance into a ballroom. A high-school girl said that when she sits down to her science homework, she's a world-renowned scientist struggling to find a cure for cancer. I don't know for sure, but from the look on my neighbor's face as he jogs down the street, I've an idea he's not plain old Bob anymore but an Olympic runner competing for the gold medal.

"Years after talking with Grandma about using one's imagination, I realized it's not only fun to become other people but you can get paid for it too. Writers play the parts of people who climb the highest mountains, suffer agonizing deaths, explore unknown planets, and rule nations. Nothing is impossible.

"Of course, using one's imagination isn't all there is to writing.

It's also sitting at a desk and putting your thoughts into words in a clear, organized, interesting way. This is WORK. And, words that to you are simply delightful, an editor may find boring. Or stupid. So, you have to rewrite or find another editor. Many editors and many rewrites later, the day may come when your story, article, or book sells. On that day you'll be flying as high as Peter Pan.

"Later, you'll hold the magazine or book and look at your words in print. That's the day you'll be so happy you could fly 'straight on till morning, even say funny things to the stars,' just like Peter Pan."

They Triumphed over Their Handicaps is intended for junior and senior high school students who read at the second-grade level. Harries has also rewritten the original texts of eight books by other authors. They comprise the series "Gateway Fact Books" and are also intended for high school students who are slow readers.

"My father was a minister, but he did free-lance writing on the side. When he was a young man he wrote articles for the *Manchester Guardian*. That was a motivating factor in my career, which began when I was in college. I wrote short features, fillers, etc., for magazines. After I began teaching I wrote my first full-length article, 'Teaching Wasn't for Me,' which was published by the *Pennsylvania School Journal*.

"Many years later, in 1976, I attended the Cape Cod Writer's Conference. One of the teachers there, Lee Wyndham, read some of the short stories I'd written. She liked them and said, 'Why don't you write a book?' So I did. I didn't sell the first five or six fiction books I wrote, but Maury Solomon, an editor at Franklin Watts, read some of my fiction and asked me to write my nonfiction book, *They Triumphed Over Their Handicaps*."

HOBBIES AND OTHER INTERESTS: Travel (Switzerland, Wales, England, Italy, Greece, France, Denmark, Sweden, and the Netherlands), swimming in Lake Champlain, Vermont.

HART, Bruce 1938-

BRIEF ENTRY: Born January 15, 1938, in New York, N.Y. A television writer and producer, lyricist, and author of books for young people, Hart received an A.B. from Syracuse University and a LL.D. from Yale University. Once a writer for the well-known "Candid Camera" television series, Hart was also on the original writing staff of "Sesame Street." With his wife Carole Hart, he was author, director, lyricist, and producer of the 1979 movie "Sooner or Later" which the two of them later adapted into a young adult novel. Also for young adults, the Harts created the "Hot Hero Sandwich" television series. They received two Emmy Awards for the series, in 1979 and 1980, for production and writing. As a lyricist, Hart has written songs like "Bang the Drum Slowly," "Can You Tell Me How to Get to Sesame Street," "Free to Be . . . You and Me" (theme song of a children's television special he produced with his wife and actress Marlo Thomas), and "You Take My Breath Away." He also wrote *The Sesame Street Song Book* and the *Sooner or Later Song Book*. According to Hart, ". . . Writing lyrics is . . . an invaluable way to prepare yourself for explorations into other forms of writing." In 1981 he and his wife wrote *Waiting Games*, a sequel to *Sooner or Later*. *Voice of Youth Advocates* described the main character,

Jesse Walters, as "warm and personable . . . [and] wonderfully refreshing," while *Book Report* commented on the "witty dialogue and . . . feeling for what it is to be young. . . ." *Office:* The Laughing Willow Co., 200 West 86th St., New York, N.Y. 10024. *For More Information See: People,* November 12, 1979; *Contemporary Authors,* Volume 107, Gale, 1983.

HART, Carole 1943-

BRIEF ENTRY: Born April 30, 1943, in Paterson, N.J. Television writer and producer, and author of books for young people. Hart graduated with honors from Barnard College in 1965. A member of the original writing staff of the "Sesame Street" show, she received an Emmy Award in 1970 for the show's pilot, "Sally Sees Sesame Street." In 1974 she was awarded her second Emmy for the children's television special "Free to Be . . . You and Me." The show was developed and produced in collaboration with her husband, lyricist Bruce Hart, and actress Marlo Thomas. Among the other television specials Hart created are "Taking Off" and "The First Annual Show of the Year," both for ABC-TV. Her credits also include several made-for-television movies like "Christine and Me," aired on NBC-TV in 1975, and "Senior Prom," a 1977 CBS-TV presentation. Also in 1977, she and Marlo Thomas again combined their talents on the ABC-TV holiday movie special "It Happened One Christmas," a successful remake of Frank Capra's classic film 'It's a Wonderful Life."

Hart's books for young people include *Deliah* (Harper, 1973), the story of a precocious ten year old. Deliah Bush beats the garbage man at a game of basketball, bangs on her drums in the park on a rainy day to chase away her "gloomies," and hints to her parents about buying her a record player for her birthday. *Bulletin of the Center for Children's Books* described Deliah as "an engaging character," adding that the book 'has a casual humor that is appealing." With her husband, Hart is the author of two young adult novels, *Sooner or Later* (Avon Flare Books, 1978) and its sequel, *Waiting Games* (Avon Flare Books, 1980). In *Waiting Games*, the Harts further explore teenager Jesse Walters's relationships with her guitar teacher (on whom she has a crush), her parents, and her best friend. *School Library Journal* found the book "dramatic, personal, and intense,' while *Voice of Youth Advocates* commented on the "realistic situations . . . [and] practical responses." In discussing her writing for young people, Hart has said: "I do find that my work aimed at this audience brings me the greatest satisfaction." *Office:* The Laughing Willow Co., 200 West 86th St., New York, N.Y. 10024. *For More Information See: People,* November 12, 1979; *Contemporary Authors,* Volume 107, Gale, 1983.

HAYWARD, Linda 1943-

BRIEF ENTRY: Born June 6, 1943, in Los Angeles, Calif. Author of books for young people. After graduating from the University of California in 1965, Hayward taught at schools in California. She was also an editor for several years in New York City, but turned to free-lance writing in 1974. Among her books for children are a number featuring Jim Henson's "Sesame Street" Muppets. All published by Golden Press, they include *The Case of the Missing Duckie,* 1980, *Going Up!: The Elevator Counting Book,* 1980, *Sesame Seasons,* 1981, and *A Day in the Life of Oscar the Grouch,* 1981. She also wrote _The Sesame Street Dictionary_ (Random House/Children's Television Workshop, 1980), which was described by _School Library Journal_ as "exploding with good fun." Similarly, _Publishers Weekly_ called _Letter, Sounds, and Words_ (Platt, 1973) "a mixture of pure fun and effective education. . . ." Recent works by Hayward include _When You Were a Baby, The Curious Little Kitten, The Curious Little Kitten: A Sniff Sniff Book, The Curious Little Kitten Gets Lost,_ and _The Simon & Schuster Picture Dictionary of Phonics from A to Zh. Residence:_ New York, N.Y. _For More Information See: Contemporary Authors,_ Volume 112, Gale, 1984.

HILL, Douglas (Arthur) 1935-
(Martin Hillman)

PERSONAL: Born April 6, 1935, in Brandon, Manitoba, Canada; son of William (a locomotive engineer) and Cora (a nurse; maiden name, Smith) Hill; married Gail Robinson (a poet and author), April 8, 1958 (divorced, 1980); children: Michael Julian. _Education:_ University of Saskatchewan, B.A. (with honors), 1957; University of Toronto, graduate study, 1957-59. _Home:_ 21 Farrer Top, Markyate, Hertfordshire, England. _Agent:_ Watson, Little, Suite 8, 26 Charing Cross Rd., London WC1H 0DG, England.

CAREER: Free-lance writer, 1959—; Aldus Books Ltd., London, England, editor, 1962-64; _Tribune_ (a London weekly), literary editor, 1971-84. Science fiction adviser to Rupert Hart-Davis, 1966-68, Mayflower Books, 1969-71, J. M. Dent & Sons, 1972-74, and to Pan Books, 1974-82.

WRITINGS: (With Pat Williams) _The Supernatural,_ Hawthorn, 1965; _The Peasants' Revolt,_ Jackdaw, 1966; (editor, and contributor under pseudonym Martin Hillman) _Window on the Future_ (anthology), Hart-Davis, 1966; _The Opening of the Canadian West,_ John Day, 1967; (editor) _The Devil His Due_ (anthology), Hart-Davis, 1967; _John Keats,_ Morgan-Grampian, 1968; _Magic and Superstition,_ Hamlyn, 1968; _Regency London,_ Macdonald, 1969.

Georgian London, Macdonald, 1970; _Return from the Dead,_ Macdonald, 1970; (under pseudonym Martin Hillman) _Bridging a Continent,_ Aldus, 1971; (editor, and contributor under pseudonym Martin Hillman) _Warlocks and Warriors_ (anthology), Mayflower, 1971; _Fortune Telling,_ Hamlyn, 1972; _The Scots to Canada,_ Gentry, 1972; _The Comet,_ Wildwood House, 1973; (reteller with wife, Gail Robinson Hill) _Coyote the Trickster: Legends of the North American Indians_ (juvenile; illustrated by Graham McCallum), Chatto & Windus, 1975, Scribner, 1976; _The English to New England,_ Gentry, 1975; (editor) _The Shape of Sex to Come_ (anthology), Pan Books, 1975; _The Exploits of Hercules_ (juvenile), Piccolo, 1977; (editor) _"Tribune" 40_ (anthology), Quartet, 1977; _Fortune Telling,_ Hamlyn, 1978; _Galactic Warlord_ (juvenile), Gollancz, 1979, Atheneum, 1980.

The Illustrated Faerie Queene (prose abridgement), Newsweek Books, 1980; (editor) _Alien Worlds: Stories of Adventure on Other Planets_ (juvenile; anthology), Heinemann, 1981; _Deathwing over Veynaa_ (juvenile), Atheneum, 1981; _Day of the Starwind_ (juvenile), Atheneum, 1981; _Planet of the Warlord_ (juvenile), Gollancz, 1981, Atheneum, 1982; _The Huntsman_ (juvenile), Heinemann, 1981, Atheneum, 1982; _Warriors of the Wasteland_ (juvenile), Atheneum, 1983; _Young Legionary_ (juvenile), Atheneum, 1983; _Alien Citadel_ (juvenile), Atheneum, 1984; _Exiles of Colsec_ (juvenile), Atheneum, 1984; _The Caves of Klydor,_ Gollancz, 1984.

Poems represented in anthologies, including _Poetmeat Anthology of British Poetry,_ edited by Dave Cunliffe, Screeches Publications, 1965; _Young British Poets,_ edited by Jeremy Robson, Poesie Vivante (Geneva), 1967; _Poems from Poetry and Jazz in Concert,_ edited by J. Robson, Souvenir Press, 1969.

Contributor of poems, book reviews, and articles to periodicals, including _Ambit, Akros, Adam International Review, Canadian Forum, Encounter, Poetry Review, New Statesman, New Worlds, Guardian, Books and Bookmen, Mayfair, Times Literary Supplement,_ and _Toronto Star._

WORK IN PROGRESS: Children's science fiction, an adult science fiction novel, and a fantasy trilogy.

SIDELIGHTS: About his work, Hill commented: "Diversity seems the keynote—recently extending it into children's fiction, science fiction, and so on, while maintaining a considerable output of literary journalism and occasional nonfiction books. [It] often seems [I work] an eight-day week and a twenty-five-hour day, but it's still the best way to live and to earn a living that I know."

HOBBIES AND OTHER INTERESTS: Television, reading, walking, cycling, photography.

HILLMAN, Priscilla 1940-

BRIEF ENTRY: Born July 24, 1940, in Newton, Mass. An author and illustrator of books for children, Hillman received her B.S. from the University of Rhode Island in 1963. For the next two years she was employed as an oceanographer at the U.S. Oceanographic Office in Suitland, Md. Her first children's book, _Minnikin, Midgie, and Moppet,_ was written with Adelaide Hall and published in 1977. Hillman has since written and illustrated a series of nine picture books aimed at preschool and early primary-grade readers. Published by Doubleday, the "Merry-Mouse" series includes: _A Merry-Mouse Christmas ABC_ (1980), _A Merry-Mouse Book of Nursery Rhymes_ (1981), _The Merry-Mouse Book of Prayers and Graces_ (1983), and _The Merry-Mouse Book of Toys_ (1983). The books convey a charming sense of country life, with woodland mice as the characters. _School Library Journal_ commented on "the delicately colored illustrations, with old-fashioned elements of country prints, mobcaps, and aprons . . . ," noting that the "mice are dressed like 19th-Century fashion models in beautiful cloaks, dresses and bonnets." Hillman's latest book is _Christmas Treasury,_ soon to be published by Doubleday. _Home:_ 11 Allen Pl., Sloatsburg, N.Y. 10974. _For More Information See: Contemporary Authors,_ Volume 108, Gale, 1983.

HILLS, C(harles) A(lbert) R(eis) 1955-

PERSONAL: Born August 21, 1955, in London, England; son of Arthur Ernest and Maria José (Reis) Hills. _Education:_ Hertford College, Oxford, B.A., 1976; University of Sussex, M.A., 1977; doctoral research at St. Antony's College, Oxford, 1977-78. _Politics:_ Conservative. _Home:_ 3 Lucas House, Albion Ave., London SW8 2AD, England. _Office:_ Business Press International, Quadrant House, The Quadrant, Sutton, Surrey, England.

CAREER: Stonehart Publications, London, England, editorial/production assistant, 1978-79; free-lance writer and editor, 1979-

81; Business Press International (formerly IPC Business Press), Sutton, England, news reporter for *Electrical and Radio Trading,* 1981—.

WRITINGS: The Rhine (juvenile), Silver Burdett, 1979; *The Danube* (juvenile), Silver Burdett, 1979; *The Fascist Dictatorships* (textbook), Batsford, 1979; *The Hitler File* (textbook), David & Charles, 1980; *World Trade* (textbook), David & Charles, 1981; *The Seine* (juvenile), Silver Burdett, 1981; *Modern Industry* (textbook), Batsford, 1982; *Growing Up in the 1950s,* David & Charles, 1983.

Contributor: John Gaisford, editor, *Atlas of Man,* Marshall Cavendish, 1978; J. P. Kenyon, editor, *A Dictionary of British History,* Secker & Warburg/Pan, 1981; *Nicholson's Historic Britain,* Nicholson Guides, 1982.

WORK IN PROGRESS: Law and Order; Living through the Second World War; Barbara Pym.

SIDELIGHTS: ''I have written mostly books for children and schools on history and geography, the two subjects in which I have university degrees. I began doing this sort of information writing while still a student by answering an advertisement for free-lance writers to work on a geographical/anthropological encyclopaedia. I found the work easy and congenial, although I realised from the beginning that it would be difficult to make a full-time living from that sort of work.

''Soon afterwards I applied for a job at a publishing house which I did not get. I wrote back to ask if they would like to consider me for free-lance work and mentioned that I had traveled widely in Germany. They wrote back and asked me if I would like to write a book for children about the Rhine River which was my first book, *The Rhine.* Since then, I have written a large number of books, mainly for the British publisher B. T. Batsford with which I have developed a close and happy working relationship.

''During this time I have developed a full-time career as a journalist and now have to fit in time for my writing in the evenings and during weekends. Sometimes, too, I have used holiday time to write. It is not easy, but I think it is a good sideline to have and I mean to continue with it.

''Although I get less time for my books now, my view of what is important in writing for school students has not changed. I try to express exactly the same insights as I would in writing for adults and I never simplify to the point of telling what I think is not the truth. Sometimes compromises are necessary, especially in matters of language, but I believe that to class readers into two fundamental groups—adults and the young— is doing both an injustice.''

Black-tailed godwits, wading birds which breed along the Danube. ■ (From *The Danube* by C. A. R. Hills.)

C. A. R. HILLS

HINTZ, (Loren) Martin   1945-

BRIEF ENTRY: Born June 1, 1945, in New Hampton, Iowa. Author of books for children. Hintz graduated from the College of St. Thomas in 1967 and received his M.A. the following year from Northwestern University. Now a free-lance writer and photographer, he has worked as a reporter/editor for the *Milwaukee Sentinel* and as contributing editor to *Group Travel*. His first book, *We Can't Afford It* (Raintree, 1977), was written with his wife Sandy. The story of a young girl who discovers her parents can't afford the shiny new bike she wants, it deals with a problem faced by many parents. *Booklist* took note of its "sensitivity to children's often unarticulated feelings. . . ." For two of his later books, Hintz drew upon past college experiences when he worked for Royal American Shows, the largest carnival in the United States. *Circus Workin's* (Messner, 1980) describes life under the big top, from set-up to performances, while *Tons of Fun: Training Elephants* (Messner, 1982) traces the history of the mammoth beasts in zoos and circuses. Both are illustrated with Hintz's own photographs. One of his latest books explores an entirely different but pertinent subject for children in today's world—computers. Also written with his wife, *Computers in Our World, Today and Tomorrow* (F. Watts, 1983) examines the upcoming roles of computers in all aspects of life, including government, education, entertainment, and the home. *For More Information See: Contemporary Authors,* Volumes 65-68, Gale, 1977.

HOLLANDER, Phyllis   1928-

PERSONAL: Born August 25, 1928, in New York, N.Y.; daughter of Harry (a lawyer) and Alice (a school principal:

The scoreboard at New York's Shea Stadium says it for a game that went 24 innings. ■ (From *The Baseball Book,* edited by Phyllis and Zander Hollander. Photograph courtesy of United Press International.)

maiden name, Root) Rosen; married Zander Hollander (a writer and editor), December 13, 1951; children: Susan, Peter. *Education:* University of Michigan, B.A., 1950; also attended Columbia University, 1950-52. *Office:* Associated Features, Inc., P.O. Box 1762, Murray Hill Station, New York, N.Y. 10156.

CAREER: Madison House Settlement, New York City, group worker, 1950-53; Associated Features Inc., New York City, senior editor, 1955—. Member of Baldwin Democratic Committee, Baldwin, N.Y., 1957-67.

WRITINGS: American Women in Sports, Grosset, 1972; (editor with husband, Zander Hollander) *They Dared to Lead: America's Black Athletes,* Grosset, 1973; (editor with Z. Hollander) *It's the Final Score That Counts,* Grosset, 1973; (editor with L. R. Herkimer) *The Complete Book of Cheerleading,* Doubleday, 1975; *One Hundred Greatest Women in Sports,* Grosset, 1976; (editor with Z. Hollander) *Touchdown!: Football's Most Dramatic Scoring Feats,* Random House, 1982; (editor with Z. Hollander) *The Baseball Book: A Complete A to Z Encyclopedia of Baseball,* Random House, 1982; *Winners under 21,* Random House, 1982; *The Masked Marvels: Baseball's Great Catchers,* Random House, 1982; (editor with Z. Hollander) *Sarajevo, 1984: The Comlete Handbook of the Olympic Winter Games,* Signet Books, 1983; (editor with Z. Hollander) *Los Angeles, 1984: The Complete Handbook of the Olympic Summer Games,* Signet Books, 1984.

WORK IN PROGRESS: The Women's Sports Encyclopedia.

HOLLINGSWORTH, Alvin C(arl) 1930-

PERSONAL: Born February 25, 1930, in New York, N.Y.; son of Charles and Cynthia (Jones) Hollingsworth; married Stephanie Knoplur, 1966; children: Steven, Kevin, Kim, Raymond. *Education:* Attended Art Students League, 1950-52; City College (now of the City University of New York), B.A., 1956, M.A., 1959; further graduate study, New York University. *Agent:* (Paintings) Lee Nordness Gallery, 236 East 75th St., New York, N.Y. 10021; and Harbor Gallery, 43 Main St., Cold Spring Harbor, N.Y. 11724. *Office:* Hostos Community College, City University of New York, New York, N.Y. 10021.

CAREER: Artist. High School of Art and Design, New York, N.Y., instructor in graphics, 1961-70; Art Students League, New York, N.Y., instructor in painting, 1969-74; Hostos Community College, New York, N.Y., assistant professor, 1971-77, associate professor of painting, 1977, currently full professor. Consultant on art and coordinator, Harlem Freedom School, Office of Economic Opportunity, 1966-67; director, Lincoln Institute of Psycho-Therapy Art Gallery, 1966-68; art supervisor, "Project Turn-On," New York Board of Education, 1968-69; artist-teacher, Scarsdale Studio Workshop, 1968; instructor, U.S.D.A.N. Center for Creative and Permanent Arts, 1970—. Has executed commissions, including Don Quixote limited edition lithographs for Original Lithographs, Inc., 1967, Don Quixote murals for Don Quixote Apartments, Bronx, N.Y., 1969, and mural for Rutgers University, 1970.

EXHIBITIONS: Work has appeared in numerous exhibitions, including: Jewish Museum, New York, 1957; "Art U.S.A.," Madison Square Garden, New York, N.Y., 1957; National Academy, 1958; Bodley Gallery, New York, 1958; Spiral Group, New York, N.Y., 1962; Emily Lowe Award Exhibition, 1963; Museum of African Art, Washington, D.C., 1964; Urban Show,

ALVIN C. HOLLINGSWORTH

New School Art Gallery, 1965, 1966; Terry Dintenfass Gallery, New York, N.Y., 1965; "Travelling Black Painters of America," University of California, Los Angeles, Calif., 1966; Koltnow Gallery, 1967; Man of LaMancha Exhibition, ANTA Theater, 1967; Oakland Museum, Oakland, Calif., 1967; Nassau Community College, Long Island, N.Y., 1968; Metropolitan Museum of Art, New York, N.Y., 1969; "New Voices," Hallmark Gallery, New York, N.Y., 1969; Bostom Museum of Fine Arts, Boston, Mass., 1970; Contemporary Arts Museum, Houston, Tex., 1970; New York State Museum, Trenton, N.J., 1970; "American Black Painters," Whitney Museum of American Art, New York, N.Y., 1971; "The Women," Interfaith Council of Churches, 1978; "Reflections of the Prophet," Pennsylvania State University, University Park, 1978. Work is represented in the permanent collections of Chase Manhattan Bank, Brooklyn Museum, IBM, Williams College, Johnson Publishing Co., and others.

One-man shows: Ward Eggleston Gallery, 1961; Harbor Gallery, 1968-69, 1971-72, 1975; Staten Island Museum, New York, N.Y., 1969; St. John's University, New York, N.Y., 1973; County College, Morris, N.J., 1973; Borough of Manhattan Community College, New York, N.Y., 1975; Afro-American Museum, Los Angeles, Calif., 1977; Penn State University, 1978; San Antonio Cultural Center, Tex., 1980; Noa Gallery, Washington, D.C., 1980; NBC Gallery, 1981; Cellar Gallery, So. Nyack, N.Y., 1983. *Member:* Artists Equity Association, Art Students League, Spiral, Phi Beta Kappa. *Awards, honors:* Recipient of awards from City Center Art Competition, 1956, Technicrafts Graphic Arts Competition,

1958, and Bodley Gallery National Drawing Competition, 1958; Emily Lowe Art Competition Award, 1963; Whitney fellowship, 1964; Artist of the Year Award from New York University, 1967; Cultural Award of the Year in Art from Alumni Association of High School of Music and Art, 1975; named NAACP Show Man of the Year, 1979; Artist of the Year Award from Bronx Museum of the Arts, 1980.

WRITINGS: (With Walter Brooks) *The Art of Acrylic Painting,* Golden Press, 1969; *I'd Like the Goo-gen-heim* (juvenile; self-illustrated), Reilly & Lee, 1970. Art critic for the *National Scene,* 1978-83. Contributor to *American Artist, Art in Society, Black Art Quarterly.*

Illustrator: Arnold Adoff, compiler, *Black Out Loud: An Anthology of Modern Poems by Black Americans* (juvenile; ALA Notable Book), Macmillan, 1970.

SIDELIGHTS: Hollingsworth writes that his recent accomplishments include: "A mural for Hostos Community College entitled, 'Hostos Odessey'; a commissioned portrait of Rose Morgan presented to her in June, 1981; a commissioned portrait of Lena Horne presented to her in May, 1982 in celebration for fifty years in show business. I am currently a full professor of art at Hostos Community College [New York]."

Hollingsworth has written and hosted television series on art, including a 1970 ten-part series, "You're Part of Art," an "Ethnic American" series shown on NBC-TV in 1973, and another series for NBC-TV, also entitled "You're Part of Art," which was completed in 1976.

FOR MORE INFORMATION SEE: New York Post, January 10, 1970; *Art Gallery,* April, 1970; *New York Amsterdam News,* October 17, 1970; *New York Times,* January 3, 1971; *Essence,* February, 1971; *Black Art Quarterly,* Fall, 1977.

HOOVER, Helen (Drusilla Blackburn) 1910-1984 (Jennifer Price)

OBITUARY NOTICE—See sketch in *SATA* Volume 12: Born January 20, 1910, in Greenfield, Ohio; died of peritonitis, June 30, 1984, in Fort Collins, Colo. Metallurgist and author. A metallurgist by profession, Hoover was the author of books on wildlife and the wilderness, including the young adult titles *The Gift of the Deer* and *Place in the Woods,* and of books for children, including *Great Wolf and the Good Woodsman* and *Animals Near and Far.* She was also an author of women's fiction and of contributions to juvenile magazines under the pseudonym Jennifer Price. *For More Information See:* Helen Hoover, *The Years of the Forest,* Knopf, 1973; *Contemporary Authors,* Volumes 21-24, revised, 1977; *The Writers Directory: 1984-1986,* St. James Press, 1983. *Obituaries: New York Times,* July 7, 1984.

HUNT, Linda Lawrence   1940- (Linda Lawrence)

PERSONAL: Born September 3, 1940, in Spokane, Wash.; daughter of Harold and Evelyn (Roth) Christensen; married James Barton Hunt (a professor of history), February 21, 1968; children: Susan Noelle, Jefferson Kim (adopted), Krista Kim-

Linda Lawrence Hunt (right) with coauthors Doris Liebert (left) and Marianne Frase (middle).

(From *Loaves and Fishes* by Linda Hunt, Marianne Frase, and Doris Liebert. Illustrated by Seho Park.)

berly. *Education:* University of Washington, Seattle, B.A., 1962, graduate study, 1968; Whitworth College, M.A.T., 1978. *Residence:* Spokane, Wash. *Office:* Department of English, Whitworth College, Spokane, Wash. 99251.

CAREER: Junior high school teacher of English and social studies in Glendora, Calif., 1962-64; high school teacher of English and social studies in Edmunds, Wash., 1967-69; Young Women's Christian Association, Spokane, Wash., director of public relations and coordinator of volunteers, 1975-77; Spokane Community College, Spokane, instructor in communications, 1978-81; Whitworth College, Spokane, coordinator of freshman writing program and teacher of writing courses, 1981—. Emory University, fellow at the Institute of Faith Development, 1983. Member of board of directors of Spokane Cooperative Health Plan, 1975-77. *Awards, honors:* Danforth associate, 1980.

WRITINGS: (With Marianne Frase and Doris Liebert) *Loaves and Fishes* (nonfiction), Herald Press, 1980; (with M. Frase and D. Liebert) *Celebrate the Seasons* (a children's gardening book), Herald Press, 1983; (with Twyla Lubben) *Christina's World,* Zondervan, 1985. Contributor to regional and national magazines, including, *Reader's Digest, Family Circle, Woman's Day, Psychology Today* and *Guideposts.* Contributing editor of *Spokane.*

SIDELIGHTS: "My husband and I took a sabbatical leave in spring of 1983, where we worked with Dr. James Fowler at

Emory University, the pioneer researcher bridging the fields of psychology and theology through his 'Stages of Faith' model. For my master's thesis I interviewed married couples, exploring the impact of family dynamics on faith development. Faith, defined by Fowler, involves everyone . . . not just specific religious definitions, but rather how people 'make meaning' out of their lives.

"Our trip to Emory was the second cross-country trip we've taken with our three children, which provided us the joy of exploring the by-ways of America again. Discovering the Great Smokey Mountains, returning to the Blue-Ridge country, talking with Cherokee Indians, Atlanta landscape designers, Morehouse College faculty, southern farmers, etc. enriched our sense of the exquisite diversity and visions of America's land and people.

"This may lead into my next writing project, which is a joint effort with my historian husband on a true story of two Spokane women who walked alone across America in 1896. They walked the rails with the promised reward of $10,000 if they succeeded within six months. Most likely, our approach will be in the form of an historical novel."

The things I want to know are in books; my best friend is the man who'll get me a book I ain't read.
—Abraham Lincoln

HUNTER, Mel   1927-

PERSONAL: Born July 27, 1927, in Oak Park, Ill.; son of Milford J. (a business executive) and Lucille (Clarkson) Hunter; married Nan Foster (divorced, April, 1969); married Nancy O'Connor (an art gallery director), August 23, 1969; children: Lisa, Scott, Amy. *Education:* Attended Northwestern University. *Home:* 60-B Lakeview Terr., Burlington, Vt. 05401. *Office:* Atelier North Star, 87-B North Ave., Burlington, Vt. 05401.

CAREER: Free-lance writer and illustrator/photographer, 1950-72; fine art printmaker, 1972-84; founder and master printer of Atelier North Star, Inc., 1983—. *Awards, honors: Strategic*

Air Command was named best aviation book of the year by Aviation and Space Writers Association, 1962.

WRITINGS—All for children; all self-illustrated; all nonfiction: *How the Earth Began,* World Publishing, 1972, reprinted as *Prehistoric Earth,* F. Watts, 1975; *How Man Began,* World Publishing, 1972, reprinted as *Prehistoric Man,* F. Watts, 1974; *How Fishes Began,* World Publishing, 1972, reprinted as *Prehistoric Fishes,* F. Watts, 1974; *How Plants Began,* World Publishing, 1972, reprinted as *Prehistoric Plants,* F. Watts, 1975.

Adult nonfiction: *The Missilemen,* Doubleday, 1960; *Strategic Air Command,* Doubleday, 1961; (editor and contributor) *The*

MEL HUNTER

At least one night a week is bowling night for many a missileman. ■ (From *The Missilemen* by Mel Hunter.)

Mylar Method Manifesto, Atelier North Star, 1979; *The New Lithography: A Complete Guide for Artists and Printers in the Use of Modern Translucent Materials for the Creation of Hand-Drawn Fine-Art Lithographic Prints,* Van Nostrand, 1983. Also contributor to *American Artist.*

Illustrator; all for children; all nonfiction, except as noted: Edward Victor, *Friction,* Follett, 1961; E. Victor, *Machines,* Follett, 1962; Alvin Silverstein and Virginia Silverstein, *Unusual Partners: Symbiosis in the Living World,* McGraw-Hill, 1968; Barbara Goodheart, *A Year on the Desert,* Prentice-Hall, 1969; Griffing Bancroft, *Snowy: The Story of an Egret,* McCall, 1970; Hayden Carruth, compiler, *The Bird/Poem Book: Poems on the Wild Birds of North America,* McCall, 1970; Vera Chaplin, *True Stories from the Moscow Zoo,* translated from the Russian by Estelle Titiev and Lila Pargment, Prentice-Hall,

1970; George K. Stone, *More Science Projects You Can Do,* Prentice-Hall, 1970.

Contributor of illustrations to *Time-Life Books* and *Encyclopaedia Americana,* and to various periodicals, including *Life, Colliers, National Geographic, Newsweek,* and others.

SIDELIGHTS: "Since 1972 I have been working entirely in the field of fine art original prints, especially hand-drawn color lithography, producing to date 113 editions, most in many colors. All during this period, I have been continuously pressing the medium for improvement in techniques and tools, to make this difficult medium much more accessible to artists. Many breakthroughs have been made, and a whole new field of color printmaking has appeared, now used by hundreds of artists who could not have made their prints by the old methods. My books are my effort to spread the how-to information as broadly as I can.

"Atelier North Star has recently been established to put the most advanced techniques of modern fine art lithography into practice in the first important professional print workshop especially equipped for the purpose. In it, all the advances described in *The New Lithography* are applied to the printing of lithographic editions by professional artists of every type, and regular college and postgraduate courses of instruction bring students and professional artists into contact, to the benefit of both."

HÜRLIMANN, Bettina   1909-1983

PERSONAL: Born June 19, 1909, in Weimar, Germany (now East Germany); died July 9, 1983, in Zollikon, Switzerland; daughter of Gustav (a publisher) and Irmgard (maiden name, Funcke) Kiepenheuer; married Martin Hürlimann (an author and publisher), February, 1933; children: Barbara (deceased), Regine, Christoph, Ulrich. *Education:* Attended Academy of Graphic Arts and Book Printing, Leipzig, Germany, c. 1928-29. *Residence:* Zurich, Switzerland.

CAREER: Author of and specialist in children's literature. Early in career, worked in Bristol, England, and as a publisher and free-lance writer for newspapers; Atlantis Verlag (publishing firm founded by husband, Martin Hürlimann), Berlin, publisher and editor, 1933-39, Zurich, Switzerland, publisher and editor, 1939-75; has also worked in numerous capacities for International Board on Books for Young People since its inception in the 1950s.

WRITINGS: (Compiler) *Eia Popeia* (juvenile verse; title means "Hushaby Baby"; illustrated by Fritz Kredel), Atlantis Verlag, 1936; *Die Jahreszeiten,* Atlantis Verlag, 1936; *Michael's Haus,* Atlantis Verlag, 1949; (author of introduction) *Kinderbilder in fünf Jahrhunderten europaischer Malerei,* Atlantis Verlag, 1949, translation published as *Children's Portraits: The World of the Child in European Painting,* Thames & Hudson, 1950; *Europaische Kinderbücher in drei Jahrhunderten,* Atlantis Verlag, 1959, translated and edited by Brian W. Alderson, published as *Three Centuries of Children's Books in Europe,* Oxford University Press, 1967, World Publishing, 1968; *Klein und Gross* (title means "Small and Big"), Atlantis Verlag, 1965; *Die Welt im Bilderbuch: Moderne Kinderbilderbücher aus 24 Ländern,* Atlantis Verlag, 1965, translated and edited by B. W. Alderson, published as *Picture-Book World: Modern Picture-Books for Children from Twenty-Four Countries,* Oxford

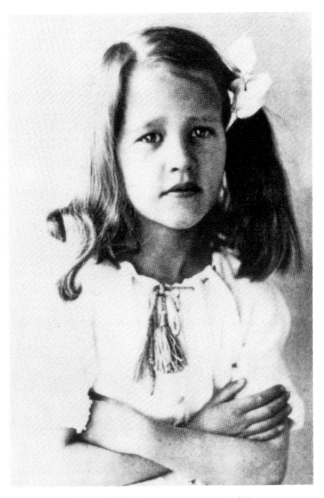

Bettina Hürlimann as a young child.

University Press, 1968, World Publishing, 1969; *Der Knabe des Tell* (juvenile; illustrated by Paul Nussbaumer), Atlantis Verlag, 1965, translated and adapted by Elizabeth D. Crawford, published as *William Tell and His Son,* Harcourt, 1967; *Barry: Ein Bilderbuch* (juvenile; illustrated by Nussbaumer), Atlantis Verlag, 1967, translation by E. D. Crawford published as *Barry: The Story of a Brave St. Bernard,* Harcourt, 1968.

(Adapter) Chiyoko Nakatani, *Fumio and die Delphine* (title means "Fumio and the Dolphins"), Atlantis Verlag, 1970; *Sieben Häuser: Aufzeichnungen einer Bücherfrau,* Artemis Verlag, 1976, translated by Anthea Bell published as *Seven Houses: My Life with Books* (autobiography), Bodley Head, 1976, Crowell, 1977; *Zwischenfall in Lerida, und andere Texte,* Atlantis Verlag, 1979. Contributor of articles to periodicals, including *Graphis* and *Horn Book.*

SIDELIGHTS: **June 19, 1909,** Born in Weimar, Germany; daughter of publishers, Gustav and Irmgard Kiepenheuer. Many years later Hürlimann reflected on her birthplace and her given name: "The accident of birth which had brought the child to a city of poets and philosophers was obviously none of her own doing, but was due to her parents. They themselves were not in fact natives of Weimar. . . . The poets' city of Weimar had lured them to settle there, and they called their daughter Bettina, which was an unusual name for a child at the time, and called to mind the romantic figure of Goethe's friend Bet-

Strong, friendly Barry had become a sad, sick dog. ■ (From *Barry: The Story of a Brave St. Bernard* by Bettina Hürlimann. Translated and adapted from the German by Elizabeth D. Crawford.)

tina Brentano.'' [Bettina Hürlimann, *Seven Houses: My Life with Books,* Crowell, 1977.[1]]

1914. Began school. ''I had been looking forward to school enormously. Hitherto I had had to depend on my mother, who read aloud with great dramatic expression, for my glimpses of the world of books. Now I was conquering it by my own efforts. But learning to read at school proved far too slow for me. The simple phrases of my primer were much inferior to what I was used to hearing my mother read aloud. However . . . my father published a book which made a satisfactory focus for my first attempts to read and also held me spellbound. It was called simply *Ein Kinderbuch* ('A Children's Book'), a collection of stories and verses by a young teacher with illustrations by his pupils. This was a completely new and astonishing venture for that time.

''It was, in fact, much later that I realized what a privilege it was to be the child of a publisher. As children, we saw more of the disadvantages, because my mother, too, became involved. This meant less story telling and fewer family outings, even when we were quite small.

'' . . . My childhood was surrounded by bookshelves, and even in those early days in Weimar, those who turned up at our house as guests were mostly artists, authors, or even printers,

like the great typographer Mardersteig, whose name I thought fascinating, and whose work at the Officina Bodoni later became a great example to me. It was only when I grew up that I realized what a unique gift all this had been.''[1]

1918. Moved to Potsdam, Germany. ''During the years we were living in our Potsdam apartment, we had a houseboat by way of refreshing contrast; for a time we even had two. The first, named *Eulalia* after our tortoise in Weimar, was my father's property. It was like a miniature ark, and I think the way for my parents' divorce was paved in that boat. My father would often disappear in it (so far as the gas shortage during the inflation would allow), and he received his authors there. Sometimes I was allowed to play hostess.

''The other and considerably larger houseboat was definitely my mother's property, and her own domain. . . .

''Not only was there my father's skiff, but a canoe, a punt, later two sailboats, and an unsinkable tub of a rowboat especially for us children. The bank of the Havel, with all these boats, was the great luxury of our childhood. It replaced the seaside holidays we almost never had, and helped us through our times of loneliness.

''We spent almost all our free time on the water, mostly in the bigger houseboat, which had living quarters comprising a large dining room, cabins, and a kitchen, and was moored to some spot on the reed-grown riverbank. From our beds, we could see waterfowl on their nests when we woke at dawn. Every now and then, however, the boat would pull free from its moorings in bad weather, and we would wake up somewhere else and have to punt our laborious way back. Life on the river was full of adventure, and our floating home was a great attraction.

"How our parents ever managed to steer us and all these boats through those times of poverty and inflation still amazes me. I suspect that my mother had convinced the owner of the boatyard that he owed it to himself to possess a library of the classics in a luxury edition, bound in pigskin, and that that was how she came by her beautiful sailboat. For book publishing was a precarious trade at the time."[1]

1922. Parents separated. "We children lived with our mother, who by now had found the most beautiful house imaginable. It was close to one of the gates of the newer part of San Souci Park, near Wildpark, and was called the Fasanerie. It had been built in the neoclassical manner around 1830 by Persius, a pupil of the great Prussian architect Schinkel.

"Throughout our adolescence this house, surrounded by one of the most beautiful parks I know, was the background to our lives. The park itself must have been far more beautiful in our day than in the age of Frederick the Great and his successors, Frederick William III and IV, who with the help of some famous gardeners created it and laid it out. The saplings they had planted were now dignified giants of trees, and the many statues and buildings nestled in a landscape that seemed almost natural, though enhanced by art. Growing up among such scenes must affect one's life significantly."[1]

During her adolescent years Hürlimann became interested in art. ". . . I began to paint watercolors of things that interested me. Though sometimes I unconsciously imitated the painter Nolde, my artistic efforts were the most original things I was producing at the time. I was always particularly happy when painting.

"On school excursions, too, painting and drawing opened my eyes to the beauties of nature and art. I kept up this early love of art, encouraged by my drawing teacher Gertrud Jackstein. She got us to study art history, and when I grew up and became a publisher, she was always, to the end of her life, urging me to write and produce an illustrated history of art for children. It was a great disappointment to her that I turned instead to children's books in general and their history.

"So I painted, immersing myself as far as possible in the great world of art, and I found that my own pictures seemed to express something that was important to me as well. I was disappointed, therefore, when a few years later I sent my collected artistic work to the Academy of Art in Leipzig, and it failed to win me a place in the painting class. This was to have a decisive influence on my life, since I then turned to typography and printing in order to go into publishing on the production side, a job covering activities that had fascinated me in my childhood and youth and led to my early attempts at designing jackets, illustrations, and text pages. The making of books was in my blood."[1]

1928-29. Attended the Academy of Graphic Arts and Book Printing in Leipzig, Germany. "Life at the Academy was very entertaining. My fellow students were mostly the sons of master painters, publishers, and typefounders, and came from all over

Hürlimann, age twenty-one.

Europe, from Poland to Spain. They also included future graphic artists, designers, and illustrators.

"As well as learning typography, we had skilled artists to teach all graphic techniques, and there were experts to instruct us in composing, printing, and bookbinding. At this time it was the only college of its kind in Europe, hence its cosmopolitan nature. There were also drawing and painting classes, which I should have liked to attend, but as I wanted to start on the practical part of my career as soon as possible, I could only go to the evening classes, where I drew with enthusiasm and some degree of success. I had some lively relationships with the students at the illustration class; even then the future publisher in me was taking note of potential children's book illustrators, though my mind was not on children's books at all yet. I was absorbed in literature and the pursuit of art.

"To all outward appearances, anyway, the composing stick was my destiny. The technical knowledge I acquired during those eighteen months was to form the basis of my career for years, indeed, for a large part of my life.

"And I almost made the composing stick my own career. Just as I had more or less mastered the technique, the Officina Bodoni, under Hans Mardersteig in Verona, was looking for a compositor. I applied for the post and was accepted, but when the manager looked more closely at my signature, which was not very clearly written, and found it was a girl's name, he turned me down. Instead I began a kind of apprenticeship in the Bibliographical Institute of Leipzig, in the encyclopedia offices, where my job included picture research as well as typographical work. Illustrations were still mostly drawings then, and I was able to put a good deal of work in the way of my poverty-stricken fellow students from the Academy. I myself had to see my boss every Saturday afternoon—this was the last Herr Meyer of Meyer's Encyclopaedia—and tell him exactly what I had learned and what I had done that week.

"From this pleasant existence, where study mingled happily with practical work and I was surrounded by a circle of friends, I was summoned home. My mother was not well, and had prescribed herself a vegetarian diet of raw foods which took a lot of preparation. As her daughter, I was needed, inexperienced as I was in this kind of thing. I was supposed to prepare juices, soups, and raw vegetable salads according to the dictates of a new and distinctly fanatical theory of nutrition, without any of the gadgets to be found in every kitchen today. When my mother did not starve to death, but actually got better, I was sent off to a domestic-science college to perfect myself in the feminine virtues.

"This did not suit me at all. I had discovered in Leipzig where my inclinations lay; I was fascinated by everything to do with the making of books—typography, illustration, paper, binding. I also read the latest modern literature with great enthusiasm, and went to see plays written by my father's authors. (I did not have the money to go to other plays for which there were no free tickets available.) Attending a domestic-science college in Potsdam was the last thing I wanted to do. I thought that what I had learned by now, coupled with my own enthusiasm, should suffice to earn me a living. So what could save me? Only a job where I actually earned money—that was the vital point."[1]

Hürlimann interviewed for a job as production assistant in the publishing house of Atlantis Verlag, which was run by Martin Hürlimann, but was turned down. "At the same time as I was so desperately looking for a job, I was getting more and more interested in literature, and in a way it would have been paradise for me to work in my father's firm, which had moved to Berlin by now. In fact, though I was so keen to learn all about book production, and was already a good typographer, neither of my parents suggested taking me into their firms."[1]

1930. Through the intervention of a close friend, Hürlimann secured a position as a private tutor to an English family. She lived and taught in England for a year.

1931. Returning to Germany, Hürlimann was accepted as a trainee at Atlantis Verlag. "So now I was employed by Atlantis Verlag, and attended the staff meetings. I can still see them all before me; accountants and packers of every shade of political opinion. The only really striking figures were the packer who called himself a 'sympathizer,' since he was not actually a communist but sympathized with the Communist Party, and the production assistant who was active in the socialist youth movement and brought out a magazine called *Das Lagerfeuer* ('The Campfire'). The secretaries regarded a new girl who could not do shorthand with some suspicion, but apart from that were very pleasant. I soon found myself doing overtime, in spite of my trainee status, since the socialist production assistant, Eberhard Koebel, soon proceeded to more interesting things, which were not connected with the publishing firm except through his magazine. Thus I took on his job as far as I was able to, and in this capacity I came to be the director's assistant. In February 1933, I became Martin Hürlimann's wife."[1]

1933. "By now, Hitler was Chancellor of the Reich; he had demonstrated his seizure of power in the symbolic shrine of Prussianism, the old Garrison Church whose bells I used to hear as a schoolgirl, and which was quite close to the hotel Zum Einsiedler, where our wedding reception was held.

"The Reichstag building went up in flames while we were on our honeymoon; several of the telegrams we received at our wedding came from Amsterdam, the place to which the first of the refugees from the Third Reich fled, among them many of my father's authors or colleagues. The landslide had begun, and we knew it. However, like any other newly married couple, we were happy and full of confidence.

"There were two of us; we were strong as lions and had publishing ideas enough to keep three firms occupied, and from now on we shared our joys and our sorrows. We were to have plenty of both.

"Our own family, consisting of our four children, Barbara (born in 1933), Regine (1935), Christoph (1938) and Ulrich (1942), became very much part of the 'publishing family,' and they seemed to have no objection. After a period of living in an old-fashioned Berlin apartment in Schöneberg, where Barbara spent the first few months of her life (this was at a time when the firm, over half its large staff cut, was trying to keep its head above water in spite of the crisis with a tiny band of workers), we moved to a villa at Roseneck in the Grünewald. This was to be our first family home as well as our first new home for the firm. In fact, the building housed only the editorial offices of *Atlantis* magazine, the production department, and the publishing offices; distribution was handled in Leipzig."[1]

1933-1939. Expanded their publishing house, Atlantis Verlag. "We were producing a great variety of books in those Berlin years. . . . The tradition of photographic volumes, a field in which the firm was prominent, embraced both European and non-European elements, and the head of the firm went on running his business along lines as cosmopolitan as possible; being a foreigner, he was able to escape the bars that the Third Reich was erecting around its people. Books on music figured with increasing frequency on our list, and later, when we started our Swiss branch, it included a number of books by Swiss authors.

"Amidst all this, our books for children, a slight but colorful constituent of our list, were really more of a hobby at first, arising from our affection for children."[1]

1935. Because of the scarcity of good children's books for their own children to read, the Hürlimanns decided to publish children's books. "Throughout most of the history of our firm . . . the Children's Book Department was like a small green meadow set in the midst of a vast landscape encompassing strange lands and their strange gods along with our own native literature, the worlds of music and ideas, and even on occasion of politics. It was a meadow I tended carefully for years. Would it ever have come into being if we ourselves had had no children. . . . I sometimes used to wonder whether children growing up, as ours were, among so much that was beautiful and creative, not to mention that element of the strange and exotic they knew from their father's Far Eastern travels, might find that this inhibited their own gifts and means of self-expression. Did it do so? It was for our elder daughter, Barbara . . . that we produced our first children's books, had them illustrated, and published them.

". . . In addition, I went on painting my own picture books; each year I made a book specially for one of the children, painting the pictures and lettering the text myself, and learning in the process how to tackle the difficulties of marrying text and illustration. We worked fast; a year later, by which time our second daughter, Regine, was reaching for picture books, too, our Children's Book Department was launched with three new publications. The first two were books of verse for children of which the first, compiled by me, contained traditional German rhymes, like that book published by my father which I had loved so much as a small child, *Die Sonne im alten Kinderlied* ('The Sun in the Old Nursery Rhyme')."[1]

1939. Left Berlin for her husband's native home in Zurich, Switzerland. "All the time we were busy keeping the firm

Tell grew pale. To shoot an apple from the head of his son? What if he missed? ■ (From *William Tell and His Son* by Bettina Hürlimann. Illustrated by Paul Nussbaumer.)

going in Berlin, living through the first years of the Nazi regime in an atmosphere of intensive work, we had been preparing for our 'return home' to Switzerland. Only for Martin was it really a homecoming; to me, it was more like going into exile, though a very pleasant exile when I compared it with the fate of the genuine emigrants from Hitler's Germany. I had formed close ties with my own country again after my return from England, and right up to the end I felt that life in Germany held the possibility of a political volte-face. I did not want to think about leaving. Martin, though he was happy in Berlin, had been more pessimistic, and had provided for the future of the firm in Zurich. . . . This Zurich office was, in a way, to be my first home in Switzerland, until I found a house for all of us.''[1]

Settled her family in a village near Zurich called Zollikon. ''This house was to be our home for the second period of our marriage, and up to the present day. Here, in a house that looked rather commonplace, but was romantically situated beside a stream, with fields, meadows, and woods not far away, our children grew up in natural freedom. Friends and authors from all over the world came to visit us in Zollikon. I cultivated our garden, doing my bit in the fight for self-sufficiency, like every other Swiss citizen who had a garden. And here, in the midst of this peaceful country, we suffered the terrors of war for those we knew and loved in the countries round about.

''Gradually, in spite of the war, our house in Zollikon was filled with new life. The stream running behind it was very noisy in wet weather, but only a cool trickle when the weather was dry; our children used to build dams across it. It was through the children that I came to know our neighbors. This was still a country community, where everyone knew everyone else; a world apparently still unharmed, one that moved me and filled me with a certain longing, and I felt that I must accept its rules and customs and learn them for myself. To a certain extent I succeeded. However, it was not easy to become genuinely Swiss, though I found that something to help me would happen every day. Best of all was when I brought a genuine little Swiss boy into the world in 1942, Ueli [Ulrich], the only one of our children to be born in his own country.''[1]

1942. Besides publishing children's books, Hürlimann wrote books for children and books on children's literature and lectured on children's literature as well. ''How was it that the world of children's books came to surround me like a second skin, like a house of my own, becoming a part of me without my actual volition? Did any action of my own set the process in motion? Hardly, since I had so many other, different interests, to which I was drawn by my reading and writing. However, one can acquire an 'image' quite involuntarily, and the fact was that I shared these other interests with a great many people, while at the time I began studying the children's lit-

Hürlimann surrounded by her grandchildren.

erature of the world all those years ago and found myself becoming involved in all the different aspects of the subject, it had previously been the province only of a few historians and educational specialists. I was not an expert of this kind, just someone with a knowledge of literature who had also learned the technique of book production. I also had children of my own, and worked in a publishing house.''[1]

As an editor and publisher, Hürlimann was largely responsible for creating an international market for children's books. She was the first to publish Indian and Japanese children's books in the West; she was instrumental in bringing many Eastern artists to international acclaim; and she was a founder of the International Board on Books for Young People, for which she was also a discoverer of new talent from around the world, whom she introduced to the ranks of children's literature. ''Some two hundred manuscripts a year would come through my door, laden with hope as if with dynamite. After the publication of my books on children's literature, many were encouraged to write to me for advice. The manuscripts might come with pictures handsomely mounted, or they might arrive by second-

class mail looking rather creased, but they always did arrive safely. Some authors decorated the wrapping paper with colorful samples of their work; in fact, our mail in the Children's Book Department was always full of color and variety, and was very international in character.''[1]

Among the list of famous artists and authors whose children's books Hürlimann first published were the Hungarian Joseph Domjan, the German Heidrun Petrides, the Englishman Brian Wildsmith, the Japanese artist Chiyoko Nakatani, the Swiss picture-book artist Paul Nussbaumer, and another Swiss author Ruth Hürlimann, who bore the same last name, but was not related to her mentor Bettina Hürlimann.

1959. An interest in children's literature prompted Hürlimann to collect rare editions of children's books and to write a book on her study of children's books entitled *Three Centuries of Children's Books in Europe*. ''I did run into one great difficulty in working on the book. I had four children who were all still at school, and while this certainly added lively interest to my work, it kept me tied to the house. I was already spending part of each day on editorial and typographical work at the firm, and I could not spend long hours in libraries reading such authorities as Comenius, von Basedow, Bertuch, Campe, and so on, in the original. Yet this was something that I had to do if I was to give a proper account of them; as for the equivalent works in other languages than German, they were even harder for me to find.

"As editor of a magazine, Martin used to spend some of his time in the city's Central Library, and he brought me home many books, but much of the material was not in the library or was kept in reference sections and could not be borrowed. So I began collecting. My original hunting ground was in secondhand bookshops of all kinds and in their catalogues. Sometimes I was lucky, but more often than not more expert collectors had been before me. In addition, friends found me books, and sometimes I got whole parcels of secondhand books as a present—rather a dusty and cumbersome sort of present, but there might be a rare nugget of gold inside. In one such apparently worthless consignment I once found the commentary to the first edition of Grimm's *Tales,* fresh as a daisy and uncut. There were times when I got almost nothing but old children's books for Christmas and my birthday. My own husband was the most resourceful of my suppliers. After we had both been looking out for it for years, Martin managed to get me the first edition of Grimm's *Tales* themselves, one of the rarest and most valuable things in German literature. This was a high point in my life as a collector; I was completely taken by surprise, and burst into tears as I held the volumes in my hands. . . ."[1]

1964-68. Made two trips to India. "My hardest task during my visits to India was to reconcile myself somehow or other, inwardly and outwardly, to the existence of these beggars, especially the children."[1]

1967. Sold Atlantis Verlag. "And then one day it all came to an end. Since none of our children was following in our footsteps, we decided, in 1967, to sell the firm, though we stayed on in the old house until 1972, and I remained faithful to my 'house of children's books.'

"I remained faithful to the firm a while longer; my desk went with me, but not my very own house or children's books. Its day was over. It stayed behind, somewhere in the old building; perhaps I ought to put up a tablet in its memory, since the frail old house has recently become subject to a protection order, and will stand for a long time yet.

"And I have done, too, with the making of books as we practiced it for thirty years in the House of Patience, along with our authors, printers, and bookbinders, though I suppose I shall never be done with it in my mind. The tools of the trade— type catalogue, slide rule, paper samples, ruler, and crayons— still have a place in my desk, as the composing stick once did. It is a pity that life is not long enough for me to teach the art to one of my grandchildren, perhaps thoughtful young Felix, who was born in this part of Zurich. I was eleven, the same age as he is now, when I began to watch my parents making books."[1]

1973. Traveled to Toronto, Canada to lecture and to the University of Missouri in Kansas to deliver the May Hill Arbuthnot Lecture. ". . . I was the first German-speaking one to have this honor. A different university stages this solemn occasion every year, attended by many enthusiasts, especially librarians from all over America. The lecture itself would be printed. When on April 27, 1973, I stood at the lecturer's desk in the

brand-new School of Education of the State University of Missouri, I felt a thrill of excitement at what I was about to do: that is, describe something of what our Middle European linguistic area had to offer in the field of children's literature. My 'fortunate moments' alternated between German and Swiss subjects, both famous and less well known, covering the ground from Comenius, through Conrad Meyer of Zurich, to the brothers Grimm, the Swiss Family Robinson, Heinrich Hoffmann, Johanna Spyri. My choice might seem banal to a German audience, and these days might even draw some protest, but here it was the right one; the examples I chose illustrated certain relationships, set right some misconceptions, and showed what Switzerland and Germany had to offer the world in the way of international understanding."[1]

1974. Appointed treasurer of the International Board on Books for Young People. ". . . This role was to give me many sleepless nights, but it happily kept me in contact with others connected with children's books in this international movement, for which I had worked previously under its founder, Jella Lepman.

"For many years I was on the committee of the International Board on Books for Young People, . . . and I sat on its jury for the Hans Christian Andersen Medal. I found it a forum for meetings with lively minded people who were to enrich my work and my whole life. I believe many of us felt the same, and perhaps it is here that the chief value of such international gatherings really lies. In any case, I am grateful to my old friend Jella Lepman, now dead, for coercing me, reluctant as I often was, to participate in these rather public activities in the cause of children's literature. The discussions of the jury, often vehement and generally conducted on a lofty plane, widened my own horizons immensely, and the effect made itself felt in my life and in my editing work. I enjoyed the fact that the jury met several times at our house."[1]

Served as a member of the jury for the Biennale Book Illustration in Bratislava. "The Biennale of Book Illustration in Bratislava, the other international institution on whose jury I served from the start, brought me into close contact with the work of illustrators from all over the world. This was my special field, and I was in my element. Particularly new was our contact with the countries of the Communist East, otherwise closed to us; it was something that made me more tolerant and understanding in general, and there was much that I liked in the East, where they are ready to sacrifice a great deal for the happiness of children."[1]

1976. Wrote her autobiography, *Seven Houses: My Life with Books.* In her book Hürlimann discussed many of her opinions of children's literature. "A masterpiece in the field of children's literature will usually look different from a masterpiece for adults. Often, though not always, its representationalism brings it close to naive art, and it may seem to go against the mainstream of modern art. But if you observe illustration for children over as many years as I have done, working with the artists, you find that at its best it is a flourishing branch of the tree of art, and as valid a manifestation of contemporary trends as, say, abstract painting or surrealism.

"In this era of the child, new modes of expression have arisen, and must be judged by artistic standards, not just educational standards or the standards of commercial art. And here there are all kinds of art forms, from naive painting and its truest offspring, the art of children themselves, to the most sophisticated of contemporary painting or graphics. . . ."[1]

July 9, 1983. Died in Zollikon after a long illness. Hürlimann's books have been translated into English, Spanish and Japanese.

FOR MORE INFORMATION SEE: Times Literary Supplement, May 25, 1967, June 6, 1968; Bettina Hürlimann, *Seven Houses: My Life with Books* (autobiography), Bodley Head, 1976, Crowell, 1977.

JAMES, Elizabeth
(Beverly Hastings, a joint pseudonym)

BRIEF ENTRY: Born in Pittsburgh, Pa. Author. After graduating from Colorado College, James worked briefly as a stewardess before moving to Los Angeles where she wrote her first screenplay, "Born Losers," under the pseudonym James Lloyd. The first of the popular "Billy Jack" movies, it was released by American International Pictures in 1967 and starred Tom Laughlin and James herself in the leading roles. Since then she has written a number of unproduced screenplays for theaters and television. In the mid-1970s she and her friend, author Carol Barkin, decided to combine their writing talents on non-fiction for young adults. The partnership has resulted in twenty books that provide useful information on a myriad of topics. Among the titles are: *The Simple Facts of Simple Machines* (Lothrop, 1975), *Slapdash Cooking* (Lothrop, 1976), *Managing Your Money* (Raintree, 1977), *The Complete Babysitter's Handbook* (Wanderer Books, 1980), *A Place of Your Own* (Dutton, 1981), and *How to Write a Great School Report* (Lothrop, 1983). Published by Raintree in 1975 as part of the "Moods and Emotions" series, four of their books deal with transitional experiences of growing up: *Are We Still Best Friends?, Doing Things Together, I'd Rather Stay Home,* and *Sometimes I Hate School.*

As a writer, James "finds it impossible to write from library research alone." Whether it be fiction or nonfiction, she thoroughly immerses herself in the subject of her current project. "If parts of the book are set in locations I'm unfamiliar with, I go there," she relates. "Similarly, if a book has projects and directions, I try everything out to make sure it works. . . . I am forced to follow the old adage, 'write what you know.'" In addition to their juvenile books, James and Barkin have collaborated on three adult mystery novels, written under the joint pseudonym Beverly Hastings: *Don't Talk to Strangers, Rated X,* and *Secrets. Residence:* Beverly Hills, Calif.

JOHNSON, Elizabeth   1911-1984

OBITUARY NOTICE—See sketch in *SATA* Volume 7: Born October 10, 1911, in Swampscott, Mass.; died August 26, 1984. Author of books for children and librarians. A graduate of Wellesley College, Johnson received her library of science degree from Simmons Library School. Her career as a children's librarian began in the mid-1930s and continued until her retirement in 1971. During that time she held positions in New York and Massachusetts public libraries. Her first book for children, *The Little Knight,* a Junior Literary Guild selection, was a result of her work as a storyteller of fairytales and fantasy. It was followed by several others, including *The Three-in-One Prince, No Magic, Thank You, Stuck with Luck,* and *Break a Magic Circle.* Johnson was a member of the American Library Association, including the Newbery-Caldecott Awards Committee, and the Women's National Book Association. *For More Information See: Authors of Books for Young People,* 2nd edi-

tion supplement, Scarecrow, 1979; *Contemporary Authors, New Revision Series,* Volume 4, Gale, 1981. *Obituaries: School Library Journal,* November, 1984.

KELLEY, True Adelaide   1946-

BRIEF ENTRY: Born February 25, 1946, in Cambridge, Mass. A free-lance illustrator and writer, Kelley received her B.A. from the University of New Hampshire and attended Rhode Island School of Design. The daughter of artists, she is an accomplished illustrator who has, thus far, over ten books to her credit. They include *The Whole World of Hands* by Gilda and Melvin Berger; *Let's Give Kitty a Bath!* by her husband, Steven Lindblom; *James Will Never Die* by Joanne Oppenheim; *Clara Cow Joins the Circus* by Michael Pellowski; *Say It Fast* by Eve Bunting; and *Sun Dogs and Shooting Stars: A Skywatcher's Calendar* by Franklyn M. Branley. Commenting on her illustrations for *Let's Give Kitty a Bath!, Publishers Weekly* stated: "The mad suspense and fun are perfectly clear in Kelley's ineffable ink drawings." She is the author of five self-illustrated books, among them *A Valentine for Fuzzboom* (Houghton, 1981) and *Buggly Bear's Hiccup Cure* (Parents Magazine Press, 1982). Kelley and her husband combined their talents to produce two amusing stories about a mouse family's disaster-filled holidays, *The Mouses' Terrible Christmas* (Lothrop, 1978) and *The Mouses' Terrible Halloween* (Lothrop, 1980). *Home and office:* Kensington Rd., Hampton Falls, N.H. 03844. *For More Information See: Contemporary Authors,* Volume 105, Gale, 1982.

KING, Tony   1947-

PERSONAL: Born March 9, 1947, in Hull, England; son of James William Henry (a ship's carpenter) and Vera (Cooney) King; married Sylvia Davies (a medical secretary), April 9, 1983. *Education:* Hull College of Art, Diploma in Graphic Design, 1966. *Home and office:* 4 Birch Meadow, Clehonger, Herefordshire, England.

CAREER: Graphic designer and illustrator at Wolff-Olins, London, England, 1966-70; free-lance graphic designer and illustrator, 1970—.

WRITINGS—All self-illustrated children's books: *Pea,* Whizzard, 1972; *The Moving Alphabet Book,* Putnam, 1982; *The Moving Animal Book,* Putnam, 1983.

Illustrator: Claire Rayner, *The Body Book* (juvenile), Whizzard, 1978.

All written by Graham Tarrant; pop-up books: *Butterflies,* Heinemann, 1982, Putnam, 1983; *Frogs,* Heinemann, 1982, Putnam, 1983; *Rabbits,* Putnam, 1984; *Bees,* Putnam, 1984.

WORK IN PROGRESS: Petrified Polar Bears, Where's Me Boots?, for children; a Christmas storybook; *Ill,* a self-illustrated juvenile book; and illustrations for *Getting Better* by Claire Rayner, a sequel to *The Body Book.*

SIDELIGHTS: "I have always liked drawing animals, watching films about them on television, and reading about them. My books were a heaven-sent opportunity to indulge my interests and create something interesting at the same time.

(From *The Moving Alphabet Book* by Tony King. Illustrated by the author.)

"I was looking for a way to do an alphabet book that hadn't been thought of before. I tried a few approaches and eventually came up with the wheel and window solution. There are eight pictures on the wheel—as you turn it a different picture comes up in the window on the page. *The Moving Alphabet Book* was successful, so I was asked to think of another using the moving idea, hence the animal and color books.

"I like working in pen and ink, pencil, watercolour, crayon, polymer. I like to change the media to fit the subject."

HOBBIES AND OTHER INTERESTS: Walking in the countryside, collecting art books, cricket, and following the horse racing season.

FOR MORE INFORMATION SEE: New York Times Book Review, September 26, 1982.

TONY KING

KLEVIN, Jill Ross 1935-

PERSONAL: Born September 7, 1935, in New York, N.Y.; daughter of George A. (an executive) and Susan Dorothy (an interior designer; maiden name, Buegeleisen) Hoffman; married Bruce M. Klevin (a mechanical engineer), April 7, 1960; children: Adam Ethan, Sloane Mallory (daughter). *Education:* Columbia University, B.S., 1961. *Home:* 12166 Laurel Terrace Dr., Studio City, Calif. 91604. *Agent:* Writers House, Inc., 21 West 26th St., New York, N.Y. 10010.

CAREER: Writer, beginning in 1956. *Member:* International P.E.N., Society of Children's Book Writers and Illustrators, National Organization for Women.

WRITINGS—For young people: *The Summer of the Sky-Blue Bikini,* Scholastic Book Services, 1978; *That's My Girl,* Scholastic Book Services, 1980; *The Best of Friends,* Scholastic Book Services, 1981; *Far from Home,* Scholastic Book Services, 1982; *The Turtle Street Trading Co.* (illustrated by Linda S. Edwards), Delacorte, 1982: *Turtles Together Forever!* (illustrated by L. S. Edwards), Delacorte, 1982; *Miss Perfect,* Scholastic Book Services, 1984; *Spoiled Rich Kids,* Putnam, in press.

WORK IN PROGRESS: A screenplay, "Little Victories"; two books in the "Turtle Street" series, *Turtles Triumphant* and *Turtles in TV Land,* to be published by Delacorte.

SIDELIGHTS: "I deal with the contemporary scene. I explore characters and relationships in today's complex society. I would very much like to write mystery novels, and think I will try my hand at one. I am an athlete, animal lover, and sometimes beach bum; I am compulsive about writing."

Two of Klevin's books about the "Turtle Street" gang deal with divorce and business. They were written for youngsters in the third to seventh grades. "I wanted to write realistically about concerns in contemporary society and how kids deal with them. Money and business are central concerns, at least to American society, and having the kids in the books go into business helped me to show some of the other things about them I felt were important to the story; for instance, how mature, capable, and resourceful kids can be and how they achieve their goals. Being successful at something kids choose to do reinforces their wish to be responsible and independent. I also wanted to indicate that money, in and of itself, isn't what matters in the end, it is just an end product of being in business, not the ultimate goal. Once these kids have it, they also have the opportunity to realize that for themselves.

"I figured that since I'm surrounded by divorcees, out of the five kids in the first Turtles book, at least two would have to have families dealing with some sort of internal stressful situation. I gave one kid the problem of adjusting to a new stepfather and dealing with a mother who really doesn't understand or accept her. Another kid comes from a home where he was loved and accepted, but where he wasn't receiving the supervision and guidance he needed.

"All of the kids are unique; however, I created the characters in this vein in order to forge a bond between them and show

JILL ROSS KLEVIN

P.J. stormed off muttering to herself about Fergy's being the extremest duress imaginable. ■
(From *The Turtle Street Trading Co.* by Jill Ross Klevin. Illustrated by Linda Strauss Edwards.)

how they form a support group for one another. They really need each other and have a big stake in staying together and making it work. Together, they have the impetus to work together toward their common goal, success.

"If the Turtles have differences, they arise out of their individual characters, personalities, and emotional make-ups, not ethnicity. The fact that staying together is so important to them helps them work those differences out equably and with a good deal of insight and maturity. I purposely never mentioned anywhere in the books the kids' ethnic backgrounds, mainly because the books were being told from their points of view, and that wasn't important to them. I hoped to let the illustrations depict the ethnic differences."

As a children's writer, Klevin observed: "Kids know when you're lying to them. It's crucial to be as honest, straightforward, and sincere as possible, without being cynical, pessimistic, or harsh. Kids are impressionable and easily influenced. I'm careful not to include information they might misconstrue, or might not be ready to accept or assimilate. Kids often don't have the experience which would give them the maturity or perspective to deal with it, and I don't want to mislead them. The important thing is to be as honest as possible with whatever subject matter you *do* include. I find that invariably, whenever I slip something in that isn't completely sincere and heartfelt, I get at least one letter from a reader pointing that fact out to me, saying, 'You were lying . . . I could tell.' That sort of thing has a way of keeping you on the track."

HOBBIES AND OTHER INTERESTS: Music, theater, ballet, movies, books.

KRAMER, Nora   1896(?)-1984

OBITUARY NOTICE—See sketch in *SATA* Volume 26: Born about 1896 in Pendleton, England; died July 4, 1984, in New York, N.Y. Children's book expert, sculptress, and author and editor of children's literature. The creator and director for ten years of the children's Little Book Shop in Macy's book department, Kramer also created the Book Plan, a personalized book selection service for children. She wrote *Storybook, Storybook: The Second Nora Kramer Storybook*, and with her son, Karl R. Kramer, *Coppercraft and Silver Made at Home*. She also edited a number of books, including *Arrow Book of Ghost Stories* and *The Ghostly Hand and Other Haunting Stories. For More Information See: Authors of Books for Young People*, 2nd edition, Scarecrow, 1971; *Contemporary Authors*, Volume 107, Gale, 1983; *Who's Who in the East*, 19th edition, Marquis, 1983. *Obituaries: New York Times*, July 6, 1984; *Publishers Weekly*, July 27, 1984.

KRULL, Kathleen   1952-
(Kathleen Cowles, Kathryn Kenny, Kevin Kenny)

BRIEF ENTRY: Born July 29, 1952, in Fort Leonard Wood, Mo. Editor and author of books for children. Since 1979 Krull has been employed as managing editor at Raintree Publishers in Milwaukee, Wis. Prior to that time, she worked as an editorial assistant at Harper & Row Publishers and as associate editor at Western Publishing. Her first book for children, *The Bugs Bunny Book* (Western Publishing, 1975), was published

under the pseudonym Kathleen Cowles. Also as Cowles, she has produced *The Seven Wishes, Golden Everything Workbook Series,* and *What Will I Be?: A Wish Book.* Under the name Kathleen Krull as well as the Cowles pseudonym, she is coauthor with Richard Allington of the "Beginning to Learn About" series which introduces basic concepts to preschool and primary grade readers. In 1980 Krull was the recipient of the Chicago Book Clinic award for *Beginning to Learn about Colors* as well as the New York Art Directors Club award for *Beginning to Learn about Shapes.* As Kevin Kenny, she coauthored *Sometimes My Mom Drinks Too Much* (Raintree, 1980) which was named outstanding social studies trade book for 1980 by the joint committee of the Children's Book Council and National Council for Social Studies. Krull is also the author of *Trixie Belden and the Hudson River Mystery* (Western Publishing, 1979), written under the house pseudonym Kathryn Kenny. She is currently working on a book about child abuse. *Office:* Raintree Publishers Ltd., 205 West Highland, Milwaukee, Wis. 53203. *For More Information See: Contemporary Authors,* Volume 106, Gale, 1982.

KUBIE, Nora (Gottheil) Benjamin   1899-
(Nora Benjamin)

PERSONAL: Born January 4, 1899, in New York, N.Y.; daughter of Paul (a ship broker) and Miriam (Rosenfeld) Gottheil; married second husband, Lawrence Schlesinger Kubie (di-

Travelers enjoy a cooling dip in this hidden spring in the limestone canyons of the Negev Desert. ■ (From *The Jews of Israel* by Nora Benjamin. Photograph courtesy of Israel Government Tourist Office.)

Nora Benjamin Kubie with her dog, Angus.

vorced); children: a son (deceased). *Education:* Attended Vassar College and Art Students League of New York; Barnard College, B.A., 1920. *Politics:* Democrat. *Religion:* Jewish. *Home:* 119 Old Saugatuck Rd., East Norwalk, Conn. 06855.

CAREER: Free-lance commercial artist, 1924-32; member of staff, Writers War Board, and Red Cross arts and crafts volunteer at Halloran Hospital during World War II; editor of United World Federalists *Newsletter,* 1948-49; has participated in ten archaeological digs; member and part-time resident at artists' village of Ein Hod, Israel. *Member:* Authors League, P.E.N., Westport-Weston Art Council, Norwalk Art Council, MacDowell Colony (fellow). *Awards, honors:* Special citation from Child Study Association of America Book Committee, 1953, for *Joel;* Juvenile Book Award of Jewish Book Council of America, 1955, for *King Solomon's Navy;* Huntington Hartford Foundation fellowship, 1960.

WRITINGS—Juvenile, except as noted: (Under name Nora Benjamin) *Hard Alee!* (self-illustrated), Random House, 1936; (under name Nora Benjamin) *Roving All the Day* (self-illustrated), Random House, 1937; (under name Nora Benjamin) *Fathom Five* (self-illustrated), Random House, 1939; *Make Way for a Sailor!* (Junior Literary Guild selection), Reynal & Hitchcock, 1946; (under name Nora Benjamin) *Remember the Valley,* Harper, 1951; *Joel,* Harper, 1952; *The First Book of Israel* (self-illustrated), F. Watts, 1953, revised edition published as *Israel,* 1978; *King Solomon's Navy* (self-illustrated), Harper, 1954; *King Solomon's Horses,* Harper, 1956; *The First Book of Archaeology,* F. Watts, 1957; *Road to Nineveh: The Adventures and Excavations of Sir Austen Henry Layard* (adult

biography), Doubleday, 1964. Editorial assistant on report of the Ashdod Expedition. Contributor of stories and articles to numerous juvenile magazines, and of travel articles to *Charm, Chicago Jewish Forum,* and *B'nai B'rith Women's News.*

WORK IN PROGRESS: An historical novel set in the time of the Third Crusade.

SIDELIGHTS: "My first 'work' was a hand-written 'Stories and Poems' illustrated by the author, aged eight or nine. And for my entire career, I've alternated between writing and painting, sometimes managing to combine the two in a book for children. When I see or experience something exciting, beautiful, amusing, or sad, I must express what I feel about it, or else I will suffer some sort of emotional indigestion. I have been lucky enough to have had a very long life, and of course I couldn't get it all down on paper or canvas, but I did my best.

"I have had what looks like a confusing number of different interests, but actually each one led to the next. My first job after college was in a book shop, which gave me the idea of drawing book jackets, end papers, sketches for the *New Yorker* and illustrations for one or two children's books. After a period of doing this it occurred to me that I might try to write and illustrate a book of my own. By this time I was living near the shore in Connecticut, married and with a young son. We were, all three, ardent sailors, and in addition to owning our own small sail boat, had several times cruised 'down to Maine' in friends' large cruising ketch. Thus the germ of my first published book, *Hard Alee!.* The central character, Sinbad, was based on Johnny, my son, as was also the hero of *Make Way for a Sailor.*

"In Westport, where we lived, the road to the yacht basin passes the statue of a Minute Man, commemorating events of the American Revolution in the area. This Minute Man, plus stories of the many Jews who fought for American independence—material which I had come across while working as researchist for the writer Carl Carmer—gave me the idea for *Joel.*

"Intrigued by another War of Independence—Israel's—I first visited the Jewish State in 1952. The landscape, the picturesque mixture of peoples from many countries, the Bible place-names and associations, and my own identification with the land of my ancestors—all cried out for expression in pictures and words. By this time, I had no more family responsibilites; I returned to Israel again and again. I bought a small ruined barn in the Artists' Village of Ein Hod, rebuilt it as my studio, and spent many months there each year. It was a beautiful, crazy, and primitive place, looking down on the sea and the ruins of a Crusader castle, and set in a garden of cactus, brambles, and crimson bougainvillea. I gardened, swam, made many dear friends, read the Old Testament avidly, wrote *King Solomon's Navy, King Solomon's Horses, The First Book of Israel,* and *The First Book of Archaeology.*

"As research for the latter, I had taken part in the digging up of a Canaanite Temple in northern Galilee, and after that, I was hooked, and went on, each season, to other digs. The biggest adventure of my life was the time spent camping in the Dead Sea desert as a member of the volunteer force that excavated the great stronghold of Masada. And one summer later on, I worked at the legendary site of Camelot in England.

"These experiences, too, may someday give birth to books. At least I hope so, for now I have grandchildren to write for; the grandchildren and the imaginary world which I create are what keep me happy, keep me from realizing how very old I actually am."

KAY KUZMA

KUZMA, Kay 1941-

PERSONAL: Born April 25, 1941, in Ogallala, Neb.; daughter of Willard J. (in real estate) and Irene (a manager; maiden name, Helm) Humpal; married Jan W. Kuzma (a biostatistician), September 1, 1963; children: Kimberly Kay, Karlene Michelle, Kevin Clark. *Education:* Loma Linda University, B.S., 1962; Michigan State University, M.A., 1963; University of California, Los Angeles, Ed.D., 1970. *Office:* School of Health, Loma Linda University, Loma Linda, Calif. 92350.

CAREER: Loma Linda University, Loma Linda, Calif., assistant professor, 1967-73, associate professor of health sciences, 1973—. Parent Scene, Inc. (publishing company), president, 1980—.

WRITINGS: Understanding Children, with study guide, Pacific Press, 1978; *Child Study Through Observation and Participation,* R & E Research Associates, 1978; *Guidelines for Child Care Centers,* Education Department, Seventh-Day Adventist General Conference, 1978; *My Unforgettable Parents,* Pacific Press, 1978; (with Clare Cherry and Barbara Harkness) *Nursery School and Day Care Center Management Guide,* Fearon, 1978; *The Kim, Kari, and Kevin Storybook* (juvenile), Pacific Press;

1979; (with husband, Jan W. Kuzma) *Building Character,* Pacific Press, 1979; *Don't Step on the Pansies* (poetry), Review & Herald, 1979; *Prime Time Parenting,* Rawson Wade, 1980; *Working Mothers: How You Can Have a Career and Be a Good Parent, Too,* Statford Press, 1981; *Filling Your Love Cup,* Parent Scene, 1982; *Living with God's Kids,* Parent Scene, 1983; *The Kim, Kari, and Kevin Storybook #2* (juvenile), Parent Scene, 1984. Editor of *Parent Scene Newsletter,* 1980—.

WORK IN PROGRESS: Curriculum guides for instructors in courses dealing with the nurturing and development of newborn and preschoolers.

SIDELIGHTS: "I never planned to be a working mother. I only wanted to be a good parent. But before I knew it, I was doing both and liking it. I believe rearing healthy, happy, competent children is the most important task anyone can be called on to perform. And I feel blessed to have had the opportunity to receive academic training in child development which has allowed me to put good theory into successful practice.

"Wherever I speak I am known by the children in the audience as Kim, Kari, and Kevin's mother. I am proud of that high distinction. *The Kim, Kari, and Kevin Storybook* began when I told the stories to my own children. They loved hearing the stories about themselves, so I wrote them down. Then, I realized that if my children enjoyed and learned to be better kids from the stories, perhaps others would enjoy them too. So, *The Kim, Kari and Kevin Storybook* was published. Now, by popular demand, *The Kim, Kari, and Kevin Storybook #2*, has been written. These stories will be about the children when they were four to eight years of age. I believe children's stories should be fun, something children can identify with—and at the same time inspire them to develop beautiful and worthwhile character traits.

''Children are my favorite people and I enjoy writing for them. I like getting letters from them and receiving their special works of art. Wherever I go I wear a special pin that says, 'I love kids.' I wish everybody did. That's why I combine my career of writing for children with writing for parents. If parents can just gain insights into what makes children 'tick,' and learn some strategies for encouraging and coping with kids, this world would certainly be a happier place in which to live.

'I believe God has a special work for each of us to do, and he can find ways and means of preparing us for that work. That's what he has done for me. I didn't start out a good writer. But with my husband's ideas, critiques, encouragement, and editing and with Esther Glaser's creative classes, my skills have developed. Writing has allowed me to have my career and be a good parent, too.''

ROSE LAGERCRANTZ

She sat on a rock right in the middle of the prickly grass, thinking. ■ (From *Tulla's Summer* by Rose Lagercrantz. Illustrated by Lady McCrady.)

LAGERCRANTZ, Rose (Elsa) 1947-

PERSONAL: Born June 12, 1947, in Stockholm, Sweden; daughter of George and Ella (Kallos) Schmidt; married Hugo Lagercrantz (a pediatrician), April 5, 1968; children: Leo, Rebecka, Samuel. *Education:* Received B.A. from Stockholm University. *Home:* Styramansgatan 7, 11454 Stockholm, Sweden. *Agent:* Rabén & Sjögren, Box 45022, 10430 Stockholm, Sweden.

CAREER: Children's Theater, Stockholm, Sweden, drama teacher, 1968-80; free-lance television scriptwriter. *Member:* Swedish Union of Authors, Swedish Union of Playwriters. *Awards, honors:* First Prize, Rabén & Sjögren, 1974, for best children's book; Astrid Lindgren Prize, 1979; Nils Holgersson Plaque, Swedish Library Association, 1980, for best children's book.

WRITINGS: Tullesommar, Rabén & Sjögren, 1973, translation by George Blecher and Lone Thygesen-Blecher published as *Tulla's Summer* (illustrated by Lady McCrady), Harcourt, 1977; *Hemligt i huvet paa Samuel Elias* (title means ''Samuel Elias' Secret''), Rabén & Sjögren, 1974; *Tröst aat Pejter* (title means ''Comfort for Peter''; illustrated by Katarina Olausson), Rabén & Sjögren, 1974; *Räddarinnan* (title means ''The Heroine''; illustrated by K. Olausson), Rabén & Sjögren, 1976; *April, April,* Rabén & Sjögren, 1978; *När den Röda Faageln Sjunger* (title means ''When the Red Bird Is Singing''), Rabén & Sjögren, 1980. Also author of *Naan Sorts Torsdag* (title means ''Some Kind of Thursday''), 1976. Author of plays for stage, radio, and television.

WORK IN PROGRESS: ''The Child of Red Riding Hood,'' a play for adults.

SIDELIGHTS: The writings of Lagercrantz have been translated into a number of languages, including English, Russian, German, French, Danish, and Norwegian.

LEACH, Maria 1892-1977

PERSONAL: Born April 30, 1892, in Brooklyn, N.Y.; died May 22, 1977, in Barrington, Nova Scotia; daughter of Benjamin H. (a lawyer) and Mary Eliza (Davis) Doane; married MacEdward Leach (a university professor), November 11, 1917; children: Macdonald Harvey. *Education:* Earlham College, B.A., 1914; University of Illinois, A.M., 1917; Johns Hopkins University, further graduate study, 1918-19. *Religion:* Society of Friends (Quakers). *Residence:* Barrington, Nova Scotia, Canada.

CAREER: Author, editor, and folklorist. Was head worker at Friends Neighborhood Guild (a settlement house), Philadelphia, Pa., and writer for Winston Publishing Co., Philadelphia, Pa.; Funk & Wagnalls Co., New York, N.Y., dictionary editor, 1936-51; editor for McGraw-Hill Book Co., Blakiston Division, 1953-58. *Member:* International Folk Music Council, American Anthropological Association, American Dialect Society, American Indian Ethnohistoric Conference, American Folklore Society, American Society for Ethnohistory, Canadian Folksong Society, Northeast Folklore Society, North Carolina Folklore Society.

WRITINGS: (Compiler and editor) *The Standard Dictionary of Folklore, Mythology, and Legend,* Funk, Volume I, 1949, Volume II, 1950, both revised in one-volume edition, 1972; *The Turnspit Dog,* Aladdin Books, 1952; *The Soup Stone: The Magic of Familiar Things,* Funk, 1954; *The Beginning: Creation Myths around the World,* Funk, 1956; *The Rainbow Book*

...His mother said, "Heavens, Sammy! You'll have to start eating lard."
"What for?" said the boy.
"Shortening." ■ (From *Noodles, Nitwits and Numbskulls* by Maria Leach. Illustrated by Kurt Werth.)

of American Folk Tales and Legends (juvenile), World Publishing, 1958; *The Thing at the Foot of the Bed and Other Scary Stories* (juvenile; illustrated by Kurt Werth), World Publishing, 1959.

Noodles, Nitwits, and Numskulls (juvenile; illustrated by K. Werth), World Publishing, 1961; *God Had a Dog: Folklore of the Dog*, Rutgers University Press, 1961; *The Luck Book* (juvenile), World Publishing, 1964; *How the People Sang the Mountains Up: How and Why Stories* (juvenile), Viking, 1967; *Riddle Me, Riddle Me, Ree* (juvenile; illustrated by William Wiesner), Viking, 1970; *Whistle in the Graveyard: Folktales to Chill Your Bones* (juvenile; illustrated by Ken Rinciari), Viking, 1974; *The Lion Sneezed: Folktales and Myths of the Cat* (juvenile; illustrated by Helen Siegl), Crowell, 1977.

SIDELIGHTS: Leach was one of America's best known folklorists, having compiled and edited the *Standard Dictionary of Folklore, Mythology and Legend*. After convincing Funk & Wagnalls to publish a folklore dictionary, Leach undertook a four-year commitment to compile, edit, and contribute to a two-volume edition of the *Standard Dictionary of Folklore, Mythology, and Legend*, first published in 1949. The books were revised into a one-volume edition in 1972. "This book is an experiment: an attempt to cut a cross section into the spiritual content of the world, an attempt to gather together in one place several thousand things heretofore scattered in learned journals, memoirs, monographs, manuscripts, rare and out-of-print books, records transcribed by working anthropologists and folklorists in the field,—and in people's heads. Completeness was an end never contemplated. . . . The archives of the nations contain folktales, songs, proverbs, riddles that would mount into millions if all totals were added. Completeness can never be an end until there comes an end to spontaneous song and creative symbol, or an end to the grim or humorous 'saw' with which the human mind meets its situation.

"The book is called a dictionary, in that, as stated above, it can not be exhaustive, and in that it deals with the terminology of a special branch of knowledge.

"Many things are included because of their great diffusion, known importance, or fame, others for their uniqueness or obscurity. Often what looks like a nonce occurrence of a motif or practice turns out to be a clue to something huge or widespread but hitherto unguessed, or a touchstone to the philosophy of a culture.

"The book belongs to no 'school' of folklore, adheres to no 'method,' advocates no 'theory.' It has tried to represent all schools, all methods, all theories, and to state their findings and dilemmas. . . . All is valid that represents the state and scope of the folklore field today. The twenty-six definitions entered under FOLKLORE in the book represent the varying and controversial points of view of modern folklore scholarship." [Maria Leach, "Preface to the Original Edition," *The Standard Dictionary of Folklore, Mythology, and Legend*, edited by Maria Leach, Funk, 1972.[1]]

Leach's interest in folklore was evident in the numerous books that she wrote for children, such as *The Lion Sneezed: Folktales and Myths of the Cat* and *Whistle in the Graveyard: Folktales to Chill Your Bones*.

During her lifetime, she lived in New York City, where she was born and raised, and in Nova Scotia, the home of her ancestors. She died at the age of eighty-five, after a long illness on May 27, 1977 in Barrington, Nova Scotia.

MARIA LEACH

FOR MORE INFORMATION SEE: Maria Leach, *The Stone Soup: The Magic of Familiar Things*, Funk, 1954; Maria Leach, "Preface to the Original Edition," *The Standard Dictionary of Folklore, Mythology, and Legend*, Funk, 1972; Doris de Montreville and Elizabeth D. Crawford, *Fourth Book of Junior Authors and Illustrators*, H. W. Wilson, 1978. *Obituaries: New York Times*, May 24, 1977; *Publishers Weekly*, June 13, 1977; *School Library Journal*, September, 1977.

LEVAI, Blaise 1919-

PERSONAL: Born April 17, 1919, in Passaic, N.J.; son of Blaise and Theresa Hatti (Neukum) Levai; married Marian Alice Korteling, September 8, 1949; children: Lynda, Kathi, Nanci, Robert, Judith. *Education:* Hope College, B.A., 1942; University of Chicago, M.A., 1946; University of Michigan, Ed.D., 1952; graduate study at Rutgers Theological Seminary, 1945, and State University of Iowa, 1959. *Office:* 475 Riverside Dr., New York, N.Y. 10027.

CAREER: Educator and writer. Ordained minister of Reformed Church in America, 1945; Voorhees College, Vellore, India, professor of English, 1946-49, professor of New Testament, 1946-49, 1953-58, head of English department, 1953-58, vice-principal, 1955-58; Vellore Christian Medical College, Vellore, professor of English, 1946-49; Arcot Theological Seminary, Vellore, professor of New Testament, 1946-49, 1953-58; Northcentral College, Orange City, Iowa, head of departments of English and journalism, 1958-60, director of public relations and director of admissions, 1958-60; American Bible

If there's anything Hungarian children will leave bread and honey for, it's a game of ball. ∎
(From *Young Hungary: Children of Hungary at Work and at Play* by Marianna Norris.
Photograph courtesy of Blaise Levai.)

Society, New York City, managing editor, department of education and information, 1960-67; United Methodist Board of Global Ministries, New York City, literary director, 1967—. Pastor, Community Church, University of Michigan Community Center, Willow Run, 1950-52; chaplain, Kodaikanal India High School, 1954-55; pastor, St. John's Church of Vellore, India, 1954-55, 1956-58; member of board of directors and chaplain, Odyssey House of New York City, 1967—.

MEMBER: American Association of University Professors, Associated Church Press, National Religion Publicity Council, Photography International, Royal Asiatic Society (fellow), Rotary Club International. *Awards, honors:* Recipient of award in recognition of outstanding creative design and craftsmanship from Printing Industries of Metropolitan New York, 1969; award for creative and religious communication from Religious Public Relations Council, 1973.

WRITINGS: (Editor) *Revolution in Missions: A Study Guide on the Subject,* Popular Press (Vellore, India), 1956, revised edition, YMCA Publishing House (Calcutta, India), 1958; (with Marianna Norris) *Young India: Children of India at Work and at Play* (juvenile; illustrated with photographs by Levai), Dodd, 1966; (with Norris) *Young Hungary: Children of Hungary at*

Work and at Play (juvenile; illustrated with photographs by Levai), Dodd, 1970; *Ask an Indian About India* (juvenile), Friendship, 1972.

Also author of *One Hundred Years in the Arcot Area*, 1954, and *Reflections of a Missionary*, 1973. Correspondent and photographer, Religious News Service. Contributor of articles to professional journals.

LIBBY, William M.   1927-1984
(Bill Libby)

OBITUARY NOTICE—See sketch in *SATA* Volume 5: Born November 14, 1927, in Atlantic City, N.J.; died of a heart attack, June 16, 1984, in Westminster, Calif. Journalist and author. Libby was a sports writer for the *Yonkers Herald-Statesman* and the *New York Post* before becoming a free-lance writer in 1960. In 1969 Libby collaborated with race-car driver Parnelli Jones on what was to become the first of more than sixty sports biographies and autobiographies (mostly written under the name Bill Libby), including those of Vida Blue, Spencer Haywood, Reggie Jackson, Nolan Ryan, and Jerry West. In addition, Libby also collaborated with celebrities other than sports figures, including Monty Hall, James Roosevelt, son of late President Franklin D. Roosevelt, and First Lady Nancy Reagan on her life story, *Nancy*. His juvenile works include *The Scrambler: The Fran Tarkenton Story*, *Rocky: The Story of a Champion*, *Superdrivers: Three Auto Racing Champions*, *Joe Louis: The Brown Bomber*, and *The Reggie Jackson Story*. *For More Information See: Authors of Books for Young People*, 2nd edition supplement, Scarecrow, 1979; *Contemporary Authors, New Revision Series*, Volume 10, Gale, 1983. *Obituaries: Los Angeles Times*, June 18, 1984; *New York Times*, June 18, 1984; *Washington Post*, June 18, 1984.

LILLINGTON, Kenneth (James)   1916-

PERSONAL: Born September 7, 1916, in Catford, London, England; son of Walter James and Eveline (Jones) Lillington; married Dulcie Elizabeth Lock, September 29, 1942; children: Susan, Elizabeth, Stephen, David. *Education:* Attended St. Dunstan's College and Wandsworth Training College in England. *Religion:* Church of England. *Home:* Bay Tree Cottage, 1 Mead Rd., Cranleigh, Surrey GU6 7BG, England. *Office:* Brooklands Technical College, Weybridge, Surrey, England.

CAREER: Temple Press Ltd., London, England, advertising copywriter, 1938-39; Walton-on-Thames School for Boys, Surrey, England, teacher, 1949-56; Brooklands Technical College, Weybridge, Surrey, England, lecturer in French and English, 1956—. Lecturer on modern literature, Workers' Educational Association, 1950—, on poetry for Poetry Society of London, 1950-57. *Military service:* Royal Army Pay Corps, 1941-43, Royal Signals, 1943-46; became sergeant. *Member:* Royal Society of Arts (fellow), International Association of Literature (fellow), Institute of Linguists (associate).

WRITINGS—All published by Heinemann, except as indicated: *The Devil's Grandson* (one-act play), 1954; *Soapy and the Pharaoh's Curse* (young adult novel), 1957; *Conjurer's Alibi*, T. Nelson, 1960; *The Secret Arrow*, T. Nelson, 1960; *Blue Murder* (one-act play), 1961; *A Man Called Hughes*, T. Nelson, 1962; *My Proud Beauty*, 1963; *The First Book of Classroom Plays* (one-act plays), R. Hale, 1967; *The Fourth Wind-*

KENNETH LILLINGTON

mill Book of One-Act Plays: Seven plays by Kenneth Lillington, Heinemann, 1967; *The Second Book of Classroom Plays*, R. Hale, 1968; *Cantaloup Crescent* (one-act play), 1968; *Olaf and the Ogre* (one-act play), 1969; *The Seventh Windmill Book of One-Act Plays: Eight plays by Kenneth Lillington*, Heinemann, 1972; *There's an End of May* (one-act play), 1973; (editor) *Nine Lives* (illustrated by Maurice Wilson), Deutsch, 1977; (editor) *For Better for Worse*, Angus & Robertson, 1979; *Young Man of Morning* (young adult novel), Faber, 1979; *What Beckoning Ghost?* (young adult novel), Faber, 1983; *Isabel's Double* (young adult novel), Faber, 1984; *Selkie* (young adult novel), Faber, 1985. Poems included in *More Comic and Curious Verse* and *Yet More Comic and Curious Verse*, both published by Penguin. Contributor to *Punch* and to education journals.

WORK IN PROGRESS: A novel.

SIDELIGHTS: "I always wanted to be a writer, but for the English grammar school boy in the 1930s there was only one kind of job, that of clerk in a city office. So I was put into an insurance company, where I spent as miserable and degrading a time as Dickens in his blacking factory, only much longer. From there I went to an advertising agency and thence to a publisher. I would not place much value on the 'experience' gained in these places, unless experience of frustration has any worth, but it may be that there I learned to sympathise with young people in their aspirations and their anxieties. This fellow-feeling with the young has never left me, and has been a strong force both in my teaching and my writing.

"After the war when I was married and had two children, I became a teacher. The fact that my writing output is not nearly

(Jacket illustration by Renate Belina from *Isabel's Double* by Kenneth Lillington.)

as large as it might be is due, I am afraid, to the coziness of my life since then. I loved my family and I loved teaching. Much of my energy was channelled into writing up 'set books' for my students, and I have a whole cupboard full of notes and essays which have now served their purpose and will never see publication. Such writing as I did 'after hours' was done unobtrusively in spare moments; writing is a supremely unsociable occupation, and few wives take kindly to their husbands locking themselves away every evening and weekend to pursue it.

"My wife solved the problem by joining in. She always reads over what I write, and her criticism is more valuable than any editor's. I have completely rewritten several books on the strength of her advice. My children have always been interested too, especially my son Stephen who, during the past six or seven years, has become a dedicated student of juvenile fiction, and indeed knows much more about the general field than I do. He buys several hardbacks a week and passes the best of them on to me. Through him I have learned what a wealth of talent there is among children's writers.

"Teaching led me into writing for the young. In 1951, having exhausted the resources of a rather skimpy school library, I

began experimenting with a teenage novel, which I read to my class at the ends of lessons. My pupils were most enthusiastic. This can be deceptive, as children, if they are on good terms with you, are too easily pleased; but it encouraged me to go on, and after tinkering with the thing for years, on and off (during which time I published several one-act plays) I eventually published it in 1957. After that I published three more novels with Nelson; but I was finding one-act plays both quicker to write and more profitable, and for the next fifteen years I spent what spare time I had on plays alone.

"I then branched out into editing anthologies, and this led me back, in a roundabout way, to teenage novels. I had written one, *Young Man of Morning,* about ancient Greece, but had never sent it out, and the publisher of one of the anthologies now encouraged me to try it out. He didn't take it, as it happened, but I was encouraged to send it to Faber, who did; and since then I have placed two more teenage novels with them. Now that I have retired from teaching I aim to produce at least one book a year.

"My last two novels are ghost stories, but their essential theme is parent-child relationship, and I don't think I could possibly have written them when I was young. Nowadays I see both sides of the case, but write from the young person's point of view. My novels are not 'protest' novels, however, nor am I in the least interested in rebels as such. The story is what matters, and any conflict among the characters must be implicit in it.

"I rewrite enormously, discarding at least four times as much as appears in print. I envy those authors who can produce ten thousand words a day on the electric typewriter and never correct a copy, but I shall never be like them. Experience does not help me much, as each new book is a new battle, as each bout must be to a boxer. Its only use is that when I get hopelessly stuck, as I do with every book I write, it counsels me that I have been so before. My method, up till now, has been appallingly inefficient; I have never made a synopsis of a book, but have made it up as I have gone along. In consequence—because the exigencies of fiction, like God, are not mocked—I have always had to track back over my work, rewriting whole chunks of it. I have learned my lesson at last, however—at the age of sixty-six—and am making a careful synopsis of my next novel, which is rather ambitious, and really must be worked out in detail before I write the story.

"I seldom reread my own books, but if ever I do, I find I am reading a stranger. Revising *Young Man of Morning* after fifteen years was a peculiar experience, like editing some other person's work. I must confess, however, that I find my earlier works entertaining, and sometimes almost echo the aging Swift: 'What genius I had then!'"

HOBBIES AND OTHER INTERESTS: Ancient Greece, swimming, collecting antiques, professional boxing and its history.

I remember, I remember,
The fir-trees dark and high;
I used to think their slender tops
Were close against the sky:
It was a childish ignorance,
But now 'tis little joy
To know I'm farther off from heav'n
Than when I was a boy.

—Thomas Hood
(From *I Remember, I Remember*)

LINDBLOM, Steven (Winther) 1946-

BRIEF ENTRY: Born March 29, 1946, in Minneapolis, Minn. A free-lance illustrator and writer, Lindblom attended St. John's College in Annapolis, Md., and received his B.F.A. from the Rhode Island School of Design. He is the author of three children's books, all illustrated by his wife, author and illustrator True A. Kelley: *The Mouses' Terrible Christmas* (Lothrop, 1978), *The Mouses' Terrible Halloween* (Lothrop, 1980), and *Let's Give Kitty a Bath!* (Addison-Wesley, 1982), an almost wordless picture book. Although most of his works are fiction, Lindblom confessed that "nonfiction writing is my first love." His self-illustrated book *The Fantastic Bicycles Book* (Houghton, 1979) reflects his interest in old bicycles. It gives detailed instructions on how to build various bikes from used and scavenged parts and offers tips on buying used parts, repairing, and maintenance. Lindblom is currently at work on three additional juvenile books on the subject of robots, croquet, and machine tools. His illustrated works include *Messing Around with Water Pumps and Siphons* by Bernie Zubrowski and *The Internal Combustion Engine* by Ross R. Olney. In reviews of Olney's book, *School Library Journal* described Lindblom's illustrations as "energetic, whimsical and understandable" while *Horn Book* found them "extremely well done and well fitted into the text." *Residence:* Warner, N.H. *For More Information See: Contemporary Authors,* Volume 106, Gale, 1982.

LOCHAK, Michèle 1936-

PERSONAL: Born June 6, 1936, in Nancy, France; daughter of Daniel (a certified public accountant) and Rose (Ditlea) Papo; married Georges Lochak (a physicist), December 22, 1956; children: Pierre, Catherine, Ivan. *Education:* Sorbonne, University of Paris, M.A., 1958. *Home:* 67 Boulevard de Picpus, 75012 Paris, France. *Office:* Gautier-Languereau, 18 rue Jacob, 75006 Paris, France.

CAREER: Chatenay-Malabry High School, Paris, France, history teacher, 1958-1970; writer, 1970—. *Awards, honors:* Loisirs-jeunes from French Specialized Press for Children's Literature, 1973, for *Les histoires d'Ivan.*

WRITINGS—Juvenile: Les histoires d'Ivan (title means "The Stories of Ivan"), Fleurus, 1973; *Vingt-watts, la petite ampoule* (title means "Twenty Watts, the Little Bulb"; illustrated by Noelle Herrenschmidt), Flammarion, 1975; *Le pain des autres* (title means "The Bread of Each and Everybody"), Flammarion, 1980; (with M. F. Mangin) *Suzette et Nicolas et le cirque des enfants,* Languereau, 1980, published as *Suzette and Nicholas and the Sunijudi Circus,* Philomel, 1981; *Ivan, Mourka et le moineau* (title means "Ivan, Mourka, and the Sparrow"), Flammarion, 1982; *Louis XIII enfant* (title means "Louis XIII as a Child"), Magnard, 1982.

MICHÈLE LOCHAK

Montmartre (comme Montparnasse) est voué aux peintres.
[Montmartre (like Montparnasse) is dedicated to painters.]

■ (From *Si tu vas . . . à Paris* by Michèle Lochak. Illustrated by Carmen Batet.)

"Si tu vas" series of children's travel guides; published by Languereau: *Si tu vas en Bretagne* (title means "If You Go to Brittany"), 1982; . . . *dans les Alpes* (title means "If You Go to the Alps"), 1982; . . . *en Provence* (title means "If You Go to Provence"), 1982; . . . *en Auvergne* (title means "If You Go to Auvergne"), 1982; . . . *à Paris* (title means "If You Go to Paris"), 1984; . . . *en Alsace* (title means "If You Go to Alsace"), 1984; . . . *au pays basque* (title means "If You Go to Basque Country"), 1984.

WORK IN PROGRESS: More books in the "Si tu vas" series: *Si tu vas en Corse* (title means "If You Go to Corsica"); . . . *en Belgique* (title means "If You Go to Belgium"); . . . *en Suisse* (title means "If You Go to Switzerland"); . . . *au Quebec* (title means "If You Go to Quebec").

SIDELIGHTS: "At the beginning, I did not understand the reasons why I wrote children's books. Wouldn't it have been easier to go on learning and teaching history? In fact, ever since I was a little girl, I had been telling stories.

"In fairy tales, a person's fate is fixed at birth. I was a storyteller then, so I became a storyteller since that was my fate.

"I have always lived in cities. Maybe that is why I am mainly interested in human beings, their past, their history, their work, their adventures, their joys and their griefs, their behaviour and their myths. Children feel closer to nature and animals. Do we have a contradiction here?

"In my opinion, not at all: nature (which I know well and love as I am a dedicated hiker, sailor and skier) is a place where children learn about life, about the rhythm of time and of the seasons, about plants and the struggle for life, and about the fleeting or perennial beauty of things. As for animals, following

the example of Aesop and many others, our poet La Fontaine gave them life in his fables and made them speak so much like human beings that every children's story refers to the cunning of the fox, the strength of the lion, the wit of the mouse—in short the character of man. One of the dangers of children's literature is that an author who is not a great moralist might produce only a set of inoffensive 'clichés,' or one who is not a real writer might just enumerate a set of unrelated facts.

"Every genre can be used in children's books and is, in fact, used. Innumerable books are published. And yet, I keep thinking of a school-teacher friend of mine, who said to me: 'So many books are published, and yet I can't find stories to tell my classes. . . . I keep using the same old ones. . . .'

"Children's books cease to belong to a marginal genre only when they reach the status of pure literature, when they succeed in re-creating the world through the bias of art, when they touch the imagination. Then and only then will they leave in the mind of children a mark so enduring as will follow them into their adult life. Very few stories and tales reach this level. And if by any chance an author or an illustrator succeeds in doing so, there is every likelihood that the result of his work will remain in his drawers after refusals from publishers on the grounds that it does not fit in with their series.

"Talent is unconventional by definition! This means it will not easily comply with ready-made moulds! Let us not be too pessimistic.

"Children are like bees: they suck the honey out of everything and anything. An average book may delight them thanks to the charm of its illustrations. The adventures of Captain 'Fracasse' (which are no longer read by French children) were decisive in the build-up of the sensitivity of a child who becomes Marcel Proust.''

About her series of travel guides, Lochak commented: "From history to stories for children, it is the same travel of human memory and its sensibilities through space and time. Here is my interest. To grow harmoniously, children need roots in the family and in the country they are from. I begin with France, but, in my collection of travel guide for children, I hope to be able to make them love foreign people and countries.

"I was asked once if I wrote for my own children. What a strange question! Naturally the fact that a two-way communication takes place is essential. One always writes for children, especially for one's own children, but this remains of secondary importance. Above all I write for myself: this is a necessity for a writer.

"Thus the story ends as it began: I was a storyteller and will remain a storyteller until the end of my life."

LORD, Athena V. 1932-

PERSONAL: Born July 21, 1932, in Cohoes, N.Y.; daughter of Athanasius (co-owner of a restaurant) and Araluka (co-owner of a restaurant; maiden name, Keramari) Vavuras; married Victor Alexander Lord (an attorney), October 3, 1954; children: Sara Matilthe, Christopher James, Victoria Marie, Alexandra Mary. *Education:* Vassar College, B.A., 1953; graduate study at Union College and University, 1975-76. *Residence:* Albany, N.Y.

ATHENA V. LORD

CAREER: Author of books for children, 1977—. Albany, N.Y., community ambassador to Spain, 1953; commissioner, Saratoga-Capital District Parks Commission, 1976-84. Lecturer and public speaker, 1953—. *Awards, honors:* Child Study Association Children's Book Committee Award, 1981, Jane Addams Children's Book Award, 1982, both for *A Spirit to Ride the Whirlwind;* named Albany Author of the Year by the Friends of the Albany Public Library, 1984.

WRITINGS—For young readers: *Pilot for Spaceship Earth: R. Buckminster Fuller, Architect, Inventor and Poet* (biography; Junior Literary Guild selection), Macmillan, 1978; *A Spirit to Ride the Whirlwind* (Junior Literary Guild selection), Macmillan, 1981; *Today's Special: Z.A.P. and Zoe,* Macmillan, 1984.

SIDELIGHTS: "I have had a long-standing love of and fascination with words, as I learned to read and write in both English and Greek before starting school at age four. The love affair continued through college, where I majored in creative writing and minored in Russian and Spanish. Writing gives me an excuse to travel, and travel gives me something to write about."

LORENZ, Lee (Sharp) 1932(?)-

BRIEF ENTRY: Born October 17, about 1932, in Hackensack, N.J. A cartoonist, editor, author, illustrator, and professional cornet player, Lorenz has worked for the *New Yorker* since 1958. Originally a staff cartoonist, he became the magazine's art editor in 1973. In addition to illustrating works by other authors, he has written and illustrated several of his own children's books. All published by Prentice-Hall, these include: *Scornful Simkin* (1980) and *Pinchpenny John* (1981), adaptations of Chaucer's "The Reeve's Tale" and "The Miller's Tale"; *The Feathered Ogre* (1981), a retelling of an Italian folktale; *Big Gus and Little Gus* (1982); and *Hugo and the Space Dog* (1983). *School Library Journal* found *Pinchpenny John* "great fun!," adding that Lorenz "made . . . [Chaucer's tale] . . . thoroughly respectable" while keeping "its lively spirit." Commenting on *Scornful Simkin, Publishers Weekly* noted Lorenz's "vigorous [drawing] style," while *School Library Journal* cited his "strikingly drafted illustrations." In a review of *The Feathered Ogre, School Library Journal* again observed: "Mass motion, velocity, gusto are the characteristics of Lorenz's dynamic virile line." In 1983 he was the recipient of the New Jersey Authors Award for *Hugo and the Spacedog.*

Lorenz's illustrated works include *The Teddy Bear Habit; or, How I Became a Winner* by James L. Collier, *Sylvester Bear Overslept* by Jan Wahl, and *Remember the a la Mode: Riddles and Puns,* compiled by Charles Keller. Lorenz has also illustrated several books for adults, among them *Real Dogs Don't Eat Leftover* (Long Shadow Books, 1983), which he edited, and Bruce Feirstein's *Real Men Don't Eat Quiche.* In addition to his work as an author and illustrator, Lorenz has performed professionally as a cornet player since 1955. *Address:* P.O. Box 131, Easton, Conn. 06612. *For More Information See: The World Encyclopedia of Cartoons,* Volume 1, Gale, 1980; *Who's Who in America: 1982-1983,* 42nd edition, Marquis, 1982.

A good tale is none the worse for being twice told.
—Proverb

ELLEN MacGREGOR

MacGREGOR, Ellen   1906-1954

PERSONAL: Born May 15, 1906, in Baltimore, Md.; died March 29, 1954, in Chicago, Ill.; daughter of George Malcolm (a physician) and Charlotte (a librarian; maiden name, Noble) MacGregor. *Education:* University of Washington, Seattle, B.S., 1926; post-graduate study, University of California, Berkeley, 1931. *Politics:* Independent. *Religion:* Protestant. *Residence:* Chicago, Ill.

CAREER: Author of books for children, best known for her "Miss Pickerell" series, among the first science-fiction books for children which combined fantasy and correct scientific information. Began her career as a librarian in the Central Hawaii School District; worked as researcher for Scott, Foresman publishers, Chicago, Ill.; library supervisor for Naval Operating Base, Key West, Fla., and for Naval Technological Training Center Library, Chicago; supervisor, Union Catalogue of Art, Chicago; serials librarian, University of Illinois, Undergraduate Division; librarian, International Harvester Co., manufacturing research division, Chicago. *Member:* Authors League, Society of Midland Authors, Illinois Women's Press Association, Children's Reading Round Table. *Awards, honors:* Pacific Northwest Library Association Young Readers' Choice Award, 1956, for *Miss Pickerell Goes to Mars.*

WRITINGS—All for children: *Tommy and the Telephone* (illustrated by Zabeth Selover), A. Whitman, 1947; *Theodore Turtle* (Junior Literary Guild selection; illustrated by Paul Galdone), Whittlesey House, 1955; *Mr. Ferguson of the Fire Department* (illustrated by P. Galdone), Whittlesey House, 1956; *Mr. Pingle and Mr. Buttonhouse* (illustrated by P. Galdone), Whittlesey House, 1957.

"Miss Pickerell" series; all for children; all published by McGraw, except as indicated: *Miss Pickerell Goes to Mars* (*Weekly Reader* Children's Book Club selection; illustrated by P. Galdone), Whittlesey House, 1951, reprinted, Pocket Books, 1980; *. . . and the Geiger Counter* (illustrated by P. Galdone), Whittlesey House, 1953, reprinted, Pocket Books, 1980; *. . . Goes Undersea* (illustrated by P. Galdone), Whittlesey House, 1953, reprinted, Pocket Books, 1981; *. . . Goes to the Arctic* (Junior Literary Guild selection; illustrated by P. Galdone), Whittlesey House, 1954, reprinted, Pocket Books, 1981.

Before her death in 1954, MacGregor had completed many boxes of notes and plans for "Miss Pickerell" books. The series was continued by Dora Pantell in 1964. Pantell and MacGregor share credit for authorship of the "Miss Pickerell" series between 1965 and 1983.

Contributor of stories to periodicals, including *Liberty, Story World, The Instructor,* and *Christian World.* Editor, *Pen Points,* 1949-50.

ADAPTATIONS: "Miss Pickerell" (television movie), starring Fran Allison, NBC-TV, March 21, 1972.

SIDELIGHTS: Ellen MacGregor was one of the first writers

She pointed to the large red book Mr. Esticott had been reading. "I'm glad to see you've finally finished reading my encyclopedia," she said. ■ (From *Miss Pickerell Goes to the Arctic* by Ellen MacGregor. Illustrated by Paul Galdone.)

A movement in the water to her left caught her attention, and she looked down. ■ (From *Miss Pickerell Goes Undersea* by Ellen MacGregor. Illustrated by Paul Galdone.)

of science fiction for young people. The creator of the popular "Miss Pickerell" series was born on **May 15, 1906** in Baltimore, Maryland. Her parents were influential in her two career choices—writing and library work. "[My parents] had an exquisite sense of fun, with a lovely feeling for the ridiculous. There was much laughter in our home. Also there was much, much reading aloud. . . ." [Helga H. Eason, "Ellen MacGregor," *Wilson Library Bulletin,* Volume 28, Number 8, April, 1954.[1]]

MacGregor majored in science at the University of Washington, earned a B.S. degree in library science in 1926, and did post-graduate work in science at the University of California. After completing her formal education, she followed her parents' advice and began a career as a librarian. Her mother, a former librarian, had travelled throughout Wisconsin establishing libraries in small towns. "Nevertheless it was with a slight lack of personal enthusiasm that I fell in with their plans for my career. What I didn't know then, was that my training as a librarian was to be the key to many interesting jobs, to many enriching experiences, and to many happy associations."[1]

During her career, MacGregor worked as a librarian for elementary schools in Hawaii, supervised the compilation of the Union Catalog of Art in Chicago, and served as librarian of the Naval Operating Base in Key West, Florida. She also served as serials' librarian of the Chicago Undergraduate Division of the University of Illinois, as a researcher in children's literature for a Chicago publishing company, and as an editor of the Illinois Women's Press Association's monthly bulletin, *Pen Points.*

It was not until **1946** that MacGregor began to write. Her first children's book was entitled *Tommy and the Telephone.* MacGregor's most famous heroine, Miss Lavinia Pickerell, was created for a short story that was published in 1950. This short story became the first book in a long series of science-fiction adventure stories that began in **1951.** The "Miss Pickerell" books were praised for their accurate scientific information. About science fiction, MacGregor once said, "It's such a satisfying form of literature . . . ! And interesting, that being scientifically logical actually frees our imaginations, rather than acting as a constraint. Of course my preference is for the scientific fantasy. . . . Stories like that are so refreshing with their combination of delightful absurdity and utter logic. . . .'' [Helga E. Eason, "Ellen MacGregor Memorial," *Wilson Library Bulletin*, September, 1954.[2]]

Although MacGregor completed only four of the Pickerell books before her early death on **March 29, 1954,** she left boxes of notes and plans for future adventures of Miss Pickerell. It wasn't until 1964, however, that an author appeared with the necessary ability to continue the adventures of Miss Pickerell. Dora Pantell has continued the series to the present day.

FOR MORE INFORMATION SEE: Chicago School Journal, May, 1951; *Wilson Library Bulletin*, April, 1954, September, 1954; *More Junior Authors*, H. W. Wilson, 1963; *Twentieth Century Children's Writers*, St. Martin's, 1978. Obituaries: *Publishers Weekly*, April 10, 1954; *Library Journal*, May 15, 1954; *Wilson Library Bulletin*, May, 1954.

MARTIN, David Stone   1913-

PERSONAL: Born June 13, 1913, in Chicago, Ill.; son of Francis James (a minister) and Grace (Hedges) Martin; married Cheri Landry (a theatrical manager), September 25, 1965; children: Tony, Stefan, Rio. *Education:* Attended public schools in Chicago, Ill. and The Art Institute of Chicago. *Home and office:* 867 Pequot Ave., New London, Conn. 06320. *Agent:* Gary Alderman, 3114 Leyton Lane, Madison, Wis. 53715.

CAREER: Chicago World's Fair, Chicago, Ill., graphic designer, architect's assistant, 1933-34; Federal Arts Project, Elgin State Hospital, Elgin, Ill., supervisor of mural projects, ca. 1934; muralist, Tennessee Valley Authority, 1936-41; set up own studio in Lambertville, N.J., 1942; Office of War Information, New York City, art director, 1942-43; artist/war correspondent, *Life*, 1945; artist/war correspondent, Abbott Laboratories, 1945; Disc Records Company of America, New York, N.Y., art director, 1944-48; Brooklyn Museum Art School, New York City, instructor in art, 1948-49; Workshop School of Advertising and Editorial Art, New York City, teacher, 1950; Art Student's League and Parson's School of Design, New York, N.Y., instructor in art, 1969-79; free-lance commercial artist, known especially for his pioneering design of jazz album covers. Work has been exhibited at various museums, including Art Institute of Chicago, Chicago, Ill.; Museum of Modern Art, New York City; and Boston Museum of Fine Arts, Boston, Mass. *Awards, honors:* Recipient of three prizes for post office murals between 1936 and 1941; recipient of five medals from New York Art Directors Annual Exhibition between 1946 and 1951.

ILLUSTRATOR: Alan Lomax, *Mister Jelly Roll: The Fortunes of Jelly Roll Martin, New Orleans Creole and "Inventor of Jazz"*, Duell, Sloan, & Pearce, 1950; Marian Cumming, *All about Marjory* (juvenile), Harcourt, 1950; Beatrice Landeck, editor, *Songs to Grow On* (juvenile), C. B. Marks, 1950; Landeck, editor, *More Songs to Grow On* (juvenile), Morrow, 1954; Henry Chapin, *Tigertail, the Game Chicken* (juvenile), W. R. Scott, 1965; Alice Low, *Kallie's Corner* (juvenile), Pantheon, 1966; Evangeline F. Morse, *Brown Rabbit: Her Story* (juvenile), Follett, 1967; Nat Hentoff, *Journey into Jazz* (juvenile), Coward, 1968; Gail Graham, *Cross-Fire: A Vietnam Novel* (juvenile), Pantheon, 1972; Bea Stadtler, *The Test*, edited by Morrison D. Bial, [Cleveland], 1973, reprinted as *The Holocaust: A History of Courage and Resistance*, Behrman, 1974.

WORK IN PROGRESS: A series of stone lithographs and oil on canvas paintings.

McCLOSKEY, (John) Robert   1914-

PERSONAL: Born September 15, 1914, in Hamilton, Ohio; son of Howard Hill and Mable (Wismeyer) McCloskey; married Margaret Durand (a children's librarian), November 23, 1940; children: Sally, Jane. *Education:* Attended Vesper George Art School, Boston, Mass., 1932-36, National Academy of Design, 1936-38. *Politics:* Democrat. *Residence:* Scott Islands, Harborside, Me.

CAREER: Executed bas relief for the municipal building, Hamilton, Ohio, 1935; did mural painting for four years; did some commercial art work; author and illustrator of children's books. Has exhibited at National Academy of Design, Tiffany Foundation, and Society of Independent Artists. *Military service:* U.S. Army, 1942-45; became technical sergeant. *Member:* American Academy in Rome (fellow), P.E.N., Authors League. *Awards, honors:* President's award, National Academy of Design, 1936; Tiffany Foundation prize; Prix de Rome, 1939; Caldecott Medal, 1942, for *Make Way for Ducklings*, and 1958, for *Time of Wonder;* Pacific Northwest Library Association's Young Readers' Choice award, 1947, for *Homer Price;* Ohioana Book award, 1949, for *Blueberries for Sal*, and 1958, for *Time of Wonder;* Caldecott Medal honor book award, 1949, for *Blueberries for Sal*, 1953, for *One Morning in Maine*, and 1954, for Ruth Sawyer's *Journey Cake, Ho!; New York Herald Tribune* Spring Festival Book Award, 1952, for *One Morning in Maine*, and 1955, for *Junket;* D.Litt., Miami University, Oxford, Ohio, 1964; Doctor of Letters, Mount Holyoke College, 1967; Regina Medal, 1974, for "continued distinguished contribution to children's literature."

WRITINGS—All self-illustrated; all published by Viking: *Lentil*, 1940; *Make Way for Ducklings* (ALA Notable Book), 1941;

ROBERT McCLOSKEY

He planted himself in the center of the road, raised one hand to stop the traffic, and then beckoned with the other, the way policemen do, for Mrs. Mallard to cross over. ■ (From *Make Way for Ducklings* by Robert McCloskey. Illustrated by the author.)

Homer Price (ALA Notable Book), 1943; *Blueberries for Sal* (ALA Notable Book), 1948; *Centerburg Tales*, 1951; *One Morning in Maine* (ALA Notable Book), 1952; *Time of Wonder* (ALA Notable Book), 1957; *Burt Dow, Deep-Water Man: A Tale of the Sea in the Classic Tradition* (*Horn Book* honor list), 1963.

Illustrator: Anne Burnett Malcolmson, *Yankee Doodle's Cousins,* Houghton, 1941; Robert Hobart Davis, *Tree Toad,* Stokes, 1942; Claire Huchet Bishop, *The Man Who Lost His Head,* Viking, 1942; Tom Robinson, *Trigger John's Son,* Viking, 1949; Ruth Sawyer, *Journey Cake, Ho!* (ALA Notable Book), Viking, 1953; Anne H. White, *Junket,* Viking, 1955; Keith Robertson, *Henry Reed, Inc.* (ALA Notable Book), Viking, 1958; K. Robertson, *Henry Reed's Journey,* Viking, 1963; K. Robertson, *Henry Reed's Baby Sitting Service,* Viking, 1966; K. Robertson, *Henry Reed's Big Show,* Viking, 1970.

ADAPTATIONS—All produced by Weston Woods, except as noted: ''Make Way for Ducklings'' (film, filmstrip and record), 1955; ''Lentil'' (film, filmstrip and record), 1957; ''Time of Wonder'' (film), 1961; ''The Doughnuts'' (film based on *Homer Price*), 1963; ''Blueberries for Sal'' (film), 1967; ''The Case of the Cosmic Comic'' (film based on *Homer Price*), 1976; ''One Morning in Maine'' (filmstrip and cassette with teacher's guide), Viking, 1979; ''Burt Dow: Deep Water Man'' (film), 1983; ''Homer Price,'' produced by Miller Brody.

SIDELIGHTS: Born **September 15, 1914,** in Hamilton, Ohio, where he attended public schools. ''I attended public school, and from the time my fingers were long enough to play the scale I took piano lessons. I started next to play the harmonica,

the drums, and then the oboe. The musician's life was the life for me—that is, until I became interested in things electrical and mechanical. I collected old electric motors and bits of wire, old clocks and Mechano sets. I built trains and cranes with remote controls, my family's Christmas trees revolved, lights flashed and buzzers buzzed, fuses blew and sparks flew! The inventor's life was the life for me—that is, until I started making drawings for the high-school paper and the high-school annual.''

''My mother and father were very sympathetic to me—provided me with brushes and paints and crayons. My mother painted china when she was a young girl.

''I conducted an harmonica band and also taught a soap carving group at the Hamilton YMCA.'' [''Robert McCloskey'' (film), Weston Woods, 1964.[1]]

In his senior year, McCloskey entered a dramatic and bold woodcut engraving in Scholastic Magazine's annual Art Award Contest and won a scholarship to the Vesper George School of Art in Boston.

Though his parents wanted him to go to college, McCloskey accepted the art scholarship in Boston. During the summers, he returned to Hamilton and worked as a counselor at the YMCA boy's camp. ''Summers I worked as a counselor at the 'Y' boy's camp, where I carved a totem pole. . . . It had eyes as big as saucers. I was carving larger and larger things, from bars of soap to trunks of trees. The chips were larger too.''[1]

1934. Received his first important commission: the execution of bas reliefs for the municipal building in Hamilton, Ohio.

About two miles outside of Centerburg, where route 56 meets route 56A, there lives a boy named Homer. ■ (From *Homer Price* by Robert McCloskey. Illustrated by the author.)

The children's section of the library in this building is now called the Robert McCloskey Room. ''An architect took a look at the totem pole and thought I had possibilities as a sculptor. I can't imagine now an architect with the courage to turn a nineteen year old boy loose to do the sculpture for one of the newest, most important buildings in town—but he did.

''. . . Having progressed from soap to wood to stone, I executed medallions depicting the arts and industry. There are also more than twenty bas reliefs . . . and two cast aluminum pieces. I finished them all in six months. I learned a lot from the job.''[1]

1935-1937. ''While living on Beacon Hill I walked through the Public Garden every day on my way to art school in the Back Bay section. I noticed the ducks in those days but no ideas in that direction ever entered my head. I was studying to be an artist, and I was hell-bent on creating *art*. My mind in those days was filled with odd bits of Greek mythology, with accent on Pegasus, Spanish galleons, Oriental dragons, and all the stuff that really and truly great art is made of. I liked those ducks, and I enjoyed feeding them peanuts, all good relaxation, I thought, for a mind heavy-laden with great art thoughts. It never would have occurred to me to *draw* those things or to *paint* them unless they were in a deep forest pool with a nude,

perhaps, and a droopy tree and a gazelle or two, just to improve the composition. That gives you a vague idea of the way things stood. But I don't regard the time and thought as wasted. I certainly got rid of a lot of ham ideas at an early age.

''It was at this time that I made my first visit to New York. I came with a list as long as my arm of things to do and see— the decorations at Radio City, the Hispanic, Metropolitan, Modern, Science and Industry, and Natural History Museums, and Grand Central Galleries, too, of course. I did it up brown, mind ticking all the time. Today there are two things from that trip I remember. I went to call on an editor of children's books. I came into her office with my folio under my arm and sat on the edge of my chair. She looked at the examples of great art I had brought along (they were woodcuts, fraught with black drama). I don't remember *just* the words she used to tell me to get wise to myself and shelve the dragons, Pegasus, limpid pool business, and learn how and what to 'art' with. I think we talked mostly of Ohio.

''The other thing I remember is that she took me out to dinner. The food was Long Island duckling.

''I went back to Boston a very puzzled art student. It was about this time that I started to draw and paint everything and anything. I lost my facility for making up droopy trees and the anatomy of non-existent dragons and gazelles. Why, I even drew ducks.'' [Bertha Mahony Miller and Elinor Whitney Field, editors, *Caldecott Medal Books: 1938-1957*, Horn Book, 1957.[2]]

Entered the National Academy of Design in New York City. Received the President's Award for creative work at the National Academy where he exhibited his work, as well as at the Tiffany Foundation and the Society of Independent Artists in Boston. During the summers he studied painting in Provincetown on Cape Cod with artist Jerry Farnsworth. ''I had never sold an oil painting—only a few water colors at most modest prices—and financially my art career was a bust. Rather than go on PWA or WPA, I took a bread and butter job doing a form of commercial art I had little interest in.''

ROBERT McCLOSKEY

By the time Uncle Ulysses and the sheriff arrived and pushed through the crowd, the lunch room was a calamity of doughnuts! ▪ (From *Homer Price* by Robert McCloskey. Illustrated by the author.)

1938. Returned to Ohio and began drawing scenes of everyday life. McCloskey brought a portfolio of new paintings to New York which helped him land a job assisting Francis Scott Bradford with murals for the Lever Brothers Building in Cambridge, Massachusetts. The murals included portrayals of the famous people of Beacon Hill.

1939. Awarded the Prix de Rome. McCloskey was unable to go abroad for his study until 1949 after the war years. During this time his first children's book, *Lentil,* was accepted for publication by Viking. "I think in pictures. All of my training has been as an artist. I don't know anything about children's literature or I've never taken any courses in writing. I fill in between pictures with words. My first book I wrote in order to have something to illustrate." [Miriam Hoffman and Eva Samuels, "Robert McCloskey, Master of Humorous Realism," *Authors and Illustrators of Children's Books,* Bowker, 1972.³]

November 23, 1940. Married Margaret Durand, a children's librarian and daughter of Newbery award-winning author, Ruth Sawyer.

1942. *Make Way for Ducklings* was awarded a Caldecott Medal. "When I started making the final sketches for this book, I

found that in spite of my various observations of mallard duck anatomy and habits, I really knew very little about them. I went first to the Natural History Museum in New York, where I took careful notice of the two stuffed mallards that were in the cases. Then I went to the Museum Library and found a top view of a duck's cranium, with minute measurements and a rough estimate of how many years ago ducks were fish. But hidden somewhere I found valuable information on the molting and mating habits of mallards.

"At this time I had the good fortune to meet an ornithologist, George Sutton, and with his kind help I found out a great deal about mallards, studying markings on skins and making notes on wings. At last I had knowledge that I could use, but not enough. I needed models.

"Time and finances would not allow such a simple solution as going where there were wild mallard ducks. I had to acquire them, so I went early one cold New York morning to Washington Market and found a poultry dealer. 'I would like to acquire some mallard ducks,' I said, and I was promptly shown a very noisy shipment that had just come in from the South. I looked in the cages and tried to pick out a pair that were not adulterated with puddle duck. I pointed to a duck and the dealer promptly made a grab in the cage, coming out with a squawking bird held tight around the neck. This process was repeated four times before the two of my choice were caught. Each time a bird was yanked out by the neck. I could not bear to see those two mistakes tossed back into the cage so I bought all four, a neat little duck cage about 3 x 5 feet in area and just high enough, and a half-bushel of mash, all for under two dollars.

"With pride I took my purchases home to the studio and displayed them to Marc Simont, my roommate at the time. (Marc is another artist who does children's illustrations once in a while.) He didn't even bat an eye when he found that all six of us were going to live together. The ducks had plenty to say—especially in the early morning.

"I spent the next weeks on my hands and knees, armed with a box of Kleenex and a sketch book, following ducks around the studio and observing them in the bath tub.

"The next step was a trip back to Boston to make sketches for my background—parks, bridges, fences, streets, stores, and book shops. Returning to New York, I brought a half-dozen ducklings home and filled more sketch books—with happy ducklings, sad ducklings, inquisitive ducklings, bored ducklings, running, walking, standing, sitting, stretching, swimming, scratching, sleeping ducklings."[2]

"You more or less have to think like a duck, too, and it helps you. You think of being just as small as you can, and just thinking back to your own childhood can help you with that."[3]

"All this sounds like a three-ring circus, but it shows that no effort is too great to find out as much as possible about the things you are drawing. It's a good feeling to be able to put down a line and know that it is right."[2]

1942-1945. Served as a Technical Sergeant of Visual Aids in the United States Army; stationed in Fort McClellan, Alabama, McCloskey was assigned to draw training pictures. "My great-est contribution to the war effort was inventing a machine to enable short lieutenants to flip over large training charts in a high breeze."[3]

1943. *Homer Price,* now an American classic, was published. "Perhaps [my favorite book is] *Homer Price,* yet I don't think I have a favorite. I cannot bear to read or even listen to anyone reading my books. They are so much a part of me and part of my past.

"Hardly a mail goes by without my getting a question about *Homer Price.* In the first story I referred to four robbers and I drew five. The book was in production, and I was being inducted into the army. I hadn't reread the story after the publisher asked me to do another drawing. I drew it, and drew five! That book came out in 1943, and I still get kids writing to me telling of their 'discovery.' When the book was translated into Japanese, they took the fifth man right out of the bed!

"Another kind of letter I receive are pictures kids have drawn of either ducks or doughnuts, and still another are from students in college asking me for the story of my life. They sometimes say, 'Add some new details and please return it to me in three days!'" [Lee Bennett Hopkins, *Books Are by People,* Citation, 1969.[4]]

"I'm not prolific—I have to wait until it bubbles out. It may take two years but I live with it. . . . I can't go at the drop of a hat. It took two years to do *Homer* and three years for the next.

"What I'm interested in is communicating with people. I like to know my work is being looked at and enjoyed. When you paint a mural in a bank or post office, you never know whether your work is being seen or not. People who frequent banks and post offices are usually busy cashing checks and licking stamps. They don't notice murals, and if they do, they seldom write and tell you so. Thirty years ago I did the sculpture for

"Trouble has come. The meal chest is low, the bin is near empty. What will feed two will not feed three." ■ (From *Journey Cake, Ho!* by Ruth Sawyer. Illustrated by Robert McCloskey.)

His favorite place to practice was in the bathtub, because there the tone was improved one hundred percent. ■ (From *Lentil* by Robert McCloskey. Illustrated by the author.)

a public building, and during all those years I received perhaps six letters from people who have noticed. On the other hand everyday brings me more letters than that from children, from parents, from teachers and librarians who've read my books.''[3]

1945. Daughter, Sally, born in Ithaca, New York.

1946. After the war, the McCloskeys made their home on an island off the coast of Maine. ''Living on an island six months a year is lots of fun and lots of work. In the spring when we first arrive, there are boats to paint, a garden to plant, the float and dock to repair, dead trees to cut down, and a thousand other things to do. But when it's a nice day, we stop our work to go fishing or sailing or picnicking. And we can picnic either on our own island or on any of the dozens of other islands around us.''

1948. Caldecott Award runner-up *Blueberries for Sal* was published. The character Little Sal was based on McCloskey's daughter, Sally. ''In my illustrations, I try to enhance and elaborate on the story I'm trying to tell. I try to utilize, to the best of my ability, the printing process and the method of reproduction available to me for the job I am doing. If there is any art in my work it is probably the art of the storyteller.'' [*Contemporary American Illustrators of Children's Books*, Rutgers, 1974.[5]]

1948-1949. Lived in Rome as a fellow of the American Academy where he studied mosaic techniques in glass and in marble.

1955. Spent two months painting in Mexico.

1957. *Time of Wonder*, McCloskey's first picture book in full-color, was published. The book, a prose poem, was developed out of family experiences on their island home. ''One element that figures very prominently in *Time of Wonder*, and several of my other stories—is the weather. Here is a lovely, soft summer day, water lapping gently on the beach; there's hardly a ripple. A few hours from now there will be a long expanse of beach there.

''This is a good day for gardening. And [wife] Peggy is in her garden working away at her plants. You can see that it's a pretty rocky garden. One of our friends calls it Peggy's rock. We scrape soil off uprooted trees and we sprinkle it liberally with seaweed and fertilizer. She grows nicotiana and daisies. We also have a large patch of squashes. Here's the ever-present wheel barrow. She tucks in a load of earth and it's off down the path. [Daughter] Sal and a friend are doing some work on a jib, getting ready for our race this afternoon. On race days we welcome some wind, by race time there is usually a good breeze. It's a good day to be out on the water, cruising, picnicking, racing, or just drifting.

''It's surprising how much food, fuel, and supplies of all kinds a family consumes. On the mainland it's not so apparent but here, where everything is brought by boat, unloaded, and wheeled across the island, it's very noticeable. Daily my wife waits for the groceries in hopes that I haven't forgotten anything. It's a long way to the grocery store.

(From the animated film, "Time of Wonder," based on the picture book by Robert McCloskey. Produced by Weston Woods, 1961.)

"Before opening up my studio in the morning I do a few chores. I check the water pump, generator engines and gasoline tanks. There's always something to do. I should climb up there and oil these doors. Today it is warm so we won't need a fire but on cool mornings in spring or fall and on damp, foggy summer mornings a few sticks of wood in this stove will warm things up."[1]

Time of Wonder won a Caldecott Medal in 1958, making McCloskey the first artist to receive the honor twice. McCloskey's award acceptance speech was impassioned—a call to Americans to put art and design to good use. "'What this country needs' is a phrase that keeps popping up. What this country needs is more exercise, or more religion, or a good five cent cigar, or, as of the moment, better education and more scientists.

"With everyone clamoring for more scientists, I should like to clamor for more artists and designers. I should like to clamor for the teaching of drawing and design to every child, right along with reading and writing. I think it is most important for everyone really to see and evaluate pictures and really to see and evaluate his surroundings.

"Stop for a moment and think how much time we all spend looking at and learning from or being influenced by pictures: pictures in magazines, pictures in newspapers, pictures in books, pictures that move, in movies or on TV. Think how much our lives are influenced by these pictures! We read these pictures. They add to and even supplant the written and spoken word. The widely quoted saying 'A picture is worth a thousand words' may be true, but a picture is really worth only as many ideas or words as someone puts into it with his brush or pen or snap of a shutter.

"Suppose we could produce a picture worth ten thousand words. It is of little use to the person who views it if he hasn't enough visual sense or experience to absorb what the picture-maker put into it. It is important that we develop people who can make worthwhile pictures, and it is important that we teach people to 'read' these pictures. That is why, in my opinion, every child, along with learning to read and write, should be taught to draw and to design.

"Do we know when someone is fooling us with pictures? With so many of our ideas being formed by pictures, it is important that we know.

". . . What are some of the elements of design? *Repetition:* as in a tree of apples, a herd of horses, a pattern of like marks made by a man with a brush or by a weaver in the cloth. As like as peas in a pod—alike, yes, but are they *exactly* alike, such as articles punched out by a machine? *Rhythm:* the rhythm of seasons, of growing shells and plants, of waves on the water and of grass in the wind. Is it the rhythm of pistons and machines? *Color:* as in the rainbow, the rocks and hills, the sea and sky and flowers, the colors of nature. Is it the color of neon lights and the colors that fluoresce? *Texture:* the textures of wood, of clay, of sand and stone, and of natural fibers. Are these like the textures of plastic, chromium and cellophane, made by machine? *Form:* the forms of plants and animals, the forms made by natural forces of wind and water, contrasting with the forms suggested by the machine—what the machine can make quickly and easily. *Space relationship:* how all of these various elements are used in relation to each other. This is the most important part of design.

"'Interesting,' you say, 'but how does this affect my life?'

"Until a few years ago, almost all design had its roots and inspiration in nature. But now there is another inspiration—the machine with its forms, its repetition, and its rhythm. Modern chemistry is providing new colors; electricity is providing new light sources. Every day there is a new material, a new texture to add to a long list. A generation of designers has been influenced by the machine and what the machine can do. Artists, architects, landscape architects, sculptors, painters, and even choreographers and musicians have been influenced by the machine. A generation of industrial designers has been busy designing furniture, gadgets, houses, filling stations, knives

(From the animated film, "Burt Dow: Deep Water Man," based on the picture book by Robert McCloskey. Produced by Weston Woods, 1983.)

(From the film, "The Case of the Cosmic Comic," based on the book *Homer Price* by Robert McCloskey. Produced by Weston Woods, 1976.)

and forks, and skyscrapers that are easy for the machine to make. A generation of highway designers has been busy altering the look of our land with the help of machines, bulldozers and earthmovers, to make it easy for cars and trucks to speed from place to place.

"I'm beginning to fear that with our machines, and machine-made materials, we are designing nature right out of our environment. In this country we have been designing, building, making things with machines, without paying the vaguest attention to the space around what we've produced.

"We're designing things without designing the space and the area around them. We are building an environment unfit for human beings to live in. Our land with government of the people, by the people, for the people is fast acquiring an environment of machines, by machines, for machines.

"Yes, I think every child ought to study design and drawing right along with reading, and writing, and arithmetic. I can't think of a scientist, minister, politician, bulldozer-operator or any other professional man or job-holder who would not be a better citizen for having had this training.

"I get mad when I see this important part of life shoved way over to one side in our curriculum and labeled 'Art.' You cannot look at the face of our country without being painfully aware of the result.

"We need a number of new professions: scientist designer, politician designer, anthropologist designer, social-scientist designer. Let us teach design, and let us get it out of the museums, let us get it off the pages and drawing boards and let us put it to work. [Lee Kingman, editor, *Newbery and Caldecott Medal Books: 1956-1965,* Horn Book, 1965.⁶]

1963. *Burt Dow, Deep-Water Man,* published. ". . . A picture book requires planning. The book starts with an idea/ideas inside my head. I imagine a lot of pictures. I almost have the book planned before I first put pencil to paper.

"From the very first minute I start I know that I am writing a sixty-four page book. I cut, I add, I paste together. This bundle of scraps with misspelled words and doodly drawings doesn't look like much but I've captured an idea. But I can't walk into a publisher's office with a bundle of scraps like this and say 'Look, I want to do a book.' I have to make a dummy, something I can take in, that will give my editor and my publisher the feeling that I want in this book. It usually takes about two years from the time I first write the story until it ends up being a completed book. The first drawing has changed but the text reads almost exactly as it did in my first draft."¹

"I used up some four boxes of pencils just making preliminary roughs for *Burt Dow.* There are sometimes as many as twenty or thirty drawings before I turn out the one you see in the book—not completed drawings, of course, but just finding out and exploring the best possible way of presenting this particular picture."³

"Burt Dow is an old deep-water man. He's retired of course, but retired or not he still keeps two boats. One is a dory so old and so leaky that it can no longer be launched. Burt has painted it red and placed it on the little patch of lawn in front of his house, overlooking the bay. He's rigged it like one of the many ships he's sailed to all corners of the seven seas. It's filled plumb to the gun'ls with earth, and every summer Burt plants it with geraniums and Indian peas. The geraniums brighten up the deck and the Indian peas climb the rigging, and sway this-a-way, and that-a-way, in a smoky sou'wester. The other boat is an old double-ender named *Tidely-Idley,* with a make-and-break engine. This boat leaks too.

"The *Tidely-Idley* is the pride and joy of Burt's life, and between odd jobs for natives and summer people he keeps her painted and patched as best he can. Every time he does a paint job, he brings home the leftover paint and uses it on the *Tidely-Idley.* 'That pink plank,' he says 'is the color of Ginny Poor's pantry . . . and the green one is the color of the floor in Dora and Doc Walton's waiting room . . . and there's the tan porch and trim color from Capt'n Haskell's house.'

"Where do I get my ideas? How did I invent these two crazy boats? How did I ever think up a character like Burt Dow? Well I'd like to have you meet Burt Dow. He lives on a neighboring island. Here he is with one of his boats. It's been a dry summer and the Indian peas haven't done too well. As a matter of fact, they're beans. Just as any old color will do for the other boat any old seeds will do to plant this one. I thought up the bright deck of geraniums, but then no, I really didn't think it up because there are front yards all up and down the coast of New England, planted with boatloads of begonias, geraniums, petunias, or you name it.'"¹

1964. Awarded an honorary degree of Doctor of Literature from Miami University. "I'm chasing a new way of life. I have been quite involved for the past three years in constructing puppets—a new type of puppet. My studio now looks like a machine shop. I had to learn a great many new techniques such as operating a lathe and cutting into rubber. I suppose I got interested in movement and in animation from watching Morton Schindel put several of my books on film and seeing the development of *The Lively Art of Picture Books,* a film produced by Weston Wood Studios, Weston, Connecticut, in 1964. I want to do something new with puppets. I think it is too bad that they are usually confined to a television box. I'd like to find a way to eliminate that. Puppets suffer from claustrophobia!"

1967. Awarded a Doctor of Letters from Mount Holyoke College.

1971. Took part in the Old Masters Program at Purdue University.

(From *Blueberries for Sal* by Robert McCloskey. Illustrated by the author.)

One morning in Maine, Sal woke up. She peeked over the top of the covers. The bright sunlight made her blink, so she pulled the covers up and was just about to go back to sleep when she remembered "today is the day I am going to Buck's Harbor with my father!"

Sal pushed back the covers, hopped out of bed, put on her robe and slippers, and hurried out into the hall.

(From *One Morning in Maine* by Robert McCloskey. Illustrated by the author.)

1974. Awarded the Regina Medal for continued distinguished contribution to children's literature from the Catholic Library Association. "I've got this all figured out now to my own satisfaction. It's a 'find your market early scheme' and closely related to the plan of selling little shavers a safety razor of practically nothing with the coming of the first fuzz. *Then* sell them razor blades for the rest of their shaving lives.

"My plan is for young artists to do children's books and find a public whose average age is about six. Fifteen years later, when that public becomes of age, there ought to be an excellent market for pictures in a right price field. A point might be brought out in an early book that no newly married couple should be without a work of art. In another fifteen years, when the artist is in his prime, the law of averages should have it that one out of every so many of his public should have become an executive, a head librarian, a banker, or a postmaster—people with lots of influence and plenty of money and wall space to dispose of. You've guessed it . . . our artist . . . sells off enough murals to retire to Provincetown and spend the rest of his days in peace and quiet, painting an occasional boat or dish of fish.

"Of course something may not work in this plan, just as some unscrupulous members of the 'razor plan' grow beards or purchase electric razors. Instead of selling that first picture to the newlyweds, our artist may find that he has become purveyor of children's picture books to a second generation. But that,

I'm sure you will agree, would be a happy ending, and I'm sure the artist would be happy, and relieved about the whole business, too."[2]

"... I'm not an authority on children's literature, or on graphic arts, or on children's illustrations. In fact, I'm not a children's illustrator. I'm just an artist who, among other things, does children's books.

"I didn't start life training with any burning desire to create little gems for the young or give my all for good old children's books. But like a musician who likes to have his music listened to, the architect who likes to build houses that are homes, I like to have my pictures looked at and enjoyed. I grew a bit tired of turning out water colors by the ream and having only one in four hundred ever find a useful spot on a wall, the others stored in portfolios in some gallery or with canvases in a dusty studio corner. Yes, I'm working on children's illustration, I'm proud of that. But I'm still for hire—to paint, sculpt, whittle, or blast if it's on some job that will bring pleasure and be used, whether it be in a bank, post office, or chicken coop."[3]

FOR MORE INFORMATION SEE: Horn Book, July, 1942, July, 1957; *Horn Book* magazine, volume XXIV, January-December, 1948; Stanley J. Kunitz and Howard Haycraft, editors, *Junior Book of Authors*, H. W. Wilson, 1951; Bertha Mahony Miller and Elinor Whitney Field, editors, *Caldecott Medal Books: 1938-1957*, Horn Book, 1957; Ruth Hill Viguers

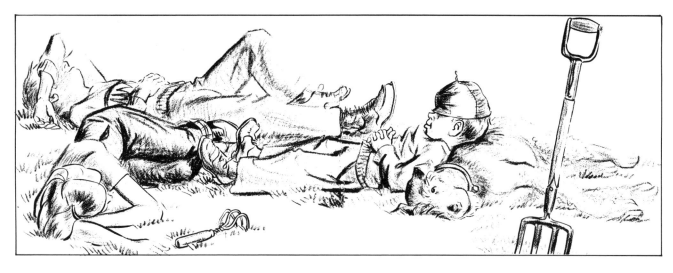

(From *Junket* by Anne H. White. Illustrated by Robert McCloskey.)

and others, compilers, *Illustrators of Children's Books: 1946-1956*, Horn Book, 1958; Ruth Sawyer, "Robert McCloskey: Good Craftsman and Fine Artist," *Publishers Weekly*, June 27, 1962; May Hill Arbuthnot, *Children and Books*, 3rd edition, Scott, Foresman, 1964; "The Lively Art of Picture Books" (film), Weston Woods, 1964; "Robert McCloskey" (film), Weston Woods, 1964; Lee Kingman, editor, *Newbery and Caldecott Medal Books: 1956-1965*, Horn Book, 1965; Child Study Association of America, *The Children's Bookshelf*, Bantam, 1965; Nancy Larrick, *A Teacher's Guide to Children's Books*, Merrill, 1966; *Books for Children, 1960-1965*, American Library Association, 1966; Lee Kingman and others, compilers, *Illustrators of Children's Books: 1957-1966*, Horn Book, 1968; Lee Bennett Hopkins, *Books Are by People*, Citation Press, 1969; Nancy Larrick, *A Parent's Guide to Children's Reading*, 3rd edition, Doubleday, 1969; Selma Lanes, *Down the Rabbit Hole*, Atheneum, 1971; Miriam Hoffman and Eva Samuels, *Authors and Illustrators of Children's Books*, Bowker, 1972; Donnarae MacCann and Olga Richard, *The Child's First Books*, Wilson, 1973; *Contemporary American Illustrators of Children's Books*, Rutgers University Press, 1974.

McNAUGHTON, Colin 1951-

PERSONAL: Born May 5, 1951, in Wallsend, Tyne, England; son of Thomas (a pattern maker) and May (Dixon) McNaughton; married Francoise Julie, June 27, 1970; children: Ben, Timothy. *Education:* Central School of Art and Design, B.A., 1973; Royal College of Art, M.A., 1976. *Home:* C 29 Odhams Walk, London, W.C. 2, England.

CAREER: Free-lance author and illustrator, London, England, 1976—. Has also worked as a part-time teacher at Cambridge School of Art. *Awards, honors:* First Prize for Didactic Literature, jointly from the Cultural Activities Board of the city of Trento and the Children's Literature Department of the University of Padua, 1978, for *C'era una volta* (title means "Once Upon a Time").

*WRITINGS—*All juvenile fiction; all self-illustrated: *Colin McNaughton's ABC and 1, 2, 3: A Book for All Ages for Reading Alone or Together*, Doubleday, 1976 (published in England separately as *Colin McNaughton's ABC and Things*

and *Colin McNaughton's 1, 2, 3 and Things*, Benn, 1976); (with Elizabeth Attenborough) *Walk, Rabbit, Walk*, Viking, 1977; *The Great Zoo Escape*, Heinemann, 1978, Viking, 1979; *The Rat Race: The Amazing Adventures of Anton B. Stanton*, Doubleday, 1978; *Anton B. Stanton and the Pirats*, Doubleday, 1979 (published in England as *The Pirats: The Amazing Adventures of Anton B. Stanton*, Benn, 1979); *Football Crazy*, Heinemann, 1980, published as *Soccer Crazy*, Atheneum, 1981; *King Nonn the Wiser*, Heinemann, 1981; *If Dinosaurs Were Cats and Dogs*, verses adapted by Alice Low, Four Winds Press, 1981; *Fat Pig*, Benn, 1981; *Crazy Bear*, Holt, 1983.

"Books of Opposites" series; all juvenile; all self-illustrated; all published by Philomel Books, 1982: *A Book of Opposites at Home; . . . at Playschool; . . . at the Party; . . . at the Park; . . . at the Stores* (series published in England by Methuen, 1982, as *Hide-Seek; Long-Short; Over-Under; In-Out; Fat-Thin*).

Also author of four color board books in the "Books of Seasons" series for Methuen/Walker Books, 1983, Dial, 1984.

Illustrator; all fiction, except as indicated: James Reeves, compiler, *The Springtime Book: A Collection of Prose and Poetry*, Heinemann, 1976; J. Reeves, compiler, *The Autumn Book: A Collection of Prose and Poetry*, Heinemann, 1977; Hester Burton, *A Grenville Goes to Sea* (juvenile), Heinemann, 1977; J. Reeves, *Eggtime Stories* (juvenile), Blackie & Son, 1978; Mary McCaffrey, *The Mighty Muddle*, Eel Pie Publishing, 1979; Jenny Hawkesworth, *A Handbook of Family Monsters* (juvenile wit and humor), Dent, 1980; Wendy Wood, *The Silver Chanter: Traditional Scottish Tales and Legends* (juvenile), Chatto Bodley Jonathan, 1980; Emil Pacholek, *A Ship to Sail the Seven Seas* (juvenile), Kestrel Books, 1980; Allan Ahlberg, *Miss Brick the Builder's Baby* (juvenile), Kestrel Books, 1981, Golden Press, 1982; A. Ahlberg, *Mr. and Mrs. Hay the Horse* (juvenile), Kestrel Books, 1981, Golden Press, 1982; Russell Hoban, *The Great Fruit Gum Robbery* (juvenile), Methuen/Walker Books, 1981, published as *The Great Gum Drop Robbery*, Philomel Books, 1982; R. Hoban, *They Came from Aargh!* (juvenile), Philomel Books, 1981; Andrew Lang, compiler, *The Pink Fairy Book* (fairy tales), edited by Brian Alderson, revised edition, Viking, 1982 (McNaughton was not associated with the previous edition); R. Hoban, *The Flight of Bembel*

COLIN McNAUGHTON

(From *A Book of Opposites at Home* by Colin McNaughton. Illustrated by the author.)

Rudzuk (juvenile), Philomel Books, 1982; R. Hoban, *The Battle of Zormla* (juvenile), Philomel Books, 1982; A. Ahlberg, *Foldaways: Monsters, Zoo, Families, Circus,* Granada, 1984.

WORK IN PROGRESS: Writing and illustrating more books; illustrations for Allan Ahlberg's *Red Nose Readers,* a series of early readers.

SIDELIGHTS: "The only picture books I knew as a child were the comic annuals I was given at Christmas: *Beano, Dandy, Topper, Eagle,* and *Lion.* Looking back it is not difficult to see that these comics were the main influence on my work. These, and the films I saw every Saturday morning at my local cinema—pirate films, knights in armour, cowboys and Indians. Although today I am married, with two wild sons and a lovely French wife, I still like the same things—the escapism of the adventure film and the crazy madness of the comic. I guess I never grew up."

FOR MORE INFORMATION SEE: Elaine Moss, *Picture Books for Young People 9-13* (bibliography), Thimble (Stroud, England), 1981; *Books for Keeps,* Number 8, May, 1981.

McVICKER, Charles (Taggart) 1930-
(Chuck McVicker)

PERSONAL: Born August 31, 1930, in Canonsburg, Pa.; son of Carl Walter (a singer) and Mary Ruth (a school teacher; maiden name, Washabaugh) McVicker; married Lucy Claire Graves (an artist and illustrator), March 20, 1954; children: Lauri, Bonnie, Heather. *Education:* Principia College, B.A., 1952; Art Center College of Design, B.F.A., 1957. *Home and office:* 4 Willow St., Princeton, N.J. 08542.

CAREER: Alexander Chaite Studios, New York, N.Y., staff artist, 1957-58; free-lance illustrator and painter, 1958—. Assistant professor, Pratt Phoenix School of Art, 1975-84, Trenton State College, 1985—. Work has been exhibited in one-man shows in Princeton, N.J., and at Thompson Gallery, New York, N.Y., 1967. Work has also been exhibited at the Greenville Gallery, Wilmington, Del. and at Back Door Gallery,

"It's unfair," I said after a few moments. "The pretty girls get everything without even trying." ■ (From *Addie and the King of Hearts* by Gail Rock. Illustrated by Charles McVicker.)

Princeton, N.J. Work is represented in permanent collections of the U.S. Capitol, Capitol Historical Society, American History Association, The White House, Society of Illustrators, U.S. Air Force, and Princeton University. *Military service:* U.S. Army, 1952-54. *Member:* Society of Illustrators (member of executive committee, 1972-74; president, 1976-78), American Watercolor Society, Graphic Artists Guild (former vice-president of national executive committee), Princeton Art Association.

ILLUSTRATOR—For children: Don Kowet, *The Soccer Book,* Random House, 1976; Gail Rock, *Addie and the King of Hearts,* Knopf, 1976; (under name Chuck McVicker) *Buck Rogers in the Twenty-fifth Century: A Pop-Up Book,* Random House, 1980. Contributor of illustrations to national magazines and various institutional publications.

WORK IN PROGRESS: Illustrations for children's music books to be published by Holt, Rinehart & Winston, Inc.

SIDELIGHTS: As a free-lance artist and illustrator, McVicker's clients include New Jersey Bell Telephone Company, American Telephone and Telegraph Company, Hertz, Ted Bates, J.

CHARLES McVICKER

Walter Thompson, as well as many magazines and publishing companies. He is a juror for the Society of Illustrator's annual national shows.

McVicker's work has taken him to Japan, Hong Kong, the Canary Islands, Germany, Greece, Turkey, Italy, and England.

MENDOZA, George   1934-

BRIEF ENTRY: Born June 2, 1934, in New York, N.Y. Poet, screenwriter, and author of over one hundred books for children. Mendoza received his B.A. from Columbia University and, pursuing an interest in sailing and fishing, did graduate study at State Maritime College. He is the recipient of a 1968 Lewis Carroll Shelf Award for his poem, *The Hunter I Might Have Been* (Astor-Honor, 1968). Among his other books is *The Lost Pony* (San Francisco Book Co., 1976), the story of a day in the life of a Parisien orphan boy who dreams of owning his own horse. *Publishers Weekly* found the book possessed a "special quality of childlike charm," and compared it to the classic story *The Red Balloon*. Mendoza's numerous writings also include *And Amedeo Asked, How Does One Become a Man?* (Braziller, 1959), *The Puma and the Pearl* (Walker & Co., 1962), *The Gillygoofang* (Dial, 1968), *Sesame Street Book of Opposites with Zero Mostel* (Platt, 1974), and *Counting Sheep* (Grosset, 1982).

As an author of screenplays, Mendoza has been involved with movies and television projects for children. With French film composer Michel Legrand, he produced the ABC-TV After-school Special "Michel's Bird" which aired in February, 1978. They adapted the program into book form as *Michel's Mixed-Up Musical Bird* (Bobbs-Merrill, 1978). Other screenplays by Mendoza include "Petals from a Poem Flower" and "You Show Me Yours and I'll Show You Mine." *For More Information See: New York Times Book Review*, May 2, 1971; *Third Book of Junior Authors*, H. W. Wilson, 1972; *Publishers Weekly*, September 29, 1976; *Contemporary Authors*, Volume 73, Gale, 1978; *Authors of Books for Young People*, supplement to the 2nd edition, Scarecrow, 1979.

MODELL, Frank B.   1917-

PERSONAL: Born September 6, 1917, in Philadelphia, Pa.; son of Irving and Daisy (Simons) Modell. *Education:* Attended Philadelphia College of Art, 1937-41. *Home:* 26 West 9th St., New York, N.Y. 10011. *Agent:* Liz Darhansoff, 1220 Park Ave., New York, N.Y. 10028. *Office:* New Yorker, 25 West 43rd St., New York, N.Y. 10036.

CAREER: Cartoonist, and author and illustrator of children's books. Worked as a cartoonist for the *Saturday Evening Post* and the *New Yorker. Military service:* U.S. Army, 1941-45. *Member:* Cartoonists' Guild. *Awards, honors:* Award from ASIFA (Association Internationale du Film d' Animation), 1971, for animated storyboards for "The Electric Company"; *One Zillion Valentines* was selected as one of *School Library Journal*'s Best Books, 1981, and as a "Children's Choice" of the International Reading Association, 1982.

WRITINGS—All for children, except as indicated; all self-illustrated: *Stop Trying to Cheer Me Up!* (adult), Dodd, 1978; *Tooley! Tooley!* (Junior Literary Guild selection), Greenwillow, 1979; *Seen Any Cats?*, Greenwillow, 1979; *One Zillion*

FRANK B. MODELL

Valentines, Greenwillow, 1981; (with Ormande De Kay) *Fractured French Encore* (adult), Doubleday, 1983; *Goodbye Old Year, Hello New Year*, Greenwillow, 1984.

Illustrator: Maxine Z. Bozzo, *Toby in the Country, Toby in the City*, Greenwillow, 1982.

WORK IN PROGRESS: Children's story about a dog who makes friends with a computer.

SIDELIGHTS: "I began drawing and liking it even earlier than kindergarten and it was the only thing I did in school that showed distinction. I drew or scribbled on everything. Copying my favorite comic characters from the Sunday papers was what probably started me on a career as a cartoonist. The simple, clear line appealed to me and seemed more within my grasp than other art work around. (I hadn't yet seen any drawings by Rembrandt, Delacroix, Daumier, or Goya.)

"I remember thinking that I had better learn as much as I could about art. I went to the Graphic Sketch Club on Saturdays while I was still in grammar school and had my first taste of real art lessons. At the Philadelphia College of Art I worked at learning to paint, draw, make lithographs, design, and so on. Four years later I graduated with the only honors any school ever bestowed on me—much to the surprise of me and my parents. I eventually found that of all the work I showed to art directors and editors, the humorous drawings were what they liked best. I was a cartoonist after all.

"I have probably written enough words to fill a good-sized novel, but they have all been published as short captions under my drawings. I once wrote some lyrics for a children's song

When summer comes to the city . . . I like to go to the beach. ■ (From *Toby in the Country, Toby in the City* by Maxine Zohn Bozzo. Illustrated by Frank Modell.)

book, and did some animation story boards for 'Sesame Street' and 'The Electric Company.' *Tooley! Tooley!* is my first published children's book. The name Tooley is after my own dog. The story occurred to me when I saw a penciled piece of paper tacked to a tree near my home. It offered a reward for a lost dog, but the description was vague and I imagined that every kid in the neighborhood interested in a reward would be picking up every dog in sight. I love kids and I love dogs and I love drawing both, so it was fun putting the story together. The real Tooley, I regret to say, passed away at a ripe old age, but I think her image and spirit are there in *Tooley! Tooley!*''

FOR MORE INFORMATION SEE: Maurice Horn, editor, *The World Encyclopedia of Cartoons,* Chelsea House, 1980.

MONTGOMERY, R(aymond) A., (Jr.) 1936- (Robert Mountain)

PERSONAL: Born March 9, 1936, in Connecticut; son of Raymond A. (an executive) and Olga Montgomery; children: Anson, Ramsey. *Education:* Williams College, B.A., 1958. *Home address:* P.O. Box 87, Waitsfield, Vt. 05673.

CAREER: Wall Street Journal, New York City, in educational services. 1961-63; Columbia University, New York City, as-

R. A. MONTGOMERY

10

You want to use your robot right away. So you take him out and show him to your friends. "I want you to meet my robot, _____," you tell them. "I fixed him myself!"

11

"Show us!" they say. You press your robot's JUMP button. Your robot jumps very high.

Turn to page 12.

(From *Your Very Own Robot* by R.A. Montgomery. Illustrated by Paul Granger.)

sistant provost. 1963-66; Vermont Crossroads Press, Waitsfield, Vt., president, 1974-78. Waitsfield Summer School, Waitsfield, Vt., co-founder, 1966. Member of board of directors of Green Mountain Valley School. *Awards, honors: The Haunted House* was chosen as one of the International Reading Association's "Children's Choices," 1982.

WRITINGS: The Energy Environment Game, Edison Institute, 1969.

"Choose Your Own Adventure" series: (Under pseudonym Robert Mountain) *Journey under the Sea* (illustrated by Paul Granger), Vermont Crossroads Press, 1977, reprinted (under name Raymond A. Montgomery), W. H. Allen, 1979; *Space and Beyond* (illustrated by P. Granger), Bantam, 1979; *The Haunted House* (illustrated by P. Granger), Bantam, 1981; *The Mystery of the Maya*, Bantam, 1981; *Abominable Snowman*, Bantam, 1981; *House of Danger*, Bantam, 1982; *The Race Forever*, Bantam, 1982; *Escape* (illustrated by Ralph Reese), Bantam, 1983; *Lost on the Amazon*, Bantam, 1983; *Prisoner of the Ant People*, Bantam, 1983; *Indian Trail*, Bantam, 1983; *Your Very Own Robot* (illustrated by P. Granger), Bantam, 1983; *Trouble on Planet Earth*, Bantam, 1984.

WORK IN PROGRESS: A novel, tentatively titled *Chrysallis*.

SIDELIGHTS: In 1975, Montgomery was president of Vermont Crossroads Press which published the first book in the "Choose

Your Own Adventure" series. "I Xeroxed 50 copies of Ed's [Packard; originator of the series] manuscript and took it to a reading teacher in Stowe. His kids—third grade through junior high—couldn't get enough of it. I published *Sugarcane Island* for $3.95 and sold an unbelievable—for a small press—8,000 copies, and sold German and Italian rights at the Frankfurt Book Fair. But we didn't have the marketing strength, so we went looking for a big publisher to take us over." [Aljean Harmetz, "'Choose Your Own Adventure' and Make Your Own Ending," *New York Times*, August 25, 1981.]

Since that time, Montgomery has written many of the books himself with a contract from Bantam Books. Some of the books in the series have been translated into fourteen different languages.

MOORE, Patrick (Alfred)   1923-

BRIEF ENTRY: Born March 4, 1923, in Pinner, Middlesex, England. Astronomer, author, editor, translator, and television host. A free-lance writer since 1952, Moore has been a familiar face to British television viewers for over twenty-five years as the host of the monthly British Broadcasting Corporation program "The Sky at Night." During that time he has witnessed such eventful happenings as the launch of Sputnik, the first moon landing, and man's first detailed look at the planets. In 1953 *A Guide to the Moon* was published; since then Moore has written over one hundred twenty-five books on the subject of astronomy, both fiction and nonfiction, for adults, young adults, and children. Many of his books have appeared in numerous revised editions since their original publications.

During the 1950s and 1960s, Moore produced over twenty science fiction novels for young readers, including *The Master of the Moon, Destination Luna: The Thrilling Story of a Boy's Adventurous Trip to the Moon, Peril on Mars, Wanderer in Space,* and *Planet of Fire.* In the late 1970s the "Scott Saunders Adventure" series appeared, with titles such as *Spy in Space, The Terror Star,* and *The Secret of the Black Hole.* The 1957 publication of Moore's *Science and Fiction* marked one of the first detailed studies of the genre by the British. In addition to his innumerable writings, Moore has also edited other works and translated several from the French. He has been the recipient of awards throughout his career, including the 1962 Lorimer Gold Medal for services to astronomy, the Goodacre Gold Medal and the Officer Order of the British Empire, both in 1968. *Home and office:* Farthings, 39 West St., Selsey, Sussex, England. *For More Information See:* Brian Ash, *Who's Who in Science Fiction,* Elm Tree Books, 1976; *Contemporary Authors, New Revision Series,* Volume 8, Gale, 1983; *The Writers Directory: 1984-1986,* St. James Press, 1983.

MURRAY, John 1923-
(Robert Combs)

PERSONAL: Born July 8, 1923, in Yonkers, N.Y.; son of William Bernard (a financier) and Ellen (Combs) Murray; married Marjorie Porcella (an attorney), February 10, 1946; children: John, Robert. *Education:* Fairleigh Dickinson University, B.S., 1950. *Politics:* Democrat. *Religion:* Roman Catholic. *Home:* R.D.1, Box 243, Little Brook Rd., Glen Gardner, N.J. 08826.

CAREER: Free-lance writer. Lecturer on national tour, 1966. Drama director, Catholic Youth Organization of Union County, N.J. *Member:* American Folklore Society. *Awards, honors:* CBS-TV Award for Script Writers, 1950; awards for one-act plays, 1950, 1960.

WRITINGS—Published by Plays, except as indicated: "The Amazing Monsieur Fabre" (unpublished), produced in Paris, France, 1952; *Mystery Plays for Young People,* 1956; *Comedies and Farces for Teen-Agers,* 1959; *One-Act Plays for Young Actors,* Denison, 1959; *Modern Monologues for Young People,* 1961, revised edition, 1982; *Comedy Round-up for Teen-Age Actors,* 1964; *Comedies and Mysteries for Young Actors,* 1972; *Fifteen Plays for Teenagers: A Collection of One-Act, Royalty-Free Comedies and Mysteries,* 1979, new edition published as *Fifteen Plays for Today's Teenagers,* 1982; *Senior Citizens Onstage,* Eldridge Publishing, 1980; *Panorama,* Johnson and Simpson, 1980; *The Sinking of the Morning Star,* 1983; *Clown-a-rama,* 1983. "The Sixth Juror" (originally published in *Comedies and Mysteries for Young Actors,* Plays, 1972), published in reading series program *Vistas,* Houghton, 1986.

Work anthologized in: *Top Flight,* Scott, Foresman, 1961; *A World of Experience,* American Book Co., 1962; *A Treasury of Holiday Plays for Teen-Agers,* Plays, 1963; *Favorite Plays for Classroom Reading,* Plays, 1965; *On Stage for Christmas,*

JOHN MURRAY

Plays, 1978; *Mystery Plays for Young Actors,* Plays, 1984. Work is also included in *Sightings,* Rand McNally, and *Top Picks,* Reader's Digest Press. Contributor of over 200 plays to magazines.

WORK IN PROGRESS: Preparing one-act plays for publication: *The Curse of Demon Creek, Flight International, The Video Game Visitors, Bed-and-Breakfast Bedlam, The Whitemarsh Affair.* "Writing and recording mysteries and romances for cassette presentation."

SIDELIGHTS: "I cannot recall the time when I didn't want to write. In elementary school, I read a chapter of my work each Friday to fellow class members, and I always managed to end the weekly session with a 'cliff hanger' in anticipation of events to follow. Perhaps I was the most apprehensive person in the class because I never knew how I would extricate the characters from the web of intrigue in which I had enmeshed them!

"I wish that I could tell you something world-shattering and illuminating about launching into a writing career, but I have found that life doesn't happen that way. In 1950, I learned about a contest launched by CBS-TV for new scripts. Those were the days when everyone sat before a six inch screen and watched Gorgeous George methodically dismember an opposing wrestler; Milton Berle; 'Robert Montgomery Presents'; and 'Studio One' with intense avidity. I sent for a contest form, wrote a thirty-minute script entitled 'Brother Zebe and Moanin' Mary,' and mailed it to the board of judges. John Steinbeck was among the illustrious names affiliated with the award. Ten days later I received a telegram stating that I had won the CBS-TV award for script writers.

"The judges mentioned that I did not spend time on elaborate camera directions or television technicalities (actually, I didn't know any!), but had written a simple, convincing story and told it well. The accompanying letter with the award check outlined: 'The judges particularly liked your true feeling for Kentucky Hill people, and your genuine, flavorsome dialogue.' It was that letter that made me aware of the sameness of people because, before writing 'Brother Zebe,' I had never been in Kentucky in my life. I was soon to learn that all people are universal—we have the same motivations, needs, love, anger, searches for fulfillment—and whether it be the exotic Indian background of Louis Bromfield novels, or the infertile earth of Pearl Buck's China, or the teeming tenement district of Betty Smith's *A Tree Grows in Brooklyn*, we are all one—we are people.

"In the fall of that same year, *Plays, the Drama Magazine for Young People* ran a one-act play contest to celebrate the tenth year of successful publication. My script, 'The Door,' won second prize, and through the efforts of the publisher, A. S. Burack, I continued to write plays. Mr. Burack became my editor, teacher and, above all, dearest friend for the next thirty years. No single person has ever given more encouragement, more strength, more purpose to my life as a writer than Mr. Burack, editor of *Plays* and *The Writer*. Whenever a crisis arises in my life, I write a play. Undoubtedly my years were filled with moments of decision because, during the ensuing years, I wrote more than two hundred published plays and eight drama anthologies.

"ENTERTAINMENT—that's the name of the game! I have tried to give plays of high entertainment value to young audiences. If a participant finds humor, emotion, and entertainment reflected in my work, then my task is well accomplished.

"I speak at numerous seminars, commencements, camp groups, schools, and drama clubs, and my rules for writing are always the same: a) Apply the seat of the trousers to the seat of the chair—and write!, and b) I don't want to know what you know—I want to know what you feel!

"Today, my entire time is absorbed in writing and helping young people in dramatic careers. I suppose that some people would classify me as a person in retirement, but I think of it as a period of adjustment. I have known young people at eighty, and old people at forty. Some people regard retirement as a period when everything starts shriveling up, hanging down, caving in, or falling out. Rubbish! Naturally, I have an awareness of mortality.

"I'll probably not write two hundred more plays or eight more drama anthologies—but a good person never retires. I have a distaste for the category 'Senior Citizen,' even though my latest collection of humorous sketches is entitled *Senior Citizens On-stage*. I will continue to turn out plays because the most rewarding declaration of the writer is, 'I'VE DONE IT!' Positive thinking is my formula for success.

"I'll never forget a statement made by my cousin, Joan Blondell, who was a brilliant star of screen and stage for fifty years: 'John, the greatest person in the entertainment field is the writer because he or she thinks—thinks—THINKS!'

"While I may be an exception to Joan's finding, I hope that the pulse beat of life around me, the association of people, and the ever-growing wonders of the world will be my heritage for all the years to come. This is my creed—for these things I pray.''

DORA PANTELL

PANTELL, Dora (Fuchs) 1915-

PERSONAL: Born December 25, 1915, in New York, N.Y.; daughter of Abraham and Jennie (Birnbaum) Fuchs; married Edward Pantell. *Education:* Hunter College, B.A., 1931; Columbia University, M.A., 1933. *Home:* 340 East 64th St., New York, N.Y. 10021.

CAREER: Author, social worker, and teacher. New York City Board of Education, New York, N.Y., teacher, 1931-34; Department of Welfare, New York, N.Y., 1934-47, became assistant publicity director; New York City Board of Education, New York, N.Y., evening school teacher of English as a second language, 1944-50, teacher-trainer, coordinator and supervisor of English as a second language and reading programs, Bureau of Continuing Education, 1951-67, curriculum writer, Bureau of Curriculum Research, 1967-70, assistant director of Office of Continuing Education, 1971-76. Interviewer and feature writer, Civilian War Assistance Unit of the United States State Department, 1946-47; feature writer, United Service for New Americans, New York, N.Y., 1947-50; radio scriptwriter for the BBC, London, England, 1950-51; instructor at Graduate School of Education, City College (now of the City University of New York), New York, N.Y., 1960-61, and Long Island University, 1961-62; writer, on loan to Department of Health, Education and Welfare, Washington, D.C., 1964-65, on loan to Department of Education, Jackson, Mississippi, 1965-66; television drama series writer and on-camera teacher, Channel

The title of the article . . . was "Cloning." ■ (From *Miss Pickerell Takes the Bull by the Horns* by Ellen MacGregor and Dora Pantell. Illustrated by Charles Geer.)

25, New York, N.Y., 1970-71. Has also taught courses in writing for children, feature writing, and English as a second language at the State University at Albany, City College, Hunter College, Long Island University, and Pace University, and has been a guest lecturer on writing for children at many colleges. *Member:* Adult Education Association of the U.S.A.

Pantell continued the ''Miss Pickerell'' series in 1964 after the death in 1954 of its originator, Ellen MacGregor. Both share the credit for authorship of the ''Miss Pickerell'' series between 1965 and 1983.

WRITINGS—''Miss Pickerell'' series; all illustrated by Charles Geer; all for children; all published by McGraw, except as noted: *Miss Pickerell on the Moon*, 1965; . . . *Goes on a Dig*, 1966; . . . *Harvests the Sea*, 1968; . . . *and the Weather Satellite*, 1971; . . . *Meets Mr. H.U.M.*, 1974; . . . *Takes the Bull by the Horns*, 1976; . . . *to the Earthquake Rescue*, 1977; . . . *and the Supertanker*, 1978; . . . *Tackles the Energy Crisis*,

1980; . . . *on the Trail*, 1982; . . . *and the Blue Whales*, 1983; . . . *and the War of the Computers*, F. Watts, 1984.

Other: *We Americans*, edited by Angelica W. Cass, Oxford Book Co., 1957, revised, 1962; (with Gladys E. Alesi) *Family Life in the U.S.A.* (young adult), Regents Publishing, 1962, revised, 1980; (with G. E. Alesi) *First Book in American English*, Books I and II, Oxford Book Co., 1962; (with G. E. Alesi) *Second Book in American English*, Oxford Book Co., 1964; *Teaching English as a New Language to Adults*, New York City Board of Education, 1964; *Language Enrichment Series*, Books 1-13, New York City Board of Education, 1964-70; *Conducting a Program of Basic Education with Adults*, New York City Board of Education, 1965; (with Leo U. Bernardo) *English: Your New Language* (teacher's edition), Silver Burdett, 1966, revised, 1972; *Teaching Dialogues: English as a New Language Program for Adults*, New York City Board of Education, 1966, new edition, 1971; *Scope and Sequence in the Teaching of English as a New Language*, New York

The fatigue lines that Mr. Squeers had mentioned were unmistakably present. ■ (From *Miss Pickerell and the Supertanker* by Ellen MacGregor and Dora Pantell. Illustrated by Charles Geer.)

City Board of Education, Book I, 1968, Book II, 1972; (with Edwin Greenidge) *If Not Now, When?: The Many Meanings of Black Power*, Delacorte, 1969; *New American English*, Books I and II, Oxford Book Co., 1972, Books III and IV, Oxford Book Co., 1974.

Ghost writer for Erich Maria Remarque, for Erica Mann, and for Julian Press (publishers). Also author of teacher-training films for the Bureau of Audio-Visual Instruction, New York City. Regular contributor to *Why* magazine and contributor of short stories and articles to *Family Circle, Journal of Gerontology, Journal of Geriatrics, Wilson Library Journal, New York City Education, Curriculum and Materials, TESOL,* to newspapers, and to educational publications.

WORK IN PROGRESS: Another "Miss Pickerell" book; a teaching text/reader based on "Miss Pickerell" adventures for Regents Publishing Co.; a mystery novel for adults; an article and a story for the magazine market.

SIDELIGHTS: Pantell was born on Christmas Day, 1915 to eastern European immigrants. "Born on the Lower East Side in Manhattan, I knew little of the ways of people outside this immigrant community. When my first grade teacher asked me to say, 'Yes, ma'am' to her, I questioned my mother as to why I should say MAN to the teacher when she was so definitely a lady. My mother could not explain. In those days, teachers in underprivileged neighborhoods did not bother to direct pupils to books beyond the standard classroom assignments. I remember adoring *A Tale of Two Cities* when I was ten, but I had no idea that Dickens had written other books which I might also love. I also remember my Saturday afternoon treks to a stationery store and finding Louisa May Alcott and Margaret Deland treasures that sold for fifty cents, probably my total weekly allowance. Margaret Deland, I now hear, has been rescued from an undeserved obscurity and hailed as a fine writer. To think that I knew it ages ago!

"I can't recall a time when I didn't write. My first opus, at

At first glance, the inside of Mrs. Miranda Prism, Antiques looked like an old-fashioned general store. ■ (From *Miss Pickerell and the Supertanker* by Ellen MacGregor and Dora Pantell. Illustrated by Charles Geer.)

the age of nine, and unfortunately long lost, was about a family very different from my own. Papa and Mama in the book never quarreled and nobody worried about money. It was a satisfying saga, not too unlike much of the escape fiction of today.

"And I continued to write. No matter what else I was doing, the writing part emerged. At the Department of Welfare, I ended up as assistant publicity director, at United Service for New Americans, I became the *chief* feature writer, at the New

An idea had come into her head. A perfectly clear, sensible idea! ■ (From *Miss Pickerell on the Trail* by Ellen MacGregor and Dora Pantell. Illustrated by Charles Geer.)

York City Board of Education, I moved out of the classroom to write curriculum, film scenarios, television scripts. All of this alongside the writing of stories and articles for magazines and books for commercial publication.

"I started to write for children quite accidentally. At the Bureau of Curriculum Research, I shared a room with Julius Schwartz, who knew a great deal about me for he always answered the telephone (on his desk) first and invariably asked who was calling. One day, he commented that most of my calls were from publishers handling my manuscripts. What bothered him was that McGraw-Hill was not among them. Why didn't I write for them, he wanted to know. 'Because they never asked me,' I told him. 'Well, I'm asking you now,' he said. It turned out that Julius Schwartz, author of a number of children's books of his own, was also science consultant for McGraw-Hill. It also seemed that McGraw-Hill had been trying unsuccessfully for ten years, ever since Ellen MacGregor, the original writer of the 'Miss Pickerell' series, had died, to find an author who could capture the mood and the charm of the books and replace her. Julie let me have one of her books to read. It was *Miss Pickerell Goes to Mars,* the first of the four books she'd written. I found it enchanting. But it was science-oriented and I was not. Julie offered to spoon-feed me the science information. He still does, but by mail during the last few years, since he now lives in Florida.

"McGraw-Hill breathed a huge sigh of relief when I submitted a sample chapter and table of contents for my first 'Miss Pickerell' book. I went on to write a total of eleven books for the company. When the junior book division was dismantled in 1983, Jon Gillett, once of McGraw-Hill and now president of Franklin Watts, took me with him. He could not bear such an

untimely demise for the 'legendary' Miss Pickerell. *Miss Pickerell and the War of the Computers* is the first book I have done for Franklin Watts.

"My illustrator was also a happy accident. McGraw-Hill found Charles Geer for me. An artist who has won a number of awards, he could not, I thought, manage to draw a cow. I was wrong; I was looking at rough drafts only. Charlie brings Miss Pickerell and all her animals to vivid life with his drawings.

"Miss Pickerell had only a cow when I inherited her. She has since accumulated a cat, a dog, a lamb, a deaf old plow horse, even a home for retired and disabled animals on or near her farm in Square Toe County. The cow came to me without a name, a fact that brought an indignant protest in eleven-year-old Nancy's fan letter. I was quick to reply. Would Nancy like me to name the cow after her? She would be delighted! But the book with the cow's name in it did not come off the press for another three years. And the reply I received when I sent Nancy a copy was a very indulgent one. How nice of me to remember a child's dream, the grown-up fourteen-year-old wrote! But her mother has since written to say that Nancy reads each new Miss Pickerell with absolute relish and that she, the mother, reads that book the minute that Nancy has finished it."

For aspiring young authors, Pantell offered the following advice: "At the 'Children's Author Weeks' where I'm often invited to talk on a 'Miss Pickerell Day,' the questions usually begin with whether I write my books in longhand or on a typewriter. The truth of the matter is that when an idea or a phrase comes into my head, I make a note on any scrap of paper I can find. I have done this on planes, in waiting rooms, or even in a theatre, when the play got dull. The note becomes

Miss Pickerell spoke soothingly to her cow. "It's all right," she told her. "Dr. Haggerty will be here soon. He'll make you feel better." ■ (From *Miss Pickerell on the Moon* by Ellen MacGregor and Dora Pantell. Illustrated by Charles Geer.)

part of a long-hand version in which I begin the book, soon to be transferred and continued on the typewriter. I am more critical when I look at a typewritten page, a very important asset for a writer. The children seem to understand this. They nod vigorously, or just thoughtfully.

"Their second question is almost always about how they can learn to write a book. I tell them that *reading lots of books* is a foundation. I also tell them about scene setting and about character and about how a plot is believable only if it comes out of the characters' needs and desires and problems, etc. One of the children in a school where I spoke last year, has just sent me a story she wrote. With a little judicious editing, it may well be accepted by a children's magazine.

"The third question is about where to find ideas. It is probably a question that has plagued authors through the years—unless something they want to say is driving them. This UNLESS bit is what I stress with the children. And when I ask them to tell me what they would like to say 'to the world,' the answers are immediate. Sometimes, I feel tempted to use a few of them."

Pantell enjoys both writing and re-reading the Miss Pickerell books. "I find her character comforting. Miss Pickerell yields to no one in standing up for what she believes and in preserving her personality or even her eccentricities."

Pantell hopes the books will go on and on. One of the recent reviews has called the character immortal. "That's a lot to say about the lady with the cow and the umbrella. But she is such a refreshing antidote in a world where even children's books are full of violence."

Pantell also laughs about the fact that for some people, she *is* Miss Pickerell. "I have my eccentricities too. And, of course, there is our love for animals." Pantell shares her Manhattan apartment with three cats and her love with every cat and dog she meets.

HOBBIES AND OTHER INTERESTS: Theatre, music, gardening, animal care.

FOR MORE INFORMATION SEE: Wilson Library Bulletin, September, 1965.

PARTCH, Virgil Franklin II   1916-1984 (Vip)

OBITUARY NOTICE: Born October 17, 1916, on St. Paul Island, Alaska; died in an automobile accident, August 10, 1984, near Valencia, Calif. Cartoonist. Partch was best known for his syndicated comic strip, "Big George," which he wrote under the pseudonym Vip. Big George was a perpetual loser in a world of traffic jams, rising meat prices, and odious puns. Partch created Big George in 1960 after years of work as a free-lance cartoonist contributing to periodicals such as *New Yorker* and *Look.* He began his career an animator at Walt Disney Studios in 1937. Partch worked there for five years before he was dismissed for refusing to adhere to studio guidelines for drawing Mickey Mouse. In 1941 he resigned from Walter Lantz Studios after a similar disagreement about guidelines for depicting Woody Woodpecker. Under the Vip pseudonym Partch wrote numerous cartoon books, including *Water on the Brain, Crazy Cartoons,* and *Dentists Are Funny People.* He also wrote the juvenile books *The Christmas Cookie Sprin-*

kle Snitcher, Shaggy Fur Face, and *Ludwig, the Dog Who Snored Symphonies. For More Information See: The World Encyclopedia of Cartoons,* Gale, 1980; *Contemporary Authors,* Volume 108, Gale, 1983; *Who's Who in American Art,* 16th edition, Bowker, 1984. *Obituaries: Los Angeles Times,* August 12, 1984; *Chicago Tribune,* August 12, 1984; *New York Times,* August 12, 1984; *Washington Post,* August 12, 1984; *Newsweek,* August 27, 1984.

PEARSON, Susan   1946-

PERSONAL: Born December 21, 1946, in Boston, Mass.; daughter of Allen M. (a Swedish masseur) and Chloris (a secretary; maiden name, Horsman) Pearson. *Education:* St. Olaf College, Northfield, Minn., B.A., 1968. *Residence:* Minneapolis, Minn.

CAREER: Author and editor. Volunteers in Service to America (VISTA), Columbia, S.C., volunteer worker, 1968-69; Quaker Oats Co., Minneapolis, Minn., sales representative, 1969-71; Viking Press, New York, N.Y., assistant, 1971-72; Dial Press, New York, N.Y., editor, 1972-78; Carolrhoda Books, Minneapolis, Minn., editor-in-chief, 1978-84. Free-lance editor and writer, 1985—. *Awards, honors: Izzie* was named one of

"What's it a list of?" said Mom.
"The things I'll need," I told her. "For running away."
■ (From *Saturday I Ran Away* by Susan Pearson. Illustrated by Susan Jeschke.)

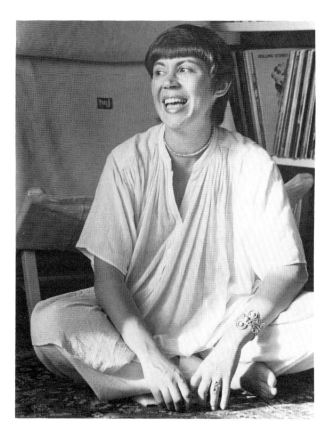

SUSAN PEARSON

New York Times Outstanding Books of the Year and one of Child Study Association's Children's Book of the Year, 1975; *Saturday I Ran Away* was selected one of International Reading Association's "Children's Choices," 1982.

WRITINGS—For children: *Izzie* (illustrated by Robert Andrew Parker), Dial, 1975; *Monnie Hates Lydia* (illustrated by Diane Paterson), Dial, 1975; *That's Enough for One Day, J.P.!* (illustrated by Kay Chorao), Dial, 1977; *Everybody Knows That!* (illustrated by D. Paterson), Dial, 1978; *Monday I Was an Alligator* (illustrated by Sal Murdocca), Lippincott, 1979; *Molly Moves Out* (illustrated by Steven Kellogg), Dial, 1979; *Karin's Christmas Walk* (illustrated by Trinka H. Noble), Dial, 1980; *Saturday I Ran Away* (illustrated by Susan Jeschke), Lippincott, 1981; *Happy Birthday Grampie, I Love You* (illustrated by Leo Dillon and Diane Dillon), Dial, in press.

WORK IN PROGRESS: Picture books and juvenile novels.

SIDELIGHTS: **December 21, 1946.** "I was born in Boston and until age nine lived in Auburndale, a suburb of Boston. We usually lived in suburbs as my father, a Swedish masseur, held jobs with the YMCAs in major metropolitan areas.

"My father and mother were thirty-six when I was born. I'm an only child. By the time I was born, my youngest cousin was already thirteen years old, making me the baby of the family, lavished with huge amounts of attention. The expectation was always that I would go to college even though nobody in the family had gone. Few restrictions were placed on me. I was never expected to play with dolls or to fit into a particular mold, and was encouraged in all my interests. What

It was getting dark now and the tree lights had come on. ■ (From *Karin's Christmas Walk* by Susan Pearson. Illustrated by Trinka Hakes Noble.)

my mother and father couldn't provide was provided by the rest of the doting family.

"My life was very much like Carrie's, the character in my book *Izzie*. My uncle lived in Portland, Maine, where we spent our Christmases and a good part of our summers eating lobster. I also spent time with another uncle on Cape Cod. I took ballet and piano lessons. It was an idyllic childhood.

"When I was nine, we moved to Newport News in southern Virginia for two years. This was during the 1950s with segregation in full force in the South. I had a hard time coping with and understanding the reasons for separate drinking fountains for blacks and whites, separate toilets, separate schools and separate swimming pools. I don't think I questioned it consciously. I was simply befuddled. When we moved to Virginia, I had already learned everything they were teaching in fourth grade except southern Confederate history and cursive handwriting. I spent the entire year practicing my long hand on the blackboard while other students were engaging in their studies.''

Pearson recollects ''writing stories as far back as second grade. I had a teacher who insisted that every subject have a booklet

connected with it. I was making science booklets, history booklets, etc. At some point in second grade, I decided I wanted my *own* booklet. The first thing I ever wrote was entitled, 'My Booklet.' It consisted of drawings, very short stories, and some poems.

"I read voraciously as a child. My favorite stories were in a book called *The Musical Seashell*. I treasured 'Live Dolls' in *The Read to Yourself Storybook*. I loved Louisa Alcott and the 'Ann of Green Gables' books. I read anything I could get my hands on.

"It was when we moved to Minnesota (where I now live) that I started writing earnestly. I think adolescence has something to do with that. Many female writers I know started writing in earnest during their adolescence, when they were too embarrassed to tell people what they were really feeling.

"By the time I reached adolescence, my mother thought my writing was becoming a bit peculiar. I would stay up after the family had gone to bed, light a candle and write secretly in my romantically lit bedroom. I don't know whether it was the candle that made her nervous or me. My parents were encouraging, however, and they were thrilled when my first book was published.

"In Minnesota I had some outstanding high school teachers. My junior year English teacher had the wonderful ability of separating what you were saying from how you were saying it. [He/She?] could disagree without marking you down, grading you instead for presentation of the argument and the logic of thinking. Many of my college professors couldn't do that.

"I was a chubby and shy teenager. By that time I was into adult books . . . Hemingway . . . Fitzgerald. I wasn't very athletic, and in Minnesota, if you're not athletic, you're in trouble. If you don't ski in the winter and swim in the summer, you end up with social problems.

"I always wanted to be something that I wasn't. If I had had any self-confidence, I probably would have been fine, but I didn't. I had many casual friends but only one or two close friends. People would have accepted me as I was, but I didn't believe that what I was was any good."

1964-1968. Attended St. Olaf College in Northfield, Minnesota. "College was a continuation of high school. I didn't grow up during that time. Part of the reason was that my father became very ill for several years before he died in 1967. Growing up and coming to terms with myself was postponed while I was dealing with his death.

"I was majoring in English and realized that I couldn't take any more English courses and still graduate. I decided to get permission from the art department to write and illustrate a children's book. Neither my English advisor, nor the director of the art department was very enthusiastic about my plan. The art teacher showed me the basic principles of using a silkscreen and left me on my own. I wrote a very simple concept book, illustrated it with silkscreen and bound it myself. I was mortified by it, thinking it a shabby effort. I would work in what was called the 'art barn,' a big room full of printmakers. I'd hang my silkscreens up facing the corner so that no one would see them. I was so embarrassed. Years later, I discovered that some of the other students became furious with my silkscreens

Just as everything was ready, Lydia walked in. . . .

"Happy birthday, sleepy head," said Daddy, still in his doughy apron.

"Happy birthday, Lydia," said Monnie. "Open my present first!" ■ (From *Monnie Hates Lydia* by Susan Pearson. Illustrated by Diane Paterson.)

which were really very good because I didn't have any art training.

"At the end of the term, I submitted my finished product, placing it under a pile in the professor's office, hoping he would get to it after I had gone home for vacation. I remember I went upstairs to clean the equipment before leaving. Somehow he had found the book, came racing up the stairs into the room in which I was working and said, 'Do you know how good this is? It's fantastic! Why didn't I notice you before? You've got more talent than half of my majors.' That was really important to me. He had somebody from the education department look it over, and then sent it off to a number of publishers. It never did get published, but now that I look back, it really wasn't bad. The professor worked with me for the remainder of my senior year, a year which instilled in me a real feeling of confidence, a feeling that, 'Gee, maybe I really could. . . .'

"Though it was not the 'in thing' to be rebellious at St. Olaf's, a very conservative, religious school, I was against Viet Nam, excited about the civil rights movement, outraged . . . , idealistic. . . . As soon as I got out of college, I joined VISTA [Volunteers in Service to America] to 'save the world,' was sent to Columbia, South Carolina for one year, and was getting as far away from my mother as soon as I possibly could. My mother and I never got along, although it's certainly better now.

"After a year with VISTA I went to work for the Columbia Office of Economic Opportunity. I was hired as an accountant and ended up spending most of my time writing programs to be funded by the federal government."

1969-1971. "When I ran out of money, I came back to Minnesota to hunt for a job. There were publishing opportunities in Minneapolis, but they tended to be concerned with specifics, such as, religious or law book publishing. One day, the employment agency called and announced that they had 'found a great job for me at Quaker Oats.' 'What do you mean?' I asked. 'I don't want to work for Quaker Oats. Doing what?' They wanted a sales representative. The money was very good. It was a man's salary, which was hard for a woman to find in those days, and it involved a company car. During the interview, they asked me why I thought I could sell Quaker Oats. 'If I can sell anything, it's Quaker Oats. For heaven's sake, I've been using it since I was six months old,' was my response. I was hired. They were looking for management possibilities, and for women. I was the first woman in a national sales force of five hundred men. They thought I was wonderful and very peculiar. I was good at the job. In fact, we used to have regional sales meetings where everybody was expected to give a sales presentation on a new product. Prizes were awarded for the best presentation. The first time I did this, I won. The prizes were a man's electric shaver and a jug of moonshine whiskey. I took the moonshine with me."

1971-1972. "As soon as I'd saved a thousand dollars, I quit Quaker Oats and moved to New York in order to write. I lived with different friends while I worked on a children's book. I wrote a book about an unhappy giraffe in a zoo. It was terrible. A girlfriend of mine was at that time dating a vice-president of William Morrow, and he asked to see my book. He loved it and wanted me to take my portfolio to see editors. For six weeks I went around New York with my portfolio. Nobody wanted to buy my book. Once again I was running out of money and in need of a job. I went to Viking who didn't like my book either, but their editor was fascinated with the fact

that I had been a sales representative for Quaker Oats and on that basis hired me as an assistant.

"Publishing was wonderful. It was glamorous. I loved it, though the feeling didn't last. I think I made it for a year before I started feeling terrible about New York. I saved a thousand dollars again and left. I traveled around the country, staying a month in Maine, a month in Washington, D.C., a month in Atlanta and in California; back to Minneapolis. Air fares were cheap in those days. I was writing a young adult novel at that time.

"Back in Minneapolis, wondering what to do next, I was pressed to find employment. Then a very peculiar sequence of events happened. The Viking editor who had hired me as an assistant called to tell me that he'd found a job for me at Dial Press. I went to New York on a Friday, was interviewed, and went to work at Dial on Monday."

1972-1978. Editor at Dial Press in New York. "Louise Fogelman, editor-in-chief, was an enormous and wonderful influence. She spent a great deal of time encouraging me, letting me make mistakes, and helping me to find out for myself how editing is done. I was also influenced by one of the finest classical children's book designers. I am not trained as an artist or designer, but we were short staffed in those days and did anything we could."

1975. *Izzie* published and named one of *New York Times* Outstanding Books of the Year for children, as well as one of Child Study Association's Books of the Year. "By then, I had been in publishing long enough to take the awards with a grain of salt. I think the award had more to do with the art work than my cat. I'd also been around long enough to know that you can get lousy reviews and win the Newbery and good reviews and never sell a copy."

Monnie Hates Lydia was published the same year. "The two characters in *Monnie Hates Lydia* were modeled after a sixth grade girlfriend and her kid sister. Susan was always beating on her kid sister, Jackie. It angered me because I had always wanted a sibling, feeling that if I had a sister like Jackie, I would never treat her that way, which is probably untrue. I think both *Monnie Hates Lydia* and *Saturday I Ran Away* [1981] come from my sympathy with the underdog, and from my own feelings of being the underdog for a long time."

1978. Editor-in-chief of Carolrhoda Books in Minneapolis, Minnesota. "Book publishing should be a wide open market. It's very upsetting to see a book get rave reviews just because it was written by somebody well known. Still, there are fantastic things being published now with an acceptance of all different kinds of formats and levels of sophistication. The problem with children's book publishing is the same as the problem with any other publishing—there aren't that many people who have a notion of what good writing really is. Perhaps children's book publishing is better off because it deals with educators and librarians who at least can tell the difference between literate and illiterate prose.

"What I look for in a children's book is *action*. I look for development—things that happen, rather than mental wanderings that go nowhere. I look for development of character, and sentence structure that is both grammatically correct and pleasing. Children's book editors usually read books aloud before publishing and look for different elements in the use of language. I find myself becoming annoyed these days when I read adult books. How could anyone publish prose which is so

It had snowed again the night before, and the snow sprayed in your face as you slid down the hill.
■ (From *Izzie* by Susan Pearson. Painting by Robert Andrew Parker.)

unlyrical, so off-beat, so disjointed? I also look for the story to move from one plane to another. I want to be someplace different when I get to the end of the story. There's a lot of teaching that goes on at a subliminal level through the nature of the characters and the story. I'm not a big fan of Aesop, however—I don't look for a moral at the end of the story.

"One of the annoyances in children's literature today is the premium placed on art as opposed to writing. There is a feeling that you can get away with virtually anything as long as you have glorious full color art accompanying it. Many publishers are falling for that. For that reason it's also more difficult for people who only write and do not do their own illustrations to become published. Apparently editors are looking for something that is 'illustratable,' something they see matching well with a certain illustrator's work.

"My own books usually begin with an idea on a piece of paper, which is stuck into a file labeled 'ideas.' One idea will stick in my mind, where a great deal of the actual writing is done, before I sit down at the typewriter. I haven't been writing much lately because my mind has been on my work at Carolrhoda.

"Some of my books have taken months and months to write. *Monnie Hates Lydia* took forever because I couldn't get the right ending. But I have also written books in an afternoon and hardly a word has been changed. "I usually write in the morning. I have a separate room, and everything is there. It's a very cheerful room and I enjoy the sunlight and the company of my cats."

For aspiring writers Pearson advises, "To be a writer you have to 'write.' You must believe that you can do it. If you want it badly enough, you can do it. But there is no point in wanting it for the glamour because writing isn't glamorous, it's a lot of hard work, and if you don't love words there's not much point in getting involved.''

Pearson's books have been illustrated by many well known illustrators. ''The child in *Izzie* is drawn as Bob Parker, the illustrator, envisioned me as a child. He asked me many questions about the neighborhood where the story takes place but I didn't give him many answers. I was taught that, at least while working on a book, it is best not to impose too many restrictions on the artist, and that the best collaboration usually comes from situations in which the artist has free reign, even if the book doesn't come out exactly as the author envisioned it.

''*Mollie Moves Out* is a 'beginning to read book.' In the story, Mollie says at one point, 'Ten rabbits living in one house are nine rabbits too many.' When I wrote the story, it read, 'Ten *blanks* living in one house are nine *blanks* too many.' I knew Mollie was supposed to have some sort of soft, furry, small animal, but I didn't have any idea what. It was Steven Kellogg who decided it should be a rabbit.

''I enjoy contact with other writers. I get a lot of it as an editor, but I miss the peers I had in New York. By the same token, when I was in New York, absolutely everybody in my life was in publishing and that drove me crazy. At least here I know some doctors, lawyers, and Indian chiefs.

''Of my own books I think *Izzie, Karin's Christmas Walk,* and *Mollie Moves Out* are my favorites, as well as *Monnie Hates Lydia,* which I think is the best writing I've done.

''I refer to certain books as a reminder of what quality is. I love the first part of Joyce's *Portrait of the Artist as a Young Man.* He has such a beautiful way of entering the child's mind. I tend to go to very complex books, which may be because I write simple stories. It would be very unlikely that I would go to Hemingway for solace, inspiration, or comfort.

''For a long time I was somewhat cynical, but not in a terrible way. I think over the years I have developed a refined sense of the absurd. Sometimes I watch a show on public television that deals with archaeology or physics or the underwater world and I think, 'Oh . . . I lost my options . . . it's not possible for me to become an archaeologist at this stage.' That makes me feel a little sad, but on the other hand, it's a continuing wonder to me that I get to spend my days doing something I enjoy so much, and that I can choose what it is I will do next.

''Right now is a time of experimentation for me. I want to try some different kinds of writing. I think there is an adult book in me, but I won't write it while I have this job. It's too complicated. I can sustain the nonfiction, but after a day at work, I couldn't go home and 'look into my soul,' as it were. I'll probably continue to do short pieces, like picture books and then branch out.''

FOR MORE INFORMATION SEE: Authors of Books for Young People, supplement to the 2nd edition, Scarecrow, 1979.

PEEK, Merle 1938-

PERSONAL: Born May 23, 1938, in Denver, Colo.; son of Jesse B. (a tire builder) and Queenie (Ridge) Peek. *Education:*

Attended University of Colorado, 1956; California College of Arts and Crafts, B.F.A., 1960. *Home:* 2329 South Ogden St., Denver, Colo. 80210.

CAREER: Time, New York, N.Y., layout artist, 1960-67; freelance illustrator, 1967-69, 1971-80, 1981—; *New York* (magazine), New York, N.Y., designer, 1969-71; *Denver* (magazine), Denver, Colo., art director, 1980-81. *Member:* Denver Botanic Gardens. *Awards, honors: Roll Over! A Counting Song* was selected as a ''Children's Choice'' by the International Reading Association, 1982.

WRITINGS—Self-illustrated: *Cricket's Tangrams* (juvenile), Random House, 1977; *Roll Over! A Counting Song* (juvenile), Houghton, 1981; *Mary Wore Her Red Dress and Henry Wore His Green Sneakers* (juvenile), Houghton, 1985.

Illustrator: Donald Nelson, *The Spotted Cow,* Parents Magazine Press, 1973; Stephen Manes, *Hooples on the Highway,* Coward, 1978; Michael O'Donoghue, *Bears* (poem), Ghost Fox, 1979; Judy Stonecipher, *Creation: For Kids and Other People Too,* Accent Publications, 1982; Martin E. Marty, *The Church in the Americas: An Illustrated History of the Church from 1500 to 1800,* Winston Press, 1983.

WORK IN PROGRESS: A juvenile fantasy, *Waterlily Lodge;* two illustrated songs for children, *The Farmer in the Dell* and *Animal Song.*

SIDELIGHTS: ''I'm satisfying a long-time ambition by adding to the not-very-old (about one hundred and fifty years) tradition of children's literature. I especially enjoy illustrating classic texts. When I was in school I was not particularly interested in history. In fact I never comprehended it at all until I was in college and studying art history. By comparing art history to world history it all fell into place. Style reflects the thinking of a period, and by getting a grasp on the thinking I was able to relate to history; whereas before memorizing dates and places had been meaningless. Consequently, my favorite movies now are costume dramas. I know I'm going to enjoy a movie if I see that it's set sometime in the past and that there's going to be lots of costumes and architecture to look at. I illustrated a story about Paul Revere by Stephen Vincent Benét for a school textbook for Houghton, and I've illustrated a number of Bible stories for Winston Press. When Winston contacted me I had been wishing to illustrate something classic; little did I think that my wish would be granted with Bible stories, which, of course, are about as classic as one can get.

''My favorite compliment is having my work described as having a timeless quality. When I was younger I was very much involved in keeping up with the trends in art. I wanted to be part of the avant-garde above all. But now I find that's not so important to me anymore. Even though I still like to see what other people are doing, I think I'm not as affected by it as I once was. Now I can let my own work just be. For having started out thinking that non-objective painting was the end-all and what I would do for the rest of my life, I'm now pursuing a style of illustration that is getting more traditional all the time.

''I enjoy both illustrating the words of others and creating the words myself. Illustrating the words of others is somewhat like solving a puzzle. The words are there and you must put a picture with them which not only makes sense, but seems right, and effortless, and hopefully furthers the story. And while satisfying all these needs you must also satisfy yourself. From this viewpoint writing the words yourself is in some ways

Merle Peek with his dog, Daisy.

simpler or easier, because you're creating your own problems for illustration.

"As much as I enjoy illustrating the words of others, the ultimate pleasure does come from conceiving the entire book—words and pictures. I like seeing my name alone on the cover.

"Though the bulk of my work has been for children, it also has a whimsical appeal to adults. I like it when I see an adult smiling with pleasure while looking at something I've done.

"Since I'm an animal lover, my visual iconography is loaded with animal forms. I like slipping animals into unexpected places such as architectural detail or as part of furniture carving. I spent a summer in Sweden, and in Stockholm I remember being enthralled by otherwise serious buildings having heads of trolls worked very subtly into the design, so subtly that only by taking a second look do you see them at all. Once I noticed this, I started looking for it, and I found it everywhere—office buildings, apartment buildings—always understated and cleverly done. In my own work I find that children invariably spot any such detail before adults do. The child is reading the picture, whereas the adult is reading the words and gives the picture only a scan.

"Communication has become a key word for me. While in college studying fine arts, I felt self-expression was it as far as art was concerned. But now I feel (and this is the point of

illustration) that communication is the point of artistic endeavor. I want the child and the adult to understand my work, not to be mystified by it. At the same time I want my work to have aesthetic appeal for those who will respond on that level—other artists particularly. Generally, it seems artists like and appreciate most the support of other artists.

"I grew up in Colorado and being so landlocked, I couldn't wait to get to the coast, to the ocean. I went to art college in California, and I loved that coast. I would stand for hours in all kinds of weather watching waves crashing against the cliffs and huge banks of fog rolling in from the sea. I thought I would always live there, I was so taken by it. But when I graduated it seemed time to take on a new horizon. And after California, the next horizon was, naturally, New York City. I had spent my childhood being dazzled by pictures and movies of New York, and I couldn't wait to get there. And I loved it. I lived in Brooklyn Heights for two years and in Manhattan for eight. In 1967 I made a trip around the world; it took nearly a year. I had been to Europe several times before, and this started out to be a year in Europe, but developed into a world tour. When I arrived back in New York, I looked around and thought that this is one of the worst places I've seen in the whole world in terms of dirt, expense, and trying to live normally and happily. And although New York is still and always will be one of my most favorite places in the world, I decided I didn't need to live *in* it anymore. Also I had gotten fanatically interested in growing plants, and I wanted to have a go at growing plants outdoors instead of just in pots indoors.

(From *Roll Over! A Counting Song,* lyrics from "Sally Go Round the Sun" by Edith Fowke. Illustrated by Merle Peek.)

"So I moved to an idyllic mountainside near Woodstock in the Catskills where I spent ten years living in a 175-year-old farm house (originally built by a Van Winkle) surrounded by 600 acres of beautiful northeastern woods. It was here that I got my first pet, or my first pet got me—a huge tailless cat wandered into the house one day and declared himself at home. I named him Bob Catskill. He's since been followed by two more cats—Felix and Lily—and by my first dog, Daisy, who is still with me. In fact Daisy is at this moment trying to get under my legs because it's thundering outside.

"While living in the Catskills I made a point of walking a mile-long trail around the house every day. I walked it every day so I could spot the smallest changes along the trail. And I walked it regardless of the weather; so sometimes I would have to put on rain gear for a summer storm or arctic gear for a blizzard. Now ordinarily we only take walks when the weather is nice, and we miss a lot because of it. It was a thrilling experience coming to know extremely well a landscape and then seeing it change under the affects of the weather, the seasons, or the time of day—early morning with the mists rising, dusk with fireflies emerging, late at night by the light of the moon—this same old walk showed me thousands of faces.

"After ten years in the woods, I felt it was again time for a change. And this time I returned to the house in which I grew up in Denver. That was a few years ago and I have planted a large perennial garden; at last count I had 104 varieties. That's all in the back garden. For the front garden I'm now planning on paper a natural garden using all native Colorado plants. I want to create a natural landscape. Right now I'm surrounded by typical city-suburb landscaping of ninety-five per cent lawn, and my country-conditioned eyes find this very *un*-natural.

"I can't seem to get enough of crossword puzzles. I became hooked on them while living in New York. There you can always spot someone doing a puzzle. Or someone will be sitting in the park and a stranger will walk by and call out, 'Did you get thirty-eight across yet?' I was pleased and relieved when I moved to Denver and saw that the Denver newspapers carry the *New York Times* puzzles which are my favorites, although occasionally I like trying the British puzzles which have you doing mental cartwheels before you've finished, if you're lucky enough to finish.

"For exercise in Denver I took up ice-dancing. I had long been interested in skating, but I hadn't lived anywhere with accessibility to an ice arena. So I started skating and after a year of classes, I started ice-dancing classes and private coaching. Skating by yourself is always a thrill, but skating with a partner and doing a set-pattern dance as well is about four times as exciting. I'm only sorry that I didn't get started much younger, because the muscles don't respond quite as well as they used to; and it takes much longer to recover from falls. Ice is really hard when you fall on it, unlike snow when you're skiing.

"I've always been fascinated by roller-coasters. As a child I built them using the garden hose as track and marbles as the coasters. A friend and I would spend the whole day building it. Then we'd actually play with it for ten minutes or so before going on to something else. I find roller coasters as thrilling to watch as to ride. I'm slowing down a bit—I used to be able to ride twenty or so times in a row; now I'm finding five times is quite enough. I'd love to design one; in fact I'd love to design a whole amusement park."

HOBBIES AND OTHER INTERESTS: Playing the piano, riding roller coasters, ice-dancing, outdoor horticulture.

Education is the ability to listen to almost anything without losing your temper or your self-confidence.
—Robert Frost

PIRSIG, Robert M(aynard) 1928-

PERSONAL: Born September 6, 1928, in Minneapolis, Minn.; son of Maynard E. (a professor) and Harriet (Sjobeck) Pirsig; married Nancy James (an administrator), May 10, 1954 (divorced, August, 1978); married Wendy Kimball (a writer), December 28, 1978; children: (first marriage) Christopher (deceased), Theodore; (second marriage) Nell. *Education:* University of Minnesota, B.A., 1950, M.A., 1958. *Address:* c/o William Morrow and Co., 105 Madison Ave., New York, N.Y. 10016.

CAREER: Montana State College (now University), Bozeman, instructor in English composition, 1959-61; University of Illinois, Chicago, instructor in rhetoric, 1961-62; technical writer at several Minneapolis, Minn., electronic firms, 1963-67; Century Publications, Minneapolis, Minn., contract technical writer, 1967-73; writer. Minnesota Zen Meditation Center, member of board of directors, 1973-77; vice-president, 1973-75. *Military service:* U.S. Army, 1946-48. *Member:* Society of Technical Communicators (past secretary and treasurer). *Awards, honors:* Guggenheim fellowship, 1974.

WRITINGS: Zen and the Art of Motorcycle Maintenance: An Inquiry into Values, Morrow, 1974.

WORK IN PROGRESS: Anthropological research intended to relate metaphysics of quality, as defined in first book, to cultural problems of today.

SIDELIGHTS: **September 6, 1928.** Born in Minneapolis. Pirsig's father was dean of the University of Minnesota Law School. Pirsig began his University studies at the age of seventeen.

1946-1948. Left college to join the U.S. Army for a two-year stint. Later Pirsig returned to college, where he received his bachelor's degree from the University of Minnesota.

1950. Traveled to India, where he lived and studied Oriental philosophy at Benares Hindu University. "As far as I know [I] didn't learn any occult secrets there. Nothing much happened at all except exposures. [I] listened to philosophers, visited religious persons, absorbed and thought and then absorbed and thought some more, and that was about all. All [my] letters show is an enormous confusion of contradictions

ROBERT M. PIRSIG

Robert Pirsig, about 1974. (Copyright © 1985 by Peter Marcus.)

and incongruities and divergences and exceptions to any rule [I] formulated about the things [I] observed. . . . However, [I had] been exposed to a lot and had acquired a kind of latent image that appeared in conjunction with many other latent images later on.'' [Robert M. Pirsig, *Zen and the Art of Motorcycle Maintenance: An Inquiry into Values,* Morrow, 1974.[1]]

1954. ''[I] returned to [my] Midwest, picked up a practical degree in journalism, married, lived in Nevada and Mexico, did odd jobs, worked as a journalist, a science writer and an industrial-advertising writer. [I] fathered two children, bought a farm and a riding horse and two cars and was starting to put on middle-aged weight. [My] pursuit of what has been called the ghost of reason had been given up. . . .''[1]

1958. Received a master's degree in journalism from the University of Minnesota.

1959. Taught English composition at Montana State College in Bozeman, Montana. During this time Pirsig began questioning modern values and investigating the idea of 'quality,' through both writing and teaching. ''The school was what could euphemistically be called a 'teaching college.' At a teaching college you teach and you teach and you teach with no time for research, no time for contemplation, no time for participation in outside affairs. Just teach and teach and teach until your mind grows dull and your creativity vanishes and you become an automaton saying the same dull things over and over to endless waves of innocent students who cannot understand why you are so dull, lose respect and fan this disrespect out into the community. The reason you teach and you teach and you teach is that this is a very clever way of running a college on the cheap while giving a false appearance of genuine education.

''The state of Montana at this time was undergoing an outbreak of ultra-right-wing politics like that which occurred in Dallas, Texas, just prior to President Kennedy's assassination. A nationally known professor from the University of Montana at Missoula was prohibited from speaking on campus on the grounds that it would 'stir up trouble.' Professors were told that all public statements must be cleared through the college public-relations office before they could be made.

''It must always be remembered that this was the nineteen-fifties, not the nineteen-seventies. There were rumblings from the beatniks and early hippies at this time about 'the system' and the square intellectualism that supported it, but hardly anyone guessed how deeply the whole edifice would be brought into doubt. . . .''[1]

1961-1962. Moved to Chicago with his family and entered a doctorate program at the University of Illinois. It was during this year that Pirsig suffered a nervous breakdown which eventually landed him in a state mental institution. ''. . . [I] took up residence near the University and, since [I] had no scholarship, began full-time teaching of rhetoric at the University of Illinois, which was then downtown at Navy Pier, sticking out into the lake, funky and hot.

''Classes were different from those in Montana. The top high-school students had been skimmed off to the Champaign and Urbana campuses and almost all the students [I] taught were a solid monotonous C. When their papers were judged in class for Quality it was hard to distinguish among them. . . .''[1]

1963-1967. Worked as a technical writer for various electronic firms in Minneapolis.

1968. With his twelve-year-old son, Chris, travelled across the country on a motorcycle trip. ''You see things vacationing on a motorcycle in a way that is completely different from any other. In a car you're always in a compartment, and because you're used to it you don't realize that through that car window everything you see is just more TV. You're a passive observer and it is all moving by you boringly in a frame.

''On a cycle the frame is gone. You're completely in contact with it all. You're *in* the scene, not just watching it anymore, and the sense of presence is overwhelming. That concrete whizzing by five inches below your foot is the real thing, the same stuff you walk on, it's right there, so blurred you can't focus on it, yet you can put your foot down and touch it anytime, and the whole thing, the whole experience, is never removed from immediate consciousness.''[1]

The motorcycle trip from their home in Minneapolis to the West Coast later formed the basis for what began as a light-hearted essay, but ended as a popular first book on values and the author's personal, psychological trials. ''Chris and I are traveling to Montana with some friends riding up ahead, and maybe headed farther than that. Plans are deliberately indefinite, more to travel than to arrive anywhere. We are just vacationing. Secondary roads are preferred. Paved county roads are the best, state highways are next. Freeways are the worst. We want to make good time, but for us now this is measured with emphasis on 'good' rather than 'time' and when you make that shift in emphasis the whole approach changes. Twisting hilly roads are long in terms of seconds but are much more enjoyable on a cycle where you bank into turns and don't get swung from side to side in any compartment. Roads with little traffic are more enjoyable, as well as safer. Roads free of drive-ins and billboards are better, roads where groves and meadows and orchards and lawns come almost to the shoulder, where kids wave to you when you ride by, where people look from their porches to see who it is, where when you stop to ask directions or information the answer tends to be longer than you want rather than short, where people ask where you're from and how long you've been riding.''[1]

1973. Member of board of directors at the Minnesota Zen Meditation Center, of which he served as vice-president from 1973-75.

1974. Received Guggenheim fellowship. Published first book, *Zen and the Art of Motorcycle Maintenance,* an autobiography that was also a philosophical treatise. ''. . . After 121 editors had turned us down, one offered a standard $3,000 advance. He said the book forced him to decide what he was in publishing for and added that, although this was almost certainly the last payment, I shouldn't be discouraged. Money wasn't the point with a book like this.

''That was true. But then came publication day, and the book's effect on readers exceeded everyone's expectations. Instead of selling hundreds of copies—or at most a few thousand—it was read by millions. Why? How could a book perform so differently from the expectations of all those publishers? What was in it they had all failed to see? Readers were perplexed too. If the book is so successful, they wondered, why is it so unusual? What is the author's motive? There was a frustrated tone. They knew there was more to this book than met the eye. They wanted to hear all.

''There really hasn't been any 'all' to tell.

''There is a Swedish word, *'kulturbarer,'* which can be translated as 'culture bearer' but still doesn't mean much. It's not a concept that has much American use, although it should have.

"A culture-bearing book, like a mule, bears the culture on its back. No one should sit down to write one deliberately. Culture-bearing books occur almost accidentally, like a sudden change in the stock market. There are books of high quality that are an important *part* of the culture, but that is not the same. They *are* a part of it. They aren't carrying it anywhere. They may talk about insanity sympathetically, for example, because that's the standard cultural attitude. But they don't carry any suggestion that insanity might be something other than sickness or degeneracy.

"Culture-bearing books challenge cultural value assumptions and often do so at a time when the culture is changing in favor of their challenge. The books are not necessarily of high quality. 'Uncle Tom's Cabin' was no literary masterpiece, but it was a culture-bearing book. It came at a time when the entire culture was about to reject slavery. People seized upon it as a portrayal of their own new values, and it became an overwhelming success.

"The success of *Zen and the Art of Motorcycle Maintenance* seems the result of this culture-bearing phenomenon. The involuntary shock treatment described here is against the law today. It is a violation of human liberty. The culture has changed.

"The book also appeared at a time of culture upheaval in the matter of material success. Hippies were having none of it. Conservatives were baffled. Material success was the American dream. Millions of European peasants have longed for it all their lives and come to America to find it—a world in which they and their descendants would at last have enough. Now their spoiled descendants were throwing that whole dream in their faces, saying it wasn't any good. What did they want?

"The hippies had in mind something that they wanted and were calling it 'freedom,' but in the final analysis, 'freedom' is a purely negative goal. It just says something is bad. Hippies weren't really offering any alternatives other than colorful short-term ones, and some of these were looking more and more like pure degeneracy. Degeneracy can be fun, but it's hard to keep up as a serious lifetime occupation.

"This book offers another, more serious alternative to material success. It's not so much an alternative as an expansion of the meaning of 'success' to something larger than just getting a good job and staying out of trouble. And also something larger than mere freedom. It gives a positive goal to work toward that does not confine. That is the main reason for the book's success, I think. The whole culture happened to be looking for exactly what this book has to offer. That is the sense in which it is a culture bearer." [Robert M. Pirsig, *Zen and the Art of Motorcycle Maintenance: An Inquiry into Values*, revised edition, Morrow, 1984.[2]]

1979. Son, Chris, was murdered in San Francisco. "He was murdered. At about 8:00 P.M. on Saturday, November 17, 1979, in San Francisco, he left the Zen Center, where he was a student, to visit a friend's house a block away on Haight Street.

"According to witnesses, a car stopped on the street beside him and two men, black, jumped out. One came from behind him so that Chris couldn't escape and grabbed his arms. The one in front of him emptied his pockets and found nothing and became angry. He threatened Chris with a large kitchen knife.

Chris said something which the witnesses could not hear. His assailant became angrier. Chris then said something that made him even more furious. He jammed the knife into Chris's chest. Then the two jumped into their car and left.

"Chris leaned for a time on a parked car, trying to keep from collapsing. After a time, he staggered across the street to a lamp at the corner of Haight and Octavia. Then, with his right lung filled with blood from a severed pulmonary artery, he fell to the sidewalk and died.

"I go on living, more from force of habit than anything else. At his funeral, we learned that he had bought a ticket that morning for England, where my second wife and I lived aboard a sailboat. Then a letter from him arrived which said, strangely, 'I never thought I would ever live to see my 23d birthday.' His 23d birthday would have been in two weeks.

"Where did Chris go? He had bought an airplane ticket that morning. He had a bank account, drawers full of clothes and shelves full of books. He was a real, live person, occupying time and space on this planet, and now suddenly where was he gone to? Did he go up the stack at the crematorium? Was he in the little box of bones they handed back? Was he strumming a harp of gold on some overhead cloud? None of these answers made any sense.

"The loops eventually stopped at the realization that before it could be asked, 'Where did he go?' it must be asked, 'What is the he that is gone?' There is an old cultural habit of thinking of people as primarily something material, as flesh and blood. As long as this idea held, there was no solution. The oxides of Chris's flesh and blood did, of course, go up the stack at the crematorium. But they weren't Chris.

"What had to be seen was that the Chris I missed so badly was not an object but a pattern and that, although the pattern included the flesh and blood of Chris, that was not all there was to it. The pattern was larger than Chris and myself and related us in ways that neither of us understood completely and neither of us was in complete control of.

"In any event, it was not many months later that my wife conceived, unexpectedly. After careful discussion we decided it was not something that should continue. I'm in my fifties. I didn't want to go through any more child-raising experiences. I'd seen enough. So we came to our conclusion and made the necessary medical appointment.

"Then something very strange happened. I'll never forget it. As we went over the whole decision in detail one last time, there was a kind of dissociation, as though my wife started to recede while we sat there talking. We were looking at each other, talking normally, but it was like those photographs of a rocket just after launching where you see two stages start to separate from each other in space. You think you're together and then suddenly you see that you're not together anymore.

"I said, 'Wait. Stop. Something's wrong.' What it was, was unknown, but it was intense and I didn't want it to continue. It was a really frightening thing, which has since become clearer. It was the larger pattern of Chris, making itself known at last. We reversed our decision, and now realize what a catastrophe it would have been for us if we hadn't.

"So I guess you could say, in this primitive way of looking at things, that Chris got his airplane ticket after all. This time he's a little girl named Nell and our life is back in perspective again. The hole in the pattern is being mended. A thousand memories of Chris will always be at hand, of course, but not a destructive clinging to some material entity that can never be here again. We're in Sweden now, the home of my mother's ancestors, and I'm working on a second book which is a sequel to [*Zen and the Art of Motorcycle Maintenance*]...."[2]

FOR MORE INFORMATION SEE: Robert M. Pirsig, *Zen and the Art of Motorcycle Maintenance: An Inquiry into Values,* Morrow, 1974; George Gent, "A Successful Pirsig Rethinks Life of Zen and Science," *The New York Times Biographical Edition,* May, 1974; *Contemporary Literary Criticism,* Volume 4, Gale, 1975; *New York Times Book Review,* March 4, 1984.

POOLE, Peggy   1925-
(Terry Roche)

PERSONAL: Born March 8, 1925, in Canterbury, Kent, England; daughter of Reginald Trelawny (National Association of Boys' Clubs) and Barbara (Tate) Thornton; married Reginald Poole (an executive), August 10, 1949; children: Catherine, Barbara, Elizabeth. *Education:* Attended Benenden School, Kent, England. *Home:* 18 Townfield Rd., West Kirby, Wirral, Merseyside L48 7EZ, England. *Agent:* Serafina Clarke, 74 Forthbridge Rd., London SW11 5HY, England. *Office:* Clarke-Conway-Gordon, 213 Westborne Grove, London W11 2SE, England.

CAREER: Worked in the Bodleian Library, Oxford, England, 1946-47; secretary for physicians in London, 1947-49; writer. Producer, hostess, and interviewer for national and local British Broadcasting Corp. programs, 1960—. Editor of poetry programme, BBC radio (Merseyside), 1977—. *Military service:* Women's Royal Naval Service, 1943-45. *Member:* International Poetry Society, Poetry Society, Society of Women Writers and Journalists, Jabberwocky, VER Poets, Merseyside Arts Association. *Awards, honors:* Edmund Blunden Award from the International Poetry Society, 1978.

WRITINGS: Never a Put Up Job (poetry), Quentin Nelson, 1970; *Cherry Stones and Other Poems,* Headland, 1983.

Under pseudonym Terry Roche; for young adults: *Brum* (illustrated by Beryl Sanders), Dobson, 1978; *Shadows on the Sand,* Dobson, 1979; *Your Turn to Put the Light Out,* Dobson, 1980.

Work has appeared in anthologies, including *All Made of Fantasy,* The Theatre, Chipping Norton Ltd., 1980. Columnist, *Deesider,* 1974-75. Contributor of short stories and articles to such publications as *Guardian, Liverpool Daily Post,* and *Woman's Weekly,* and of poetry to periodicals, including *Countryman, Country Quest, New Poetry,* and *Poetry Nottingham.*

WORK IN PROGRESS: Young adult book, *Sydney Sparrow,* under name Terry Roche; sequence of poems, photographs, and art work of a family childhood in Kent during the 1920s and 30s; *A Husk of Meaning;* a series of letters from an R.A.F. chaplain serving in World War II written to a girl seventeen years younger than himself.

SIDELIGHTS: "I was brought up on a farm situated on the Roman road between Canterbury and Hythe in Kent. I spent

(Jacket design by Beryl Sanders from *Shadows on the Sand* by Terry Roche.)

three years living in the Channel Islands before I went to Merseyside, where I have spent the next phase of my life in an Edwardian house looking across the Dee Estuary to the hills of Wales.

"Poetry has been a part of me since I was a child. For the last ten years I have been responsible for organizing Jabberwocky, a group of poetry lovers who come from all over the northwest for an evening of poetry, old and new. Jabberwocky has also published four collections of poetry by people who have read their own work at our gatherings over the years, including such V.I.P.'s as Stephen Spender, Ted Hughes, Thom Gunn, and Alan Brownjohn. The title of my own first collection, *Never a Put Up Job* (which incidentally I now feel was premature), is taken from a quote of Robert Frost's in a letter to Louis Untermeyer.

"In my books for children, fact mixes with fiction. Apart from a few brief years, I have always owned a dog, and this, combined with six successive holidays on the canals, resulted in *Brum.* It is set on the Shropshire Union Canal, while *Shadows on the Sand* is set in Merseyside. In these books, the best part for me as author, occurs when the fictional characters take over the story; the controversial ending in *Your Turn to Put the Light Out* was 'dictated' in the night to me. *A Husk of Meaning* is an anthology of experience, good and bad, relating to godparents and godchildren—a much neglected subject. The mass

PEGGY POOLE

of material waiting to be brought together kept me busy for years.

"I have produced and performed in amateur productions; I love the theater. I have also been a potter, mostly on the wheel. I greatly enjoy driving and have travelled extensively in the British Isles, Eire, Zimbabwe (when it was Rhodesia), and Switzerland. I belong to no political party or church because, for me, there are no clear answers in life, but I do have a basic belief in people and in a pattern."

PORTER, Katherine Anne   1890-1980

PERSONAL: Born May 15, 1890, in Indian Creek, Tex.; died September 18, 1980, in Silver Spring, Md.; daughter of Harrison Boone and Mary Alice (Jones) Porter; married John Henry Koontz, 1906 (divorced, June 21, 1915); married Ernest Stock, 1925 (divorced, 1926); married Eugene Dove Pressly, 1933 (divorced April 19, 1938); married Albert Russel Erskine, Jr. (a professor of English), 1938 (divorced, 1942). *Education:* Educated at home and in Southern girls' schools.

CAREER: Professional writer. Lecturer and teacher at writers' conferences; speaker at more than 200 universities and colleges in the United States and Europe. Writer-in-residence, or member of the faculties of English, at Olivet College, Olivet, Mich., 1940, Stanford University, Stanford, Calif., 1948-49, University of Michigan, Ann Arbor, 1953-54, University of Virginia, Charlottesville, 1958, and Washington and Lee University, Lexington, Va., where she was first woman faculty member in the school's history, 1959. Ewing Lecturer, University of California, Los Angeles, 1959; first Regents Lecturer, University of California, Riverside, 1961. Member, President Johnson's Committee on Presidential Scholars.

MEMBER: National Institute of Arts and Letters (vice-president, 1950-52), American Academy of Arts and Letters. *Awards, honors:* Guggenheim fellowship for literature, 1931, 1938; Society of the Libraries of New York University first annual gold medal, 1940, for *Pale Horse, Pale Rider;* fellow of the Library of Congress in regional American literature, 1944; chosen one of six representatives of American literature at International Expositions of the Arts in Paris, France, 1952; Ford Foundation grant, 1959-61; State Department grant for international exchange of persons to Mexico, 1960, 1964; first prize, O. Henry Memorial Award, 1962, for "Holiday"; Emerson-Thoreau Bronze Medal for Literature of American Academy of Arts and Sciences, 1962; Pulitzer Prize, 1966, and National Book Award, 1966, both for *The Collected Stories of Katherine Anne Porter;* National Institute of Arts and Letters gold medal for fiction, 1967. Honorary degrees include D.Litt. from University of North Carolina, 1949, Smith College, 1958, and Wheaton College; D.H.L. from University of Michigan, 1954, and University of Maryland, 1966; D.F.A. from LaSalle College.

WRITINGS: My Chinese Marriage, Duffield, 1921; *Outline of Mexican Popular Arts and Crafts,* Young & McCallister, 1922; *What Price Marriage,* Sears, 1927; *Flowering Judas* (Book-of-the-Month Club selection), Harcourt, 1930, 2nd edition with added stories published as *Flowering Judas and Other Stories,* 1935; (translator and compiler) *Katherine Anne Porter's French Songbook,* Harrison Co., 1933; *Hacienda: A Story of Mexico,* Harrison Co., 1934; *Noon Wine,* Schuman's, 1937; *Pale Horse, Pale Rider* (three novelettes), Harcourt, 1939; (translator) Fernandez de Lizardi, *The Itching Parrot,* Doubleday, 1942; (author of preface) Flores and Poore, *Fiesta in November,* Houghton, 1942; *The Leaning Tower, and Other Stories,* Harcourt, 1944; *The Days Before: Collected Essays and Occasional Writings,* Harcourt, 1952, revised and enlarged edition published as *The Collected Essays and Occasional Writings of Katherine Anne Porter,* Delacorte, 1970; *Old Order: Stories of the South,* Harcourt, 1955; *A Defense of Circe,* Harcourt, 1955; *Fiction and Criticism of Katherine Anne Porter,* University of Pitts-

Katherine Anne Porter (far right) at eighteen months with sister, Annie Gay, and brother, Harry Ray.

burgh Press, 1957, revised edition, 1962; *Ship of Fools* (novel; Book-of-the-Month Club selection), Little, Brown, 1962; *The Collected Stories of Katherine Anne Porter*, Harcourt, 1965; *A Christmas Story* (illustrated by Ben Shahn), Dial, 1967; *The Never Ending Wrong*, Little, Brown, 1977. Contributor to anthologies including *The Second American Caravan*, edited by Alfred Kreymborg and others, 1928 and *Best Short Stories of 1930, . . .1933,* and *. . .1936,* all edited by Edward J. O'Brien. Contributor to numerous magazines.

ADAPTATIONS: "Pale Horse, Pale Rider" (play), first produced at the Jan Hus Theatre, 1959, (film) starring Joan Hackett and Keir Dullea, Canadian Broadcasting Corporation, 1964; "Ship of Fools" (movie), starring Simone Signoret and Oskar Werner, Columbia Pictures, 1965; "Noon Wine" (film), starring Jason Robards and Olivia de Havilland, written and directed by Sam Peckinpah, first broadcast on "ABC Stage 67," 1966, starring Fred Ward, first broadcast on "American Playhouse," PBS, January 21, 1985; "The Jilting of Granny Weatherall" (film), starring Geraldine Fitzgerald, first broadcast on PBS, March 3, 1980.

SIDELIGHTS: ". . . I was born on **May 15, 1890,** in Indian Creek, Texas, near Austin—I should say sixty-five miles away. This was in central Texas, black land farming country, but I didn't stay there long. Until I was eleven I lived mostly in either San Antonio or in a small town named Kyle that was about five miles from my grandmother's farm. She had quite a large landholding there; little by little she dispersed it by giving it to her children and by the time she died she had a very small farm, a few hundred acres.

"After that I was in San Antonio and New Orleans. I went to girls' schools and convents and had quite a classical and ornamental education, the kind girls got then, and I don't think it took very well. I seem to have spent most of my time 'bootlegging' literature. When they were trying to make us read St. Thomas Aquinas, I was reading *Confessions of St. Augustine*. I read and read and read. I got most of my education from books. We had a good collection at home; most old-fashioned literate families had. I think mine was the very last generation with a certain sort of upbringing. After Grandmother died everything was scattered—the books, furniture, the family life and all—and the next two generations were brought up on radio and records and cars, no books at all, nothing that we would have called education. It seemed an extraordinarily savage kind of upbringing, but they didn't seem to miss anything so I suppose it was all right for them. It was very disappointing for me.

"I remember once telling somebody who asked me about my education that by academic standards I was an illiterate. My father read this and his feelings were hurt and he said, 'Well, we did our best to educate you but you were proof against it.' He was right. I really was proof against the kind of education they wanted to give me and I never went to college. I left school when I was about sixteen and never set foot in a university until I went there to teach." [Roy Newquist, *Conversations*, Rand McNally, 1967.[1]]

Writing and reading were two pastimes Porter indulged in as a young girl. ". . . I really started writing when I was six or seven years old. But I had such a multiplicity of half-talents too: I wanted to dance, I wanted to play the piano, I sang, I drew. It wasn't really dabbling—I was investigating everything. And then, for one thing, there weren't very many amusements in those days. If you wanted music, you had to play the piano and sing yourself. . . .

Katherine Anne Porter, 1933.

". . . I was reading Shakespeare's sonnets when I was thirteen years old, and I'm perfectly certain that they made the most profound impression upon me of anything I ever read. For a time I knew the whole sequence by heart; now I can only remember two or three of them. That was the turning point of my life, when I read the Shakespeare sonnets, and then all at one blow, all of Dante—in that great big book illustrated by Gustave Doré. The plays I saw on the stage, but I don't remember reading them with any interest at all. Oh, and I read all kinds of poetry—Homer, Ronsard, all the old French poets in translation. We also had a very good library of—well, you might say secular philosophers. I was incredibly influenced by Montaigne when I was very young. And one day when I was about fourteen, my father led me up to a great big line of books and said, 'Why don't you read this? It'll knock some of the nonsense out of you!' It happened to be the entire set of Voltaire's philosophical dictionary with notes by Smollett. And I plowed through it; it took me about five years.

"And of course we read all the eighteenth-century novelists, though Jane Austen, like Turgenev, didn't really engage me until I was quite mature. I read them both when I was very young, but I was grown up before I really took them in. And I discovered for myself *Wuthering Heights;* I think I read that book every year of my life for fifteen years. I simply adored it. Henry James and Thomas Hardy were really my introduction to modern literature; Grandmother didn't much approve of it. She thought Dickens might do, but she was a little against Mr. Thackeray; she thought he was too trivial. So that was as far as I got into the modern world until I left home!" ["Katherine Anne Porter," *Writers at Work: The Paris Review Interviews,* second series, Viking, 1963.[2]]

(From the film "The Jilting of Granny Weatherall," starring Geraldine Fitzgerald. First broadcast on PBS-TV, March 3, 1980, as part of the thirteen-week television series "The American Short Story." Photograph by Ken Howard.)

1906. "At sixteen I ran away from New Orleans and got married. And at twenty-one I bolted again, went to Chicago, got a newspaper job, and went into the movies."[2]

Porter's first marriage ended in divorce, as did her three other marriages. "My first . . . [marriage] was a plain disaster, I was so terribly young and it took all my resources to get me out of the scrape, but I got out of it and I've forgotten about it, really. He went off and married somebody else and seems to have done very nicely; he was several years older than I. . . . He was from the Deep South. There was nothing wrong with him; he just wasn't the man for me and I had no business bolting off with him. He was rather a nice man—I know that now—but I didn't like him, and that's no foundation for marriage.

"He wasn't the most composed of men, come to think of it, but it was a typical thing on my part because I've always loved men like that, high-strung, moody, fickle—impossible, in a word. Once when I was in a very bad state, having great trouble

with life, just trying to exist, to survive, I said to a doctor, 'Do you know I attract insane people?'—and I do, the hysterical, lost people, often quite clinically mad, who come to fasten themselves around my neck, and I have to deal with them. So I said to the doctor, 'Do you suppose it's deep calling to deep? That they know I'm just as crazy as they are if I would only break down and admit it?' And he said, 'No, on the contrary. They're looking for sanity, a stable sort of relation, a person who stands firm.' So I've been certified as hopelessly sane, and I can't get out of anything.

"I used to get fits and leap up and down and tear my hair and say to my second husband, when we were traveling about in Europe and we'd have to pull up stakes and go somewhere else—he was with the foreign service—'I'm going to wind up in Bellevue if this goes on!' And he'd say, 'Don't be silly; you're never going to enjoy the advantages of Bellevue.' Sure enough, I never have, and I've sometimes longed for it.

"At any rate, I've been married to three very passable men and couldn't make any of the marriages work. I suppose the

(From the movie "Noon Wine," starring Fred Ward and Lise Hilboldt, based on the novel by
Katherine Anne Porter. First broadcast on "American Playhouse," PBS-TV, January 21, 1985.
Movie still by Deana Newcomb.)

The feast in the beginning was meant to celebrate with joy the birth of a Child, an event of such importance to this world that angels sang from the skies in human language to announce it. ∎
(From *A Christmas Story* by Katherine Anne Porter. Illustrated by Ben Shahn.)

contrary demands of career, my husbands' and mine, got in the way. . . .''[1]

1921. Went to Mexico to study Aztec and Mayan art designs and became involved in the Obregon Revolution. Her experiences in Mexico resulted in her first published short story, "Maria Concepción." "I rewrote 'Maria Concepción' fifteen or sixteen times. That was a real battle, and I was thirty-three years old. I think it is the most curious lack of judgment to publish before you are ready. If there are echoes of other people in your work, you're not ready. If anybody has to help you rewrite your story, you're not ready. A story should be a finished work before it is shown. And after that, I will not allow anyone to change anything, and I will not change anything on anyone's advice. 'Here is my story. It's a finished story. Take it or leave it!' ''[2]

1930. First book, *Flowering Judas,* published when the author was forty. The story was based on actual experience. "That story had been on my mind for years, growing out of this one little thing that happened in Mexico. . . . A girl I knew had asked me to come and sit with her, because a man was coming to see her, and she was a little afraid of him. And as I went through the courtyard, past the flowering judas tree, I glanced in the window and there she was sitting with an open book on her lap, and there was this great big fat man sitting beside her. Now Mary and I were friends, both American girls living in this revolutionary situation. She was teaching at an Indian school, and I was teaching dancing at a girls' technical school in Mexico City. And we were having a very strange time of it. I was more skeptical, and so I had already begun to look with a skeptical eye on a great many of the revolutionary

leaders. Oh, the idea was all right, but a lot of men were misapplying it.

"And when I looked through that window that evening, I saw something in Mary's face, something in her pose, something in the whole situation, that set up a commotion in my mind. Because until that moment I hadn't really understood that she was not able to take care of herself, because she was not able to face her own nature and was afraid of everything. I don't know why I saw it. I don't believe in intuition. When you get sudden flashes of perception, it is just the brain working faster than usual. But you've been getting ready to know it for a long time, and when it comes, you feel you've known it always.

"The first time someone said to me, 'Why did you write *Flowering Judas* in the historical present?' I thought for a moment and said, 'Did I?' I'd never noticed it. Because I didn't *plan* to write it any way. A story forms in my mind and forms and forms, and when it's ready to go, I strike it down—it takes just the time I sit at the typewriter. I never think about form at all. In fact, I would say that I've never been interested in anything about writing after having learned, I hope, to write. That is, I mastered my craft as well as I could. There is a technique, there is a craft, and you have to learn it. Well, I did as well as I could with that, but now all in the world I am interested in is telling a story. I have something to tell you that I, for some reason, think is worth telling, and so I want to tell it as clearly and purely and simply as I can. But I had spent fifteen years at least learning to write. I practiced writing in every possible way that I could. I wrote a patische of other people, imitating Dr. Johnson and Laurence Sterne, and Petrarch and Shakespeare's sonnets, and then I tried writing my own way. I spent fifteen years learning to trust myself: that's what it comes to. Just as a pianist runs his scales for ten years before he gives his concert: because when he gives that concert, he can't be thinking of his fingering or of his hands; he has to be thinking of his interpretation, of the music he's playing. He's thinking of what he's trying to communicate. And if he hasn't got his technique perfected by then, he needn't give the concert at all.''[2]

1931. Went to Europe on a Guggenheim fellowship for literature. Porter's voyage by ship later inspired her novel, *Ship of Fools*. ''While I was living in Basel, after my first trip to Europe, I made some notes. Then there was a sort of log, or long letter, that I'd kept on my first trip, sailing from Veracruz to Bremerhaven. . . . I read it over, began thinking, and what I believed would be a short novel began forming in my mind. So when I came back to the United States in 1936, I had several things all ready to go. I went to a publisher and made a contract for four short novels, the titles to be *Noon Wine, Old Mortality* [eventually included in *Pale Horse, Pale Rider*], *Pale Horse, Pale Rider,* and *Ship of Fools.*

''I wrote *Noon Wine* in one week, from Saturday to Saturday, and that very evening I started *Old Mortality* and wrote that

in a week. Then I got interrupted somehow; I'd gone up into the country and had taken a room in an inn and in fourteen days had written those two short novels; but the interruption finished that. The thing that is death to me is to have my time frittered away; I must have absolute concentration, no breaks until the vein is worked out. So I went to New Orleans and found another hidey-hole (an old Scotch word). It took me nine days to produce *Pale Horse, Pale Rider* [1959], and I rolled up my sleeves and said, 'Here goes the big voyage,' because I knew it couldn't be a short novel. I worked and worked, month after month, and the notes piled up incredibly.

''Oddly enough, everything you see in the book [*Ship of Fools*] was there at the start, except that the novel itself is five or six times as long as I'd intended it to be. . . .''[1]

1940. Member of the English faculty at Olivet College in Michigan. Porter later taught at Stanford University, University of Michigan, University of Virginia, University of California, and Washington and Lee University. ''Art is not a religion, it's not a substitute for religion, and though it can be a friend of religion, or an enemy, it's strictly of this world. But you have to be sure of your vocation. You can't just say, 'I'm going to be a painter,' or 'I'm going to be a writer,' without being so

[The Captain] said with rancor . . . "It is a pity she did not respond better to your treatment. Indeed, I gather that her condition worsened very much in your hands. . . .A doctor cannot afford to let his failures weigh upon his mind!" ■ (From *Ship of Fools* by Katherine Anne Porter. Photograph from the movie adaptation starring Oskar Werner and Charles Korvin. Copyright © 1965 by Columbia Pictures, Inc.)

. . . The waves just beneath rolled and washed back upon themselves in white foam in the rayed lights from the ship. What am I to do, she asked herself, where am I to go? ■ (From *Ship of Fools* by Katherine Anne Porter. Photograph from the movie adaptation starring Vivien Leigh. Copyright © 1965 by Columbia Pictures, Inc.)

The international cast of "Ship of Fools" : (left to right) Vivien Leigh, Simone Signoret, José Ferrer, Lee Marvin, Oskar Werner, Elizabeth Ashley, George Segal, José Greco, Michael Dunn, Charles Korvin, and Heinz Ruehann.

sure of yourself you can't be thrown off. You've got to have a certainty beyond rationalization or question. Nobody can help you and nobody can promise you anything. You've got to take your life in your own hands, and you can't go showing manuscripts to other people and asking advice. You've got to work on your own without letting anyone else touch your work.

"I suppose, like all advice, this is not to be taken. I told a friend not long ago that I will never again attempt to tell any young person what to do—the really gifted don't need advice and the others can't take it.

"Life is short and art is long and what is needed is a living touch with reality, a tangible proof in a way, which an older artist can sometimes give to a young one. But I'm the last person who should give advice; I'm anywhere from fifteen to twenty years older than my contemporaries—or so-called contemporaries—because I was a late starter. The others started out to go their way—they knew something of what they wanted; they saw writing as an active way of life in which you advance from one point to another—and I never saw it that way at all. I still don't even when it seems as if I've lived forever. I've stayed with the ship, and heaven only knows what glorious islands I'd have found if I'd got off somewhere along the route.

"But perhaps every young artist has to do it one way, his way, and the hell with patterns. Remember who you are and where you are and what you're doing. Nobody else can do anything for you and you really wouldn't want them to, anyway. And never take advice. . . ."[1]

1962. Critically acclaimed as a short story writer, Porter published her only novel, *Ship of Fools*. "I didn't know how to write it. I looked upon myself as a short-story writer. I started with short stories and gradually expanded them; whatever a story took, I gave it its own head, so to speak, and gradually went from little things like "Magic," all of 1,400 words, to *Flowering Judas*, five or six thousand words, to "The Cracked Looking Glass," which is thirteen thousand. As I became more practiced and worked easier with length, the publishers kept shouting for a novel. When I took *The Leaning Tower*, the third collection of short stories, to Donald Brace, he said, 'Oh, we can't publish any more short stories.' I somehow emerged with three short novels. They are not novellas; they are not novelettes; they are short novels. Every time I see the word 'novella' my hair stands on end. I have tried so hard to keep that pretentious, slack, boneless word out of the language."[1]

Ship of Fools took over twenty years to write. At times, Porter would cease writing on the book for two or three years. "I was determined to finish that book so I went into the country and leased a house, an inexpensive country house on a hill, and I lived there for three years and every single blessed day I worked on that murderous, entrancing book. Then the lease ran out so I had to do something else; I went to the University of Virginia, then to Washington and Lee University, and tried to write in the hours I didn't face amiable shiny faces, but I couldn't. To me the situation was getting ridiculous; they'd started advertising the book and set up a false clamor.

"Somebody told me that when the book came out I'd get a

(From the movie "Ship of Fools," starring Simone Signoret and Oskar Werner, based on the novel by Katherine Anne Porter. Copyright © 1965 by Columbia Pictures, Inc.)

Time magazine cover. I had always heard that a *Time* cover is the kiss of death, but by the time the book came out they were so crashingly bored with the whole subject they hardly mentioned it, at first. I got what they called a 'take-out' but it was the most casual, superficial treatment imaginable.

"In the meantime I had left Harcourt, Brace; they were tired of me and I was certainly good and tired of them. Seymour Lawrence came along and said he was going to *Atlantic Monthly* and Little, Brown, and asked me to come with him, so I went along. Little, Brown, took me on with magnificence. They bailed me out of Harcourt, Brace, gave me an advance, and I was $35,000 in debt to them by the time *Ship of Fools* was published. Very few publishers will do all that. But Book-of-the-Month Club in turn bailed me out and erased all the deficits.

"At any rate, with all the clamor about the book going on, I decided that I couldn't put off finishing it any longer so I went to an expensive (I didn't know how expensive at the time) place on Cape Ann overlooking the sea. I had a great glass wall, a stunning view, and I sat there for three months. They'd send me my breakfast on a tray, and when I didn't skip lunch I'd walk a few steps for it. Nobody came near me, and when the girls came to sweep the room I'd just move into a corner and let them work around me. No telephone calls, no visitors,

no telegrams, nothing. And I finished the thing, but I think I sprained my soul. . . .

"*Ship of Fools* was like Mark Twain's tight shoes; he was having an argument with a friend, I think it was William Dean Howells, who said, 'Say something in favor of tight shoes.' And Mark Twain replied, 'Well, they make you forget all your other troubles.' This was my book, you know. As long as I had it to worry over I couldn't have other troubles, but now a sea full of other things has washed up to haunt me.' "[1]

1966. Won the Pulitzer Prize and the National Book Award for *The Collected Stories of Katherine Anne Porter*. "I've been called a stylist until I really could tear my hair out. And I simply don't believe in style. The style is you. Oh, you can cultivate a style, I suppose, if you like. But I should say it remains a cultivated style. It remains artificial and imposed, and I don't think it deceives anyone. A cultivated style would be like a mask. Everybody knows it's a mask, and sooner or later you must show yourself—or at least, you show yourself as someone who could not afford to show himself, and so created something to hide behind. Style is the man. Aristotle said it first, as far as I know, and everybody has said it since, because it is one of those unarguable truths. You do not create a style. You work, and develop yourself; your style is an emanation from your own being. Symbolism is the same way.

I never consciously took or adopted a symbol in my life. . . .''[2]

September 18, 1980. Died at the age of ninety in the Carriage Hill Nursing Home in Silver Spring, Maryland, after several years of ill health. ''There seems to be a kind of order in the universe, in the movement of the stars and the turning of the earth and the changing of the seasons, and even in the cycle of human life. But human life itself is almost pure chaos. Everyone takes his stance, asserts his own rights and feelings, mistaking the motives of others, and his own. . . . Now, nobody knows the end of the life he's living, and neither do I. . . . We don't really know what is going to happen to us, and we don't know why. Quite often the best we can do is to keep our heads, and try to keep at least one line unbroken and unobstructed. . . .''[2]

HOBBIES AND OTHER INTERESTS: Outdoor life (she was the great-great-great granddaughter of Jonathan Boone, the younger brother of Daniel Boone), old music, medieval history, reading, cookery, gardening.

FOR MORE INFORMATION SEE: New Republic, April 19, 1939, December 4, 1965; Robert van Gelder, *Writers and Writing,* Scribner, 1946; Edmund Wilson, *Classics and Commercials,* Farrar, Straus, 1950; *Virginia Quarterly Review,* autumn, 1960; *New York Times Book Review,* April 1, 1962; Harry John Mooney, editor, *The Fiction and Criticism of Katherine Anne Porter,* University of Pittsburgh Press, 1962; ''Katherine Ann Porter,'' *Writers at Work: The Paris Review Interviews,* second series, Viking, 1963; Ray B. West, Jr., *Katherine Anne Porter* (pamphlet), University of Minnesota Press, 1963; *Current Biography,* H. W. Wilson, 1963; *Paris Review,* number 29, 1963-64; William L. Nance, *Katherine Anne Porter and the Art of Rejection,* University of North Carolina Press, 1964; George Hendrick, *Katherine Anne Porter,* Twayne, 1965; *Harper's,* September, 1965; *New York Times,* March 16, 1966; John W. Aldridge, *Time to Murder and Create,* McKay, 1966; *Partisan Review,* spring, 1966; *Twentieth Century Literature,* April, 1967; Roy Newquist, *Conversations,* Rand McNally, 1967; L. C. Hartley and G. Core, editors, *Katherine Anne Porter,* University of Georgia

Porter, on her eighty-fifth birthday.

Press, 1969; *Washington Post,* May 15, 1970; John Edward Hardy, *Katherine Anne Porter,* Ungar, 1973; *Contemporary Literary Criticism,* Gale, Volume I, 1973, Volume III, 1975, Volume VII, 1977, Volume X, 1979, Volume XIII, 1980; *Sewanee Review,* spring, 1974; *American Writers: A Collection of Literary Biographies,* Scribner, 1974; *Washington Star,* May 11, 1975; *Authors in the News,* Volume II, Gale, 1976; *Dictionary of Literary Biography,* Volume 4: *American Writers in Paris, 1920-1939,* Gale, 1980; Joan Givner, *Katherine Anne Porter: A Life,* Simon & Schuster, 1982. *Obituaries: Time,* September 29, 1980; *Newsweek,* September 29, 1980; *Publishers Weekly,* October 3, 1980.

RABINOWITZ, Sandy   1954-

BRIEF ENTRY: Born October 22, 1954, in New Haven, Conn. An author and illustrator of children's books, Rabinowitz received a certificate of illustration from Parsons School of Design. Describing herself as a "full-time horsewoman," she has owned horses since she was eight and has trained at least three foals. Her books, all self-illustrated, feature horses as characters. They include: *The Red Horse and the Bluebird* (Harper, 1975), *What's Happening to Daisy?* (Harper, 1977), *A Colt Named Mischief* (Doubleday, 1979), and *How I Trained My Colt* (Doubleday, 1981). Rabinowitz is currently at work on another children's book, *The Nature of Wild Horses. Residence:* Bethany, Conn. *For More Information See: Contemporary Authors,* Volume 103, Gale, 1982.

We are now at the point where we must educate people in what nobody knew yesterday, and prepare in our schools for what no one knows yet but what some people must know tomorrow.

—Margaret Mead

READY, Kirk L.   1943-

PERSONAL: Born December 29, 1943, in Louisville, Ky.; son of Ernest W. (sales executive in automotive field) and Lowis (a teacher; maiden name, Ross) Ready; married Sandra Kohan (a librarian), July 29, 1967; children: Karen, Ray. *Education:* Stout State University, B.A., 1967; Mankato State University, M.A., 1968, Specialist's degree, 1979. *Home:* 108 Tami Lane, Mankato, Minn. 56001. *Office:* Mankato State University, Box 48, Mankato, Minn. 56001.

CAREER: Jordan Ford, Excelsior, Minn., auto mechanic, 1966; North High School, Minneapolis, Minn., instructor in metals, 1966-67; Florida Junior College, Jacksonville, instructor in drafting, 1968-69; Mankato State University, Mankato, Minn., associate professor of automotive engineering, 1971—, department chairman of the Industrial Technical Studies, 1984—. Faculty advisor, Society of Automotive Engineers, 1974—; consultant on fuel economy to City of Mankato until 1977. Autocross director, Sports Car Club of America, 1974-75; president, Basso Presto Sports Car Club, 1977-79. *Military service:* U.S. Army, 1969-71; became sergeant. *Member:* American Industrial Arts Association, Society of Automotive Engineers, International Association of Vehicle Design. *Awards, honors:* Driver of the Year, Land-O-Lakes Region of the Sports Car Club of America, 1974 and 1977; Blue Flame Ecology Salute, Blue Flame Gas Association, 1975; Merit Teaching Award, Mankato State University, 1982.

WRITINGS: Custom Cars (juvenile), Lerner, 1982.

SIDELIGHTS: "Growing up in an 'automotive family,' my interest in that area was natural. The decision to teach at the college level in the automotive area came after exposure to many automotive careers."

HOBBIES AND OTHER INTERESTS: Sports car racing and building experimental fuel economy vehicles.

(From *Custom Cars* by Kirk L. Ready. Photograph courtesy of Gary Garnett.)

KIRK L. READY

ROBERTS, Bruce (Stuart) 1930-

BRIEF ENTRY: Born February 4, 1930, in Mount Vernon, N.Y. Photographer, editor, and author. Since 1978 Roberts has been director of photography for *Southern Living* magazine. Before that time he worked as a reporter, editor, publisher, photographer, and director of photography for several newspapers in Florida and North Carolina. He has also been employed as a free-lance photographer and as director of Carolina Illustrated, Inc., a photographic service. All of Roberts' books are self-illustrated with photographs, and many have been done in collaboration with his wife, Nancy Correll Roberts. Together they wrote *Where Time Stood Still: A Portrait of Appalachia* (Crowell-Collier, 1970), which was chosen as one of the outstanding children's books of 1970 by the *New York Times* editorial board. Other juvenile books by the husband-and-wife team include *This Haunted Land* (McNally & Loftin, 1970) and *Ghosts of the Wild West* (Doubleday, 1976). Roberts has supplied photographs for numerous books written by others, such as his wife's *A Week in Robert's World: The South* and *Southern Ghosts,* and Joel Rothman's *At Last to Ocean* and *Once There Was a Stream.* For adults, he and his wife are the authors of *You and Your Retarded Child* (Concordia, 1974); he has also produced a history entitled *The Carolina Gold Rush: America's First* (McNally & Loftin, 1971). *Home:* 5018 Juita Dr., Irondale, Ala. 35210. *For More Information See:* William Powell, *North Carolina Lives,* Historical Record Association, 1962; *U.S. Camera,* May, 1962; *Editor and Publisher,* March 2, 1963; *Contemporary Authors, New Revision Series,* Volume 6, Gale, 1982.

ROCKWOOD, Joyce 1947-

PERSONAL: Born June 1, 1947, in Ames, Iowa, daughter of Frank Bradford (an Episcopalian priest) and Katherine (Graves) Rockwood; married Charles Hudson (a professor of anthropology), May 28, 1968. *Education:* University of Georgia, A.B. (cum laude), 1969; also attended University of Wisconsin. *Residence:* Georgia.

CAREER: Writer. *Member:* Authors Guild, Authors League of America, Southern Anthropological Society, Phi Beta Kappa. *Awards, honors:* International Reading Association's Children's Book Award honor book, 1977, for *To Spoil the Sun.*

WRITINGS—All juvenile novels; all published by Holt, except as noted: *Long Man's Song,* 1975; *To Spoil the Sun,* 1976; *Groundhog's Horse* (illustrated by Victor Kalin), 1978; *Enoch's Place,* 1980; *The Midnight Horse,* Scholastic, 1980. Contributor to *Appalachian Journal.*

SIDELIGHTS: ''I consider myself an anthropologist as well as a novelist. In my writing I attempt to draw the reader into the drama of other worlds, real worlds where the characters are as human and as moving and as rational as in our own. I write primarily about the American Indians, setting my stories in the cultures of the past, relying heavily on anthropological and historical research in order to recreate the reality that has since been shattered by the European invasion. Yet I strive above all to entertain. My purpose is not to teach, but to offer a powerful human experience.''

JOYCE ROCKWOOD

Without another word he jumped up behind the boy, sprawling belly first across Midnight's rump. ■ (From *Groundhog's Horse* by Joyce Rockwood. Illustrated by Victor Kalin.)

ROSS, Wilda (S.)   1915-

BRIEF ENTRY: Born October 23, 1915, in Santa Barbara, Calif. A scientist and author, Ross received her A.B. from the University of California. Since 1974 she has been employed as a medical abstractor for Kaiser Permanente Medical Group and before that served as an instructor in natural history and as a technician for the Bureau of Insect Identification in Washington, D.C. She has also developed natural history programs for schools and junior museums. Her science books are designed to expose young children to the intricacies of flora, fauna, and ecology. *Can You Find the Animal?* (Coward, 1974), a Golden Junior Literary Award winner, is an introduction to shape and color camouflage. *Who Lives in this Log?* (Coward, 1971) depicts the plant and animal life living in and on a log in the forest while tracing the changes in the log as it decays and eventually becomes nourishment for soil. Ross's other books include *What Did Dinosaurs Eat?* (Coward, 1972), *Cracks and Crannies: What Lives There?* (Coward, 1975), and *The Rain Forest: What Lives There?* (Coward, 1977). She is currently working on a book about tigers born in an animal park. In addition to her juvenile books, Ross is the author of a history column for the *San Francisco Examiner* and editor of a local

newsletter for the California Native Plant Society. Her memberships include the Sierra Club and the Audubon Society. *Address:* P.O. Box 845, San Rafael, Calif. 94901. *For More Information See: Authors of Books for Young People,* supplement to the second editon, Scarecrow, 1979; *Contemporary Authors,* Volumes 85-88, Gale, 1980; *The Writers Directory, 1984-86,* St. James Press, 1983.

SALDUTTI, Denise   1953-

PERSONAL: Born July 24, 1953, in Newark, N.J.; daughter of Felix A. (executive of Tredways Express) and Doris (Laurenzano) Saldutti; married Richard Egielski (an illustrator), May 8, 1977. *Education:* B.F.A. from Parsons School of Design, New York, N.Y. *Home and office:* West Beth Artists Co-op, 463 West St., New York, N.Y. 10014.

CAREER: Illustrator, 1974—. *Exhibitions:* Society of Illustrators Annual Exhibition, 1975, 1976; "200 Years of American

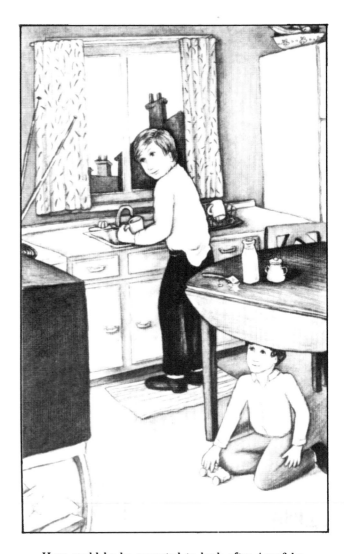

How could he be expected to look after Ange? he wondered. How could *anybody* look after a brother who behaved like a loony duck? ■ (From *My Brother Ange* by Mary McCaffrey. Illustrated by Denise Saldutti.)

Illustration," 1977-78; New York Historical Society Museum; Children's Book Artists for Peace ("And Peace Attend Thee"), City Gallery, New York, N.Y., 1984.

ILLUSTRATOR: (Contributor) Henry Pitz, *200 Years of American Illustration,* edited by Bob Crozier, Random House, 1977; Elizabeth Winthrop, *I Think He Likes Me,* Harper, 1980; Mary McCaffrey, *My Brother Ange,* Crowell, 1982; Robert Louis Stevenson, *The Moon,* Harper, 1984.

WORK IN PROGRESS: Research for a new picture book; paintings for exhibitions.

SIDELIGHTS: "I grew up in a suburban town in New Jersey, the oldest child of a large family. Being a shy yet imaginative child, I found expressing myself visually with pictures a good thing for a non-verbal person to do. I enjoyed drawing and painting and was much encouraged to do so.

"Attending art school in New York City, I began training as an illustrator. There, while studying with Maurice Sendak [1973-1974], I learned that illustrating children's books seemed to offer the most freedom to the artist's imagination.

"When I illustrate a picture book I begin by visualizing the manuscript and how I think the pictures should look. Then it's much like directing a play, casting its characters and creating the sets and costumes. I try to make a story flow from page to page with more happening in the pictures than just mirroring the text. My finished illustrations are executed in egg tempera on gessoed boards. In some books I have pre-separated the colors which makes them easier to be printed, but I would much rather work in full color-camera separated.

"Doing a book is hard work—time consuming, calling for a lot of patience and inspiration, but the finished product makes it all worthwhile. It's always a thrill to hold the printed and bound book in your hands knowing that it's part of you and that it will give enjoyment to others."

SEARCY, Margaret Zehmer 1926-

BRIEF ENTRY: Born October 26, 1926, in Raleigh, N.C. Educator and author of books for children. A graduate of Duke University, Searcy received her M.A. from the University of Alabama where, since 1964, she had been employed as an instructor in anthropology. Also a visiting and public lecturer, in 1973 she received grants from the Alabama Consortium for Higher Education for study in Mexico and Guatemala. She has incorporated her anthropological background into her writings for children, a series of six books based on Southeastern North American Indian myths that are designed to expose readers to the lifestyles, flora, and fauna of ancient tribes. In 1975 the first book in the series, *Ikwa of the Temple Mounds* (University of Alabama Press, 1974) received the Charlton W. Tebeau Literary Award from the Florida Historical Society. Three years later, both *Ikwa* and *The Race of Flitty Hummingbird and Flappy Crane: An Indian Legend* (Portals Press, 1978) were adapted for presentation on Alabama Public Television. In addition, Searcy was the recipient of the 1980 Author's Award from the Alabama Library Association for her rendition of a contest between two rival groups of animals, *Tiny Bat and the Ball Game* (Portals Press, 1978). The other books in the series are: *Alli Gator Gets a Bump on His Nose* (Portals Press, 1978), *The Charm of the Bear Claw Necklace: A Story of Stone-Age Southeastern Indians* (University of Alabama Press, 1981), and

Wolf Dog of the Woodland Indians (University of Alabama Press, 1982). *Office:* Department of Anthropology, University of Alabama, University, Ala. 35486. *For More Information See: Contemporary Authors,* Volumes 81-84, Gale, 1979.

SEBESTYEN, Ouida 1924-
(Igen Sebestyen)

PERSONAL: Name is pronounced "WEE-da See-best-yen"; born February 13, 1924, in Vernon, Tex.; daughter of James E. (a teacher) and Byrd (a teacher; maiden name, Lantrip) Dockery; married Adam Sebestyen, December 22, 1960 (divorced, 1966); children: Corbin. *Education:* Attended University of Colorado. *Home:* 115 South 36th St., Boulder, Colo. 80303.

CAREER: Writer. *Awards, honors: Words by Heart* was selected as one of the best books by *New York Times* and *School Library Journal,* 1979, named as a best book for young adults by American Library Association, 1979, received International Reading Association Children's Book Award, 1980, and American Book Award, 1982; *Far from Home* was named best book for young adults by the American Library Association, 1980, named *School Library Journal* Best Books of the Year, 1980, American Book Award nomination, 1981, Child Study Association Recommended Titles, 1981, William Allen White Master list, 1982-83, and Dutch Children's Book Award "Silver Honours," 1984; *IOU's* was named best book for young adults by the American Library Association, 1982, Library of Congress Children's Books, 1982, Child Study Children's Book Committee list, 1983, Texas Institute of Letters Children's Book award, 1983, and Mark Twain Award List, nominee, 1985.

WRITINGS—All juvenile; published by Little, Brown: *Words by Heart* (ALA Notable Book), 1979; *Far from Home,* 1980; *IOU's,* 1982. Contributor to anthology, *Sixteen,* edited by Don-

OUIDA SEBESTYEN

The crazy old bird didn't know what he meant. Changes, worries, nothing like that meant anything. Maybe geese were lucky. ■ (Jacket illustration by Wendell Minor from *Far from Home* by Ouida Sebestyen.)

ald R. Gallo, Delacorte, 1984. Also author of short stories under pseudonym, Igen Sebestyen.

WORK IN PROGRESS: A young adult book ''set in turn-of-the-century Colorado during the early labor movements''; research on early efforts to unionize miners; adaptation of *Words by Heart* as a dramatic special for PBS-TV.

SIDELIGHTS: ''When my life got too small, in the little Texas town where I grew up, I enlarged it at the library or the movies. My favorite dream was to sit in a theater someday, watching people react with gasps and laughter to a story I had created. Now when people tell me they were crying so hard reading *Words by Heart* that they missed their bus—I'm delighted!

''Because I grew up reading Mark Twain and Dickens and Keats and Shakespeare, I can't understand why my son and his friends look blank when I quote someone who lived and wrote only a couple of centuries ago. I guess I went at reading strangely, stumbling over *Winnie-the-Pooh* and *Bambi* when I was thirty, and joyfully discovering Lloyd Alexander and all the other richly gifted contemporary writers for young people when I was past fifty.

''I went at writing strangely, too. When I wrote my first novel at twenty, I was sure I would be published in a matter of weeks. Actually, it took thirty-five years. But after four unaccepted

novels and four hundred rejection slips for stories, plays, poems—even true confessions—I finally got the hang of it.

''I write because I love words. And maybe because I was a shy only child and books gave me happiness that I wanted to repay. I write about children, and pets, and the West, and past times because they are special and important to me. It's fun to do the research that creates careful little worlds to set my books in. While I write, I listen to ragtime or whatever music my characters might listen to. I write in longhand first, so I can follow the sun from the east window to the west window during the day, then I type, revising like mad, over and over. In the summer I can't bear to stay indoors, so I type under a tree, with interruptions for watering the garden or sneaking off on a picnic.

''I owe a deep debt of gratitude to my son and mother, who supported me in a warm three-generation family while I struggled to be a writer. It is, paradoxically, much easier *and* much harder to 'suffer for your art' when others you love are doing without too.

''I hope I write for readers of all ages, because I want to nourish the child's idealism and delight in life that we all have in us. It's rewarding to be writing at a mellow age, with an actual history of my own to draw from. Having my first published book so generously honored and loved has balanced all the lean years. And now, if my Cinderella story can keep another writer trying—never, never giving up—that will be frosting on the cake.''

FOR MORE INFORMATION SEE: Publishers Weekly, May 28, 1979; *English Journal,* October, 1980; *New York Times Book Review,* January 18, 1981, July 26, 1981; Sally Holmes Holtze, editor, *Fifth Book of Junior Authors and Illustrators,* H. W. Wilson, 1983.

SHEEDY, Alexandra (Elizabeth)   1962-
(Ally Sheedy)

PERSONAL: Born June 13, 1962, in New York, N.Y.; daughter of John J. (an executive) and Charlotte (a writer and literary agent; maiden name, Baum) Sheedy. *Education:* Currently attending the University of Southern California. *Home:* 145 West 86th St., New York, N.Y. 10024. *Agent:* Charlotte Sheedy, 145 West 86th St., New York, N.Y. 10024.

CAREER: Writer and actress.

WRITINGS: She Was Nice to Mice (juvenile; illustrated by Jessica Ann Levy), McGraw, 1975. Contributor of articles to periodicals, including *New York Times, Seventeen, Ms., Young Miss,* and *Village Voice.*

WORK IN PROGRESS: Poetry, collection of stories, and articles.

SIDELIGHTS: ''I was born in New York City. My mother is a writer and a literary agent, and my father is in advertising. I have a younger sister, Meghan, and a brother, Patrick, both of whom I am very close to. When I was nine years old, my parents divorced. We used to spend half the week at my mom's house and half the week at my dad's.

''I read tons of books when I was growing up, and saw many plays in New York. When I was very young, perhaps in first grade, my dad taught me how to read and write. My parents always encouraged my writing.

''I remember I used to read a book, then retell the story in my own way to friends. I played with the same group of kids on Fire Island summer after summer, reading books, then acting them out as plays. Writing, acting, and retelling stories have always been an interest.

''I liked Maurice Sendak and Grimm's fairy tales as a young girl, and all of the 'Ramona the Pest' books by Beverly Cleary, and the classics like *Little Women.* I read whatever was around the house.''

Sheedy studied dance with the American Ballet Theatre for many years. ''I started dancing when I was six years old. I went to the ballet and decided I wanted to become a ballerina. I danced with the American Ballet Theatre for ten years and used to perform at Lincoln Center during the summers, which was the first time I was ever on stage.

''At a certain point, I realized that dancing was going to take a bigger commitment than I was ready to give. I had too many other interests to keep me from concentrating on dance alone.''

ALEXANDRA SHEEDY

Sheedy wrote her first published book, *She Was Nice to Mice,* when she was twelve years old. ''I had always loved princesses and queens and at that time was fascinated by Elizabethan history. I saw the movie 'Anne of a Thousand Days' and began to have dreams in which I was Princess Elizabeth and my mother Anne Boleyn. My mother was going to school at the time and I used to walk around the university while she was in class pretending I was Elizabeth I. I started to write a story about her. The idea for the mouse came from a book about little people called, *The Borrowers.* I used my hamster, Samantha, as a model for the mouse and narrator of *She Was Nice to Mice.*

''The Elizabethan period seemed very theatrical. The idea of having a king and a queen came right out of the fairy tales I had read as a kid. When I began to read English history, I learned about the people who had interested me: Elizabeth I, Anne Boleyn, Henry VIII and all of his six wives, and Eleanor of Aquitaine. Studying them was like having all of my favorite people brought to life. It was another fairy tale.

''By the time I wrote *She Was Nice to Mice* I knew so much about the Elizabethan era that I didn't have to do too much research. But I did research costumes, Shakespearean plays and even their diet. As a matter of fact, the pudding in the story was originally going to be potato pudding, but my editor said 'No . . . I don't think the English had potatoes then.' I had to drag out a book on Elizabethan food and found an essay explaining that potatoes were eaten in Ireland by the peasants and were never allowed in the court. Potatoes had, in fact, not been brought to England at that time.

''I worked on the book in the same way I had always worked on my stories. I would write and then read out loud. My mother

(From the movie "War Games," starring Matthew Broderick and Ally Sheedy. Released by Metro-Goldwyn-Mayer, 1983.)

would sit with me and help with typing. If she thought it was too long in one section, she would tell me so. But the person who really sat down with me and told me what needed change was the editor. One Saturday, I remember, we bought bagels and cream cheese and spent the entire day at her house, going over the manuscript. She said, 'Okay, I'm going to chop this . . . fill this out more. . . .' At first I was upset, as I always am when I'm criticized or corrected. 'What do you mean I did it wrong?' I'd think. But when I worked on it, I discovered that she was right.

"Jessica Ann Levy, the illustrator of *She Was Nice to Mice,* is one year older than I am. We grew up together and are very good friends. It was fun to work on the book together. At the time, we lived outside of New York, so we only met once every two weeks. It was my mom's idea to get Jessica to do the illustrations. She was only thirteen, but had already sold some of her art work.

"I remember when my mom finally handed me the finished book and said, 'This is it.' The book was all bound . . . very exciting, but it was back to daily life. I was only thirteen and school was my priority.

"The publicity, the articles and the interviews that came out when *She Was Nice to Mice* was published put some of my friends off, but I didn't make a big deal out of it. I wanted to be one of them. I wanted to belong. Being in the public eye

at such a young age was an annoyance more than anything else. I remember asking my mother to tell the school not to cut stories out of the newspaper and not to say anything about the book because I didn't want to become alienated from my friends. I never thought of writing the book as something special or different. I did something I really wanted to do.

"Later *Seventeen* excerpted the book and I met the magazine's editor, Phyllis Snyder, who has been my mentor in many ways.

"My mother is a writer who owns her own literary agency. She has been a good role model and critic. She looks at my work with the same objective eye she brings to manuscripts from any of her other clients. My writing in some ways sounds similar to hers. Because she knows her own weaknesses and flaws as a writer, she can immediately point out mine."

Sheedy, who, aside from writing, has acted in many films, plays, and on televison, feels that those early years of dance training have helped her to become a disciplined actress. "Acting is a lot like dancing. In dance, you must do exercises and repetitions all the time to achieve the freedom and agility on stage. The movement can flow out of you. For me, acting requires the same discipline. I work on my craft by attending classes where we do exercises and work on technique. Then when I take on a role, everything can come through because I have tuned up, just like an instrument."

An accomplished actress, she has worked on many films, plays, and television shows including, "Hill Street Blues," "Bad Boys," "War Games," and Mark Medoff's "The Magic Kid." "I have been working as an actress professionally since I was fifteen. I loved working on 'War Games.' It was exciting for me and I learned a lot. I also enjoyed working with Matthew Broderick. It was the second film role I had done. I think of acting jobs in terms of a role to work on. Right now I lead a nice student-type existence. Doing 'War Games' only changed my life in terms of what roles I may now be eligible for, but my life is not completely blown into different proportions.

"Perhaps I can keep celebrity in perspective because I grew up in a household where writers were always walking in and out of the door. I could pick up a book from the bookshop, read it, and then have the writer walk in the next morning. So I was never in awe of writers. What I did respect was the work they did. Sometimes I would listen to them come over in tears about a part of a book that wasn't working—but they were artists and kept trying.

"The writers I knew lived in a different world from the actors. The public never saw their faces; they read their work. It was what they did that counted, not how they appeared. That's how I think actors should be. I don't want to go around thinking, 'Oh, my hair is out of place.' That has nothing to do with acting. Acting like writing is a creative process, a technique.

"Acting and writing have always been co-existing interests for me. Now I am studying acting as a drama major at the Uni-

versity of Southern California; writing I do on my own time. Lately I have written more poems than anything else. When I write fiction I like narrative, I like to write people's thoughts more than dialogue.

"In the future, I think I will take any challenges that come up. Right now, I am working on a Sam Shepard play at school, and I have done two other plays this year. I think there is a difference between film acting and stage acting and the ideal would be to have an acting range, like actress Glenn Close, who can adapt to any medium. I would love to be able to do that with writing as well. I would like to try writing theatre plays some day. My favorite playwrights are Sam Shepard, Carson McCullers, Tom Stoppard, Shakespeare, Chekov, Ibsen, Williams, Miller, and Tina Howe.

"I have been working on a project which is a combination of many different writings. I don't want to call it a 'book,' because I endanger myself when I feel I have to finish something. I start thinking about what I'm writing instead of just writing. I'm able to write so much more when I think no one will ever read it.

"When I moved to Los Angeles I didn't like it right away, but I've adapted. I do miss the plays in New York, and my friends, though I have made new friends here.

"My advice to young people who might want to write is to do it! Write a lot, read as much as you can, and learn from what you read. Don't be discouraged by thoughts like 'Oh, I can't do it, it's dumb.' Live and travel and take chances with people because it all comes back in your writing, your acting, dancing, photography—whatever it is you do. Just keep going and bring everything that you experience to what you do."

FOR MORE INFORMATION SEE: People, September 29, 1983.

I always could tell just what our Queen was thinking, even though she never showed it by her expression. ■
(From *She Was Nice to Mice* by Alexandra Sheedy. Illustrated by Jessica Ann Levy.)

SHELDON, Muriel 1926-
(Muriel Batherman)

BRIEF ENTRY: Born October 16, 1926, in New York, N.Y. Author and illustrator of books for children. After attending Pratt Institute from 1944 to 1947, Sheldon spent one year as promotional designer for Helena Rubinstein in New York City and the next seven years as assistant art editor of *Charm* magazine. In 1964 she illustrated her first children's book, *The Alphabet Tale* by Jan Garten. It was followed by illustrations for three films produced in 1969 by Silver Burdett, Inc.: "Little Overcoat," "Sheep Shearing," and "One Little Blackbird." Since then, Sheldon has illustrated about a dozen children's books, including four that she wrote herself: *Big and Small, Short and Tall* (Scholastic Book Services, 1972), *Some Things You Should Know about My Dog* (Prentice-Hall, 1976), *Animals Live Here* (Greenwillow, 1979), and *Before Columbus* (Houghton, 1981). In her writing, she strives to expand the vocabularies of primary-grade readers through brief yet informative texts. *Publishers Weekly* described her as "a talented, respectful creator of children's fare, . . . laudably impatient with 'controlled vocabularies'" who, as an illustrator, "shapes deceptively vague lines into dandy drawings, set against pleasing hues. . . ."

The recipient of numerous awards, Sheldon has received three certificates of excellence from the American Institute of Graphic

Arts (AIGA) and an award of merit from the Art Directors Club of New York. *The Alphabet Tale* was named among one hundred best children's books of 1964 by the AIGA; in 1972 *Hey, Riddle Riddle* by Ann Bishop was a winner in the Printing Industries of America's graphic arts competition. In addition, *Some Things You Should Know about My Dog* was included in the 1977 Children's Book Showcase while *Animals Live Here* was named an outstanding science trade book by the National Teachers Association. All of Sheldon's work as an author and an illustrator are published under her maiden name, Batherman. *Home and office:* 37 Ogden Place, Morristown, N.J. 07960. *For More Information See: Contemporary Authors,* Volume 101, Gale, 1981.

SHORE, Robert   1924-

PERSONAL: Born February 27, 1924, in New York, N.Y.; *Education:* Attended Cranbrook Academy of Art and Art Students League. *Residence:* New York, N.Y.

CAREER: Painter, sculptor, and illustrator of books for children. Teacher at School of Visual Arts, New York, N.Y. Work has been exhibited at Detroit Institute of Fine Arts, Smithsonian Institution, and National Gallery in Washington, D.C. *Awards, honors:* Fulbright fellow, 1952; Boys' Club Junior Book Award, 1965, for *Ramlal;* recipient of gold medal from Society of Illustrators, 1966, for *Billy Budd* [*and*] *Benito Cereno.*

ILLUSTRATOR—All for children, except as indicated: Herman Melville, *Moby Dick* (young adult), Macmillan, 1962; Rudyard Kipling, *The Jungle Books,* Macmillan, 1964; H. Melville,

(From *Moby Dick* by Herman Melville. Illustrated by Robert Shore.)

Billy Budd [*and*] *Benito Cereno* (young adult), Limited Editions Club, 1965; Albert T. W. Simeons, *Ramlal,* Atheneum, 1965; Walter Morey, *Home Is the North,* Dutton, 1967; William Wise, *When the Saboteurs Came: The Nazi Sabotage Plot against America in World War II* (young adult), Dutton, 1967; Eleanor Clymer, *The Big Pile of Dirt,* Holt, 1968; Thomas Matthews, *Stories of the World's Great Operas,* Golden Press, 1968; Joseph Conrad, *Heart of Darkness* (young adult), Limited Editions Club, 1969; Florette Henri and Richard Stillman, *Bitter Victory: A History of Black Soldiers in World War I,* Doubleday, 1970; Reginald Rose, *The Thomas Book,* Harcourt, 1972; Alfred Hitchcock, compiler, *Alfred Hitchcock's Supernatural Tales of Terror and Suspense,* Random House, 1973; Polly Curren, *Army of Two,* Scholastic Book Services, 1976.

SIDELIGHTS: Shore becomes totally immersed in the time, setting, and characters when illustrating a book. "When I illustrate a story I play all the parts. This can be wearing on the family, particularly when old Captain Ahab is the creature you are involved with. It all starts humorously enough but pretty soon you start walking as though you have a peg leg. You harpoon the breakfast pancakes and start peppering your daily conversation with words like 'avast,' 'ahoy,' and of course, 'belay!' You can get away with a lot of this stuff if you make believe you're kidding, but deep down . . . you know the truth—an artist prepares!" [Robert Shore, "When I Illustrate a Story I Play All the Parts," *Publishers Weekly,* February 26, 1968.[1]]

The artist describes the rigorous hours of research spent to prepare the most authentic illustrations possible for his books,

ROBERT SHORE

Moby Dick and *Billy Budd*. "Off to Mystic, Connecticut, to peruse the whaler *Charles W. Morgan* with the rest of the tourists, but with one serious difference. Everyone else is a gawking tourist while I—I am Ahab. When no one is looking I proceed to plan dark happenings, take photographs and make sketches—in short, I look like a tax assessor!

"A trip to the Coney Island Aquarium to see the beluga whales merely added to the confusion. The belugas are quite adorable and I found it hard to understand how Ahab could be so mad at Moby Dick. Nevertheless, I tried to sketch them with as much ease as one can draw a fleeting, two-ton whale in a darkened aquarium.

"The publication of Moby Dick led to an invitation to illustrate Melville's *Billy Budd* for the Limited Editions Club. I was, of course, delighted. However . . . I sensed a new problem. I was considered something of a nautical expert. This was a

fallacy. But I was flattered and proceeded to pursue some level of expertise. I therefore embarked for Polk's Hobby Shop on Fifth Avenue—where else? At Polk's I bought a plastic model of Nelson's ship *Victory*. This was a ship of the same period as Billy Budd's. . . .

"When finished with the model I did indeed know a great deal more about old ships; after all, I had started from zero. . . . My new-found knowledge, meagre as it was, helped me know where and what Melville was talking about. This was extremely important because often the location of the action, the very shape of things within the physical locale, can evoke a pictorial idea."[1]

When asked to illustrate his first book for younger children, *The Big Pile of Dirt,* Shore felt a little hesitant. "Until that time I had mostly illustrated the aforementioned dreadnoughts of literature. All those gloomy, wonderful masterpieces hardly

(From "The Pram" by A. W. Bennett in *Alfred Hitchcock's Supernatural Tales of Terror and Suspense.* Illustrated by Robert Shore.)

prepared me to think in terms of pictures of frolicking kids. I then read the manuscript of *The Big Pile of Dirt* by Eleanor Clymer. It was poignant and charming. I put aside my harpoon and took up my finger paints. . . . I started a sketchbook that I filled full of drawings of little ones, children from memory, children I saw in the streets, and of course my own kids. . . . [The children] became people, small people, joyful people, sad people, little people with an infinite number of expressions and movements. I also noticed how children like to build and live in their own little worlds. A fancy toy is completely neglected for an old empty cookie box, a house built from cardboard and lavishly decorated with crayon definitely preempts a spiffy store-bought job. My mind wandered back to my own pre-Snoopy Sopwith Camel, made from kitchen chairs, with a rolling pin as a machine gun. . . . I was remembering things old and learning things new. The kids were becoming my people.

"The children of *Pile of Dirt* are so-called disadvantaged, but this is almost beside the point. The child always seems to feel disadvantaged when overwhelmed by the incomprehensible adult world. To these children their problems are real and intense, their joy, despair and imagination boundless. The adult world is at its cruelest in thinking that the feelings and ideas of children are to be ignored or handled with a smiling condescension. You see, I've taken sides. The kids have become the good guys and the adults the bad guys. It was inevitable. The bad guys are always busy trying to destroy the good guys'

dreams and laughter. . . . The good guys beat the bad guys through compromise, and in that compromise grow up a little sadder, a little wiser, but with the dream still in sight and touch.''[1]

FOR MORE INFORMATION SEE: American Artist, September, 1960; Robert Shore, ''When I Illustrate a Story I Play All the Parts,'' *Publishers Weekly,* February 26, 1968; Lee Kingman and others, compilers, *Illustrators of Children's Books: 1957-1966,* Horn Book, 1968.

SIEGEL, Robert (Harold) 1939-

PERSONAL: Born August 18, 1939, in Oak Park, Ill.; son of Frederick William (a personnel manager) and Lucille (Chance) Siegel; married Roberta Ann Hill, August 19, 1961; children: Anne Lenaye, Lucy Blythe, Christine Elizabeth. *Education:* Attended Denison University, 1957-59; Wheaton College, Wheaton, Ill., B.A., 1961; Johns Hopkins University, M.A., 1962; Harvard University, Ph.D., 1968. *Religion:* Christian. *Residence:* Milwaukee, Wis. *Office:* Department of English, University of Wisconsin, Milwaukee, Wis. 53201.

CAREER: Trinity College, Bannockburn, Ill., instructor in English, 1962-63; Dartmouth College, Hanover, N.H., assistant professor of English, 1967-75; University of Wisconsin-Mil-

ROBERT SIEGEL

Prince Harold and Gwendolyn followed him across a beach of round, white stones. ■ (From *The Kingdom of Wundle* by Robert Siegel. Illustrated by Marilyn Churchill Theurer.)

waukee, Milwaukee, assistant professor, 1976-79, associate professor of English, 1979-83, professor of English, 1983—. Visiting lecturer in creative writing, Princeton University, 1975-76; poet-in-residence and visiting professor of English, Wheaton College, 1976. Resident poet at Greenlake (Wis.) Writers' Conference, 1974. *Member:* Modern Language Association of America, Conference on Christianity and Literature (director, 1969-72), Associated Writing Programs. *Awards, honors:* Foley Award, 1970, for "The Rock"; Dartmouth faculty fellowship, 1971-72; *Transatlantic Review* fellowship from Breadloaf Writers' Conference, 1974; Yaddo resident, 1974, 1975; Chicago Poetry Award from Society of Midland Authors and Illinois Council for the Arts, and Cliff Dwellers Arts Foundation Award, both 1974, for *The Beasts and the Elders;* "To Market, to Market" included in *Best Poems of 1976: The Borestone Mountain Poetry Awards;* Jacob Glatstein Memorial Prize from *Poetry,* 1977; *Prairie Schooner* poetry prize, 1977; University of Wisconsin research grant for poetry, 1978; Ingram Merrill Foundation award, 1979; National Endowment for the Arts creative writing fellowship, 1980; book of the year award, 1980, from *Campus Life* magazine, first prize for juvenile fiction from the Council of Wisconsin Writers, 1981, and gold medallion for fiction from the EPA, 1981, all for *Alpha Cen-*

tauri; poetry prize from the Society of Midland Authors, 1981, for *In a Pig's Eye;* Matson Award from Friends of Literature, 1982, for *Whalesong.*

WRITINGS: The Beasts and the Elders (poetry), University Press of New England, 1973; *In a Pig's Eye* (poetry), University Presses of Florida, 1980; *Alpha Centauri* (fiction), Cornerstone Books, 1980; *Whalesong* (fiction), Crossway Books, 1981; *The Kingdom of Wundle,* Crossway Books, 1982; *The Wyrm of Grog,* Crossway Books, in press. Contributor of poetry to magazines and journals, including *Poetry, Prairie Schooner, Atlantic Monthly, Beloit Poetry Journal, Sewanee Review,* and *New York Quarterly.* Work included in ten anthologies, including *Contemporary American Poets: The Generation of 2000.*

WORK IN PROGRESS: A third collection of poems and two book-length fantasies.

SIDELIGHTS: "I began to write fantasy because of certain unforgettable experiences I had reading fantasies, from *Stuart Little* to *The Faerie Queene.* There is a portion of reality absent from ordinary fiction which one finds in tales of the marvelous. Writers of fantasy cast a wider net and sometimes, like Wynken, Blynken, and Nod in the poem, draw in a star.

"Fantasy can take the reader into a universe of splendors too bright to look upon and horrors too terrible to dream of—into a universe where the marvelous is not only possible, but unnervingly probable—in short, into the *real* universe filled with the wonders of angels and fallen men, of black holes, quasars, stars, moonlight, fire, stone, tree, bread, and wine.

"It is in fantasy that the blinkers of our materialistic mind-set are taken off and we see the wide meadows of reality on either side. Happily, modern physics seems to have regained a sense of wonder in the face of the universe's mysteries. It was Einstein, after all, who speculated that near the speed of light each of us would shrink to one inch in size and live a hundred years while aging only one. Before Einstein, such thoughts were only the stuff of fantasy. Astronomers say that if we were to enter a black hole, we might emerge on the other side of the universe, or in another time entirely. Fantasists have dreamed of such wonders for millenia.

"Even more important, fantasy can change the world right around us. C. S. Lewis wrote that once we have visited the woods of elfland, every ordinary wood is enchanted for us. The poet W. H. Auden remarked that when he was a boy he didn't believe in giants, ogres, or dragons, but when he grew older, he found the world was filled with them. In college, I myself discovered in Spenser's *Faerie Queene,* the variety, the confusion, and the beauty, the treachery, the splendor and the danger characteristic of the world we live in. Compared to this great fantasy, the so-called 'realistic' novels of the last two hundred years seem to follow one small thread of reality and miss the whole tapestry.

"There is another quality in fantasy that I can hardly begin to describe. The best of it furnishes something akin to what C. S. Lewis felt while staring at a flowering currant bush, as he recalls in *Surprised by Joy:* 'It is difficult to find words strong enough for the sensation which came over me; Milton's "enormous bliss" of Eden (giving the full, ancient meaning to "enormous") comes somewhere near it.' For this experience of bliss he chooses the German word *Sehnsucht,* which means *yearning* or *longing*—but more than these. I believe a statement by a medieval mystic may shed light on such an experience: 'The desiring is the having and the having's the desiring.'

"I have experienced moments similar to this one while reading good fantasy. Again, I fall back on Lewis' words to describe them: 'We do not want merely to *see* beauty. . . . We want something else which can hardly be put into words—to be united with the beauty we see, to pass into it, to receive it into ourselves, to bathe in it, to become part of it.'

"I grew up in a very flat part of the midwest. My hometown was filled with tall, infinitely various elms, and furnished with green, endless summers. These did much for my imagination. The surrounding cornfields were flat, and I discovered mountains, streams, and forests mostly in books. Perhaps because of this introduction, when I later lived among these, they were already enchanted for me. I remember spending the hottest part of an afternoon in the town pool and then going home water-logged to read on our leaf-shadowed front porch. To this day the parched smell of chlorine drying on the skin is more inviting to me than all the perfumes of Arabia.

"On that porch I consumed many books, including the 'Oz' stories. When I grew older and went to college, a professor or two made me want to spend my life reading and talking about books, as well as writing them. I write both poetry and fantasy. For me, writing is a serious kind of play, and while I'm doing it I can't imagine doing anything else. It is the most wonderful thing in the world to do. Poetry and fantasy are very similar. Among the best lines of poetry ever written is the old ballad refrain, 'Over the hills and far away.' It stirs my heart and wakens an ancient longing in me. For me, writing a fantasy is an attempt to follow that longing over the hills and far away.

"I wrote my first fantasy, *Alpha Centauri,* because of what a horse did. My wife, daughters, and I were living in England some ten years ago. A friend invited us down to his small farm in Surrey, part of the Green Belt surrounding London. It was a chilly December week-end and we had to inch along in our Volkswagon through a fog the British call a pea-souper. Our friend Steve kept a few horses in a barn and paddock connected to his house. One of the mares on which my daughters rode that week-end was named Rebecca. It is to Rebecca that I owe a great and unpayable debt.

"My wife and I had just turned out the light in the guest room when, *bang,* the window swung open and a dark silhouette moved into the room. I leaped out of bed and switched on the light to find the large white head of a mare thrust over our sill, doing its best to reach an ashtray filled with horse treats. I gave the mare the treat and managed to convince her to withdraw her head. Our host Steve laughed so hard the next morning that to this day I suspect him of planning the surprise for us.

"Several years later the image of the huge white shape frightening us in the dark began to haunt me. Behind Steve's house is a forest of pine trees, and the combination of forest, fog, and the startling horse—together with Steve's great love of horses—began to work a magic in me.

"'Someday,' I said to myself, 'I'll write the story of what would have happened if one of my daughters had mounted that horse and ridden into the forest.'

"One summer while spending a month on the rocky coast of Maine, I told the incident to a friend and she said, 'Write the story.' So I began. Since then I have completed that story and four more, and I have no desire to stop."

HOBBIES AND OTHER INTERESTS: Cross-country walking, travel.

FOR MORE INFORMATION SEE: Times Literary Supplement, March 29, 1974; *Poetry,* September, 1974, May, 1982; *Los Angeles Book Review,* November 30, 1980; *Publishers Weekly,* June 5, 1981; *Chicago Tribune Book World,* October 11, 1981; *Los Angeles Times,* December 10, 1981; *Wisconsin Academy Review,* June, 1982.

SMITH, Jacqueline B. 1937-

PERSONAL: Born September 15, 1937, in Abington, Pa.; daughter of John and Mary (Decker) Bardner; married Walter R. Smith (a dockmaster), June 14, 1958; children: W. David, Susan Lynn. *Education:* Attended Pennsylvania Academy of Fine Arts, 1971, and Philadelphia College of Art, 1973-74. *Home:* 3446 Marinatown La. N.W., N. Fort Myers, Fla. 33903. *Agent:* Phil Veloric, 128 Beechtree Dr., Broomall, Pa. 19008.

CAREER: Taught art in local galleries and home studio, 1969-81; free-lance illustrator, 1974—; *South Jersey Sandflea,* designer and publisher, 1976—. *Exhibitions:* Gaslight Gallery, Runnemede, N.J., 1974; The Art Den, Westville, N.J., 1976.

ILLUSTRATOR: Barbara S. Hazen, *Gorilla Wants to Be the Baby,* Atheneum, 1978; Margaret Teibl, *Davey Come Home,* Harper, 1979. Also illustrator of book jacket of Marilyn Gould's *Golden Daffodils,* Addison-Wesley, 1982.

WORK IN PROGRESS: Several porcelain projects for Lenox and Hamilton; *More than One,* self-illustrated; series of sleeping cats in pastels.

SIDELIGHTS: "My childhood is remembered by a collection of recalled moments in a kaleidoscope of wonderful colors and mediums, that allowed a small child to express herself in a world where 'little children were seen but not heard.' At three-and-a-half years of age, I can remember the joy of freely col-

JACQUELINE B. SMITH

(From *Davey Come Home* by Margaret Teibl. Illustrated by Jacqueline B. Smith.)

oring a haystack in the coloring book an exotic pink, and the enthusiasm I felt as I mixed green and aqua for the little boy's hair as he slid down the pink haystack quite unaffected by his colorful situation.

"Bright cubes of red, yellow and blue in a little wooden box recall sunny days spent in kindergarten at Yorkship School. While most of the other kids chose to listen to stories and slide down the wooden slide that sat in the middle of the large airy room, I would sit for great periods of time arranging the cubes to create one fascinating pattern after another.

"I remember the waxy smell and the dull click of worn crayons in an over used cardboard box. Grey clay, with its oil spreading into the newsprint paper it was served on, became lumpy, misshapen pigs and elephants at the mercy of my small hands.

"And the best times of all were when the traveling art teacher came each week with a new project for us to attempt. How much more bearable school became because of these sessions. We were each given our own set of paints and brushes that were kept in the closet in the back of each room. How sad I would feel when the class came to an end and I'd carefully clean off the paint cakes and wipe out the little enamel water

pan. It always seemed like forever until the teacher would return the following week.

"In my senior year, I was offered an art scholarship to the University of Miami. However, to attain this, it was necessary to bring my grades up. (A feat I did not feel up to working at.) In not doing so, I made a decision that I was to regret for the remainder of my days.

"Not long after my graduation from Camden High School, I met and married my husband and we raised two lovely children.

"When the children were little, I began to feel the necessity to involve myself in the arts and joined the local art league where I exhibited on a regular basis. It was through the league that I befriended and took watercolor lessons from a respected watercolorist, Donn Hettel. Donn was later to open his own gallery along with his wife and they invited me to have a one-woman show. Shortly afterward, I began teaching art in the gallery and continued instructing there and in another local gallery for twelve years.

"Through the next few years, I had another one-woman show and attended various colleges for courses in life study.

"Beginning to feel the need to grow further artistically, I attended an evening course at Philadelphia College of Art. It was there I met an enthusiastic and talented illustrator of children's books, Carolyn Croll. It was through Carolyn that my introduction to the exciting world of children's books began.

"The road was difficult and long, but never without enthusiasm as I pursued my new goal of illustrating a published children's book. Finally the persistence paid off in the fourth year, after having written and illustrated no less than eleven of my own unpublished creations and designing and publishing a regional children's magazine called *South Jersey Sandflea*. Finally the first opportunity, a thirty-two page, two-color children's book to illustrate for Atheneum Publishing presented itself. While the deadline was short and I had the pressure of time upon my shoulders, I involved myself totally, and through it learned how to deal with deadlines.

"This published book and another that followed from Harper & Row, led to fascinating free-lance jobs designing and illustrating plates, porcelains and jewelry for companies like the Franklin Mint, Hamilton Collections, and Lenox.

"Now that my children are grown and responsibilities are lightened, my husband and I live aboard a boat in Florida where he is a dockmaster and I manufacture regional stationery.

"I have taken a studio in downtown Fort Myers in a building with several other artists. The experience is proving to be quite exhilarating as the group is very prolific, talented and willing to share ideas.

"A new book is forming in my mind, and will be the next project, after I finish some free-lance work that has piled up, and paint a large watercolor for an upcoming show.

"For hobbies, I am exploring the art of porcelain dollmaking and hope to create my own for future production. Another project is a thirty-six piece (all different) chess set sculpted in clay, based on *Alice through the Looking Glass*. Alice is one of the white pawns and, of course, Lewis Carroll is the white knight.''

Smith commented on her favorite authors and illustrators. "I love to follow my husband through the boat reading *Winnie the Pooh* as he shaves or tries to accomplish little jobs. Someone once said A. A. Milne puts words into shapes. I guess of all children's book authors, I enjoy him the most. There are so many current illustrators in the field that I admire, it would be difficult to pick any one as my favorite. But at the top of that long list, I would have to mention Michael Hague, Kay Chorao, Nancy Ekholm Burkert, and Trina S. Hyman.

"Things are finally falling into place and, as I sit writing this, the smell of the bakery below wafts through my large studio windows and a local feline, who visits me regularly, sits sunning himself in the middle of the floor and I think that at age forty-five, life now offers much to be thankful for."

FOR MORE INFORMATION SEE: Philadelphia Bulletin, March 21, 1976.

SPINELLI, Jerry 1941-

PERSONAL: Born February 1, 1941, in Norristown, Pa.; son of Louis A. (a printer) and Lorna Mae (Bigler) Spinelli; married Eileen Mesi (a writer), May 21, 1977; children: Kevin, Barbara, Lana, Jeffrey, Molly, Sean, Ben. *Education:* Gettysburg College, A.B., 1963; Johns Hopkins University, M.A., 1964; attended Temple University, 1964. *Home:* 35 Yale Rd., Havertown, Pa. 19083. *Agent:* Mrs. Ray Lincoln, Ray Lincoln Literary Agency, 4 Surrey Rd., Melrose Park, Pa. 19126. *Office:* Chilton Co., Chilton Way, Radnor, Pa. 19089.

CAREER: Chilton Co. (magazine publisher), Radnor, Pa., editor, 1966—. *Military service:* U.S. Naval Air Reserve, 1966-72. *Member:* Philadelphia Writers Organization.

WRITINGS—For young people: *Space Station Seventh Grade,* Little, Brown, 1982; *Who Put That Hair in My Toothbrush?,* Little, Brown, 1984; *Night of the Whale,* Little, Brown, 1985. Work represented in anthologies, including *Best Sports Stories of 1982,* Dutton.

SIDELIGHTS: "After my high school football team won a big game, I went home to write a poem about it while the town celebrated and blared in the streets. The poem was published in the local newspaper, and I've been a writer ever since."

JERRY SPINELLI

STERN, Philip Van Doren 1900-1984
(Peter Storme)

OBITUARY NOTICE—See sketch in *SATA* Volume 13: Born September 10, 1900, in Wyalusing, Pa.; died of a heart attack, July 31, 1984, in Sarasota, Fla. Advertiser, designer, historian, editor, and author. Stern wrote more than forty books for adults and children, including several works on the Civil War era, among them *The Man Who Killed Lincoln, An End to Valor, The Drums of Morning,* and *Secret Missions of the Civil War.* He was best known, however, as the author of *The Greatest Gift,* a short story about a despondent, suicidal man who discovers how much his life has meant to others and thereby rediscovers the joy of living. Stern's story, originally written as a Christmas greeting, was adapted by filmmaker Frank Capra as the motion picture "It's a Wonderful Life." Under the pseudonym Peter Storme, Stern wrote the novel *The Thing in the Brook* and was the co-author of the novel *How to Torture Your Friends.* He also worked as an editor for Pocket Books, Simon & Schuster, and Alfred A. Knopf. Volumes he edited include *The Portable Edgar Allan Poe, Tales of Horror and the Supernatural,* and *The Pocket Reader.* In addition, Stern wrote *The Beginnings of Art,* which was selected for the American Institute of Graphic Arts Children's Book Show of 1973-1974. *For More Information See: Authors of Books for Young People,* 2nd edition supplement, Scarecrow, 1979; *Contemporary Authors, New Revision Series,* Volume 6, Gale, 1982. *Obituaries: Chicago Tribune,* August 3, 1984; *Los Angeles Times,* August 3, 1984; *Time,* August 13, 1984; *AB Bookman's Weekly,* September 24, 1984.

JON STONE

STONE, Jon 1931-

PERSONAL: Born April 13, 1931, in New Haven, Conn.; son of Emerson Law (a physician) and Grace (a nurse) Stone; married Beverley Ogg, June 27, 1966 (divorced, June, 1984); children: Polly, Katherine. *Education:* Williams College, B.A., 1952; Yale University, M.F.A., 1955. *Home:* Sandgate, Arlington, Vt. 05250. *Office:* c/o Children's Television Workshop, One Lincoln Plaza, New York, N.Y. 10023.

CAREER: Columbia Broadcasting System, Inc., producer of "Captain Kangaroo," 1961-63, producer of "Children's Film Festival," 1964-65; Public Broadcasting Service, Children's Television Workshop, executive producer, head writer, and director of "Sesame Street," 1968-78, creative consultant, 1978-80. *Awards, honors:* Recipient of five Emmy Awards for the production of "Sesame Street," two Emmy Awards for writing "Sesame Street," one Emmy Award for the special "Christmas Eve on Sesame Street," and one Emmy for the special "Big Bird in China," all granted by the National Academy of Television Arts and Sciences; two Writer's Guild of America Television Award nominations, for "Julie on Sesame Street" and "John Denver and the Muppets"; honorary L.H.D. from Williams College, 1976; Writer's Guild of America award for best children's script, 1983, for "Big Bird in China."

WRITINGS—All for children: *The Monster at the End of This Book* (illustrated by Mike Smollin), Western Publishing, 1976; *Would You Like to Play Hide and Seek in This Book with Loveable, Furry Old Grover?* (illustrated by M. Smollin), Random House, 1976; (with Joe Bailey) *Christmas Eve on Sesame Street* (illustrated by Joe Mathieu), Random House, 1981; *Resting Places* (illustrated by M. Smollin), Random House, 1983;

Big Bird in China (photographs by Victor DiNapoli), Random House, 1983.

Author of the pilot program for "The Muppet Show" and several television specials, including "Julie on Sesame Street" and "John Denver and the Muppets"; writer and director of "Christmas Eve on Sesame Street"; writer, executive producer, and director of "Big Bird in China."

SIDELIGHTS: **1931.** Stone was born and raised in New Haven, Connecticut. "It was wonderful to grow up in Connecticut. The town of New Haven, where I grew up, was to hockey what so many Indiana towns are to basketball. I was a fanatic—played hockey morning, noon, and night.

"My father, in addition to being an obstetrician/gynecologist, was a concert pianist. He was a real Renaissance man and even founded an orchestra of business and professional men who played music as a hobby. He also worked for the neighborhood music school for poor children. Musicians would come in to teach the children how to play various instruments, and formed a little orchestra. He did most of his concert work for the New Haven Symphony. I, too, was very involved in music. I sang and played the horn.

"My mother was very supportive and kept me out of my father's hair. That was her main function. I have an older brother, who is now a CBS vice-president, and a younger sister who teaches school.

"I didn't write as a child. I'm somewhat dyslexic, so words come with difficulty. I'm not a reader, and consequently not much of a writer."

"Big Bird" with Jon Stone.

1952. Received a bachelor's degree from Williams College. "In college I studied music, partly because it interested me, but mainly because the music department was in the basement of the theater, and there was no theater major. I was the only music major during my senior year, so I got a lot of individual attention. I used to hang out around the theater—it was shameful, but interesting. Williams is not an art school. It turns out lawyers and Wall Street brokers. When Watergate hit the front pages, the list of Williams' alumni who were involved was very impressive. A lot of them were classmates of mine.

"Williams has now become co-educational. When I was there, there were fifteen hundred men stuck on a tiny campus. It was like a penitentiary. Bennington, happily, was only a few miles away, and Smith was an hour and a half's drive, so we got out on weekends when studies would allow it. But it's so much more convenient when everyone lives and works and studies together."

"After Williams I went to Yale School of Drama and majored in directing because it is the 'catch-all' major. You can study costume design, lighting, acting, writing, etc. But if you major in acting, you must concentrate on acting alone."

"I came to New York, like everyone else, to become an actor. With my master of fine arts degree, I got a job as an office boy at CBS. I remember the interview very well. Bob Claver, who later became a good friend, was then the associate producer of 'Captain Kangaroo.' I came in with my non-existent resume in hand, and he asked, 'You really want this job?' I said, 'Yes sir, I need the money.' It was $43.00 a week! 'Well, you can start Monday morning then,' he said. I thanked him, and just as I was bowing and scraping my way back out of the office, he said, 'Wait a minute! Come back here!' I thought, 'Oh God, he's found out something that will blow the whole job.' Then he added, 'Want some advice? If you don't make it in this business in two years, why don't you put the "h" back in your name and forget about it.'

"As an office boy I ran the mimeograph machine for the secretaries. The purple ink came off all over my hands, my shirt, everything. It smelled awful. You couldn't go out with anyone after work. It was a terrible job, but I worked my way into other fields. I became a production assistant, and a stage manager. While a stage manager for the 'Jimmy Dean Show' at CBS, I got a part in the Maxwell Anderson play, 'The Golden Six.' I arranged my CBS schedule so that I could work shows that didn't conflict with rehearsals or performances at the theater.

1961-1963. "All of the production work I did for CBS was an education. In those days, television was live, and the 'Kangaroo' show did things like ultra-violet puppet work and musical numbers that were up-to-date and more varied than most programs at the time. I was exposed to a real cross-section of production and it was wonderful training; tougher than the old drama school.

"Producing is the ultimate area of work, because you make the rules and you can become involved in a little of everything. You can hire yourself as a writer, a director, and as an actor, too.

"I produced 'Captain Kangaroo' for two years. Producing varies from program to program. There was very little to do on 'Kangaroo.' In the first place, there was an executive producer over me, who made most of the major decisions. My function was the day-to-day operation of the show. At that time, since

the show had been on the air for seven years, there were very few decisions to make. It had a format, a schedule of writing and directing and no casting; so it ran itself.

"I wrote two scripts a week for 'Kangaroo,' and that was really my first writing job. I came into the organization as an associate producer, began writing, became a producer, and then left."

1964. Formed an association with puppeteer Jim Henson. "Jim Henson had just come to New York with his 'Muppets' and though I've forgotten exactly how we met, I do remember that we just kept getting thrown together in various situations. I had just sold a pilot to ABC for a children's program based on *Cinderella*. I asked Jim to do the puppets, and when the show didn't go to series, Jim picked up the property and rewrote it as the special, 'Hey Cinderella,' which played in Canada.

"'Hey Cinderella' came and went. Then Jim and I did a show for NBC's 'Experiment in Television,' and it was at that time that I was invited to collaborate on 'Sesame Street.' When I was working on the format, of course, the first person I called was Jim. Happily for all of us, he agreed to help.

"I was one of the four original producers of 'Sesame Street.' Each of us gravitated into our own individual field of interest. The executive producer, Dave Connell, took over the animation for 'Sesame Street.' The other three were a producer from Philadelphia who had worked in live film, myself, and Sam Gibbon. Gibbon, a Rhodes scholar, became the liaison between the educational community and the rest of us, who were one-syllable-word-type-television producers. I took over the television programming and casting, and was the original head writer as well as producer.

"Joan Ganz Cooney raised the initial funding for the program on this premise: She knew that children were watching upwards to forty and fifty hours of television a week and that superficial evidence showed that they were learning quite a bit from what they were watching. That is, a two-and-a-half-year-old could go to the supermarket and read the word 'Jello' on the box. Joan reasoned, quite logically, that if children were watching that much television, and were learning from it, there had to be a way to find out what it is they like to watch and what would be good for them to know once they enter school. On the basis of that combination, she raised eight million dollars.

"There isn't another show that has been organized the way 'Sesame Street' was. We spent over a year preparing. It was expensive and time consuming—a real luxury. In the summer of '68, we held five seminars at Harvard, inviting people who were related in the field of pre-school education. We held seminars on subjects like numbers and counting skills, letters and pre-reading skills, pre-cognitive organization, and the social behavior of pre-schoolers. We invited educational experts, teachers, motivated ghetto parents—some interested artists like Jim Henson and Maurice Sendak—people who knew about kids. We spent three days just kicking ideas around, trying to decide what we should be doing with this television show.

"When we came back to New York, we spent a long time researching what children were watching on television. We tested everything from existing children's shows to Walter Cronkite. Then we married the two. That is, we found out what kids liked to watch, and put it together with what they ought to be learning. Gradually, we came up with the elements that would be useful to a television show. I knew I didn't want it to be another clubhouse in the back yard or a cute little show set in a hollow tree. One day I was watching an urban coalition public service spot on television, which had been filmed on a Harlem street, showing all the garbage cans. All of a sudden, everything clicked. I thought, if we really want to reach an urban black pre-school child (which was the bulls-eye of our target audience) we should use the street outside his home. The street outside of his window is where it's all happening, where the action is—where the older kids get to play. It's an environment he can identify with. I decided to hire a movie (rather than television) designer immediately to make the set. I wanted a real street. I wanted a building. In fact, the original steps to the brownstone were stage steps made of wood, but it *sounded* wrong, so we sent them back to be recast in concrete at about 600 pounds a piece. The stage hands were ready to kill me every time they had to strike the set.

"In most cases, the characters were written first, and then Jim Henson came up with the puppets. I invented many of the 'Sesame Street' characters. 'Oscar the Grouch' evolved because I really wanted something to represent the dark side of all of us. I didn't want everything to be cute and wonderful and bright and sunny, because life isn't that way. Oscar was originally so awful that we had to soften his character. Jim and I had talked about creating a whole family of these scruffy little things. I wanted a manhole cover in the street which would lift to show eyes staring at you. The camera would tilt down a drippy long sewer pipe where stuff is flowing under the street and then in half-darkness, these scruffy unidentifiable things would scurry around, picking up what floats by, eating it—talking some unintelligible language. The more we talked, the better we loved it, but we decided we'd never get away with it, and settled on Oscar, who would live in a trash can on the street. I also created 'Ernie' and 'Burt.' 'Grover,' developed by Frank Oz, was an existing puppet. 'Cookie Monster' came out of a sketch we were working on about a quiz show called 'Pick Your Pet.' Jerry Jewel, who wrote the sketch, hadn't come up with an ending, so we improvised at the studio. The quiz master offered the winning contestant his choice of prizes of either an all-expenses paid vacation to Hawaii for two and a brand new house and car and $20,000, or—a cookie. This character went crazy trying to decide, but finally chose the cookie. That was the first appearance of the 'Cookie Monster,' and all because we didn't have an ending to a sketch. A lot of things happened that way—totally unplanned. It was great fun.''

Stone was executive producer of ''Sesame Street'' for eight years, and in this capacity won five Emmy Awards. As a member of the writing staff, he shared in two other Emmys.

About the development of ''Sesame Street,'' Stone commented: ''There's an innocence to many of the characters. 'Big Bird' is really the surrogate within the show for the four-year-old audience. He sees things the way a four-year-old would. We needed a peer, because the rest of the cast is rather adult. 'Big Bird' was not in the test show. When we did the pilot, there were no puppets on the street. The original intention was to place the actors in a real place and cut away to puppets and films—always returning to the street for reality. We had been given a lot of research advice which said that children of that age have a difficult time separating reality from fantasy. The advisors felt we should not mix the two elements. On paper that looks wonderful. But we tested the show and found the kids loved the puppets, the animation, the films, and the street and real people simply couldn't compete. We decided to mix the fantasy with the street. As we did repeatedly over the years, where education and entertainment were in conflict, we dumped the education.

''What we were most interested in was what children liked to watch. It was very gratifying when we guessed right, and very educational when we guessed wrong. Some things were easy to predict; we knew kids would love the puppets, the animation, the fast moving things. But if anyone had asked me before we did any testing if a black ghetto child could relate to Mister Rogers, I would have said 'Not in a million years. . . .' Curiously, he tested very high. As best as we could determine, it was because so many of these children lived in fatherless homes and found it very unusual to have a grown-up man, and a white one at that, speaking very softly and quite directly to *them*. The kids were mesmerized. That made us think about format, about whether to have our characters *always* talk directly to the camera, or use a more conventional presentation style. We decided on a compromise. Basically, 'Sesame Street' is presentational—the children are observing other people in action, but we also break out of that and talk directly to them.

''We tested many television commercials as well. Children love them. They're fast moving, have a nice time frame of thirty seconds or one minute, and a lot of repetition, which children enjoy. The whole segmented nature of 'Sesame Street' was really based on children's enjoyment of these very short commercials. We've been highly criticized for that, because we were not lengthening the child's attention span. Over the years, we have built in more and more long segments or plot lines which can run the entire hour of the show.

''We had no idea that this show was going to last as long or be as successful as it turned out to be. It never even occurred to me that it would go beyond the initial two years we had planned. When we began to read our press releases, we discovered we were a big hit.

''My daughter Polly was two when we went on the air, and Kate came along after, so the first seven years of the show I had a built-in test audience at home. They used to shoot down all my best stuff, and tell me how they liked Mister Rogers better than 'Sesame Street.' Rotten kids.

''I never read my scripts to them—I couldn't compete with Muppets—but I would talk to them about the show. Their mother did commercials, so they grew up in this strange world where Mommy makes commercials, and you see her on television selling things, while Daddy goes off and works with the 'Cookie Monster.' It's not a bad way to grow up.

'''Sesame Street' always worked on a satirical double-level. We knew that the toddler was not usually in charge of the television set, and also felt that the ideal viewing situation for 'Sesame Street' would be the child watching with somebody older, who could reinforce the messages, answer questions, and guide the viewing. So we put all kinds of adult humor in the show; in that sense, it is very sophisticated. Some of what's going on is way over the child's head, especially with the Muppets. The only limit I ever imposed on the writers was when the material made the child feel, 'Something is going on that I don't understand.' If the child could even get a whiff of the fact that it was no longer *his* show, I blew the whistle.''

1978. ''In the late seventies, I went to Joan [Ganz Cooney] and told her I felt the show really needed a kick in the tail. It was getting harder and harder to make Friday's show not look exactly like Tuesday's. I told her I had two solutions. One was to take the show out of production for a year, to re-do the whole process that helped us conceive it in the first place, and to reassess the audience after 'Sesame Street' had been running for eight years. I also wanted to test our shows against other

(From *The Monster at the End of This Book* by Jon Stone. Illustrated by Mike Smollin.)

children's programs to find out what was working and what wasn't. Secondly, I wanted quite ruthlessly to drop things that weren't working, change the sets, the cast—the whole format. But we didn't have the resources or the courage, so I suggested an alternative—new leadership. I'd used up my bag of tricks. I wanted to stay with the show in some capacity but I knew we needed people who could approach the work with fresh ideas. I worked very closely with the new staff for a year, and saw that the transition was smooth. I'm still involved in 'Sesame Street,' and it has been a very good transition for me too. It gives me lots of time to work on my own projects.''

May, 1983. Writer, executive producer and director of a ninety-minute NBC-TV special filmed in China. To create the program, Stone visited China three times. '''Big Bird in China' began after Carrol Spinney [the puppeteer who plays 'Big Bird'] went to China with Bob Hope years ago. He was very impressed with China, and told me that it would be great to do a project there. I spoke with Joan who encouraged me to 'Go ahead and try it.' I then wrote to Chairman Zhang, the head of Chinese television and radio and a high-ranking party member. The letter was very florid—I spoke about the need for understanding between the future generations in America and China and how a co-production for children might foster this. People told me not to expect an answer for six months because of the bureaucracy, but inside of three weeks I received a letter from the Chairman himself saying that he loved the idea. He invited us to come to China and discuss the project. We organized a tour, and went dashing over for a week in September of '81. I offered my proposals of what I expected of them, and what we would

bring into the country in terms of money and assets. I expected them to provide personnel, not money. I agreed to take care of the underwriting, but I needed co-producers to help me scout locations, travel with us, and provide interpreters. The Chinese agreed. I returned to the States, and began to put the business aspects of the project together. I approached head of NBC Fred Silverman who agreed to finance the project. I finally secured the permission from Children's Television Workshop and went back to China to set things up.

''I sent ahead a list of places I wanted to visit, and things I'd wanted to see. It was just a random list of elements that I thought would be interesting on a children's program about China. I was there for five weeks. We toured, and I kept a very careful daily diary of everything that might be interesting to use as part of the show. When I came back, I went through my journal and made a list of 85 to 90 elements which I thought the script should include. Every time I incorporated one of the elements on the list, I'd cross it off. When I got to the last one, the script was finished. It worked out very well. We went back to shoot in the spring of '82.

''The Chinese wanted us to use their own people for any of the roles which were Chinese. I had originally planned to use a Chinese-American girl who was bi-lingual for the lead which would have made my life much simpler.

''I told the producers in China exactly what I wanted as far as the age and look of the part. They went out to day care centers

Cookie Monster shows a fondness for the works of Cezanne. ■ (From the television special "Don't Eat the Pictures: Sesame Street at the Metropolitan Museum of Art." Directed by Jon Stone. First broadcast on PBS-TV, November 16, 1983.)

The guard (Paul Dooley) protecting "The Storm" in the Andre Meyer Gallery at the Metropolitan Museum of Art looks with disapproval as Oscar the Grouch walks by. ■ (From the television special "Don't Eat the Pictures: Sesame Street at the Metropolitan Museum of Art." Directed by Jon Stone. First broadcast on PBS-TV, November 16, 1983.)

"So how's a guy like Santa Claus, who's built like a dump truck, how's he going to get down all those skinny chimneys? Huh?" Big Bird had to think about that. ■ (From *Christmas Eve on Sesame Street* by Jon Stone. Illustrated by Joe Mathieu.)

and kindergartens all over Peking. After interviewing all of these children, they selected thirty, brought them into a television studio, and taped them talking and singing a little children's song in Chinese. Six of the best were sent to me. I chose Ouyang Lien-Tze right away.

"When I finished the script I recorded all of her sixty lines and sent her a little Walkman, headphones, and the tape. Every night before she went to bed, she learned two lines of dialogue in English, not even knowing what it meant. Her grandmother spoke a little English, and her father helped her learn the part.

"She was wonderful, and very fragile. She came down with the flu during part of the shooting, so we let her sleep whenever she could—but when she worked, she *really* worked. She studied all the time, paid close attention and was very disciplined. But she was still six years old, a very little girl—all giggly and happy and ready to play tricks on people. Her character name was Xiau Foo which means 'little lotus.' She loved to

call me Lau Foo. It literally means 'old lotus,' which she thought was just hysterical! She was an infectious giggler."

Stone received his ninth Emmy Award for "Big Bird in China." "The Emmy for 'Big Bird in China' was the culmination of a lot of work. But my first Emmy for 'Sesame Street' was very gratifying too. That first year, we walked away with everything. I remember Bill Cosby hosted the awards. He lost his Emmy for 'I Spy,' and during the ceremonies after we'd won two or three, he came out and said, 'Next year, the only show I'm going to do is "Sesame Street."' It got a big laugh, and the next day, I sent him a telegram which said 'eighty million people heard you say it. . . .' He wired back immediately, and flew into New York that weekend. We fired up a studio and he came in and did a lot of pieces that are still running on the show.

"I made a coffee table out of my Emmy Awards. I took some Vermont barn boards, set the Emmy Awards on them and put

(From "Big Bird in China," the first joint project between Children's Television Workshop—creators of "Sesame Street"—and China Central Television. Written, produced, and directed by Jon Stone. This ninety-minute musical adventure was presented as an NBC-TV special on May 29, 1983.)

Jon Stone, on the set of "Big Bird in China."

a piece of plexiglass on top. What else could I do with nine Emmys? I have a tiny apartment, I don't have enough doors to use them as doorstops.''

August, 1983. Directed the hour-long ''Sesame Street'' special, ''Don't Eat the Pictures,'' filmed in the Metropolitan Museum of Art in New York City. '''Don't Eat the Pictures' was wonderful to direct. We could only shoot in the museum at night and on Mondays when it was closed. Often we worked from seven p.m. to four a.m. It was great fun, but we had to be very careful. The nightmare was that some gaffer was going to shove a boom through a Picasso. Happily nothing like that occurred, and the museum staff was very patient and understanding. In fact, we worked with a young woman who impressed me tremendously. She was knowledgeable, thoughtful, friendly, and knew her business. That woman was Caroline Kennedy. She had majored in art at Harvard, and is the film and television liaison at the Metropolitan Museum, so naturally, she worked with us.''

Stone has also written several children's books, including *The Monster at the End of This Book,* which has sold over five million copies. ''I wrote *The Monster at the End of This Book*

on an airplane between New York and Denver. It was an idea that had been floating around in my head. I believe that books for young children should be very kinetic. *The Monster at the End of This Book* was really based on the assumption that an adult would read to the child. The premise was simply to teach the child that the way you read a book is to start at the beginning and turn one page at a time.''

When asked how he began writing for children, Stone replied: ''I really *fell* into writing, and then I found out that I was pretty good at it. Writing is a knack. I've talked with Maurice Sendak about this before; most of people seem to push down their feelings as they get older—and then there are a few of us who never grow up. That sounds pretentious, but it's a quality which is essential if you are to be involved in kids' worlds through writing, or anything else.

''In my estimation, there are remarkably few good children's writers. I like Maurice Sendak, Margaret Wise Brown, Richard Scarry, and for older kids, Dr. Seuss.

''Every time I do a book, I also make a layout of the artwork. I draw it the way I see it, and later the artist comes in and makes it pretty. I see everything in terms of a frame. In the case of books, the frame is a page.

"Using a word processor has changed my life. It has eliminated the paper nightmare that all scripts are. For someone like myself, who really doesn't *like* writing, it's nice to have a toy to play with while you are doing that otherwise unpleasant lonely task. The typewriter was never a toy—for me, it was an instrument of torture.

"I get very upset with writers who don't think visually. Writing for television has been helpful in that way. Most writers think in terms of words; it's their weapon. Many scripts come through which are much too word-oriented. It takes a lot of undoing to get them to where they ought to be. Writers have to learn to trust the actors and the director. Television is 90% visual and ten percent words. But it is also 100% storytelling. So the best directors come from the ranks of writing, not from MTV or commercials.

"I've often been asked about violence on television, and I have mixed feelings about it. There are various kinds of violence, some of which I object to. I think there is a difference between 'Cookie Monster' driving a train through a wall and the 'Texas Chain Saw Massacre.' Any kind of violence that could be a negative model or lead the child to physical harm is dangerous. But the kind of violence we do with puppets is really harmless, and has been the basis of comedy for hundreds of years.

"For fun I play with the computer, go out with friends . . . but I'm something of a workaholic, because I really enjoy what I do, except for some of the writing aspects. When I'm writing, I work for as short a period as possible. I write very early in the morning. Usually I get up at five a.m. and work until eight or nine. Then I'm done for the day. I also like collaborating. It makes writing a little less lonely."

FOR MORE INFORMATION SEE: Women's Wear Daily, May 25, 1983; *Time,* May 30, 1983.

NANCY TAFURI

TAFURI, Nancy 1946-

PERSONAL: Born November 14, 1946, in New York, N.Y.; daughter of Otto George (a naval officer) and Helen (Kruger) Haase; married Thomas M. Tafuri (a graphic designer), June 14, 1969. *Education:* School of Visual Arts, New York, N.Y., completed three-year program, 1964-67. *Home:* 286 Tophet Rd., Roxbury, Conn. 06783. *Office:* One Plus One Studio, 105 West 55th St., New York, N.Y. 10019.

CAREER: Graphic designer; children's book illustrator. Simon & Schuster, New York, N.Y., assistant art director, 1967-69; One Plus One Studio, New York, N.Y., co-owner, 1969—. *Exhibitions:* Society of Illustrators, 1977. *Awards, honors: The Piney Woods Peddler* was chosen one of the International Reading Association's "Children's Choices," 1982; *Early Morning in the Barn* was selected by *School Library Journal* as one of "Best Books 1983"; *If I Had a Paka: Poems in Eleven Languages* was selected as a Jane Addams honor book.

WRITINGS—All self-illustrated: *All Year Long,* Greenwillow, 1983; *Early Morning in the Barn,* Greenwillow, 1983; *Have You Seen My Duckling?,* Greenwillow, 1984; *Rabbit's Morning,* Greenwillow, 1985.

Illustrator: Jean Holzenthaler, *My Hands Can,* Dutton, 1977;

George Shannon, *The Piney Woods Peddler* (ALA Notable Book), Greenwillow, 1981; Charlotte Pomerantz, *If I Had a Paka: Poems in Eleven Languages,* Greenwillow, 1982; Charlotte Zolotow, *The Song,* Greenwillow, 1982; Mirra Ginsburg, *Across the Stream* (ALA Notable Book), Greenwillow, 1982; C. Pomerantz, *All Asleep,* Greenwillow, 1984; Crescent Dragonwagon, *Coconut,* Harper, 1984.

WORK IN PROGRESS: Illustrating Helen Griffith's *Nata.*

SIDELIGHTS: "My life began in 1946. Being a daughter of a naval officer, I spent a great deal of time with my mother until father retired eleven years later. During this time I learned to enjoy my own company—coloring in my books, trying earnestly never to go out of the lines or break a crayon. Painting was fun, too, and mother would always set me up with whatever I needed for long hours of enjoyment.

"So, I guess it stood to reason that when I reached the age to decide on a career, an artistic one would be the direction I would follow. I entered the School of Visual Arts in New York in 1964 taking a journalistic design course which included graphic design, book design, type, magazine illustration and children's book illustration just to name a few. I was fascinated by the children's book course and knew in my heart that some day I wanted to devote my life to illustrating for children.

(From *Across the Stream* by Mirra Ginsburg. Illustrated by Nancy Tafuri.)

"I met my husband in art school taking the same course. We were married two years after finishing school and opened our own graphic design firm shortly after—we have been working together ever since; concerning ourselves with the designing of book jackets for both hardcover and paperback books, logo and letterhead design as well as editorial layout. Our business has done very well, so now at this point in time I can take that turn in my career to devote more time to creating books for young children.

"To date the basic medium I have been working with has been colored concentrated inks with black line."

VERRONE, Robert J. 1935(?)-1984

OBITUARY NOTICE: Born about 1935; died August 4, 1984, in Mt. Kisco, N.Y. Publishing executive and editor. A vice-president of Macmillan Publishing, Verrone was considered one of the leading publishers of children's books. In 1968 he co-founded Bradbury Press where he was publisher and editor of picture books. When the firm was acquired by Macmillan in 1982, Verrone became vice-president. Prior to his work at Bradbury Press, he had served as a vice-president of Prentice-Hall publishers. At one time he was also president of the Children's Council and the Publishers' Library Promotion Group. *Obituaries: Publishers Weekly,* August 17, 1984.

A wise system of education will at least teach us how little man yet knows, how much he has still to learn.
—Sir John Lubbock

WATANABE, Shigeo 1928-

PERSONAL: Born March 20, 1928, in Shizuoka, Japan; son of Yuzo (a photographer) and Seki (Imai) Watanabe; married Kazue Nagahara, June 29, 1958; children: (three sons) Tetsuta, Mitsuya, Khota. *Education:* Keio University, Tokyo, B.A., 1953; Case Western Reserve University, M.S.L.S., 1955. *Home:* 2-40-8 Sakuragaoka, Tamashi, Tokyo 206, Japan.

CAREER: New York Public Library, New York, N.Y., children's librarian, 1955-57; Keio University, Tokyo, Japan, associate professor, 1957-69, professor of children's literature, 1970-75; author, translator, and critic of books for children. Vice-president, International Board on Books for Young People, 1976-78. Visiting lecturer at numerous institutions, including University of Illinois, Western Michigan University, Pratt Institute, Library of Congress, and Case Western Reserve University. *Member:* Japan Library Association. *Awards, honors:* Chosen as one of the outstanding storytellers for the Storytelling Festival at the American Library Association, Miami Beach Conference, 1956; chosen May Hill Arbuthnot Honor Lecturer by the Children's Services Division of the American Library Association, 1977; Fifteenth Mobil Children's Culture Award (Japan), 1980.

WRITINGS—Works translated into English; all for children; "I Can Do It All By Myself" series; all illustrated by Yasuo Ohtomo: *Dosureba Iinokana,* Fukuinkan, 1977, published in America as *How Do I Put It On?: Getting Dressed,* Collins (New York), 1979 (published in England as *How Do I Put It On?,* Bodley Head, 1979); *Kon'nichiwa,* Fukuinkan, 1980, published in England as *Hallo! How Are You?*, Bodley Head, 1980, published in America as *Where's My Daddy?*, Philomel Books, 1982; *Itadakimaasu*, Fukuinkan, 1980, published in America as *What a Good Lunch!: Eating*, Collins, 1980 (published in England as *How Do I Eat It?*, Bodley Head, 1980); *Yoi Don!*, Fukuinkan, 1980, published in America as *Get Set! Go!*, Philomel Books, 1981 (published in England as *Ready, Steady, Go!*, Bodley Head, 1981); *Doronko, Doronko*, Fukuinkan, 1981, published in America as *I'm the King of the Castle!: Playing Alone*, Philomel Books, 1982 (published in England as *I'm the King of the Castle*, Bodley Head, 1982); *I Can Ride It!: Setting Goals*, Philomel Books, 1982 (published in England as *I Can Do It!*, Bodley Head, 1982); *Boku Ouchi o Tsukurunda*, Fukuinkan, 1982, published in America as *I Can Build a House!*, Philomel Books, 1983; *I Can Take a Walk*, Philomel Books, 1984 (published in England as *I'm Going for a Walk*, Bodley Head, 1984).

Other; all illustrated by Yasuo Ohtomo; all published by Akane-Shobo, except as indicated: *Oisha-san nanka Kowakunai* (title means "I Dare to See a Doctor!"), 1976; *Okaimono Daisuki* (title means "I Love to Go Shopping"), 1978; *Boku Pato-car ni Nottanda!* (title means "I Rode in a Police Car"), 1979; *Boku Oyogerunda!* (title means "I Can Swim Well!"), 1979; *Ice-Cream ga Futtekita* (title means "Ice-Cream Has Fallen"), 1979; *Boku maigo ni nattanda* (title means "I Got Lost in the Crowd"), 1980; *Kumata-kun no Orusuban* (title means "Kumata Looks after the House While Parents Are Away"), 1980; *Boku Shin'kansen ni Nottanda* (title means "Fun on the Shin-'kansen Line"), 1981; *Boku Camp ni Ittanda* (title means "Nice Camping"), 1981; *Kiiroi Taxi* (title means "The Yellow Taxi Cab"), Fukuinkan, 1982.

Translator of children's books from English into Japanese, including *A Visit from St. Nicholas* by Clement Moore, *A Wrinkle in Time* by Madeleine L'Engle, *The Moffats* by Eleanor Estes, *Make Way for Ducklings* by Robert McCloskey, and *Scrambled Eggs Super* by Dr. Seuss (pseudonym of Theodor Seuss Geisel), and of critical works such as *The Unreluctant Years: A Critical Approach to Children's Literature* by Lillian H. Smith. Contributor of articles on children's literature and library services to numerous professional journals.

SIDELIGHTS: **March 20, 1928.** Born in Shizuoka City, Shizuoka Prefecture in Japan. "I was born and brought up in the family of [a] poor photographer. I have only seven brothers and four sisters though my father married twice because my mother died when I was five years old. My father had to support his family with anything he was able to obtain cheaper by the dozen. My stepmother, who was really a nice mother to all the children, had to work very hard in bringing up the children and keeping the house clean. I remember one night she fainted after she had done all the washing in the bathroom. She had, of course, no washing machine.

"The photographer was a very stern father as he was a pious believer in Buddhism who tried to practice his faith all through his life. He actually practiced Buddhist austerities with the monks in a temple, and, once in a while, took some of us to the temple with him. He built a sizable altar in the house and made all in the household, even his apprentice, observe morning and evening worship services. His children did not enjoy this at all but listened attentively when he told them mystic stories of the incarnation of Buddha. They must have been from the *Jataka* or the *Panchatantra*. He told us not only Buddhistic fables but also other folktales and legends of Japan and sometimes stories of heroic events in other lands.

SHIGEO WATANABE

"He told us stories not only in the evenings at home but out in the field, by the beach, and on the dried riverbed when we went for a walk. On summer evenings when the air had cooled off, people in the neighborhood used to bring out their bamboo benches in the street and play *shogi*, Japanese chess. Then my father became very popular among the neighborhood children. It was a thrilling and chilling experience to hear him tell, in the dark, a ghost story written by Lafcadio Hearn.

"This kind of scene disappeared a long time ago from the streets in Japan as TV came into the houses. I still wonder how and when my father had learned all these stories while he had received only an elementary education. It was a miracle how my parents had managed to keep the family surviving all through those years. Our house was burnt down in a big fire which swept away the whole town when I was twelve years old. And toward the end of World War II, the whole city was burnt to ashes again. Twice in his life my father had to confront an impossible fate; a dozen children, no house in which to live, nothing to feed the children, and no work to earn his living.

"I am his third son. The third son in any fairy tale sets out on a quest, realizing his ignorance, knowing himself to be a sim-

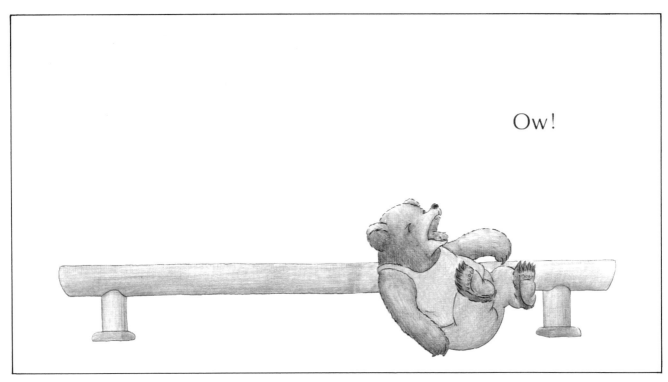

(From *Ready, Steady, Go!* by Shigeo Watanabe. Illustrated by Yasuo Ohtomo.)

pleton. Now years have passed. The third son has traveled to many parts of the world, met many people from all walks of life, and has returned home. He is happily married and has three sons of his own.'' [Shigeo Watanabe, ''May Hill Arbuthnot Honor Lecture, One of the Dozens,'' *Top of the News,* spring, 1977.[1]]

1953. Graduated from Keio University of Tokyo. As an exchange student for two years in the United States, Watanabe attended Case Western Reserve University. ''I was very tense . . . coming from a faraway country, and not comprehending everything spoken to me in English at the school. I did not know how to behave in the unfamiliar atmosphere of the classes specializing in literature and services for children. Every time I entered the classroom I waited at the door until all my classmates had entered. When the class was dismissed I stood at the door just like a doorman again until all my classmates had gone out. Some classmates smiled at me and said 'Thank you.' Some classmates did not notice me at all. And some other considerate classmates said, 'Oh, don't wait, you go ahead!' Even when I was told to I still felt awkward to go ahead of any one of my classmates, because I had been told when I was still a student in Japan that 'Ladies First' was quite an important manner for men in the U.S.A. But in the first few classes I took at Case Western Reserve University women's liberation had gone to its extremity and I found myself the only man in these classes. My state of tension was not eased until at one of the class gatherings a classmate patted me on the back and she said, 'Oh, forget about being a man.' ''[1]

1955-1957. Worked as the only male children's librarian in the New York Public Library system, where he gained recognition as an outstanding storyteller. ''As soon as I started working as a children's librarian in the New York Public Library, I became rather popular among my small patrons. I liked them very much. To my surprise, they were very friendly from the beginning. They were much more sociable and talkative than children I had known in Japan. They bombarded me with questions Japanese children would never ask an adult whom they met for the first time, such as 'Where are you from?' 'What's your name?' 'How come? You're a man!'

''To the first question I answered, 'I am from Tokyo.' As soon as a child heard my answer he said, 'I know Tokyo. My uncle has been to Tokyo, you see. Tokyo is a big city in China.'

''To the second question I said, 'My name is Mr. Shigeo Watanabe.' To this answer the children responded differently. 'What?' said one. 'That's a funny name!' said another. 'Mr. Wantang?' said still another. This sounded to me like a kind of Chinese soup.

''What a cultural difference, I thought while these questions and answers were going back and forth between the children and me. In a tightly closed community like Japan's, we would never directly ask a stranger or a newcomer where he is from. Until he introduced himself we would wait or try to find out from somebody within our circle who knew him, or not ask at all but gossip about him among ourselves. This means that a newcomer must try to find a way to integrate himself into the new surroundings. Everybody knows or is supposed to know each other in the old society where classes, status, families, friends, enemies, and prejudice have lived together for centuries. In old established communities in Japan, we used to greet each other by saying 'Good morning.' Then, instead of 'How are you?' we used to say 'Where are you going?' Since then, urbanization in Japan has been drastic, however, and many folks left their hometowns, moved to so-called new housing projects, and started asking each other, 'Where are you from?'

''But from the question where I was from, I sensed instantly

Hello, Milkman.
Have you seen my daddy?

No!

(From *Where's My Daddy?* by Shigeo Watanabe. Illustrated by Yasuo Ohtomo.)

that the children were ready to accept me, and I thought that it must be a cultural trait naturally inherited by these children.

"My name, both given name and family name, is popular in Japan like John Smith or David Brown is in this country. But the unfamiliar sound of my name must have surprised or puzzled the children. They were more intrigued when I wrote it down on a piece of paper both in the Japanese alphabet and in *kanji*, which is Japanese writing using Chinese characters.

"The third question, 'How come? You are a man!' was a very puzzling one to me. So I said, 'I beg your pardon.' The child repeated the same question, kindly rephrasing it for me: 'How come a man like you is working in the children's room?' Then I understood his question and remembered again that I was a man. Even to a child it must have been a unique thing for a man to be a children's librarian. It was indeed so for the New York Public Library at that time because I was the only male children's librarian among more than one hundred qualified children's librarians working throughout the system. Thanks to this, I had to be very popular among female children's librarians. . . .

"I still do remember very fondly all the children I came across while I worked as a children's librarian at St. George, Port Richmond, Harlem, Fordham, and a few other branches. And the books that I shared the pleasure of reading with these children mean so much to my life. *Harry, the Dirty Dog, My Father's Dragon, Make Way for Ducklings, Tke Moffats, The Twenty-One Balloons,* and many others gave me everlasting pleasure in working with books and children. These books I brought back to Japan and shared the pleasures once more with our children by translating them into Japanese. Most of them are still being widely read by Japanese children."[1]

1957-1969. Returned to Japan, where he became associate pro-

fessor at Keio University. "When my period of study as an exchange student was over and I had to leave New York, the children asked, 'Mr. Watanabe, are you leaving us for good?' 'I don't want to,' I said, 'But I have to, for the good of Japanese children.' 'Yes,' they said. 'Please come back!' . . ."[1]

1958. Married Kazue Nagahara, and had three sons. "It is very difficult to observe one's own children intellectually and objectively, even for a person whose profession is in the realm of children. This is particularly true when the parents are young and the children are small. We were not exceptions. When we had the first two sons . . . we were living a hand-to-mouth existence. My wife was occupied with the physical care of our children and I was busy with my work away from my family. We did not have time to look at our children with calm thoughts about their future in relation to our own society and their future society. But to have a new child in our middle age as we have is just like receiving a gift from God. This child is the greatest pleasure in our family, and he has freshly stimulated my professional interests. I have always marveled at the natural affinity between the childhood of the human race and the childhood of individual human beings. . . ."[1]

1970-1975. Made full professor at Keio University. Watanabe has traveled and lectured extensively as a specialist of children's literature and library services. "There are two ways to make a trip to a place where you have never visited before. The place may be a village, a town, or even a country. It may be the site of a ruined civilization, a house where a famous poet once lived, or even a garden where a tale of fantasy took place. One way to visit such a place is to make a thorough study beforehand, the other is to go there without any preparation except for your genuine interest in the place.

"I have gone both ways but my personal preference is the latter because I can enjoy the trip far better if I go unprejudiced. If

I visit a place thoroughly informed, I will see almost everything as I expect to see and feel it, as if I am confirming everything I know. I gain only the satisfaction of having visited the place and seen the things with my own eyes. I had this kind of trip to the U.S. Library of Congress, Stratford-on-Avon in England, the Acropolis in Athens, the Toshogu Shrine in Nikko in Japan, and a few other places. None of the places was as striking as I had expected. The Library of Congress was smaller than the one I had dreamed of. Shakespeare's birthplace was exactly as I had studied it in a guide book. The Acropolis blurred by smog was indeed a distressing sight. At the Toshogu Shrine in Nikko I was more interested in watching the foreign visitors.

"But a trip without any prejudice or any expectation will give you the genuine pleasure of finding things which in themselves will reveal many things to your eyes: they are hidden treasures, hidden beauties, hidden histories, and hidden meanings. I was awe-struck by the history of the Tower of London. I was astounded countless times by the beauty and the power of the works of fine art at the British Museum. I was speechless when I saw the people who were living practically in the water of the Menam in Bangkok. I was horror-struck when I thought about the end of the pueblos at the top of Mesa Verde National Park in Colorado. I was angered to the bottom of my heart for the sake of the proud Indios when I thought about the fall of the Inca Empire at Cuzco and Machu Picchu in Peru.

"You won't be able to cry or be awe-struck if you are prepared. But if you cried or were awe-struck by what you saw, then you will never forget the incident or the situation which moved you.

"I have traveled my life, like my trips, to different places without making a solid preliminary study or keeping a detailed record afterward. I have not tried to memorize everything I have encountered or to write it down in my notebook. . . ."[1]

1976. Began a two-year term as vice-president of the International Board on Books for Young People. The following year he was selected as the May Hill Arbuthnot Honor Lecturer by the Children's Services Division of the American Library Association.

1980. Received the Fifteenth Mobil Children's Culture Award. Besides being a specialist of children's literature, Watanabe has written seventy-two children's books in Japan that have not been translated into English. His children's books published in England and the United States are all part of the "I Can Do It All By Myself" series. Watanabe is known in Japan as one of the leading translators of children's literature. "In the world today, many children share similar experiences, but each child has his or her own life. Children are very sensitive about their homes and their worlds. And in reality it is a mistake to suppose that the same virtues and vices reside in different peoples. That is the reason why 'international understanding through children's books' is very important. To understand and appreciate the differences among peoples correctly—the difference in origin, the difference in belief, the difference in history, the difference in manner, the difference in expression, the difference in art, the difference in language, the difference in taste, and the differences in many other things that influence peoples to live differently—is to understand the world."[1]

FOR MORE INFORMATION SEE: Bookbird, February, 1976, March, 1977; *Top of the News,* April, 1976, spring, 1977.

WESTMAN, Paul (Wendell) 1956-

PERSONAL: Born October 27, 1956, in Minneapolis, Minn.; son of Bert Fabian (a laborer; in sales and small business) and Irene Geneva (a cost estimator; maiden name, Taxdahl) Westman. *Education:* University of Minnesota, B.A., 1979; University of North Dakota, J.D., 1984. *Politics:* Democrat. *Religion:* Lutheran. *Home:* 905 8th Ave. N.W., Waseca, Minn. 56093.

CAREER: Free-lance writer, 1978—. *Member:* National Taxpayers Union, University of Minnesota Alumni Association, Norwegian-American Historical Association, Phi Beta Kappa, Phi Kappa Phi. *Awards, honors:* Scholastic Writing Award from Scholastic Magazines, 1970, for article "Tornado!," and 1973, for short story "A Christmas Story"; NCTE Achievement Award in Writing from National Council of Teachers of English, 1974.

*WRITINGS—*Juvenile; published by Dillon, except as noted: *Hubert Humphrey: The Politics of Joy,* 1979; *Alan Shepard: First American in Space,* 1979; *Neil Armstrong: Space Pioneer,* Lerner, 1980; *Ray Kroc: Mayor of McDonaldland,* 1980; *Walter Cronkite: The Most Trusted Man in America,* 1980; *John Glenn: Around the World in Ninety Minutes,* 1980; *Jacques Cousteau: Free Flight Undersea,* 1980; *Jesse Jackson: I Am Somebody,* 1980; *Jimmy Carter: From Farm Boy to President,* Lerner, 1981; *Billy Graham: Reaching Out to the World,* 1981; *Frank Borman: To the Moon and Back,* 1981; *John Young: Space Shuttle Commander,* 1982; *Andrew Young: Champion*

PAUL WESTMAN

Another of Jacques's inventions was an electric car. He built the car when he was thirteen. ∎
(From *Jacques Cousteau: Free Flight Undersea* by Paul Westman. Illustrated by Reg Sandland.)

of the Poor, 1982; *Thor Heyerdahl: Across the Seas of Time,* 1982; *Walter Mondale: Serving All the People,* 1984. Contributor to *Current Biography.*

WORK IN PROGRESS: Defense and Foreign Policy for a Free Society, "the first in a projected series of books explicating and updating the classical, individualist liberalism of Locke, Montesquieu, Jefferson, Mill, and Gladstone for modern readers."

SIDELIGHTS: "As a youngster, my reading habits ran heavily to juvenile biographies and American history. So when I decided to write for children, my choice of subject matter was a natural one.

"I grew up in southern Minnesota, and even in grammar school was an avid patron of the local libraries. During these youthful years I was a special fan of Bobbs-Merrill's 'Childhood of Famous Americans' series, and of Augusta Stevenson, a remarkably gifted Indiana writer and ex-school teacher whose books in fact inaugurated the 'Childhood' series.

"I began writing professionally in college, and my biographies formed the nucleus of both the 'Achievers' series at Lerner Publications and the 'Taking Part' series at Dillon Press. *(Neil Armstrong,* the first book I wrote, was written in 1976, but not published until several years later.) The proceeds from these books and from the articles I wrote at that time for the reference periodical *Current Biography,* to which I was a regular contributor for several years, helped defray tuition expenses at the University of Minnesota, where I majored in political science and history.

"One reason for writing *Neil Armstrong* and its successor biographies was my belief that they would fill a gap in the literary marketplace: the unavailability of brief, informative biographies of contemporary figures of substantial accomplishment for approximately third grade readers.

"A subsidiary aim was to dramatize the exciting and path-breaking experiences of major astronauts for young readers, which is the reason you will find so many astronauts as the subjects of my books. These biographies were among the first books for young readers, I think, to attempt to humanize—or to 'detechnologize,' the pioneering era of space flight.

"Otherwise, my only intention has been to produce brief, well-crafted, informative, carefully researched and historically accurate biographies of selected contemporary individuals that youthful readers can profit from in an educational sense, and enjoy at the same time. I hope that in some measure I have succeeded in this.

HOBBIES AND OTHER INTERESTS: Reading, genealogical research, old movies.

WHITE, Ruth C.   1942-
(Ruth White Miller)

PERSONAL: Born March 15, 1942, in Whitewood, Va.; daughter of John Edward (a coal miner) and Olive (a hospital food server; maiden name, Compton) White; divorced; children: Dee Olivia. *Education:* Montreat-Anderson College, A.A., 1962; Pfeiffer College, A.B., 1966; Queens College, Charlotte, N.C., Library Media Specialist, 1976. *Politics:* Democrat. *Home:*

2409 Radium Springs Rd., Albany, Ga. 31705. *Office:* Dougherty Junior High School, 1800 Massey Dr., Albany, Ga. 31705.

CAREER: Mt. Pleasant Middle School, Mt. Pleasant, N.C., teacher of English, 1966-76; Boys Town, Pineville, N.C., house mother, 1976-77; Harleyville-Ridgeville High School, Dorchester, S.C., librarian, 1977-81; Dougherty Junior High School, Albany, Ga., librarian, 1981—. *Awards, honors:* Citation for the best children's book by a North Carolinian from the North Carolina chapter of the American Association of University Women, 1977, for *The City Rose; The City Rose* was also nominated for the Georgia Children's Book Award and voted favorite book by six thousand Indiana school children.

WRITINGS: (Under name Ruth White Miller) *The City Rose* (juvenile), McGraw, 1977.

WORK IN PROGRESS: Under name Ruth C. White, "I am presently working on an autobiographical book tentatively titled *Ghost Come Back Again* which will be classified as fiction."

SIDELIGHTS: "Born in the poverty-stricken coal mining region of Virginia, I was the fourth daughter of a coal miner who died when I was six. Our school years were painful because we were so poor, but each one of us managed to get the most out of the public school system and go on to a better life. For this reason I am a great believer and a great supporter of

RUTH C. WHITE

the public education system in our country. I will always work in the public school system and try to give back something of what was given to me. I love children. I love working with children and writing for children. I work with and write for adolescent girls because that was the time in my life when I was most confused and unhappy. I can relate to these girls now because I remember the pain of trying to grow up, trying to find my identity, and trying to be an individual in a conformist's worlds. Adolescents today have basically the same problems, only more of them. It is a very hard time in which to grow up.

"After finishing high school in Virginia's coal region, I went to a small mountain college in North Carolina. I spent two glorious years there feeling that I had at last escaped my miserable childhood. I went on to finish college in Misenheimer, North Carolina; then later I took a teaching post nearby and stayed for ten years.

"I grew restless with teaching and decided to become a school librarian, so I went back to school in 1975 at Queens College in Charlotte and became certified in library media, but I could not find a post. It was then I decided to become a house parent at Boys Town in Pineville, North Carolina. For a year I worked with troubled adolescent boys, then moved on to Charleston, South Carolina, where I found a post as a high school librarian. After four years there I moved on to Albany, Georgia, to live with my sister. Here I am a junior high librarian at an excellent school, and I really enjoy my work. I have no plans to leave.

"I have been very lucky to live in four of the most beautiful states in the United States. The South is rich in story material, and I expect to go on writing for a long, long time."

The author added that her future works will be written under the name Ruth C. White.

WILKINSON, Sylvia (J.) 1940-

BRIEF ENTRY: Born April 3, 1940, in Durham, N.C. A novelist, educator, and author of children's books, Wilkinson received her B.A. from the University of North Carolina at Greensboro and her M.A. from Hollins College. She later did graduate study at Stanford University. During the 1960s she worked as an English instructor at several universities and was writer-in-residence at Hollins College, Richmond Humanities Center, and Sweet Briar College. Critics have praised her powerful characterization in adult novels like *Moss on the North Side* (Houghton, 1966) and *Bone of My Bones* (Putnam, 1982). Wilkinson has also written several children's books on the subject of auto racing, a sport that has interested her since childhood. Each of the books includes quotes from professionals in the field, giving readers what *School Library Journal* termed an "insider's view" of the sports car world. All published by Children's Press, the titles include: *Formula One,* 1981, *Formula Atlantic,* 1981, *Endurance Racing,* 1981, *Champ Cars,* 1982, and *Trans-Am,* 1983. In the 1970s Wilkinson began ghost-writing a boys' adventure-mystery series that centers around auto racing. *Address:* 514 Arena St., El Segundo, Calif. 90245. *For More Information See: Akron Beacon Journal,* July 7, 1974; *Contemporary Authors,* Volumes 17-20, revised, Gale, 1976; *Authors in the News,* Volume 1, Gale, 1976; *The Writers Directory: 1984-1986,* St. James Press, 1983.

WILLIAMS, Louise Bonino 1904(?)-1984

OBITUARY NOTICE: Born about 1904; died September 11, 1984. Publishing executive and editor. A former vice-president and editor-in-chief of Random House Books for Young Readers, Williams's association with the publishing company spanned over thirty years. During that time she pioneered the concept of series publishing for young people with Noel Streatfeild's "Shoes" books, helped to establish Landmark Books, and edited works by such authors as Jean de Brunhoff, Laurent de Brunhoff, Theodor Geisel (Dr. Seuss), and Walter Farley. She was also a former president of the Children's Book Council. *Obituaries: Publishers Weekly,* October 12, 1984; *School Library Journal,* November, 1984.

WINSTON, Clara 1921-1983

OBITUARY NOTICE: Born December 6, 1921, in New York, N.Y.; died of leukemia, November 7, 1983, in Northampton, Mass. Translator and author. Winston is best known for her collaborative translations with her husband, Richard Winston. Among the more than one hundred fifty volumes they translated are psychologist's Carl G. Jung's *Memories, Dreams, Reflections,* novelist Herman Hesse's *The Glass Bead Game,* and convicted war criminal Albert Speer's *Inside the Third Reich.* For young people their translations include *Blue Mystery* by Margot Benary-Isbert and *The Magic Stone* by Leonie Kooiker, which appeared on the International Board on Books for Young People (IBBY) Translator's Honor List in 1980. The Winstons also received awards for their other books. On her own, Winston wrote the adult novels *The Closest Kin There Is* and *The Hours Together.* At the time of her death, she was translating a book by Goethe with her daughter, Krishna Winston-Billingsley. *For More Information See: Contemporary Authors,* Volumes 25-28, revised, Gale, 1977; *Who's Who in America,* 42nd edition, Marquis, 1982; *Who's Who of American Women,* 13th edition, Marquis, 1983. *Obituaries: New York Times,* November 10, 1983.

ZELAZNY, Roger (Joseph Christopher) 1937-
(Harrison Denmark)

BRIEF ENTRY: Born May 13, 1937, in Cleveland, Ohio. Science fiction novelist, short story writer, and editor. Zelazny burst upon the scene of science fiction writing in 1965 with two Nebula award-winning works: a novella, "He Who Shapes," and a novelette, "The Doors of His Face, the Lamps of His Mouth." The following year he received the Hugo award for ". . . And Call Me Conrad"; in 1968 he again received the award for his novel, *Lord of Light.* Critics have lauded Zelazny's use of allegory, psychology, myth, and "double vision" in his stories of fantasy and high adventure. Although most critics agree that his best works were written during the 1960s, he remains a prolific and popular artist of the science fiction genre.

Zelazny began free lancing in 1962 while working for the Social Security Administration in Cleveland, Ohio. From that time until he became a full-time writer in 1969, he produced a multitude of stories that appeared in magazines like *Amazing*

Stories and *Fantastic,* sometimes under the pseudonym Harrison Denmark. During those years he received sixteen nominations for the Hugo and Nebula awards, winning each one twice. In 1972 he was the recipient of the Prix Apollo for the French edition of *Isle of the Dead;* "Home Is the Hangman" garnered him both the Hugo and Nebula for best novella of 1975. More recently, "Unicorn Variations" was a 1982 Hugo winner. In the 1970s Zelazny began devoting more of his time to writing novels rather than the shorter novelettes or stories. Among these are the well-known "Amber" series *(Nine Princes in Amber, The Guns of Avalon, Sign of the Unicorn, The Hand of Oberon,* and *Courts of Chaos), Jack of Shadows,* and *To Die in Italbar.* His works have appeared in numerous anthologies, including *Four for Tomorrow* (Ace, 1967), *The Last Defender of Camelot* (Pocket Books, 1980), and *Unicorn Variations* (Pocket Books, 1983). *Agent:* Kirby McCauley Ltd., 60 East 42nd St., New York, N.Y. 10017. *For More Information See: Contemporary Authors,* Volumes 21-24, revised, Gale, 1977; *Dictionary of Literary Biography,* Volume 8, Part 2, Gale, 1981; *Contemporary Literary Criticism,* Volume 21, Gale, 1982; *Who's Who in America,* 42nd edition, Marquis, 1982.

ZEMACH, Kaethe   1958-

BRIEF ENTRY: Born March 18, 1958, in Boston, Mass. The second generation of authors and illustrators of children's books in her family, Zemach is the daughter of Harvey Fischtrom (who writes under the pseudonym Harve Zemach) and Caldecott award-winning illustrator Margot Zemach. Her first book, *The Princess and Froggie* (Farrar, Straus, 1975) was a family affair—written with her father and illustrated by her mother. In 1978 Kaethe made her debut as an illustrator with Norman Rosten's *The Wineglass: A Passover Story* (Walker & Co., 1978). It was followed by *The Beautiful Rat* (Four Winds, 1979), a Japanese folktale that she adapted and illustrated. Her "interpretive illustrations, swirling and rhythmic . . . in shades of blues and oranges," were noted by *Horn Book* as having an effect of "a free and original response to traditional material." In her next book, Yuri Suhl's *The Purim Goat* (Four Winds, 1980), Kaethe used black wash drawings to accompany the humorous story of a poor widow and a troublesome goat, set in a small shtetl in Eastern Europe. Commenting on her latest work, Eve Bunting's *The Traveling Men of Ballycoo* (Harcourt, 1983), *Publishers Weekly* observed: "In Zemach's vividly colored pictures, it's plain to see that she has created her own, high-spirited style, influenced but not dominated by the prize-winning illustrations of her mother." *Home:* 2423 Oregon St., Berkeley, Calif. 94705. *For More Information See: Contemporary Authors, New Revision Series,* Volume 8, Gale, 1983.

His studies were pursued but never effectually overtaken.

—H.G. Wells

CUMULATIVE INDEX TO
ILLUSTRATIONS AND AUTHORS

Illustrations Index

(In the following index, the number of the volume in which an illustrator's work appears is given *before* the colon, and the page on which it appears is given *after* the colon. For example, a drawing by Adams, Adrienne appears in Volume 2 on page 6, another drawing by her appears in Volume 3 on page 80, another drawing in Volume 8 on page 1, and another drawing in Volume 15 on page 107.)

YABC

Index citations including this abbreviation refer to listings appearing in *Yesterday's Authors of Books for Children,* also published by the Gale Research Company, which covers authors who died prior to 1960.

Kramer, Anthony, *33:* 81
Kramer, Frank, *6:* 121
Krantz, Kathy, *35:* 83
Kraus, Robert, *13:* 217
Kredel, Fritz, *6:* 35; *17:* 93-96;
    22: 147; *24:* 175; *29:* 130; *35:* 77;
    YABC 2: 166, 300
Krementz, Jill, *17:* 98
Kresin, Robert, *23:* 19
Krush, Beth, *1:* 51, 85; *2:* 233; *4:* 115;
    9: 61; *10:* 191; *11:* 196;
    18: 164-165; *32:* 72; *37:* 203
Krush, Joe, *2:* 233; *4:* 115; *9:* 61;
    10: 191; *11:* 196; *18:* 164-165;
    32: 72, 91; *37:* 203
Kubinyi, Laszlo, *4:* 116; *6:* 113;
    16: 118; *17:* 100; *28:* 227; *30:* 172
Kuhn, Bob, *17:* 91; *35:* 235
Künstler, Mort, *10:* 73; *32:* 143
Kurchevsky, V., *34:* 61
Kurelek, William, *8:* 107
Kuriloff, Ron, *13:* 19
Kuskin, Karla, *2:* 170
Kutzer, Ernst, *19:* 249

LaBlanc, André, *24:* 146
Laboccetta, Mario, *27:* 120
Laceky, Adam, *32:* 121
La Croix, *YABC 2:* 4
Laimgruber, Monika, *11:* 153
Laite, Gordon, *1:* 130-131; *8:* 209;
    31: 113
Lamb, Jim, *10:* 117
Lambert, J. K., *38:* 129; *39:* 24
Lambert, Saul, *23:* 112; *33:* 107
Lambo, Don, *6:* 156; *35:* 115; *36:* 146
Landa, Peter, *11:* 95; *13:* 177
Landau, Jacob, *38:* 111
Landshoff, Ursula, *13:* 124
Lane, John, *15:* 176-177; *30:* 146
Lane, John R., *8:* 145
Lang, Jerry, *18:* 295
Langler, Nola, *8:* 110
Lantz, Paul, *1:* 82, 102; *27:* 88;
    34: 102
Larsen, Suzanne, *1:* 13
Larsson, Carl, *35:* 144, 145, 146, 147,
    148-149, 150, 152, 153, 154
Larsson, Karl, *19:* 177
La Rue, Michael D., *13:* 215
Lasker, Joe, *7:* 186-187; *14:* 55;
    38: 115; *39:* 47
Latham, Barbara, *16:* 188-189
Lathrop, Dorothy, *14:* 117, 118-119;
    15: 109; *16:* 78-79, 81; *32:* 201,
    203; *33:* 112; *YABC 2:* 301
Lattimore, Eleanor Frances, *7:* 156
Lauden, Claire, *16:* 173
Lauden, George, Jr., *16:* 173
Laune, Paul, *2:* 235; *34:* 31
Lawrence, John, *25:* 131; *30:* 141
Lawrence, Stephen, *20:* 195
Lawson, Carol, *6:* 38
Lawson, George, *17:* 280
Lawson, Robert, *5:* 26; *6:* 94; *13:* 39;
    16: 11; *20:* 100, 102, 103;
    YABC 2: 222,
    224-225, 227-235, 237-241

Lazarevich, Mila, *17:* 118
Lazarus, Keo Felker, *21:* 94
Lazzaro, Victor, *11:* 126
Leacroft, Richard, *6:* 140
Leaf, Munro, *20:* 99
Leander, Patricia, *23:* 27
Lear, Edward, *18:* 183-185
Lebenson, Richard, *6:* 209; *7:* 76;
    23: 145
Le Cain, Errol, *6:* 141; *9:* 3; *22:* 142;
    25: 198; *28:* 173
Lee, Doris, *13:* 246; *32:* 183
Lee, Manning de V., *2:* 200; *17:* 12;
    27: 87; *37:* 102, 103, 104;
    YABC 2: 304
Lee, Robert J., *3:* 97
Leech, John, *15:* 59
Lees, Harry, *6:* 112
Legrand, Edy, *18:* 89, 93
Lehrman, Rosalie, *2:* 180
Leichman, Seymour, *5:* 107
Leighton, Clare, *25:* 130; *33:* 168;
    37: 105, 106, 108, 109
Leisk, David, *1:* 140-141; *11:* 54;
    30: 137, 142, 143, 144
Leloir, Maurice, *18:* 77, 80, 83, 99
Lemke, Horst, *14:* 98; *38:* 117, 118,
    119
Lemon, David Gwynne, *9:* 1
Lenski, Lois, *1:* 144; *26:* 135, 137,
    139, 141
Lent, Blair, *1:* 116-117; *2:* 174;
    3: 206-207; *7:* 168-169; *34:* 62
Lerner, Sharon, *11:* 157; *22:* 56
Leslie, Cecil, *19:* 244
Levai, Blaise, *39:* 130
Levin, Ted, *12:* 148
Levit, Herschel, *24:* 223
Levy, Jessica Ann, *19:* 225; *39:* 191
Lewin, Betsy, *32:* 114
Lewin, Ted, *4:* 77; *8:* 168; *20:* 110;
    21: 99, 100; *27:* 110; *28:* 96, 97;
    31: 49
Lewis, Allen, *15:* 112
Leydon, Rita Flodén, *21:* 101
Lieblich, Irene, *22:* 173; *27:* 209, 214
Liese, Charles, *4:* 222
Lignell, Lois, *37:* 114
Lilly, Charles, *8:* 73; *20:* 127
Lilly, Ken, *37:* 224
Lincoln, Patricia Henderson, *27:* 27
Lindberg, Howard, *10:* 123; *16:* 190
Linden, Seymour, *18:* 200-201
Linder, Richard, *27:* 119
Line, Les, *27:* 143
Linell. *See* Smith, Linell
Lionni, Leo, *8:* 115
Lipinsky, Lino, *2:* 156; *22:* 175
Lippman, Peter, *8:* 31; *31:* 119, 120,
    160
Lisker, Sonia O., *16:* 274; *31:* 31
Lissim, Simon, *17:* 138
Little, Harold, *16:* 72
Little, Mary E., *28:* 146
Lively, Lorna, *19:* 216
Llerena, Carlos Antonio, *19:* 181
Lloyd, Errol, *11:* 39; *22:* 178
Lo, Koon-chiu, *7:* 134
Lobel, Anita, *6:* 87; *9:* 141; *18:* 248

Lobel, Arnold, *1:* 188-189; *5:* 12;
    6: 147; *7:* 167, 209; *18:* 190-191;
    25: 39, 43; *27:* 40; *29:* 174
Loefgren, Ulf, *3:* 108
Loescher, Ann, *20:* 108
Loescher, Gil, *20:* 108
Lofting, Hugh, *15:* 182-183
Loh, George, *38:* 88
Lonette, Reisie, *11:* 211; *12:* 168;
    13: 56; *36:* 122
Longtemps, Ken, *17:* 123; *29:* 221
Looser, Heinz, *YABC 2:* 208
Lopshire, Robert, *6:* 149; *21:* 117;
    34: 166
Lord, John Vernon, *21:* 104; *23:* 25
Loretta, Sister Mary, *33:* 73
Lorraine, Walter H., *3:* 110; *4:* 123;
    16: 192
Loss, Joan, *11:* 163
Louderback, Walt, *YABC 1:* 164
Low, Joseph, *14:* 124, 125; *18:* 68;
    19: 194; *31:* 166
Lowenheim, Alfred, *13:* 65-66
Lowitz, Anson, *17:* 124; *18:* 215
Lowrey, Jo, *8:* 133
Lubell, Winifred, *1:* 207; *3:* 15; *6:* 151
Lubin, Leonard B., *19:* 224; *36:* 79,
    80; *YABC 2:* 96
Ludwig, Helen, *33:* 144, 145
Lufkin, Raymond, *38:* 138
Luhrs, Henry, *7:* 123; *11:* 120
Lupo, Dom, *4:* 204
Lustig, Loretta, *30:* 186
Lydecker, Laura, *21:* 113
Lynch, Charles, *16:* 33
Lynch, Marietta, *29:* 137; *30:* 171
Lyon, Elinor, *6:* 154
Lyon, Fred, *14:* 16
Lyons, Oren, *8:* 193
Lyster, Michael, *26:* 41

Maas, Dorothy, *6:* 175
Macdonald, Alister, *21:* 55
MacDonald, Norman, *13:* 99
MacDonald, Roberta, *19:* 237
Macguire, Robert Reid, *18:* 67
Machetanz, Fredrick, *34:* 147, 148
MacInnes, Ian, *35:* 59
MacIntyre, Elisabeth, *17:* 127-128
Mack, Stan, *17:* 129
Mackay, Donald, *17:* 60
MacKaye, Arvia, *32:* 119
MacKenzie, Garry, *33:* 159
Mackinlay, Miguel, *27:* 22
Mackinstry, Elizabeth, *15:* 110
Maclise, Daniel, *YABC 2:* 257
Madden, Don, *3:* 112-113; *4:* 33, 108,
    155; *7:* 193; *YABC 2:* 211
Maddison, Angela Mary, *10:* 83
Maestro, Giulio, *8:* 124; *12:* 17;
    13: 108; *25:* 182
Magnuson, Diana, *28:* 102; *34:* 190
Mahony, Will, *37:* 120
Mahood, Kenneth, *24:* 141
Maik, Henri, *9:* 102
Maisto, Carol, *29:* 87
Maitland, Antony, *1:* 100, 176; *8:* 41;
    17: 246; *24:* 46; *25:* 177, 178;
    32: 74

Author Index

The following index gives the number of the volume in which an author's biographical sketch, Brief Entry, or Obituary appears.

This index includes references to all entries in the following series, which are also published by Gale Research Company.

YABC—*Yesterday's Authors of Books for Children: Facts and Pictures about Authors and Illustrators of Books for Young People from Early Times to 1960,* Volumes 1-2

CLR—*Children's Literature Review: Excerpts from Reviews, Criticism, and Commentary on Books for Children,* Volumes 1-7

Author Index